DIONYSIUS OF HALICARNASSUS

THE ROMAN ANTIQUITIES

V

LCL 372

DIONYSIUS OF HALICARNASSUS

THE ROMAN ANTIQUITIES

BOOKS VIII–IX.24

WITH AN ENGLISH TRANSLATION BY

EARNEST CARY

ON THE BASIS OF THE VERSION OF
EDWARD SPELMAN

HARVARD UNIVERSITY PRESS

CAMBRIDGE, MASSACHUSETTS
LONDON, ENGLAND

First published 1945
Reprinted 1956, 1962, 1986, 2005

LOEB CLASSICAL LIBRARY® is a registered trademark
of the President and Fellows of Harvard College

ISBN 0-674-99410-8

Printed and bound by Edwards Brothers, Ann Arbor, Michigan
on acid-free paper made by Glatfelter, Spring Grove, Pennsylvania

CONTENTS

THE ROMAN ANTIQUITIES
OF
DIONYSIUS OF HALICARNASSUS

ΔΙΟΝΥΣΙΟΥ

ΑΛΙΚΑΡΝΑΣΕΩΣ

ΡΩΜΑΙΚΗΣ ΑΡΧΑΙΟΛΟΓΙΑΣ

ΛΟΓΟΣ ΟΓΔΟΟΣ

I. Οἱ δὲ μετὰ τούτους ἀποδειχθέντες ὕπατοι κατὰ τὴν ἑβδομηκοστὴν καὶ τρίτην ὀλυμπιάδα, ἣν[1] ἐνίκα στάδιον Ἀστύλος Κροτωνιάτης, ἄρχοντος Ἀθήνησιν Ἀγχίσου, Γάιος Ἰούλιος Ἰοῦλος[2] καὶ Πόπλιος Πινάριος Ῥοῦφος, ἄνδρες ἥκιστα πολεμικοὶ καὶ διὰ τοῦτο μάλιστα τῆς ἀρχῆς ταύτης παρὰ τοῦ δήμου τυχόντες, εἰς πολλοὺς καὶ μεγάλους ἠναγκάσθησαν κινδύνους καταστῆναι, πολέμου καταρραγέντος ἐκ[3] τῆς ἐκείνων ἀρχῆς δι' ὧν ἡ 2 πόλις ὀλίγου ἐδέησεν ἐκ βάθρων ἀναιρεθῆναι. ὁ γὰρ Μάρκιος ἐκεῖνος ὁ Κοριολανός, ὁ τὴν ἐπὶ τῇ τυραννίδι αἰτίαν σχὼν[4] καὶ φυγῇ ἀιδίῳ ἐλαθείς, ἀγανακτῶν τε ἐπὶ τῇ συμφορᾷ καὶ τιμωρίαν παρὰ τῶν ἐχθρῶν βουλόμενος λαβεῖν, δι' οὗ δ' ἂν αὐτῇ γένοιτο τρόπου καὶ δι' οἵας δυνάμεως ἀνασκοπῶν,

---

[1] ἣν Jacoby : καθ' ἣν O. [2] Kiessling : ἰοῦλλος O.
[3] ἐκ O : ἐπὶ Kiessling. [4] Cobet : ἔχων O.

---

[1] For chaps. 1-2, 3 cf. Livy ii. 35, 6-8. [2] 487 B.C.

2

THE ROMAN ANTIQUITIES

OF

DIONYSIUS OF HALICARNASSUS

BOOK VIII

I. The consuls[1] who were chosen after these were
Gaius Julius Iulus and Publius Pinarius Rufus, who
entered upon their magistracy in the seventy-third
Olympiad[2] (the one in which Astylus of Croton won
the foot-race), when Anchises was archon at Athens.
These magistrates, who were not in the least warlike
men and for that reason chiefly had obtained the
consulship from the people, were involved against
their will in many great dangers, a war having broken
out as a result of their rule[3] which came near destroying the commonwealth from its foundations. For
Marcius Coriolanus, the man who had been accused
of aiming at tyranny and condemned to perpetual
banishment,[4] resented his misfortune and at the same
time desired to avenge himself upon his enemies ;
and considering in what manner and with the aid of
what forces he might accomplish this, he found that

[3] Or, following Kiessling's emendation, "in their consulship."
[4] See vi. 92-94, vii. 21-64.

μίαν εὕρισκε Ῥωμαίοις τότε ἀντίπαλον ἰσχὺν τὴν
Οὐολούσκων, εἰ κοινῇ χρησάμενοι γνώμῃ καὶ
τυχόντες ἡγεμόνος ἔμφρονος ἐνστήσονται πρὸς
3 αὐτοὺς τὸν πόλεμον. ἐλογίζετο μὲν οὖν,[1] ὡς εἰ
πείσειε τοὺς Οὐολούσκους δέξασθαί τε αὐτὸν καὶ
τὴν ἡγεμονίαν ἐπιτρέψαι τοῦ πολέμου, ῥᾳδίως
αὐτῷ διαπεπράξεται τὸ ἔργον· ἐτάραττε δ' αὐτὸν
ἡ συνείδησις ὅτι πλειστάκις κατὰ τὰς μάχας δεινὰ
δεδρακὼς ἦν αὐτοὺς καὶ πόλεις συμμαχίδας ἀφῃρη-
μένος. οὐ μὴν ἀπέστη γε τῆς πείρας διὰ τὸ τοῦ
κινδύνου μέγεθος, ἀλλ' εἰς αὐτὰ τὰ δεινὰ χωρεῖν
4 ἐβουλεύσατο καὶ πάσχειν ὑπ' αὐτῶν ὁτιοῦν. φυ-
λάξας δὲ νύκτα καὶ ταύτην σκοταίαν ἧκεν εἰς
Ἄντιον, τὴν ἐπιφανεστάτην τῶν ἐν Οὐολούσκοις
πόλεων, ἡνίκα περὶ δεῖπνον ἦσαν οἱ κατὰ τὴν
πόλιν, καὶ παρελθὼν εἰς οἰκίαν ἀνδρὸς δυνατοῦ,
δι' εὐγένειάν τε καὶ πλοῦτον καὶ τὰς ἐν τοῖς πολέμοις πράξεις μέγα ἐφ' ἑαυτῷ φρονοῦντος καὶ τὸ
ἔθνος ὅλον ἄγοντος ὡς τὰ πολλά, ᾧ Τύλλος Ἄττιος
ὄνομα ἦν, ἱκέτης τοῦ ἀνδρὸς γίνεται καθεζόμενος
5 ἐπὶ τῆς ἑστίας. διηγησάμενος δ' αὐτῷ τὰς κατα-
σχούσας αὐτὸν ἀνάγκας δι' ἃς ὑπέμεινεν ἐπὶ τοὺς
ἐχθροὺς καταφυγεῖν, μέτρια ἠξίου φρονῆσαι καὶ
ἀνθρώπινα περὶ ἀνδρὸς ἱκέτου καὶ μηκέτι πολέμιον
ἡγεῖσθαι τὸν ὑποχείριον μηδ' εἰς τοὺς ἀτυχοῦντας
καὶ τεταπεινωμένους ἀποδείκνυσθαι τὴν ἰσχύν,
ἐνθυμούμενον ὡς οὐ μένουσιν ἐπὶ τοῖς αὐτοῖς
6 πράγμασιν αἱ τῶν ἀνθρώπων τύχαι. " Δύναιο δ'
ἄν," ἔφη, " τοῦτο ἐξ αὐτοῦ μάλιστα μαθεῖν ἐμοῦ,
ὃς ἐν τῇ μεγίστῃ πόλει κράτιστός ποτε εἶναι τῶν
ἄλλων δοκῶν, νῦν ἔρημος καὶ ἄπολις καὶ ταπεινὸς

---

[1] μὲν οὖν Garrer : γοῦν O, οὖν Sintenis.

4

the only army which was then a match for the Romans was that of the Volscians, if these would agree together and make war upon them under an able general. He reasoned, therefore, that if he could prevail on the Volscians to receive him and to entrust to him the command of the war, his purpose would easily be accomplished. On the other hand, he was disturbed by the consciousness that he had often brought calamities upon them in battle and had forced many cities to forsake their alliance with them. However, he did not desist from the attempt because of the greatness of the danger, but resolved to encounter these very perils and suffer whatever might be the consequence. Having waited, therefore, for a night—and a dark one—he went to Antium, the most important city of the Volscians, at the hour when the inhabitants were at supper ; and going to the house of an influential man named Tullus Attius, who by reason of his birth, his wealth and his military exploits had a high opinion of himself and generally led the whole nation, he became his suppliant by sitting down at his hearth. Then, having related to him the dire straits which had forced him to take refuge with his enemies, he begged of him to entertain sentiments of moderation and humanity toward a suppliant and no longer to regard as an enemy one who was in his power, nor to exhibit his strength against the unfortunate and the humbled, bearing in mind that the fortunes of men are subject to change. "And this," he said, "you may learn most clearly from my own case. For though I was once looked upon as the most powerful of all men in the greatest city, I am now cast aside, forsaken, exiled and abased,

ἐρριμμένος, τοῦτο πείσομαι[1] ὅ τι ἂν ἐχθρῷ ὄντι σοι
δοκῇ. ὑπισχνοῦμαι δέ σοι τοσαῦτα ἀγαθὰ ποιήσειν
Οὐολούσκους φίλος τῷ ἔθνει γενόμενος ὅσα κακὰ
εἰργασάμην ἐχθρὸς ὤν. εἰ δέ τι ἄλλο γινώσκεις
περὶ ἐμοῦ, χρῆσαι τῇ ὀργῇ παραχρῆμα καὶ θάνατον
χάρισαί μοι τὸν τάχιστον αὐτοχειρίᾳ τε καὶ ἐπὶ τῆς
ἑστίας τῆς ἑαυτοῦ[2] καθιερεύσας τὸν ἱκέτην."

II. Ἔτι δ' αὐτοῦ ταῦτα λέγοντος ἐμβαλὼν τὴν
δεξιὰν ὁ Τύλλος καὶ ἀπὸ τῆς ἑστίας ἀναστήσας
θαρρεῖν τε αὐτὸν ἐκέλευσεν, ὡς μηδὲν ἀνάξιον τῆς
ἰδίας ἀρετῆς πεισόμενον, καὶ πολλὰς αὐτῷ χάριτας
εἰδέναι τῆς πρὸς ἑαυτὸν ἀφίξεως ἔφη, τιμήν τινα
οὐ μικρὰν εἶναι καὶ ταύτην ἀποφαινόμενος· Οὐολούσκους τε αὐτῷ πάντας ὑπισχνεῖτο ποιήσειν
φίλους ἀρξάμενος ἀπὸ τῆς ἑαυτοῦ πατρίδος· καὶ
2 οὐδεμίαν ἐψεύσατο τῶν ὑποσχέσεων. χρόνου δέ
τινος οὐ πολλοῦ διελθόντος βουλευομένοις τοῖς
ἀνδράσι κατὰ σφᾶς, Μαρκίῳ τε καὶ Τύλλῳ, κινεῖν
ἐδόκει τὸν πόλεμον. ὁ μὲν οὖν Τύλλος αὐτίκα
μάλα ἐβούλετο πᾶσαν τὴν Οὐολούσκων δύναμιν
παραλαβὼν ἐπὶ τὴν Ῥώμην χωρεῖν ἕως ἐστασίαζέ
τε καὶ ἡγεμόνας ἀπολέμους εἶχεν, ὁ δὲ Μάρκιος
αἰτίαν πρῶτον ᾤετο δεῖν εὐσεβῆ καὶ δικαίαν
ἐνστήσασθαι τοῦ πολέμου, διδάσκων ὡς ἁπάσαις
μὲν πράξεσι θεοὶ συλλαμβάνουσι, μάλιστα δὲ ταῖς
κατὰ πολέμους, ὅσῳ μείζους τέ εἰσι τῶν ἄλλων
καὶ εἰς ἀδήλους φιλοῦσι κατασκήπτειν τύχας.
ἐτύγχανον δὲ τότε Ῥωμαίοις καὶ Οὐολούσκοις
ἐκεχειρίαι τοῦ πολέμου καὶ ἀνοχαὶ πρὸς ἀλλήλους

---

[1] πείσομαι Tauchnitz ed. : πεισόμενος O. Kiessling proposed ἔρριμμαι τοῦτο πεισόμενος.
[2] ἑαυτοῦ AB : σεαυτοῦ C, Jacoby.

6

and destined to suffer any treatment you, who are my enemy, shall think fit to inflict upon me. But I promise you that I will perform as great services for the Volscians, if I become their friend, as I occasioned calamities to them when I was their enemy. However, if you have any other purpose concerning me, let loose your resentment at once and grant me the speediest death by sacrificing the suppliant with your own hand and at your own hearth."

II. While he was yet speaking these words Tullus gave him his hand and, raising him from the hearth, bade him be assured that he should not be treated in any manner unworthy of his valour, and said he felt himself under great obligations to him for coming to him, declaring that he looked upon even this as no small honour. He promised him also that he would make all the Volscians his friends, beginning with those of his own city; and not one of his promises did he fail to make good. Soon afterwards Marcius and Tullus conferred together in private and came to a decision to begin war against the Romans. Tullus proposed to put himself immediately at the head of all the Volscians and march on Rome while the Romans were still at odds and had generals averse to war. But Marcius insisted that they ought first to establish a righteous and just ground for war; for he pointed out that the gods take a hand in all actions, and especially in those relating to war, in so far as these are of greater consequence than any others and their outcome is generally uncertain. It happened that there was at that time an armistice and a truce existing between the Romans and the Volscians and

οὖσαι σπονδαί τε διετεῖς ὀλίγῳ πρότερον χρόνῳ
3 γενόμεναι. "᾽Εὰν μὲν οὖν ἀπερισκέπτως," ἔφη,
"καὶ διὰ τάχους τὸν πόλεμον ἐπιφέρῃς, τοῦ
λελύσθαι τὰς σπονδὰς αἴτιος ἔσῃ καὶ τὸ δαιμόνιον
οὐχ ἕξεις εὐμενές· ἐὰν δὲ περιμείνῃς[1] ἕως ἐκεῖνοι
τοῦτο ποιήσωσιν, ἀμύνεσθαι δόξεις καὶ λελυμέναις
σπονδαῖς βοηθεῖν. ὅπως δ᾽ ἂν τοῦτο γένοιτο, καὶ
ὅπως ἂν ἐκεῖνοι μὲν ἄρξειαν παρασπονδεῖν, ἡμεῖς
δὲ δόξαιμεν ὅσιον καὶ δίκαιον ἐπιφέρειν τὸν πόλεμον, ἐγὼ σὺν πολλῇ φροντίδι ἀνεύρηκα. δεῖ δ᾽
ὑφ᾽ ἡμῶν αὐτοὺς ἐξαπατηθέντας ἄρξαι τῆς παρα-
4 νομίας. ὁ δὲ τρόπος τῆς ἐξαπάτης, ὃν ἐγὼ τέως
μὲν ἀπόρρητον ἐφύλαττον ἀναμένων τὸν οἰκεῖον
αὐτοῦ καιρόν, νῦν δὲ σοῦ σπουδάζοντος ἔργου
ἔχεσθαι θᾶττον ἐκφέρειν εἰς[2] μέσον ἀναγκάζομαι,
τοιόσδε ἐστίν· θυσίας ἐπιτελεῖν Ῥωμαῖοι μέλλουσι
καὶ ἀγῶνας ἄγειν ἀπὸ πολλῶν χρημάτων σφόδρα
λαμπρούς, ἀφίξονταί τε κατὰ θέαν ἐπὶ τούτους
5 πολλοὶ τῶν ξένων. τοῦτον ἀναμείνας τὸν χρόνον
ἴθι καὶ σὺ καὶ Οὐολούσκων ὅσους δύνασαι πλείστους παρασκεύασον ἐλθεῖν ἐπὶ τὴν θέαν· ὅταν δ᾽ ἐν
τῇ πόλει γένῃ, τῶν ἀναγκαιοτάτων τινά σοι φίλων κέλευσον ἐλθεῖν ὡς τοὺς ὑπάτους καὶ δι᾽ ἀπορ-
ρήτων εἰπεῖν ὅτι μέλλουσιν ἐπιτίθεσθαι τῇ πόλει
Οὐολοῦσκοι νύκτωρ καὶ ἐπὶ τοῦτο ἥκουσι τὸ ἔργον ἀθρόοι. εὖ γὰρ ἴσθι ὡς εἰ τοῦτο ἀκούσειαν
οὐδὲν ἔτι ἐνδοιάσαντες ἐκβαλοῦσιν ὑμᾶς ἐκ τῆς
πόλεως καὶ παρέξουσιν ἀφορμὴν δικαίας ὀργῆς."
III. ῾Ως δ᾽ ἤκουσε ταῦτα ὁ Τύλλος, ὑπερηγάσθη
τε καὶ τὸν παρόντα καιρὸν τῆς στρατείας ὑπερβαλό-

---

[1] περιμείνῃς Β : ἐπιμένῃς Α.　　　　[2] εἰς Reiske : ἐπὶ Ο.

[1] For chaps. 2, 4–4, 4 cf. Livy ii. 37 f.

also a treaty for two years which they had made a short time before : " If, therefore, you make war upon them inconsiderately and hastily," he said, " you will be to blame for the breaking of the treaty, and Heaven will not be propitious to you ; whereas, if you wait till they do this, you will seem to be defending yourselves and coming to the aid of a broken treaty. How this may be brought about and how they may be induced to violate the treaty first, while we shall seem to be waging a righteous and just war against them, I have discovered after long consideration. It is necessary that the Romans should be deceived by us, in order that they may be the first to commit unlawful acts. The nature of this deceit,[1] which I have hitherto kept secret while awaiting the proper occasion for its employment, but am now forced, because of your eagerness for action, to disclose sooner than I wished, is as follows. The Romans are intending to perform sacrifices and exhibit very magnificent games at vast expense, at which great numbers of strangers will be present as spectators. Wait for this occasion, and then not only go thither yourself, but engage as many of the Volscians as you can to go also and see the games. And when you are in Rome, bid one of your closest friends go to the consuls and inform them privately that the Volscians are intending to attack the city by night and that it is for this purpose that they have come to Rome in so great numbers. For you may be assured that if they hear this they will expel you Volscians from the city without further hesitation and furnish you with a ground for just resentment."

III. When Tullus heard this, he was highly pleased, and letting that opportunity for his expedition pass,

9

μενος[1] περὶ τὴν παρασκευὴν ἐγίνετο τοῦ πολέμου. ἐπεὶ δὲ καθῆκεν ὁ τῆς ἀρχῆς[2] καιρός, Ἰουλίου τε καὶ Πιναρίου τὴν ὑπατείαν ἤδη παρειληφότων, ἡ κρατίστη τῶν Οὐολούσκων νεότης ἐξ ἁπάσης πόλεως, ὡς ὁ Τύλλος ἠξίου, παρῆν ἐπὶ τὴν τῶν ἀγώνων θέαν· καὶ κατεσκήνουν οἱ πλείους ἐν ἱεροῖς τε καὶ δημοσίοις τόποις οὐκ ἔχοντες καταγωγὰς ἐν οἰκίαις τε καὶ παρὰ ξένοις, καὶ ὁπότε διὰ τῶν στενωπῶν πορεύοιντο, κατὰ συστροφὰς καὶ ἑταιρίας ἀθρόοι διεξῇεσαν, ὥστε καὶ λόγον ἤδη γίνεσθαι περὶ αὐτῶν ἀνὰ τὴν πόλιν καὶ ὑποψίας 2 ἀτόπους. ἐν δὲ τούτῳ προσέρχεται τοῖς ὑπάτοις ὁ κατασκευασθεὶς ὑπὸ τοῦ Τύλλου μηνυτής, ὡς ὁ Μάρκιος ὑπέθετο, καὶ ὡς δὴ ἀπόρρητον πρᾶξιν κατὰ τῶν ἑαυτοῦ φίλων ἐχθροῖς μέλλων ἐκφέρειν ὅρκοις καταλαμβάνεται τοὺς ὑπάτους ὑπὲρ ἀσφαλείας τε τῆς αὐτὸς[3] αὑτοῦ[4] καὶ τοῦ μηδένα Οὐολούσκων μαθεῖν ὅστις ἦν ὁ τὴν μήνυσιν κατ' αὐτῶν πεποιημένος. καὶ μετὰ τοῦτ' ἐκφέρει[5] τὴν περὶ τῆς ἐπιθέσεως τῆς κατεψευσμένης μήνυσιν. 3 ἐδόκει τοῖς ἀνδράσιν ἀληθὴς εἶναι ὁ λόγος, καὶ αὐτίκα ἡ βουλὴ κατ' ἄνδρα ὑπὸ τῶν ὑπάτων κληθεῖσα συνῆκτο, καὶ παραχθεὶς ὁ μηνυτὴς τοὺς αὐτοὺς εἶπε καὶ πρὸς ἐκείνην τὰ πιστὰ λαβὼν λόγους. τοῖς δὲ καὶ πάλαι μὲν εἶναι τὸ πρᾶγμα ἐδόκει μεστὸν ὑποψίας τοσαύτην νεότητα ἐξ ἑνὸς ἔθνους διαφόρου σφίσιν ἐπὶ τὴν θέαν ἐλθεῖν,[6] προσελθούσης δὲ μηνύσεως, ἧς τὴν ἀπάτην ἠγνόουν, ἰσχὺν βεβαίαν ἡ δόξα ἔλαβεν, ἐδόκει τε ἅπασιν ἀπαλλάττειν τοὺς ἄνδρας ἐκ τῆς πόλεως πρὶν ἥλιον

---

[1] Enthoven : ἀναβαλόμενος O, Jacoby.
[2] ἀρχῆς O : ἑορτῆς Sylburg.　　　[3] αὐτὸς B : om. A.

employed himself in preparing for the war. When the time for the beginning of the festival had come, Julius and Pinarius having already succeeded to the consulship, the flower of the Volscian youth came from every city, as Tullus requested, to see the games ; and the greater part of them were obliged to quarter themselves in sacred and public places, as they could not find lodgings in private houses and with friends. And when they walked in the streets, they went about in small groups and companies, so that there was already talk about them in the city and strange suspicions. In the mean time the informer suborned by Tullus, pursuant to the advice of Marcius, went to the consuls, and pretending that he was going to reveal a secret matter to his enemies against his own friends, bound the consuls by oaths, not only to insure his own safety, but also to insure that none of the Volscians should learn who had given the information against them. Thereupon he gave his information concerning the alleged plot. The consuls believed his story and immediately convened the senate, summoning the members individually ; and the informer, being brought before them and receiving their assurances, gave to them also the same account. The senators even long before this had looked upon it as a circumstance full of suspicion that such numbers of young men should come to see the games from a single nation which was hostile to them, and now that information too was given, the duplicity of which they did not perceive, their opinion was turned into certainty. It was their unanimous decision, therefore, to send the men out of the city

---

⁴ αὑτοῦ Post : αὐτοῦ O, Jacoby.   ⁵ Reiske : ἐπιφέρει O.
⁶ Kiessling : προσελθεῖν O, παρελθεῖν Sylburg, Jacoby.

δῦναι, τοῖς δὲ μὴ πεισθεῖσιν ἐπικηρύξαι θάνατον, ἐπιμεληθῆναι δὲ τῆς ἀπαλλαγῆς αὐτῶν, ἵνα χωρὶς ὕβρεως καὶ μετ᾽ ἀσφαλείας γένοιτο, τοὺς ὑπάτους.

IV. Ταῦτα τῆς βουλῆς ψηφισαμένης οἱ μὲν ἐκήρυττον διὰ τῶν στενωπῶν διεξιόντες ἀπιέναι[1] Οὐολούσκους ἐκ τῆς πόλεως αὐτίκα μάλα κατὰ μίαν ἅπαντας ἐξιόντας πύλην τὴν καλουμένην Καπυνὴν, ἕτεροι δὲ παρέπεμπον τοὺς ἀπαλλαττομένους ἅμα τοῖς ὑπάτοις· ἔνθα μάλιστα ὤφθη ὅσον αὐτῶν τὸ πλῆθος ἦν καὶ ὡς ἀκμαῖον ἅπαν ὑφ᾽ ἕνα καιρὸν καὶ κατὰ μίαν ἐξιόντων πύλην. πρῶτος δ᾽ αὐτῶν ὁ Τύλλος ἐξῄει διὰ ταχέων καὶ καταλαβὼν οὐ πρόσω τῆς πόλεως τόπον ἐπιτήδειον 2 ἐν τούτῳ τοὺς ὑστεροῦντας ἀνελάμβανεν. ἐπειδὴ δὲ πάντες συνήχθησαν, ἐκκλησίαν ποιησάμενος πολλῇ καταβοῇ τῆς Ῥωμαίων πόλεως ἐχρήσατο, δεινὴν καὶ ἀφόρητον ἀποφαίνων τὴν ὕβριν ἣν ὑβρισμένοι πρὸς αὐτῶν ἦσαν Οὐολοῦσκοι μόνοι τῶν ἄλλων ξένων ἐξελαθέντες ἐκ τῆς πόλεως· καὶ λέγειν ἠξίου ταῦτα πρὸς τὴν ἑαυτοῦ πόλιν ἕκαστον καὶ πράττειν ὅπως παύσωνται τῆς ὕβρεως Ῥωμαῖοι δίκας παρασχόντες τῆς παρανομίας· ταῦτα εἰπὼν καὶ παραθήξας ἀνθρώπους ἀγανακτοῦντας 3 ἐπὶ τῷ πάθει διέλυσε τὴν ἐκκλησίαν. ὡς δ᾽ ἀπαλλαγέντες εἰς τὰς ἑαυτῶν ἕκαστοι πατρίδας ἐδήλωσαν τοῖς ἄλλοις τὸν προπηλακισμὸν ἐπὶ μεῖζον ἐξαίροντες τὰ γενόμενα, ἠγανάκτει τε πᾶσα πόλις καὶ κατέχειν τὴν ὀργὴν οὐκ ἠδύνατο· δια-

----

¹ Sylburg : ἀπεῖναι O.

----

¹ The Porta Capena. The real etymology of the name Capena is not known.

before sunset and to order proclamation to be made
that all who did not obey should be put to death;
and they decreed that the consuls should see to it
that their departure took place without insult and
in safety.

IV. After the senate had passed this vote some
went through the streets making proclamation that
the Volscians should depart from the city immediately
and that they should all go out by a single gate, the
one called the Capuan gate,[1] while others together
with the consuls escorted them on their departure.
And then particularly, when they went out of the
city at the same time and by the same gate, it was
seen how numerous they were and how fit all were
for service. First of them to depart was Tullus, who
went out in haste, and taking his stand in a suitable
place not far from the city, picked up those who
lagged behind. And when they were all gathered together, he called an assembly and inveighed at length
against the Roman people, declaring that it was an
outrageous and intolerable insult that the Volscians
had received at their hands in being the only
strangers to be expelled from the city. He asked
that each man should report this treatment in his
own city and take measures to put a stop to the
insolence of the Romans by punishing them for their
lawless behaviour. After he had spoken thus and
sharpened the resentment of the Volscians, who were
already exasperated at the usage they had met with,
he dismissed the assembly. When they returned to
their several cities and each related to his fellow
citizens the insult they had received, exaggerating
what had occurred, every city was angered and unable to restrain its resentment; and sending ambas-

πρεσβευομένη δ' ἄλλη πρὸς ἄλλην εἰς μίαν ἀγορὰν
ἅπαντας[1] ἠξίου Οὐολούσκους συνιέναι,[2] ἵνα κοινῇ
4 χρήσαιντο γνώμῃ περὶ τοῦ πολέμου. ἐγίνετο δὲ
ταῦτα τοῦ Τύλλου μάλιστα ἐνάγοντος, καὶ συνῄεσαν ἐξ ἁπάσης πόλεως οἵ τε ἐν τοῖς τέλεσι καὶ
πολὺς ἄλλος ὄχλος εἰς τὴν Ἐχετρανῶν πόλιν· αὕτη
γὰρ ἐδόκει ἐν καλλίστῳ κεῖσθαι συνόδου[3] ταῖς
ἄλλαις ἡ πόλις. ῥηθέντων δὲ πολλῶν λόγων, οὓς
εἶπον οἱ δυναστεύοντες ἐν ἑκάστῃ πόλει, ψῆφος
ἀνεδόθη τοῖς παροῦσι, καὶ ἦν ἡ νικῶσα γνώμη
κινεῖν τὸν πόλεμον, ὡς Ῥωμαίων ἀρξάντων τῆς
περὶ τὰς σπονδὰς παρανομίας.

V. Ὑπὲρ δὲ τοῦ τίνα χρὴ πολεμεῖν αὐτοῖς τρόπον προθέντων σκοπεῖν τῶν ἐν τοῖς τέλεσι παρελθὼν ὁ Τύλλος συνεβούλευσεν αὐτοῖς καλεῖν τὸν
Μάρκιον καὶ παρ' ἐκείνου πυνθάνεσθαι πῶς ἂν ἡ
Ῥωμαίων καταλυθείη δύναμις· κράτιστα γὰρ ἁπάντων ἀνθρώπων εἰδέναι πῇ τε κάμνει τὰ τῆς πόλεως
πράγματα καὶ πῇ μάλιστα ἔρρωται. ἐδόκει ταῦτα,
καὶ αὐτίκα πάντες ἐβόων καλεῖν τὸν ἄνδρα. καὶ ὁ
Μάρκιος ἧς ἐβούλετο ἀφορμῆς λαβόμενος ἀνέστη
κατηφὴς καὶ δεδακρυμένος καὶ μικρὸν ἐπισχὼν
χρόνον τοιούτους διέθετο λόγους·

2   "Εἰ μὲν ἡγούμην ὑμᾶς ἅπαντας ὅμοια γινώσκειν
περὶ τῆς ἐμῆς συμφορᾶς, οὐκ ἂν ὑπελάμβανον
ἀναγκαῖον εἶναι περὶ αὐτῆς ἀπολογεῖσθαι· ἐνθυμούμενος δ', ὡς ἐν πολλοῖς καὶ διαφόροις ἤθεσιν
εἰκός, εἶναί τινας οἷς παραστήσεται δόξα οὔτε
ἀληθὴς οὔτε προσήκουσα περὶ ἐμοῦ,[4] ὡς οὐκ ἂν

---

[1] Kiessling : πάντας O.
[2] Reiske : ἰέναι O.
[3] ἐν καλλίστῳ κεῖσθαι συνόδου Reiske, κάλλιστα κεῖσθαι

sadors to one another, they demanded that all the
Volscians should meet together in a single assembly
in order to adopt a common plan concerning war.
All this was done chiefly at the instigation of Tullus.
And the authorities from every city together with a
great multitude of other people assembled at Ecetra ;
for this city seemed the most conveniently situated
with respect to the others for a general assembly.
After many speeches had been made by the men in
power in each city, the votes of all present were
taken ; and the view which carried was to begin war,
since the Romans had first transgressed in the matter
of the treaty.

V. When the authorities had proposed to the
assembly to consider in what manner they ought to
carry on the war against them, Tullus came forward
and advised them to summon Marcius and inquire of
him how the power of the Romans might be over-
thrown, since he knew better than any man both the
weakness and the strength of the commonwealth.
This met with their approval, and at once they all
cried out to summon the man. Then Marcius,
having found the opportunity he desired, rose up
with downcast looks and with tears in his eyes and
after a brief pause spoke as follows :

" If I thought you all entertained the same opinion
of my misfortune, I should not think it necessary to
make any defence of it ; but when I consider that,
as is to be expected among many men of different
characters, there are some to whom will occur the
notion, neither true nor deserved by me, that the

συνόδου Kayser : ἐν (om. ἐν Ba) καλλίστῃ κεῖσθαι συνόδῳ AB,
Jacoby.
⁴ περὶ ἐμοῦ B : om. R.

ἄτερ αἰτίας ἀληθοῦς καὶ δικαίας ἐξήλασέ με ὁ
δῆμος ἐκ τῆς πατρίδος, παντὸς μάλιστα οἴομαι
δεῖν πρῶτον ὑπὲρ τῆς ἐμῆς φυγῆς ἐν κοινῷ πρὸς
3 ἅπαντας ὑμᾶς ἀπολογήσασθαι. ἀλλ' ἀνάσχεσθέ
μου, πρὸς θεῶν, καὶ οἱ κράτιστα ἐγνωκότες, ἃ
πέπονθα ὑπὸ τῶν ἐχθρῶν καὶ ὡς οὐ προσῆκόν μοι
ταύτης πεπείραμαι τῆς τύχης διεξιόντος, καὶ μὴ
πρότερον ποθεῖτε ὅ τι χρὴ πράττειν ἀκοῦσαι πρὶν
ὁποῖός τίς εἰμι ὁ τὴν γνώμην ἀποδειξόμενος[1]
ἐξετάσαι. ἔσται δὲ βραχὺς ὁ περὶ αὐτῶν, κἂν
πρόσωθεν ἄρξωμαι, λόγος.

4 " Ῥωμαίοις τὸ μὲν ἐξ ἀρχῆς πολίτευμα ἦν μικτὸν[2] ἔκ τε βασιλείας καὶ ἀριστοκρατίας· ἔπειτα
ὁ τελευταῖος βασιλεὺς Ταρκύνιος τυραννίδα τὴν
ἀρχὴν ἠξίου ποιεῖν. συστάντες οὖν ἐπ' αὐτὸν οἱ
τῆς ἀριστοκρατίας ἡγεμόνες ἐκεῖνον μὲν ἐξέβαλον
ἐκ τῆς πόλεως, αὐτοὶ δὲ τὰ κοινὰ κατέσχον ἀρίστην
καὶ σωφρονεστάτην, ὡς ἅπαντες ὁμολογοῦσι,
καταστησάμενοι πολιτείαν. χρόνοις δ' οὐ πολλοῖς
τῶν νῦν πρότερον, ἀλλὰ τρίτον ἢ τέταρτον τοῦτ'
ἔτος, οἱ πενέστατοί τε καὶ ἀργότατοι τῶν πολιτῶν
πονηροῖς χρησάμενοι προστάταις ἄλλα τε πολλὰ
ἐξύβρισαν καὶ τελευτῶντες καταλύειν τὴν ἀριστο-
5 κρατίαν ἐπεχείρουν. ἐφ' οἷς ἅπαντες μὲν οἱ τῆς
βουλῆς προεστηκότες ἤχθοντο καὶ ὅπως παύσωνται
τῆς ὕβρεως οἱ κινοῦντες τὴν πολιτείαν σκοπεῖν
ἠξίουν, ὑπὲρ ἅπαντας δὲ τοὺς ἀριστοκρατικοὺς ἐκ
μὲν τῶν πρεσβυτέρων[3] Ἄππιος ἀνὴρ πολλῶν
ἄξιος ἕνεκα[4] ἐπαινεῖσθαι, ἐκ δὲ τῶν νεωτέρων

---

[1] Steph. : προσδειξάμενος AB.
[2] μικτὸν B : om. R.
[3] Reiske : πρεσβυτάτων O.

people would not have banished me from my country without a real and just cause, I think it necessary above all things first to clear myself publicly before you all in the matter of my banishment. But have patience with me, I adjure you by the gods, even those of you who are best acquainted with the facts, while I relate what I have suffered from my enemies and show that I have not deserved this misfortune which has befallen me; and do not be anxious to hear what you must do before you have inquired what sort of man I am who am now going to express my opinion. The account I shall give of these matters will be brief, even though I begin from far back.

"The original constitution of the Romans was a mixture of monarchy and aristocracy. Afterwards Tarquinius, their last king, thought fit to make his government a tyranny; for which reason the leading men of the aristocracy, combining against him, expelled him from the state, and taking upon themselves the administration of public affairs, formed such a system of government as all men acknowledge to be the best and wisest. Not long ago, however, but only two or three years since, the poorest and idlest of the citizens, having bad men as their leaders, not only committed many other outrages, but at last endeavoured to overthrow the aristocracy. At this all the leaders of the senate were grieved and thought they ought to consider how the insolence of these disturbers of the government could be stopped; but more active in this regard than the other aristocrats, were, of the older senators, Appius, a man deserving of praise on many accounts, and,

---

ⁱ ἕνεκα ACmg, ἕνικα B, om. C : ἕνεκεν Jacoby.

ἐγώ· καὶ λόγους ἐποιούμεθα διὰ παντὸς ἐπὶ τῆς
βουλῆς ἐλευθέρους, οὐ δήμῳ πολεμοῦντες ἀλλὰ
πονηροκρατίαν ὑφορώμενοι, οὐδὲ καταδουλώσασθαί
τινα βουλόμενοι¹ Ῥωμαίων ἀλλὰ τὸ μὲν ἐλεύθερον
ἅπασιν ἀξιοῦντες ὑπάρχειν,² τὴν δὲ προστασίαν
τῶν κοινῶν ἀποδεδόσθαι τοῖς κρείττοσι.

VI. '' Ταῦθ' ὁρῶντες οἱ πονηρότατοι τοῦ πλήθους ἐκεῖνοι προστάται πρώτους ἔγνωσαν ἡμᾶς
τοὺς φανερώτατα ἐναντιουμένους σφίσιν ἐκποδὼν
ποιήσασθαι, οὐχ ἅμα ἀμφοτέροις ἐπιχειρήσαντες,
ἵνα μὴ ἐπίφθονόν τε καὶ βαρὺ τὸ πρᾶγμα γένηται,
ἀλλ' ἀπ' ἐμοῦ τοῦ νεωτέρου τε καὶ εὐμεταχειρισ-
τοτέρου ἀρξάμενοι. τὸ μὲν οὖν πρῶτον ἄκριτόν
με ἐπεχείρησαν ἀπολέσαι, ἔπειτα ἔκδοτον παρὰ τῆς
βουλῆς ἠξίουν ἐπὶ θανάτῳ λαβεῖν· ἀποτυχόντες δ'
ἀμφοτέρων προὐκαλέσαντο ἐπὶ δίκην, ἣν αὐτοὶ
δικάσειν ἔμελλον, τυραννίδος ἐπιβαλόντες αἰτίαν.
2 καὶ οὐδὲ τοῦτ' ἔμαθον, ὅτι δήμῳ τύραννος οὐδεὶς
πολεμεῖ μετὰ τῶν ἀρίστων συστάς, ἀλλὰ τἀναντία
μετὰ τοῦ δήμου τὸ κράτιστον ἐκ τῆς πόλεως
ἀναιρεῖ μέρος· δικαστήριόν τε οὐχ ὅπερ ἦν πάτριον
ἀπέδωκάν μοι τὴν λοχῖτιν καλέσαντες ἐκκλησίαν,
ἀλλ' ὃ πάντες ὁμολογοῦσι πονηρότατον εἶναι δικασ-
τήριον³ καὶ ἐπ' ἐμοῦ πρώτου καὶ μόνου γενόμενον, ἐν ᾧ πλέον ἔχειν ἔμελλον οἱ θῆτες καὶ
ἀνέστιοι καὶ τοῖς ἀλλοτρίοις ἐπιβουλεύοντες βίοις
τῶν ἀγαθῶν καὶ δικαίων καὶ τὰ κοινὰ σώζεσθαι
3 βουλομένων. τοσοῦτο δ' ἄρα μοι περιῆν τοῦ μηδὲν

---

¹ βουλόμενοι B : om. R.
² ὑπάρχειν Reiske : ἔχειν R, om. B.
³ δικαστήριον O : om. Reudler, Jacoby.

---

¹ The tribunes.　　　² The aristocracy.

of the younger men, I myself. And the speeches which on every occasion we made before the senate were frank, not by way of making war upon the populace, but from a suspicion we had of government by the worst elements ; nor again from a wish to enslave any of the Romans, but from a desire that the liberty of all might be preserved and the management of public affairs be entrusted to the best men.

VI. " This being observed by those most unprincipled leaders of the populace,[1] they resolved to remove first out of their way the two of us who most openly opposed them—not, however, by attacking us both at once, lest the attempt should appear invidious and odious, but beginning with me who was the younger and the easier to be dealt with. In the first place, then, they endeavoured to destroy me without a trial ; and after that they demanded that I be delivered up by the senate in order to be put to death. But having failed of both purposes, they summoned me to a trial in which they themselves were to be my judges, and charged me with aiming at tyranny. They had not learned even this much— that no tyrant makes war upon the populace by allying himself with the best men,[2] but, on the contrary, destroys the best element in the state with the aid of the populace. And they did not give me the tribunal that was traditional, by summoning the centuriate assembly, but rather a tribunal which all admit to be most unprincipled—one set up in my case and mine alone—in which the working class and vagabonds and those who plot against the possessions of others were sure to prevail over good and just men and such as desire the safety of the commonwealth. This profit, then, and no more did I gain from my

19

ἀδικεῖν, ὥστ' ἐν ὄχλῳ κρινόμενος, οὗ τὸ πλέον
μισόχρηστον ἦν καὶ διὰ τοῦτ' ἐχθρὸν ἐμοί, δυσὶ
μόνον ἑάλων ψήφοις, ἀποτιθεμένων τὴν ἐξουσίαν
τῶν δημάρχων εἰ μὴ καταδικασθείην ἐγώ, καὶ τὰ
ἔσχατα πείσεσθαι πρὸς ἐμοῦ λεγόντων καὶ πάσῃ
σπουδῇ καὶ προθυμίᾳ παρὰ τὸν ἀγῶνα κατ' ἐμοῦ
4 χρησαμένων. τοιαῦτα δὴ πεπονθὼς ἐγὼ πρὸς τῶν
ἐμαυτοῦ πολιτῶν ἀβίωτον ἡγησάμην τὸν λοιπὸν
ἔσεσθαί μοι βίον, εἰ μὴ λάβοιμι παρ' αὐτῶν δίκας·
καὶ διὰ τοῦτ' ἐξόν μοι ζῆν ἀπραγμόνως, εἴτ' ἐν ταῖς
Λατίνων πόλεσιν ἠβουλόμην κατὰ τὸ συγγενές, εἴτ'
ἐν ταῖς νεοκτίστοις ἃς οἱ πατέρες ἡμῶν ἀπῴκισαν,
οὐκ ἠβουλήθην, ἐφ' ὑμᾶς δὲ κατέφυγον, οὓς ἠπιστάμην[1] πλεῖστά τε ὑπὸ Ῥωμαίων ἠδικημένους
καὶ μάλιστα αὐτοῖς ἀπεχθομένους, ἵνα κοινῇ μεθ'
ὑμῶν τιμωρησαίμην αὐτούς, ὅση μοι δύναμις,
λόγοις τε, ἔνθα δεῖ λόγων, καὶ ἔργοις, ὅταν ἔργων
δέῃ. χάριν τε ὑμῖν μεγάλην[2] οἶδα τῆς τε ὑποδοχῆς
μου καὶ ἔτι μᾶλλον τῆς τιμῆς ᾗ με τιμᾶτε, οὐθὲν
οὔτε μνησικακήσαντες οὔτε ὑπολογισάμενοι ὧν
ὑπ' ἐμοῦ πολεμίου ποτὲ ὄντος ἐπάθετε[3] κατὰ τοὺς
πολεμίους.

VII. " Φέρε δή, τίς ἂν εἴην ἀνήρ, εἰ δόξης καὶ
τιμῶν ὧν προσῆκέ μοι παρὰ τοῖς ἐμαυτοῦ πολίταις
τυγχάνειν πρὸς[4] τῶν εὖ παθόντων ἀποστερηθείς,
πρὸς δὲ τούτοις πατρίδος τε καὶ οἴκου καὶ φίλων
καὶ θεῶν πατρῴων καὶ τάφων προγονικῶν καὶ

---

[1] οὓς ἠπιστάμην R : ἠπιστάμην γὰρ A.

[2] ὑμῖν μεγάλην Reiske, τὴν μεγάλην ὑμῖν Jacoby   τὴν μεγάλην AB.

[3] ὑπ' ἐμοῦ πολεμίου ποτὲ ὄντος ἐπάθετε Jacoby, ὑπ' ἐμοῦ ἔτι
πολεμίου ὄντος ἐπάθετε Reiske, ὑπ' ἐμοῦ πρότερόν γε ἐπάθετε
Kiessling : ὑπ' ἐμοῦ ποτε ὄντες ἐπάθετε AB.

innocence, that, though tried by the mob, of which the greater part were haters of the virtuous and for that reason hostile to me, I was condemned by two votes only, even though the tribunes threatened to resign their power if I were acquitted, alleging that they expected to suffer the worst at my hands, and though they displayed all eagerness and zeal against me during the trial. After meeting with such treatment at the hands of my fellow citizens I felt that the rest of my life would not be worth living unless I took revenge upon them ; and for this reason, when I was at liberty to live free from vexations either in any of the Latin cities I pleased, because of our ties of kinship, or in the colonies lately planted by our fathers, I was unwilling to do so, but took refuge with you, though I knew you had suffered ever so many wrongs at the hands of the Romans and had conceived the greatest resentment against them, in order that in conjunction with you I might take revenge upon them to the utmost of my power, both by words where words were wanted, and by deeds, where deeds were wanted. And I feel very grateful to you for receiving me, and still more for the honour you show me, without either resenting or taking into account the injuries which you received from me, your erstwhile enemy, during the wars.

VII. " Come now, what kind of man should I be if, deprived as I am of the glory and honours I ought to be receiving from my fellow citizens to whom I have rendered great services, and, in addition to this, driven away from my country, my family, my friends, from the gods and sepulchres of my ancestors and

---

* Cobet : παρὰ O, Jacoby, ὑπὸ Prou.

παντὸς ἄλλου ἀπελαθεὶς ἀγαθοῦ, παρ' ὑμῖν δ'
ἅπαντα ταῦτα εὑρών, οἷς ἐκείνων χάριν ἐπολέμουν,
εἰ[1] μὴ γενοίμην χαλεπὸς μὲν οἷς ἀντὶ πολιτῶν
ἐχθροῖς κέχρημαι, χρηστὸς δ' οἷς ἀντὶ πολεμίων
φίλοις; ἀλλ' ἔγωγε οὐδ' ἐν ἀνδρὸς μοίρᾳ θείην ἂν
ὅστις μήτε τὸ πολεμοῦν δι' ὀργῆς ἔχει μήτε τὸ
σῶζον ἑαυτὸν δι' εὐνοίας. πατρίδα τε ἡγοῦμαι οὐ
τὴν ἀπαρνησαμένην με πόλιν, ἀλλ' ἧς ἀλλότριος
ὢν πολίτης γέγονα, γῆν τε οὐκ ἐν ᾗ ἠδίκημαι
2 φίλην, ἀλλ' ἐν ᾗ τὸ ἀσφαλὲς ἔχω. καὶ ἂν θεός τε
συλλαμβάνῃ καὶ τὰ ὑμέτερα ὡς[2] εἰκὸς πρόθυμα ᾖ,
μεγάλην καὶ ταχεῖαν ἐλπίζω γενήσεσθαι μεταβολήν.[3] εὖ γὰρ ἴστε ὅτι πολλῶν ἤδη πολεμίων[4]
πειραθέντες Ῥωμαῖοι οὐθένας μᾶλλον ἔδεισαν
ὑμῶν, οὐδ' ἔστιν ἐφ' ᾧ μᾶλλον σπουδάζοντες
διατελοῦσιν ἢ ὅπως τὸ ὑμέτερον ἔθνος ἀσθενὲς ἀπο-
3 δείξουσι. καὶ διὰ τοῦτο τὰς μὲν πολέμῳ λαβόντες
ὑμῶν ἔχουσι[5] πόλεις, τὰς δὲ φιλίας ἐλπίδι παρα-
κρουσάμενοι, ἵνα μὴ καθ' ἓν ἅπαντες γενόμενοι
κοινόν ἐξενέγκητε κατ' αὐτῶν πόλεμον. ἐὰν οὖν
τἀναντία ὑμεῖς ἀντιφιλοτιμούμενοι διατελῆτε καὶ
μίαν ἅπαντες ἔχητε περὶ[6] τοῦ πολέμου γνώμην, ὃ
ποιεῖτε νυνί, ῥᾳδίως αὐτῶν τὸ κράτος παύσετε.

VIII. "Ὃν δὲ τρόπον ἀγωνιεῖσθε καὶ πῶς
χρήσεσθε τοῖς πράγμασιν, ἐπειδὴ γνώμην ἀξιοῦτέ
με ἀποφήνασθαι, εἴτ' ἐμπειρίαν μοι μαρτυροῦντες
εἴτ' εὔνοιαν εἴτε καὶ ἀμφότερα, φράσω καὶ οὐκ
ἀποκρύψομαι. πρῶτον μὲν οὖν ὑμῖν παραινῶ

---

[1] εἰ B by correction : om. R.   [2] ὡς Steph. : om. AB.
[3] μεταβολήν O : τὴν μεταβολήν Jacoby.
[4] Sylburg : πολέμων O.
[5] ἔχουσι Steph. : ἀποδείξουσι ABC.
[6] περὶ added by Kiessling.

from every enjoyment, and if, finding all these things among you against whom I made war for their sake, I should not become harsh toward those whom I have found enemies instead of fellow citizens, and helpful to those whom I have found friends instead of enemies? For my part, I could not count as a real man anyone who feels neither anger against those who make war upon him nor affection for those who seek his preservation. And I regard as my fatherland, not that state which has renounced me, but the one of which I, an alien, have become a citizen ; and as a friendly land, not the one in which I have been wronged, but that in which I find safety. And if Heaven lends a hand and your assistance is as eager as I have reason to expect, I have hopes that there will be a great and sudden change. For you must know that the Romans, having already had experience of many enemies, have feared none more than you, and that there is nothing they continue to seek more earnestly than the means of weakening your nation. And for this reason they hold a number of your cities which they have either taken by war or deluded with the hope of their friendship, in order that you may not all unite and engage in a common war against them. If, therefore, you will strive unceasingly to counteract their designs and will all be of one mind about war, as you are now, you will easily put an end to their power.

VIII. " As to the manner in which you will wage the contest and how you will handle the situation, since you ask me to express my opinion—whether this be a tribute to my experience or to my goodwill or to both—I shall give it without concealing anything. In the first place, therefore, I advise you to

σκοπεῖν ὅπως εὐσεβῆ καὶ δικαίαν πορίσησθε τοῦ
πολέμου πρόφασιν. εὐσεβὴς δὲ καὶ δικαία τοῦ
πολέμου πρόφασις ἥτις ἂν γένοιτο καὶ ἅμα συμ-
2 φέρουσα ὑμῖν, ἀκούσατέ μου. Ῥωμαίοις ἡ μὲν ἐξ
ἀρχῆς ὑπάρξασα γῆ βραχεῖά ἐστι καὶ λυπρά, ἡ δ'
ἐπίκτητος, ἣν τοὺς περιοίκους ἀφελόμενοι κατέχουσι,¹ πολλὴ καὶ ἀγαθή· καὶ εἰ τῶν ἠδικημένων
ἕκαστοι τὴν ἑαυτῶν ἀξιοῖεν ἀπολαβεῖν, οὐδὲν οὕτως
μικρὸν οὐδ' ἀσθενὲς οὐδ' ἄπορον ὡς τὸ Ῥωμαίων
ἄστυ γενήσεται. τούτου δ' οἶμαι δεῖν ὑμᾶς ἄρξαι.
3 πέμπετε οὖν πρέσβεις ὡς αὐτοὺς ἀπαιτοῦντες ἃς
κατέχουσιν ὑμῶν πόλεις καὶ ὅσα τείχη ἐν τῇ
ὑμετέρᾳ γῇ ἐνετειχίσαντο ἀξιοῦντες ἐκλιπεῖν, καὶ
εἴ τι ἄλλο βίᾳ σφετερισάμενοι τῶν ὑμετέρων ἔχουσι
πείθοντες ἀποδιδόναι. πολέμου δὲ μήπω ἄρχετε
πρὶν ἢ λαβεῖν τὰς παρ' αὐτῶν ἀποκρίσεις. ἐὰν
γὰρ ταῦτα ποιήσητε, δυεῖν ὧν βούλεσθε ὑπάρξει
θάτερον ὑμῖν· ἢ τὰ ἑαυτῶν ἀπολήψεσθε ἄνευ
κινδύνων καὶ δαπάνης, ἢ καλὴν καὶ δικαίαν πρόφασιν εἰληφότες ἔσεσθε τοῦ πολέμου. τὸ γὰρ μὴ
τῶν ἀλλοτρίων ἐπιθυμεῖν, ἀλλὰ τὰ ἑαυτῶν ἀπαιτεῖν
καὶ μὴ τυγχάνοντας τούτου πολεμεῖν, ἅπαντες
4 ὁμολογήσουσιν² εἶναι καλόν. φέρε δή, τί ποιήσειν
οἴεσθε Ῥωμαίους ταῦθ' ὑμῶν προελομένων; πότερον ἀποδώσειν τὰ χωρία ὑμῖν; καὶ τί κωλύσει
πάντων αὐτοὺς ἀποστῆναι τῶν ἀλλοτρίων; ἥξουσι
γὰρ Αἰκανοί τε καὶ Ἀλβανοὶ καὶ Τυρρηνοὶ καὶ
πολλοὶ ἄλλοι τὴν ἑαυτῶν ἕκαστοι γῆν ἀποληψό-
μενοι. ἢ καθέξειν τὰ χωρία καὶ μηθὲν τῶν δικαίων

---

¹ κατέχουσι added by Sylburg, ἔχουσι by Cmg, Sintenis.
² ἂν ὁμολογήσουσιν B : ἀνομολογήσουσιν A, ἂν ὁμολογήσαιεν
Reiske.

consider how you may provide yourselves with a righteous and just pretext for the war. And what pretext for war will be not only righteous and just but also profitable to you at the same time, you shall now learn from me. The land which originally belonged to the Romans is of small extent and barren, but the acquired land which they possess as a result of robbing their neighbours is large and fertile ; and if each of the injured nations should demand the return of the land that is theirs, nothing would be so insignificant, so weak, and so helpless as the city of Rome. In doing this I think you ought to take the lead. Send ambassadors to them, therefore, to demand back your cities which they are holding, to ask that they evacuate all the forts they have erected in your country, and to persuade them to restore everything else belonging to you which they have appropriated by force. But do not begin war till you have received their answer. For if you follow this advice, you will obtain one of two things you desire : you will either recover all that belongs to you without danger and expense or will have found an honourable and a just pretext for war. For not to covet the possessions of others, but to demand back what is one's own and, failing to obtain this, to declare war, will be acknowledged by all men to be an honourable proceeding. Well then, what do you think the Romans will do if you choose this course ? Do you think they will restore the places to you ? And if they do, what is to hinder them from relinquishing everything that belongs to others ? For the Aequians, the Albans, the Tyrrhenians, and many others will come each to get back their own land. Or do you think they will retain these places and refuse all your just demands ?

ποιήσειν; ὅπερ ἐγὼ νομίζω. οὐκοῦν ἀδικεῖσθαι
πρότεροι[1] λέγοντες ὑπ' αὐτῶν κατὰ τὸ ἀναγκαῖον
ἐπὶ τὰ ὅπλα χωρήσετε καὶ συμμάχους ἕξετε ὅσοι
τὰ ἑαυτῶν ἀφαιρεθέντες ἀπεγνώκασιν ἄλλως ἂν
5 ἔτι αὐτὰ ἢ πολεμοῦντες οὐκ ἀπολήψεσθαι. κράτι-
στος δ' ὁ καιρὸς καὶ οἷος οὐχ ἕτερος ἐπιθέσθαι
Ῥωμαίοις, ὃν ἡ τύχη τοῖς ἀδικουμένοις οὐδ' ἂν
ἐλπισθέντα παρεσκεύασεν, ἐν ᾧ στασιάζουσι καὶ
ὑποπτεύουσιν ἀλλήλους καὶ ἡγεμόνας ἔχουσιν ἀ-
πείρους πολέμου. ἃ μὲν οὖν ὑποτίθεσθαι ἔδει λόγοις καὶ παραινεῖν φίλοις, μετὰ πάσης εὐνοίας καὶ
πίστεως εἰρημένα ὑπ' ἐμοῦ, ταῦτ' ἐστίν· ἃ δὲ
παρ' αὐτὰ τὰ ἔργα ἑκάστοτε προορᾶσθαί τε καὶ
μηχανᾶσθαι δεήσει, τοῖς ἡγεμόσι τῆς δυνάμεως
6 ἐπιτρέψατε διανοεῖσθαι. πρόθυμον γὰρ καὶ τοὐμὸν
ἔσται ἐν ᾧ ἄν με τάττητε τόπῳ, καὶ πειράσο-
μαι μηδενὸς εἶναι χείρων μήτε στρατιώτου μήτε
λοχαγοῦ μήτε ἡγεμόνος· ἀλλὰ καταχρῆσθέ μοι
λαβόντες ὅπου ἂν μέλλω τι ὑμᾶς ὠφελήσειν, καὶ
εὖ ἴστε ὅτι, εἰ πολεμῶν ὑμῖν μεγάλα βλάπτειν
δυνατὸς ἦν, καὶ σὺν ὑμῖν ἀγωνιζόμενος μεγάλα
δυνήσομαι ὠφελεῖν."

IX. Τοιαῦτα μὲν ὁ Μάρκιος εἶπεν. οἱ δὲ Οὐολοῦσκοι λέγοντός τε τοῦ ἀνδρὸς ἔτι δῆλοι ἦσαν
ἀγάμενοι τοὺς λόγους, καὶ ἐπειδὴ ἐπαύσατο, μεγάλῃ βοῇ πάντες ἐπεσήμηναν ὡς τὰ κράτιστα
ὑποθεμένῳ[2] λόγον τε οὐθενὶ προθέντες ἐπικυροῦσι
τὴν γνώμην. γραφέντος δὲ τοῦ δόγματος εὐθὺς ἐξ
ἑκάστης πόλεως τοὺς ἐπιφανεστάτους ἄνδρας ἑλό-

---

[1] Sylburg : πρότερον O.
[2] Reudler : ὑποτιθεμένῳ Ba, ὑποτιθεμένου ABb.

26

That is my opinion. Protesting, therefore, that they wronged you first, you will of necessity have recourse to arms, and you will have for your allies all who, having been deprived of their possessions, despair of recovering them by any other means than by war. This is a most favourable and a unique opportunity which Fortune has provided for the wronged nations, an opportunity for which they could not even have hoped, of attacking the Romans while they are divided and suspicious of one another and while they have generals who are inexperienced in war. These, then, are the considerations which it was fitting to suggest in words and urge upon friends, and I have offered them in all goodwill and sincerity. But when it comes to the actual deeds, what it will be necessary to foresee and contrive upon each occasion, leave the consideration of those matters to the commanders of the forces. For my zeal also shall not be wanting in whatever post you may place me, and I shall endeavour to do my duty with no less bravery than any common soldier or captain or general. Pray take me and use me wherever I may be of service to you, and be assured that if, when I fought against you, I was able to do you great mischief, I shall also be able, when I fight on your side, to be of great service to you."

IX. Thus Marcius spoke. And the Volscians not only made it clear while he was yet speaking that they were pleased with his words, but, after he had done, they all with a great shout signified that they found his advice most excellent; and permitting no one else to speak, they adopted his proposal. After the decree had been drawn up they at once chose the most important men out of every city and sent them

μένοι πρεσβευτὰς εἰς τὴν Ῥώμην ἀπέστειλαν· τῷ
δὲ Μαρκίῳ ψηφίζονται βουλῆς τε μετουσίαν ἐν
ἁπάσῃ πόλει καὶ ἀρχὰς ἐξεῖναι πανταχόσε μετιέναι
καὶ τῶν ἄλλων ὁπόσα τιμιώτατα ἦν παρ' αὐτοῖς
2 μετέχειν. καὶ πρὶν ἢ τὰς Ῥωμαίων ἀποκρίσεις
ἀναμεῖναι, πάντες ἔργου εἴχοντο παρασκευαζόμενοι
τὰ πολέμια· ὅσοι τε ἦσαν αὐτῶν ἄθυμοι τέως
κακωθέντες ἐν ταῖς προτέραις μάχαις, τότε πάντες
ἐπερρώσθησαν[1] ὡς τὴν Ῥωμαίων καθαιρήσοντες
3 ἰσχύν. οἱ δ' εἰς τὴν Ῥώμην ἀποσταλέντες ὑπ'
αὐτῶν πρέσβεις καταστάντες ἐπὶ τὴν βουλὴν ἔλεγον
ὅτι Οὐολούσκοις περὶ πολλοῦ ἐστι καταλύσασθαι
τὰ πρὸς Ῥωμαίους ἐγκλήματα καὶ τὸν λοιπὸν
χρόνον εἶναι φίλοις καὶ συμμάχοις ἄνευ δόλου καὶ
ἀπάτης. ἔσεσθαι δὲ τὸ πιστὸν αὐτοῖς τῆς φιλίας
βέβαιον ἀπέφαινον, εἰ κομίσαιντο γῆν τε τὴν ἑαυτῶν καὶ πόλεις ἃς ὑπὸ Ῥωμαίων ἀφῃρέθησαν·
ἄλλως δ' οὔτε εἰρήνην οὔτε φιλότητα βεβαίαν
ὑπάρξειν αὐτοῖς· τὸ γὰρ ἀδικούμενον ἀεὶ πολέμιον
εἶναι τῷ πλημμελοῦντι φύσει. ἠξίουν τε μὴ καταστῆσαι σφᾶς εἰς ἀνάγκην πολέμου τῶν δικαίων
ἀποτυγχάνοντας.

X. Ὡς δὲ ταῦτ' εἶπον οἱ πρέσβεις, ἐβουλεύοντο
κατὰ σφᾶς οἱ σύνεδροι μεταστησάμενοι τοὺς ἄνδρας. καὶ ἐπειδὴ ἔκριναν ἃς χρὴ ἀποκρίσεις ποιήσασθαι, καλέσαντες αὐτοὺς πάλιν ἐπὶ τὸν σύλλογον
ταύτην ἔδοσαν τὴν ἀπόφασιν· "Οὐ λανθάνετε
ἡμᾶς, ὦ Οὐολοῦσκοι, φιλίας μὲν οὐδὲν δεόμενοι,
πρόφασιν δ' εὐπρεπῆ λαβεῖν βουλόμενοι τοῦ πολέμου. ἃ γὰρ ἥκετε παρ' ἡμῶν ἀπαιτοῦντες, καλῶς

---

[1] Kiessling : ἐρρώσθησαν O.

to Rome as ambassadors. As for Marcius, they voted that he should be a member of the senate in every city and have the privilege of standing for magistracies everywhere, and should share in all the other honours that were most highly prized among them. Then, without waiting for the Romans' answer, they all set to work and employed themselves in warlike preparations ; and all of them who had hitherto been dejected because of their defeats in the previous battles now took courage, feeling confident that they would overthrow the power of the Romans. In the mean time the ambassadors they had sent to Rome, upon being introduced into the senate, said that the Volscians were very desirous that their complaints against the Romans should be settled and that for the future they should be friends and allies without fraud or deceit. And they declared that it would be a sure pledge of friendship if they received back the lands and the cities which had been taken from them by the Romans ; otherwise there would be neither peace nor secure friendship between them, since the injured party is always by nature an enemy to the aggressor. And they asked the Romans not to reduce them to the necessity of making war because of their failure to obtain justice.

X. When the ambassadors had thus spoken, the senators ordered them to withdraw, after which they consulted by themselves. Then, when they had determined upon the answer they ought to make, they called them back into the senate and gave this decision : " We are not unaware, Volscians, that it is not friendship you want, but that you wish to find a specious pretext for war. For you well know that you will never obtain what you have come to demand

ἐπίστασθε οὐδέποτε ληψόμενοι· χρήζετε γὰρ ἀδί-
2 κων τε καὶ ἀδυνάτων. εἰ μὲν οὖν δόντες ἡμῖν
τὰ χωρία ἔπειτα μεταδόξαν[1] ὑμῖν νῦν ἀπαιτεῖτε,
ἀδικεῖσθε μὴ κομιζόμενοι, εἰ δὲ πολέμῳ ἀφαιρεθέντες οὐκέτι αὐτῶν ὄντες κύριοι, ἀδικεῖτε τῶν
ἀλλοτρίων ἐφιέμενοι. ἡμεῖς δὲ κρατίστας ἡγού-
μεθα κτήσεις ἃς ἂν πολέμῳ κρατήσαντες λάβωμεν,
οὔτε πρῶτοι καταστησάμενοι νόμον τόνδε οὔτε
αὐτὸν ἀνθρώπων ἡγούμενοι εἶναι μᾶλλον ἢ οὐχὶ
θεῶν· ἅπαντάς τε καὶ Ἕλληνας καὶ βαρβάρους
εἰδότες αὐτῷ χρωμένους οὐκ ἂν ἐνδοίημεν ὑμῖν
μαλακὸν οὐδὲν οὐδ' ἂν ἀποσταίημεν ἔτι τῶν δορι-
3 κτήτων. πολλὴ γὰρ ἂν εἴη κακότης, εἴ τις ἃ μετ'
ἀρετῆς καὶ ἀνδρείας ἐκτήσατο, ταῦτα ὑπὸ μωρίας
τε καὶ δειλίας ἀφαιρεθείη. πολεμεῖν τε οὔτε μὴ
βουλομένους ὑμᾶς ἀναγκάζομεν, οὔτε προθυμου-
μένους παραιτούμεθα· ἂν δ' ἄρξησθε, ἀμυνούμεθα.
ταῦτα Οὐολούσκοις ἀπαγγέλλετε καὶ λέγετε ὅτι
λήψονται μὲν πρότεροι τὰ ὅπλα ἐκεῖνοι, θήσομεν
δ' ἡμεῖς ὕστεροι."

XI. Ταύτας οἱ πρέσβεις τὰς ἀποκρίσεις λαβόντες
ἀπήγγειλαν τῷ πλήθει τῶν Οὐολούσκων. συναχθείσης οὖν αὖθις ἐκκλησίας μετὰ τοῦτο κυροῦται
δόγμα κοινὸν τοῦ ἔθνους προειπεῖν Ῥωμαίοις τὸν
πόλεμον. ἔπειτα αἱροῦνται στρατηγοὺς αὐτοκράτορας τοῦ πολέμου Τύλλον τε καὶ Μάρκιον δυνάμεις τε ψηφίζονται καταγράφειν καὶ χρήματα
εἰσφέρειν καὶ τἆλλα παρασκευάσασθαι ὅσων ὑπ-
2 ελάμβανον δεήσειν τῷ πολέμῳ. μελλούσης δὲ
διαλύεσθαι τῆς ἐκκλησίας ἀναστὰς ὁ Μάρκιος ἔφη[2]·

---

[1] μεταδόξαν B : δόξαν R.
[2] ἔφη O : ἔφησεν Jacoby

of us, since you desire things that are unjust and impossible. If, indeed, having made a present to us of these places, you now, having changed your minds, demand them back, you are suffering a wrong if you do not recover them ; but if, having been deprived of them by war and no longer having any claim to them, you demand them back, you are doing wrong in coveting the possessions of others. As for us, we regard as in the highest degree our possessions those that we gain through victory in war. We are not the first who have established this law, nor do we regard it as more a human than a divine institution. Knowing, too, that all nations, both Greeks and barbarians, make use of this law, we will never show any sign of weakness to you or relinquish any of our conquests hereafter. For it would be great baseness for one to lose through folly and cowardice what one has acquired by valour and courage. We neither force you to go to war against your will nor deprecate war if you are eager for it ; but if you begin it, we shall defend ourselves. Return this answer to the Volscians, and tell them that, though they are the first to take up arms, we shall be the last to lay them down."

XI. The ambassadors,[1] having received this answer, reported it to the Volscian people. Another assembly was accordingly called and a decree of the whole nation was passed to declare war against the Romans. After this they appointed Tullus and Marcius generals for the war with full power and voted to levy troops, to raise money,[2] and to prepare everything else they thought would be necessary for the war. When the assembly was about to be dismissed, Marcius rose up

---

[1] For chaps. 11-13 cf. Livy ii. 39, 1 f.
[2] That is, by war taxes (εἰσφοραί).

" "Α μὲν ἐψήφισται τὸ κοινὸν ὑμῶν ἔχει καλῶς,
καὶ γινέσθω κατὰ τὸν οἰκεῖον ἕκαστα καιρόν· ἐν
ὅσῳ δὲ τὰ στρατεύματα μέλλετε καταγράφειν καὶ
τἆλλα εὐτρεπίζειν ἕξοντά τινας, ὥσπερ εἰκός,
ἀσχολίας καὶ διατριβάς, ἐγὼ καὶ Τύλλος ἔργου
ἐχώμεθα. ὅσοις οὖν ὑμῶν βουλομένοις ἐστὶ προ-
νομεῦσαι τὴν τῶν πολεμίων καὶ πολλὴν ἀποτεμέ-
σθαι λείαν, ἴτε σὺν ἡμῖν. ὑποδέχομαι δ' ὑμῖν, ἐὰν
θεὸς συλλάβῃ, πολλὰς καὶ καλὰς δώσειν ὠφελείας.
3 ἔτι γὰρ ἀπαράσκευοί εἰσι Ῥωμαῖοι δύναμιν οὔπω
συνεστηκυῖαν ὁρῶντες ὑμετέραν, ὥστε ἀδεῶς ἡμῖν
ὑπάρξει πᾶσαν ὅσην ἂν βουλώμεθα τῆς ἐκείνων
χώρας καταδραμεῖν."

XII. Ἀποδεξαμένων δὲ καὶ ταύτην τὴν γνώμην
τῶν Οὐολούσκων ἐξῄεσαν οἱ στρατηγοὶ διὰ ταχέων,
πρὶν ἔκπυστα γενέσθαι Ῥωμαίοις τὰ βουλεύματα,
πολλὴν ἐπαγόμενοι στρατιὰν ἑκούσιον· ἧς μέρος
μὲν ὁ Τύλλος ἔχων εἰς τὴν Λατίνων χώραν ἐνέβαλεν, ἵνα περισπάσειε τῶν πολεμίων τὴν ἐκεῖθεν
ἐπικουρίαν, τὸ δὲ λοιπὸν ὁ Μάρκιος ἄγων ἐπὶ τὴν
2 Ῥωμαίων ἤλασεν. οἷα δ' ἀπροσδοκήτου τοῦ[1]
κακοῦ τοῖς κατὰ τὴν χώραν διατρίβουσιν ἐπιπεσόντος πολλὰ μὲν ἑάλω σώματα Ῥωμαίων
ἐλεύθερα, πολλὰ δ' ἀνδράποδα, βοῶν τε καὶ ὑποζυγίων καὶ τῶν ἄλλων βοσκημάτων χρῆμα οὐκ
ὀλίγον· σῖτός τε ὅσος ἐγκατελήφθη καὶ σίδηρος καὶ
ὅσοις ἄλλοις χώρα[2] γεωργεῖται τὰ μὲν ἡρπάσθη,
τὰ δὲ διεφθάρη. τελευτῶντες γὰρ καὶ πῦρ εἰς τὰς
αὐλὰς φέροντες ἐνέβαλλον Οὐολοῦσκοι, ὥστε πολλοῦ χρόνου μηδ' ἀναλαβεῖν αὐτὰς δύνασθαι τοὺς

---

[1] τοῦ added by Grasberger.
[2] Sintenis : χωρία Β, τὰ χωρία Α.

and said : " What your league has voted is all well and good ; and let each provision be carried out at the proper season. But while you are planning to enrol your armies and making other preparations which, in all probability, will involve some trouble and delay, let Tullus and me set to work. As many of you, therefore, as wish to plunder the enemy's territory and to gain much booty, come with us. I undertake, with the assistance of Heaven, to give you many rich spoils. For the Romans, observing that your forces have not yet been assembled, are as yet unprepared ; so that we shall have an opportunity of overrunning as large a part of their country as we please without molestation."

XII. The Volscians having approved of this proposal also, the generals marched out in haste at the head of a numerous army of volunteers before the Romans were informed of their plans. With a part of this force Tullus invaded the territory of the Latins, in order to cut off from the enemy any assistance from that quarter ; and with the remainder Marcius marched against the Romans' territory. As the calamity fell unexpectedly upon the inhabitants of the country, many Romans of free condition were taken and many slaves and no small number of oxen, beasts of burden, and other cattle ; as for the corn that was found there, the iron tools and the other implements with which the land is tilled, some were carried away and others destroyed. For at the last the Volscians set fire to the country-houses, so that it would be a long time before those who had lost

3 ἀποβαλόντας. μάλιστα δὲ τοῦτ' ἔπασχον αἱ τῶν δημοτῶν κτήσεις, αἱ δὲ τῶν πατρικίων ἔμειναν ἀσινεῖς· εἰ δέ τινες ἐβλάβησαν, εἰς ἀνδράποδα καὶ βοσκήματα ἔδοξαν βλαβῆναι. τοῦτο γὰρ ὑπὸ τοῦ Μαρκίου παρηγγέλλετο τοῖς Οὐολούσκοις, ἵνα δι' ὑποψίας ἔτι μᾶλλον οἱ πατρίκιοι γένωνται[1] τοῖς δημοτικοῖς καὶ μὴ ἐξαιρεθείη τὸ στασιάζον ἐκ τῆς 4 πόλεως· ὅπερ καὶ συνέβη. ὡς γὰρ ἠγγέλθη τοῖς Ῥωμαίοις ἡ καταδρομὴ τῆς χώρας, καὶ ἔγνωσαν οὐκ ἐξ ἴσου γεγονυῖαν ἅπασι τὴν συμφοράν, κατεβόων μὲν τῶν πλουσίων οἱ πένητες ὡς ἐπαγόντων σφίσι τὸν Μάρκιον, ἀπελογοῦντο δ' οἱ πατρίκιοι καὶ κακουργίαν τινὰ τοῦ στρατηγοῦ ταύτην ἀπέφαινον. βοηθεῖν δὲ τοῖς ἀπολλυμένοις ἢ σώζειν τὰ περιόντα δι' ὑποψίαν τε ἀλλήλων καὶ δέος προδοσίας οὐθεὶς ἠξίου· ὥστε κατὰ πολλὴν ἄδειαν ὁ Μάρκιος ἀπῆγε τὴν στρατιὰν καὶ κατέστησεν ἅπαντας ἐπὶ τὰ οἰκεῖα παθόντας μὲν οὐδὲν δεινόν, δράσαντας δ' ὅσα ἠξίουν, καὶ πολλῶν εὐπορή- 5 σαντας χρημάτων. ἧκε δὲ καὶ ὁ Τύλλος ὀλίγον ὕστερον ἐκ τῆς Λατίνων χώρας πολλὰς ἐπαγόμενος ὠφελείας· οὐδὲ γὰρ ἐκεῖνοι[2] δύναμιν ἔσχον ὁμόσε χωρεῖν τοῖς πολεμίοις[3] ἀπαράσκευοί τε ὄντες καὶ παρ' ἐλπίδα τοῦ δεινοῦ σφίσιν ἐπιπεσόντος. ἐκ δὲ τούτου πᾶσα πόλις ἐπήρτο ταῖς ἐλπίσι, καὶ θᾶττον ἢ ὡς ἄν τις ὑπέλαβεν ἥ τε καταγραφὴ τῶν στρατιωτῶν ἐγίνετο, καὶ τἄλλα ὑπηρετεῖτο ὅσων τοῖς στρατηγοῖς ἔδει.

XIII. Ἐπειδὴ δὲ συνῆκτο ἤδη[4] πᾶσα ἡ δύναμις,

---

[1] γένωνται O : γένοιντο Jacoby.
[2] Kiessling : ἐκεῖ O.
πολεμίοις Ba : πολεμίοις μαχησόμενοι BbR.

them could restore them. The farms of the plebeians suffered most in this respect, while those of the patricians remained unharmed, or, if they received any damage, it seemed to fall only on their slaves and cattle. For Marcius thus instructed the Volscians, in order to increase the suspicion of the plebeians against the patricians and to keep the sedition alive in the state ; and that is just what happened. For when this raid upon the country was reported to the Romans and they learned that the calamity had not fallen upon all alike, the poor clamoured against the rich, accusing them of bringing Marcius against them, while the patricians endeavoured to clear themselves by declaring that this was some malicious trick on the part of the general. But neither of them, because of mutual jealousy and fear of treachery, thought fit either to come to the rescue of what was being destroyed or to save what was left ; so that Marcius had full liberty to withdraw his army and to bring all his men home after they had done as much harm as they pleased, while suffering none themselves, and had enriched themselves with much booty. Tullus also arrived a little later from the territory of the Latins, bringing with him many spoils ; for there too the inhabitants had no army with which to engage the enemy, since they were unprepared and the calamity fell upon them un-expectedly. As a result of this every city of the Volscians was buoyed up with hope, and more quickly than anyone would have expected not only were the troops enrolled, but everything else was supplied that the generals needed.

XIII. When all their forces were now assembled,

---

⁴ ἤδη B : om. R.

ἐβουλεύετο μετὰ τοῦ συνάρχοντος ὁ Μάρκιος ὅπως χρηστέον τοῖς λοιποῖς πράγμασιν. ἔφη δ' οὖν λέγων· "Ἐμοὶ δοκεῖ, ὦ Τύλλε, κράτιστον εἶναι νείμασθαι τὰς δυνάμεις ἡμᾶς διχῇ· ἔπειτα τὸν μὲν ἕτερον ἡμῶν ἄγοντα τοὺς ἀκμαιοτάτους καὶ προθυμοτάτους ὁμόσε χωρεῖν τοῖς πολεμίοις,[1] καὶ εἰ μὲν ὑπομενοῦσιν εἰς χεῖρας ἡμῖν ἰέναι, μιᾷ κρῖναι τὸν ἀγῶνα μάχῃ, εἰ δ' ἀποκνήσουσιν, ὡς ἐγὼ πείθομαι, στρατιᾷ νεοσυλλέκτῳ καὶ ἡγεμόσιν ἀπείροις πολέμου τὸν ὑπὲρ τῶν ὅλων κίνδυνον ἐπιτρέπειν, τήν τε χώραν αὐτῶν ἐπιόντα πορθεῖν καὶ τοὺς συμμάχους περισπᾶν καὶ τὰς ἀποικίας ἀν-

2 αιρεῖν καὶ πᾶν ἄλλο κακὸν ὅ τι δύναιτο ποιεῖν. τὸν δ' ἕτερον ἐνθάδε ὑπομένοντα φυλακὴν ποιεῖσθαι τῆς τε χώρας καὶ τῶν πόλεων, μὴ λάθωσιν ἀφυλάκτοις ἐπιπεσόντες αὐτοῖς οἱ πολέμιοι, καὶ πρᾶγμα αἴσχιστον πάθωμεν, ἐν ᾧ τῶν ἀπόντων ἐφιέμεθα τὰ παρόντα ἀφαιρεθέντες. ἀλλὰ χρὴ τὸν ἐνθάδε ὑπομένοντα ἤδη τείχη τε ἀνορθοῦν[2] ὅσα πέπτωκε καὶ τάφρους ἀνακαθαίρειν καὶ φρούρια ὀχυροῦν, ἵνα τοῖς γεωργοῦσι τὴν χώραν ὑπάρχωσι καταφυγαί, στρατιάν τε ἄλλην προσκαταγράφειν καὶ τροφὰς τοῖς ἔξω οὖσιν ἐπιχορηγεῖν καὶ ὅπλα χαλκεύειν καὶ εἴ τι ἄλλο ἀναγκαῖον ἔσται πρᾶγμα

3 ὀξέως ὑπηρετεῖν. δίδωμι δέ σοι τὴν αἵρεσιν, εἴτε τῆς ὑπερορίου στρατιᾶς εἴτε τῆς ἐνθάδε ὑπομενούσης ἐθέλεις στρατηγεῖν." ταῦτα λέγοντος αὐτοῦ σφόδρα ἠγάσθη τὴν γνώμην ὁ Τύλλος, καὶ τὸ δραστήριον τοῦ ἀνδρὸς εἰδὼς καὶ ἐπιτυχὲς ταῖς μάχαις[3] ἐπέτρεψεν ἐκείνῳ τῆς ἔξω στρατιᾶς ἄρχειν.

---

[1] μαχησόμενον after πολεμίοις deleted by Cobet.
[2] Steph. : ὀρθοῦν AB.

Marcius took counsel with his colleague how they should conduct their future operations ; and he said to him : " In my opinion, Tullus, it will be best for us to divide our army into two bodies ; then one of us, taking the most active and eager of the troops, should engage the enemy, and if they can bring themselves to come to close quarters with us, should decide the contest by a single battle, or, if they hesitate, as I think they will, to stake their all upon a newly raised army and inexperienced generals, then he should attack and lay waste their country, detach their allies, destroy their colonies, and do them any other injury he can. And the other should remain here and defend both the country and the cities, lest the enemy fall upon these unawares, if they are unguarded, and we ourselves suffer the most shameful of all disgraces in losing what we have while endeavouring to gain what we have not. But it is necessary that the one who remains here should at once repair the walls of the cities that have fallen in ruin, clear out the ditches, and strengthen the fortresses to serve as places of refuge for the husbandmen. He should also enrol another army, supply the forces that are in the field with provisions, forge arms, and speedily supply anything else that shall be necessary. Now I give you the choice whether you will command the army that is to take the field, or the one which is to remain here." While he was speaking these words Tullus was greatly delighted with his proposal, and knowing the man's energy and good fortune in battle, yielded to him the command of the army that was to take the field.

---

³ ταῖς μάχαις AC : om. B, Jacoby.

XIV. Καὶ ὁ Μάρκιος οὐθὲν ἔτι διαμελλήσας
ἧκεν ἄγων τὴν δύναμιν ἐπὶ Κιρκαίαν πόλιν, ἐν ᾗ
κληροῦχοι Ῥωμαίων ἦσαν ἅμα τοῖς ἐπιχωρίοις
πολιτευόμενοι, καὶ παραλαμβάνει τὴν πόλιν ἐξ
ἐφόδου. ὡς γὰρ ἔγνωσαν οἱ Κιρκαῖοι κρατουμένην
σφῶν τὴν χώραν καὶ προσάγουσαν τῷ τείχει τὴν
στρατιάν, ἀνοίξαντες τὰς πύλας ἐξῄεσαν ὁμόσε τοῖς
πολεμίοις ἄνοπλοι παραλαβεῖν τὴν πόλιν ἀξιοῦντες·
ὅπερ αὐτοῖς αἴτιον τοῦ μηδὲν παθεῖν ἀνήκεστον
2 ἐγένετο. οὔτε γὰρ αὐτῶν ἀπέκτεινεν ὁ στρατηγὸς
οὐδένα οὔτε ἐξήλασεν ἐκ τῆς πόλεως· ἐσθῆτα δὲ
τοῖς στρατιώταις καὶ τροφὰς εἰς μῆνα ἱκανὰς καὶ
ἀργύριόν τι μέτριον λαβὼν ἀπῆγε τὴν δύναμιν
ὀλίγην μοῖραν ἐν τῇ πόλει καταλιπὼν τῆς τε
ἀσφαλείας τῶν ἐνοικούντων ἕνεκα, μή τι ὑπὸ
Ῥωμαίων πάθωσι κακόν, καὶ τοῦ μηδὲν ὕστερον
νεωτερίσαι.

3 Εἰς δὲ τὴν Ῥώμην ὡς ἠγγέλθη τὰ γενόμενα
πολὺ πλείων ταραχὴ καὶ θόρυβος ἦν, τῶν μὲν
πατρικίων ὃν δῆμον ἐχόντων δι᾽ αἰτίας ὅτι πολεμιστὴν ἄνδρα καὶ δραστήριον καὶ φρονήματος
εὐγενοῦς μεστὸν ψευδεῖ περιβαλόντες αἰτίᾳ τῆς πόλεως ἀπήλασαν καὶ παρεσκεύασαν ἡγεμόνα Οὐο-
4 λούσκοις γενέσθαι, τῶν δὲ προεστηκότων τοῦ
δήμου κατηγορίας τοῦ συνεδρίου ποιουμένων καὶ
τὸ πρᾶγμα ὅλον ἐξ ἐπιβουλῆς ὑπ᾽ ἐκείνων κατ-
εσκευάσθαι λεγόντων τόν τε πόλεμον οὐ κοινὸν
ἅπασιν, ἀλλὰ σφίσι μόνοις ἐπάγεσθαι σκηπτο-
μένων· καὶ ἦν τὸ κακοηθέστατον τοῦ δήμου μέρος
ἅμα τούτοις. στρατιὰς δὲ καταγράφειν ἢ καλεῖν

XIV. Marcius,[1] without losing any more time, came with his army to the city of Circeii, in which there were Roman colonists living intermingled with the native residents ; and he took possession of the town as soon as he appeared before it. For when the Circeians saw their country in the power of the Volscians and their army approaching the walls, they opened their gates, and coming out unarmed to meet the enemy, asked them to take possession of the town—a course which saved them from suffering any irreparable mischief. For the general put none of them to death nor expelled any from the city ; but having taken clothing for his soldiers and provisions sufficient for a month, together with a moderate sum of money, he withdrew his forces, leaving only a small garrison in the town, not only for the safety of the inhabitants, lest they should suffer some harm at the hands of the Romans, but also to restrain them from beginning any rebellion in the future.

When news of what had happened was brought to Rome, there was much greater confusion and disorder than before. The patricians reproached the populace with having driven from the state a man who was a great warrior, energetic, and full of noble pride, by involving him in a false charge and having thus caused him to become general of the Volscians ; and the leaders of the populace in turn inveighed against the senate, declaring that the whole affair was a piece of treachery devised by them and that the war was being directed, not against all the Romans in common, but against the plebeians only ; and the most evil-minded element among the populace sided with them. But neither party gave so much as a

---

[1] For chaps. 14-21 *cf.* Livy ii. 39, 2-4.

τοὺς συμμάχους ἢ παρασκευάσασθαι[1] τὰ κατεπεί
γοντα διὰ τὰ πρὸς ἀλλήλους ἔχθη καὶ τὰς ἐν ταῖς
ἐκκλησίαις κατηγορίας οὐδ' εἰς νοῦν ἐλάμβανον.

XV. Τοῦτο καταμαθόντες οἱ πρεσβύτατοι τῶν
Ῥωμαίων συστραφέντες ἔπειθον ἰδίᾳ τε καὶ ἐν
κοινῷ τοὺς στασιωδεστάτους τῶν δημοτικῶν παύ
σασθαι τῶν εἰς τοὺς πατρικίους ὑποψιῶν τε καὶ
κατηγοριῶν, διδάσκοντες ὡς[2] εἰ δι' ἑνὸς ἀνδρὸς
ἐπιφανοῦς φυγὴν τοσοῦτος κίνδυνος κατέσχε τὴν
πόλιν, τί χρὴ προσδοκᾶν, ἐὰν ἀναγκασθῶσιν οἱ
πολλοὶ τῶν πατρικίων προπηλακισθέντες ὑπὸ τοῦ
δήμου ταὐτὸ φρονῆσαι· καὶ κατέσχον οὗτοι τὴν
2 ἀκοσμίαν τοῦ πλήθους. παυσαμένου δὲ τοῦ πολλοῦ
θορύβου συνελθοῦσα ἡ βουλὴ τοῖς μὲν ἀπὸ τοῦ
κοινοῦ τῶν Λατίνων παροῦσι πρεσβευταῖς ἐπὶ
συμμαχίας αἴτησιν ἀπεκρίνατο· μὴ ῥᾴδιον εἶναι
σφίσι βοήθειαν ἀποστέλλειν κατὰ τὸ παρόν, αὐτοῖς
δ' ἐκείνοις ἐπιτρέπειν τὴν ἑαυτῶν στρατιὰν κατα
γράφειν καὶ ἡγεμόνας τῆς δυνάμεως ἰδίους ἐκ
πέμπειν ἕως ἂν[3] αὐτοὶ ἐκπέμψωσι δύναμιν. ἐν γὰρ
ταῖς συνθήκαις αἷς ἐποιήσαντο πρὸς αὐτοὺς περὶ
3 φιλίας ἀπόρρητον ἦν τούτων ἑκάτερον. τοῖς δ'
ὑπάτοις ἐφῆκαν στρατόν τε συναγαγεῖν ἐκ κατα
λόγου καὶ τὴν πόλιν διὰ φυλακῆς ἔχειν καὶ τοὺς
συμμάχους παρακαλεῖν, εἰς ὕπαιθρον δὲ μήπω τὰς
δυνάμεις ἐξάγειν ἕως ἂν ἅπαντα εὐτρεπῆ γένηται.
καὶ ὁ δῆμος ταῦτα ἐπεκύρωσεν. ἦν δὲ βραχὺς ὁ
λειπόμενος τῆς ἀρχῆς τοῖς ὑπάτοις χρόνος, ὥστε
οὐδὲν ἔφθασαν τῶν ἐψηφισμένων ἐπὶ τέλος ἀγαγεῖν,

---

[1] Kiessling : κατασκευάσασθαι O.
[2] ὡς O : om. Sylburg, Jacoby.
[3] ἐκπέμπειν ἕως ἂν Cary, ἀποδεῖξαι ἕως ἂν Kiessling : ἐκ-

thought to raising armies, summoning the allies, or making the necessary preparations, by reason of their mutual hatreds and their accusations of one another in the meetings of the assembly.

XV. This being observed by the oldest of the Romans, they joined together and sought to persuade the most seditious of the plebeians both in public and in private to put a stop to their suspicions and accusations against the patricians. If, they argued, by the banishment of one man of distinction the commonwealth had been brought into so great danger, what were they to expect if by their abusive treatment they forced the greater part of the patricians to entertain the same sentiments? Thus these men appeased the disorderliness of the populace. After the great tumult had been suppressed, the senate met and gave the following answer to the ambassadors who had come from the Latin League to ask for armed assistance: That it was not easy for them to send assistance for the time being; but that they gave the Latins leave to enrol their own army themselves and to send out their own generals in command of their forces until the Romans should send out a force; for by the treaty of friendship they had made with the Latins both these things were forbidden. The senate also ordered the consuls to raise an army by levy, to guard the city, and to summon the allies, but not to take the field with their forces till everything was in readiness. These resolutions were ratified by the people. Only a short time now remained of the consuls' term of office, so that they were unable to carry to completion any of the measures that had been voted,

πέμπειν τε ὅταν Jacoby, ἐκπέμπειν τε ὅσην (σην in ras. B) ἂν AB.

ἀλλὰ παρέδοσαν ἡμιτελῆ πάντα[1] τοῖς μεθ᾽ ἑαυτοὺς ὑπάτοις.

XVI. Οἱ δὲ παρὰ τούτων τὴν ἀρχὴν παραλαβόντες, Σπόριος Ναύτιος καὶ Σέξτος Φούριος, στρατιάν τε ὅσην ἐδύναντο πλείστην ἐκ τοῦ πολιτικοῦ κατεστήσαντο καταλόγου, καὶ φρυκτωρίας καὶ σκοποὺς ἐν τοῖς ἐπικαιροτάτοις φρουρίοις ἔταξαν, ἵνα μηδὲν ἀγνοήσωσι τῶν ἐπὶ τῆς χώρας πραττομένων· χρήματά τε καὶ σῖτον καὶ ὅπλα ἐν 2 ὀλίγῳ χρόνῳ πολλὰ ἡτοιμάσαντο. τὰ μὲν οὖν οἰκεῖα παρεσκεύαστο αὐτοῖς ὡς ἐνῆν ἄριστα, καὶ οὐδὲν αὐτῶν ἔτ᾽ ἐνδεῖν[2] ἐδόκει· τὰ δὲ συμμαχικὰ οὐχ ἅπαντα ὑπήκουε προθύμως ἑκούσιά τε οὐκ ἦν οἷα συνάρασθαι τοῦ πολέμου, ὥστε οὐδὲ προσαναγκάζειν αὐτὰ ἠξίουν φοβούμενοι προδοσίαν. ἤδη δέ τινα καὶ ἀφίστατο αὐτῶν ἐκ τοῦ φανεροῦ 3 καὶ τοῖς Οὐολούσκοις συνελάμβανε. πρῶτοι δ᾽ ἦρξαν Αἰκανοὶ τῆς ἀποστάσεως, ἅμα τῷ συστῆναι τὸν πόλεμον εὐθὺς ἐλθόντες ὡς τοὺς Οὐολούσκους καὶ συμμαχίαν μεθ᾽ ὅρκων συνθέμενοι, στρατιάν τε ἀπέστειλαν οὗτοι τῷ Μαρκίῳ πλείστην τε καὶ προθυμοτάτην. ἀρξαμένων δὲ τούτων πολλοὶ καὶ τῶν ἄλλων συμμάχων κρύφα συνελάμβανον τοῖς Οὐολούσκοις οὐκ ἀπὸ ψηφισμάτων οὐδ᾽ ἀπὸ κοινοῦ δόγματος ἀποστέλλοντες αὐτοῖς τὰς συμμαχίας, εἰ δέ τισιν ἦν βουλομένοις μετέχειν τῆς στρατείας τῶν σφετέρων, οὐχ ὅπως ἀποτρέποντες, ἀλλὰ καὶ 4 παρορμῶντες. ἐγεγόνει τ᾽ ἐν[3] οὐ πολλῷ χρόνῳ τοσαύτη δύναμις περὶ τοὺς Οὐολούσκους ὅσην οὐ πώποτ᾽ ἔσχον ὅτε μάλιστα ἤκμαζον ταῖς πόλεσιν[4]·

---

[1] Kiessling : ἅπαντα O.
[2] ἔτ᾽ ἐνδεῖν Reiske : ἔτι δεῖν O, Jacoby.

but handed over everything half finished to their successors.

XVI. Those who assumed office after them, Spurius Nautius and Sextus Furius,[1] raised as large an army as they could from the register of citizens, and placed beacons and lookouts in the most convenient fortresses, in order that they might not be unaware of anything that passed in the country. They also got ready a great quantity of money, corn and arms in a short time. Their preparations at home, then, were made in the best manner possible, and nothing now seemed to be wanting; but the allies did not all obey their summons with alacrity nor were they disposed to assist them voluntarily in the war, so that the consuls did not think fit to use compulsion either with them, for fear of treachery. Indeed, some of the allies were already openly revolting from them and aiding the Volscians. The Aequians had begun the revolt by going at once to the Volscians as soon as the war arose and entering into an alliance with them under oath; and these sent to Marcius a very numerous and zealous army. After these had taken the lead, many of the other allies also secretly assisted the Volscians and sent them reinforcements, though not in pursuance of any votes or general decree, but if any of their people desired to take part in the campaign of Marcius, they not only did not attempt to dissuade them, but even encouraged them. Thus in a short time the Volscians had got so large an army as they had never possessed when their cities had been in the most flourishing state. At the head of this

----

[1] Cf. Livy ii. 39, 9.

----

[3] τ' ἐν Hertlein : τε O.
[4] ταῖς πόλεσιν O : τοῖς πλήθεσιν Post, ἐν τοῖς πολέμοις Reiske.

ἣν ἐπαγόμενος ὁ Μάρκιος ἐνέβαλεν αὖθις εἰς τὴν
Ῥωμαίων γῆν, καὶ ἐγκαθεζόμενος ἡμέρας συχνὰς
ἐδῄου τῆς γῆς ὅσην ἐν τῇ πρότερον εἰσβολῇ παρ-
5 έλιπε. σωμάτων μὲν οὖν ἐλευθέρων οὐκέτι πολλῶν
ἐγκρατὴς ἐγένετο κατὰ ταύτην τὴν στρατείαν· οἱ
γὰρ ἄνθρωποι τὰ πλείστου ἄξια συσκευασάμενοι
παλαίτερον ἔτι κατεπεφεύγεσαν, οἱ μὲν εἰς τὴν
πόλιν, οἱ δ' εἰς τὰ πλησίον φρούρια, εἴ τινα[1] ἦν
ἐχυρώτατα· τὰ δὲ βοσκήματα αὐτῶν, ὅσα οὐχ οἷοί
τε ἦσαν ἀπελάσαι, καὶ τοὺς νέμοντας θεράποντας
λαμβάνει τόν τε σῖτον τὸν[2] ἐπὶ ταῖς ἅλωσιν ἔτι κείμενον καὶ τοὺς ἄλλους καρπούς, τοὺς μὲν ἐν χερσὶν
ὄντας, τοὺς δὲ καὶ συγκεκομισμένους ἀναιρεῖται.
6 προνομεύσας δὲ καὶ διαπορθήσας ἅπαντα οὐθενὸς
ὁμόσε χωρῆσαι τολμήσαντος ἀπῆγεν ἐπ' οἴκου τὴν
στρατιὰν βαρεῖαν οὖσαν ἤδη τῷ πλήθει τῶν ὠφελειῶν καὶ σχολῇ πορευομένην.

XVII. Οἱ δὲ Οὐολοῦσκοι τὸ μέγεθος τῆς κομιζο-
μένης λείας ὁρῶντες καὶ περὶ τῆς Ῥωμαίων
ἀτολμίας ἀκούοντες, οἳ δὴ τέως τὴν ἀλλοτρίαν
ληλατοῦντες ἀδεῶς τότε τὴν αὑτῶν γῆν ἠνείχοντο
δῃουμένην ὁρῶντες, αὐχήματός τε μεγάλου ἐν-
επίμπλαντο καὶ ἐν ἐλπίδι ἦσαν ἡγεμονίας, ὡς δὴ
ῥᾴδιον καὶ ἐν ἑτοίμῳ σφίσιν ὂν καταλῦσαι τὴν τῶν
ἀντιπάλων ἰσχύν, θυσίας τε χαριστηρίους τοῖς
θεοῖς ἐποιοῦντο καὶ σκύλων ἀναθέσει τοὺς νεὼς καὶ
τὰς ἀγορὰς ἐκόσμουν καὶ ἦσαν ἅπαντες ἐν ἑορταῖς
καὶ εὐπαθείαις, τόν τε Μάρκιον ἀγάμενοι καὶ ὑμ-
νοῦντες διετέλουν, ὡς εἴη τά τε πολέμια δεινότατος
ἀνθρώπων καὶ στρατηγὸς οἷος οὔτε Ῥωμαῖος οὔτε

army Marcius made another irruption into the territory of the Romans, and encamping there for many days, laid waste all the country which he had spared in his former incursion.   He did not, it is true, capture many persons of free condition on this expedition ; for the inhabitants had long since fled, after getting together everything that was most valuable, some to Rome and others to such of the neighbouring fortresses as were most capable of defence ; but he took all the cattle they had not been able to drive away, together with the slaves who tended them, and carried off the corn, that still lay upon the threshing-floors, and all the other fruits of the earth, whether then gathering or already gathered.   Having ravaged and laid everything waste, as none dared to come to grips with him, he led homeward his army, which was now heavily burdened with the great amount of its spoils and was proceeding in leisurely fashion.

XVII. The Volscians, seeing the vast quantity of booty that was being brought home and hearing reports of the craven spirit of the Romans who, though they had hitherto been wont to ravage their neighbours' country, could now bear to see their own laid waste with impunity, were filled with great boastfulness and entertained hopes of the supremacy, looking upon it as an easy undertaking, lying ready to their hands, to overthrow the power of their adversaries.   They offered sacrifices of thanksgiving to the gods for their success and adorned their temples and market-places with dedications of spoils, and all passed their time in festivals and rejoicings ; while as for Marcius, they continued to admire and celebrate him as the ablest of all men in warfare and a general

---

ἄλλος στρατηγὸς[1] Ἑλλήνων ἢ βαρβάρων οὐδείς.
2 μάλιστα δὲ τῆς τύχης αὐτὸν ἐμακάριζον ἅπαντα
ὅσοις ἐπιχειρήσειε κατὰ γνώμην αὐτῷ προχω-
ροῦντα ὁρῶντες δίχα πόνου· ὥστ᾽ οὐδεὶς ἦν τῶν
ἐχόντων τὴν στρατεύσιμον ἡλικίαν ὃς ἀπολείπεσθαι
τοῦ ἀνδρὸς ἠξίου, ἀλλὰ πάντες ὥρμηντο μετέχειν
τῶν πράξεων καὶ συνῄεσαν ὡς αὐτὸν ἐξ ἁπάσης
3 πόλεως. ὁ δὲ στρατηγός, ἐπειδὴ τὴν προθυμίαν
τῶν Οὐολούσκων ἐπέρρωσε καὶ τὸ τῶν πολεμίων
ἀνδρεῖον εἰς ταπεινὴν καὶ ἄνανδρον κατέκλεισεν ἀμη-
χανίαν, ἐπὶ τὰς συμμαχίδας αὐτῶν πόλεις[2] ὅσαι τὸ
πιστὸν διεφύλαττον ἦγε τὴν δύναμιν· καὶ αὐτίκα
ἑτοιμασάμενος ὅσα εἰς πολιορκίαν χρήσιμα ἦν, ἐπὶ
4 Τολερίνους ἐλαύνει τοῦ Λατίνων ὄντας ἔθνους. οἱ
δὲ Τολερῖνοι πρὸ πολλοῦ παρασκευασάμενοι τὰ εἰς
πόλεμον[2] καὶ τὰ ἐκ τῆς χώρας εἰς τὴν πόλιν συγ-
κεκομικότες ἐδέχοντο αὐτὸν ἐπιόντα καὶ χρόνον μέν
τινα ἀντεῖχον ἀπὸ τῶν τειχῶν μαχόμενοι καὶ πολλοὺς τῶν πολεμίων κατέτρωσαν· ἔπειτα ὑπὸ τῶν
σφενδονητῶν ἀναστελλόμενοι καὶ μέχρι δείλης
ὀψίας ταλαιπωροῦντες πολλὰ μέρη τοῦ τείχους
5 ἐξέλιπον. τοῦτο καταμαθὼν ὁ Μάρκιος τοῖς μὲν
ἄλλοις στρατιώταις παρήγγειλε κλίμακας προσφέρειν κατὰ τὰ γυμνούμενα μέρη τοῦ περιβόλου,
αὐτὸς δὲ τοὺς κρατίστους τῆς στρατιᾶς ἀναλαβὼν[4]
ἐπὶ τὰς πύλας ἵεται βαλλόμενος ἀπὸ τῶν πύργων,
καὶ διαρρήξας τοὺς μοχλοὺς παρέρχεται πρῶτος εἰς
τὴν πόλιν. ἦν δ᾽ ὑφεστηκὸς ταῖς πύλαις πολὺ καὶ
καρτερὸν στῖφος τῶν πολεμίων, οἳ δέχονταί τε
αὐτὸν ἐρρωμένως καὶ μέχρι πολλοῦ διεκαρτέρουν

---

[1] στρατηγὸς deleted by Reiske, Jacoby.
[2] πόλεις B : om. R.

without an equal either at Rome or in the Greek or
barbarian world. But above all they admired him
for his good fortune, observing that everything he
undertook easily succeeded according to his desire;
so that there was no one of military age who was
willing to be left behind by him, but all were eager
to share in his exploits and flocked to him from every
city. The general, after he had strengthened the
zeal of the Volscians and reduced the manly fortitude
of the enemy to a helplessness that was abject and
anything but manly, led his army against the cities
of their allies that still remained faithful to them;
and having promptly prepared everything that was
necessary for a siege, he marched against the
Tolerienses, who belonged to the Latin nation.
These, having long before made the necessary preparations for war and transported all the effects they
had in the country into the city, withstood his attack
and held out for some time, fighting from their walls
and wounding many of the enemy; then, after
being driven back by the slingers and enduring
hardships till the late afternoon, they abandoned
many parts of the wall. When Marcius was informed
of this, he ordered some of the soldiers to plant
ladders against those parts of the wall that were left
unprotected, while he himself with the flower of his
army hastened to the gates amid a shower o spears
that were hurled at him from the towers; and
breaking the bars asunder, he was the first to enter
the city. Close to the gates stood a large and strong
body of the enemy's troops, who stoutly withstood his
attack and continued to fight for a long time; but

---

³ εἰς τὸν πόλεμον Sylburg, Jacoby.
⁴ ἀναλαβὼν placed here by Sylburg : after πύλας by O.

ἀγωνιζόμενοι· πολλῶν δ' ἀναιρεθέντων τρέπονται
οἱ λοιποὶ καὶ σκεδασθέντες ἔφευγον ἀνὰ τοὺς
6 στενωπούς. ὁ δ' ἠκολούθει κτείνων τοὺς[1] κατα-
λαμβανομένους, ὅσοι μὴ τὰ ὅπλα ῥίψαντες εἰς
ἱκεσίας ἐτράποντο· ἐν δὲ τούτῳ καὶ οἱ διὰ τῶν
κλιμάκων ἀναβαίνοντες ἐκράτουν τοῦ τείχους. τοῦτον δὴ[2] τὸν τρόπον ἁλούσης τῆς πόλεως ἐξελό-
μενος ὁ Μάρκιος ἐκ τῶν λαφύρων ὅσα θεοῖς τε
ἀναθήματα καὶ κόσμος ταῖς Οὐολούσκων πόλεσιν
ἔμελλε γίνεσθαι,[3] τὰ λοιπὰ τοῖς στρατιώταις ἐφῆκε
7 διαρπάσαι. ἦν δὲ πολλὰ μὲν αὐτόθι σώματα, πολλὰ
δὲ χρήματα, πολὺς δὲ σῖτος, ὥστε μὴ ῥᾴδιον εἶναι
μιᾷ πάντα[4] ἐκκομίσαι τοὺς κρατήσαντας ἡμέρᾳ,
ἀλλ' ἐκ διαδοχῆς ἄγοντες καὶ φέροντες τὰ μὲν
αὐτοί, τὰ δ' ἐπὶ τῶν ὑποζυγίων, πολὺν ἠναγκάσθησαν διατρῖψαι χρόνον.

XVIII. Ὁ δὲ στρατηγός, ἐπειδὴ τὰ σώματα καὶ
τὰ χρήματα πάντα ἐξεκεκόμιστο, τὴν πόλιν ἔρημον
καταλιπὼν ἀπῆγε τὴν δύναμιν ἐπὶ Βῶλαν Λατίνων[5]
ἑτέραν πόλιν. ἔτυχον δὲ καὶ οἱ Βωλανοὶ προεγνω-
κότες αὐτοῦ τὴν ἔφοδον καὶ παρεσκευασμένοι
πάντα τὰ πρὸς τὸν ἀγῶνα ἐπιτήδεια. ὁ μὲν οὖν
Μάρκιος ὡς ἐξ ἐφόδου τὴν πόλιν αἱρήσων κατὰ
πολλὰ μέρη τοῦ τείχους ἐποιεῖτο τὰς προσβολάς·
οἱ δὲ Βωλανοὶ περιμείναντες καιρὸν ἐπιτήδειον
ἀνοίγουσι τὰς πύλας, καὶ φερόμενοι κατὰ πλῆθος
ἐν τάξει τε καὶ κόσμῳ συρράττουσι τοῖς κατὰ
μέτωπον, καὶ πολλοὺς αὐτῶν ἀποκτείναντες, ἔτι δὲ
πλείους[6] κατατραυματίσαντες τούς τε λοιποὺς αἰσχρῶς ἀναγκάσαντες φυγεῖν ἀνέστρεψαν εἰς τὴν

[1] τούς B : τοὺς πολεμίους R.
[2] Kiessling : δὲ O.

when many of them had been killed, the rest gave way and, dispersing themselves, fled through the streets. Marcius followed, putting to death all whom he overtook except those who threw away their arms and had recourse to supplications. In the meantime the men who had ascended by the ladders were making themselves masters of the wall. The town being taken in this manner, Marcius set aside such of the spoils as were to be consecrated to the gods and to adorn the cities of the Volscians, and the rest he permitted the soldiers to plunder. Many prisoners were taken there, also a great deal of money and much corn, so that it was not easy for the victors to remove everything in one day, but they were forced to consume much time while, working in relays, they drove or carried away the booty, either on their own backs or using beasts of burden.

XVIII. The general, after all the prisoners and effects had been removed out of the city, left it desolate and drew off his forces to Bola, another town of the Latins. The Bolani also, as it chanced, had been apprised of his intended attack and had prepared everything necessary for the struggle. Marcius, who expected to take the town by storm. delivered his attacks upon many parts of the wall. But the Bolani, after watching for a favourable opportunity, opened their gates, and sallying out in force in regular array, engaged the front ranks of the enemy; then, after killing many of them and wounding still more and after forcing the rest to a shameful flight, they

---

³ Hertlein : γενέσθαι O, Jacoby, ἔσεσθαι Cobet.
⁴ πάντα B : πάντας R.
⁵ Βῶλαν Λατίνων Sintenis : βωλανῶν O.
⁶ πλείους B : πλείους τούτων R.

2 πόλιν. ὡς δ' ἔγνω τὴν τροπὴν τῶν Οὐολούσκων ὁ Μάρκιος, οὐ γὰρ ἔτυχε παρὼν ἐν ᾧ χωρίῳ[1] τὸ πάθος ἐγένετο, παρὴν σὺν ὀλίγοις κατὰ σπουδὴν καὶ τοὺς ἐκ τῆς τροπῆς σκεδασθέντας ἀναλαβὼν συνίστα τε[2] καὶ παρεθάρρυνε, καὶ ἐπειδὴ κατέστησεν εἰς τάξεις, ὑποδείξας ἃ δεῖ πράττειν, ἐκέλευσε προσβάλλειν τῇ πόλει κατὰ τὰς αὐτὰς πύλας.

3 χρησαμένων δὲ πάλιν τῶν Βωλανῶν τῇ αὐτῇ πείρᾳ καὶ κατὰ πλῆθος ἐκδραμόντων οὐ δέχονται αὐτοὺς οἱ[3] Οὐολοῦσκοι, ἀλλ' ἐγκλίναντες ἔφευγον κατὰ τοῦ πρανοῦς, ὡς ὁ στρατηγὸς αὐτοῖς ὑπέθετο· καὶ οἱ Βωλανοὶ τὴν ἀπάτην οὐκ εἰδότες ἐδίωκον ἄχρι πολλοῦ. ἐπεὶ δὲ πρόσω τῆς πόλεως ἐγένοντο, ἔχων τοὺς ἐπιλέκτους τῶν νέων ὁ Μάρκιος ὁμόσε τοῖς Βωλανοῖς ἐχώρει· καὶ γίνεται πολὺς αὐτῶν ἐνταῦθα φόνος τῶν μὲν ἀμυνομένων, τῶν δὲ φευγόντων.

4 ὁ δ' ἀκολουθῶν τοῖς ἐπὶ τὴν πόλιν ὠθουμένοις φθάνει πρὶν ἐπιρραχθῆναι τὰς πύλας εἰσβιασάμενος[4] εἰς τὸ τεῖχος. ὡς δ' ὁ στρατηγὸς ἅπαξ ἐγκρατὴς τῶν πυλῶν ἐγένετο, ἠκολούθει καὶ τὸ ἄλλο τῶν Οὐολούσκων πλῆθος, οἱ δὲ Βωλανοὶ τὸ τεῖχος ἐκλιπόντες ἔφευγον ἐπὶ τὰς οἰκίας. γενόμενος δὲ καὶ ταύτης κύριος τῆς πόλεως ἐπέτρεψε τοῖς στρατιώταις τά τε σώματα ἐξανδραποδίσασθαι καὶ τὰ χρήματα διαρπάσαι, καὶ τὸν αὐτὸν τρόπον ὥσπερ καὶ πρότερον ἅπασαν ἐκκομίσας τὴν λείαν σὺν χρόνῳ τε καὶ κατὰ πολλὴν ἐξουσίαν, μετὰ τοῦτο τὴν πόλιν ἐνέπρησεν.

XIX. Ἐντεῦθεν δὲ τὴν δύναμιν ἀναλαβὼν ἦγεν ἐπὶ τοὺς καλουμένους Λαβικανούς. ἦν δὲ καὶ αὕτη[5] τότε Λατίνων ἡ πόλις, Ἀλβανῶν ὥσπερ αἱ

¹ χωρίῳ B : om. R.

retired into the city. When Marcius learned of the
rout of the Volscians—for it chanced that he was not
present in the place where this defeat occurred—he
came up in all haste with a few of his men, and rally-
ing those who were dispersed in the flight, he formed
them into a body and encouraged them. Then,
having got them back in their ranks and indicated
what they were to do, he ordered them to attack the
town at the same gates. When the Bolani once
more tried the same expedient, sallying out in force,
the Volscians did not await them, but gave way and
fled down hill, as their general had instructed them
to do; and the Bolani, ignorant of the ruse, pursued
them a considerable way. Then, when they were at
a distance from the town, Marcius fell upon them
with a body of chosen youth; and many of the Bolani
fell, some while defending themselves and others
while endeavouring to escape. Marcius pursued those
who were being pushed back toward the town and
forced his way inside the walls before the gates could
be slammed shut. When the general had once made
himself master of the gates, the rest of the Volscian
host followed, and the Bolani, abandoning the walls,
fled to their houses. Marcius, having possessed himself of this city also, gave leave to the soldiers to make
slaves of the inhabitants and to seize their effects ;
and after carrying away all the booty at his leisure
and with full liberty, as before, he set fire to the town.

XIX. From there he took his army and marched
against the place called Labici. This city too belonged then to the Latins and was, like the others, a

² συνίστα τε R : συνίσταται B, συνίστατο Jacoby.
³ οἱ B : om. R.   ⁴ Cobet : ἐκβιασάμενος O.
⁵ Sylburg : αὐτὴ O.

ἄλλαι[1] ἄποικος. καταπλήξασθαι δὲ βουλόμενος
τοὺς ἔνδον ἔκαιεν αὐτῶν τὴν χώραν εὐθὺς ἐπιὼν
ὅθεν μάλιστα ἔμελλον ὄψεσθαι τὴν φλόγα. οἱ δὲ
Λαβικανοὶ τεῖχος εὖ κατεσκευασμένον[2] ἔχοντες
οὔτε κατεπλάγησαν αὐτοῦ τὴν ἔφοδον οὔτε μαλακὸν ἐνέδοσαν οὐδέν, ἀλλ' ἀντεῖχον ἀπομαχόμενοι
γενναίως καὶ πολλάκις ἐπιβαίνοντας τοῦ τείχους
2 τοὺς πολεμίους ἀπήραξαν. οὐ μὴν εἰς τέλος γε
ἀντέσχον ὀλίγοι πρὸς πολλοὺς ἀγωνιζόμενοι καὶ
χρόνον οὐδὲ[3] τὸν ἐλάχιστον ἀναπαυόμενοι. πολλαὶ
γὰρ προσβολαὶ καὶ καθ' ὅλην τὴν πόλιν ἐγίνοντο
ὑπὸ τῶν Οὐολούσκων ἐκ διαδοχῆς ὑποχωρούντων
μὲν αἰεὶ τῶν κεκμηκότων, ἑτέρων δὲ προσιόντων
νεαρῶν· πρὸς οὓς ἀγωνιζόμενοι δι' ὅλης ἡμέρας
καὶ οὐδὲ τὸν τῆς νυκτὸς ἀναπαυσάμενοι[4] χρόνον
ἐκλιπεῖν ἠναγκάσθησαν τὸ τεῖχος ὑπὸ κόπου.
παραλαβὼν δὲ καὶ ταύτην ὁ Μάρκιος τὴν πόλιν
ἐξηνδραποδίσατο καὶ τοῖς στρατιώταις ἐφῆκε μερί-
3 σασθαι τὰς ὠφελείας. ἀναστήσας δὲ τὴν δύναμιν
ἐκεῖθεν ἐπὶ τὴν Πεδανῶν πόλιν (ἦν δὲ καὶ αὕτη[5]
τοῦ Λατίνων γένους), συντεταγμένην ἔχων τὴν
στρατιὰν ἀφικνεῖται καὶ αὐτὴν ἅμα τῷ πλησίασαι
τοῖς τείχεσιν αἱρεῖ κατὰ κράτος. καὶ ταὐτὰ δια-
θεὶς ὅσα τὰς πρότερον ἁλούσας ἔωθεν εὐθὺς ἀνα-
4 στήσας τὴν δύναμιν ἦγεν ἐπὶ Κορβιῶνα. ὄντι δ'
αὐτῷ πλησίον τοῦ τείχους τὰς πύλας ἀνοίξαντες οἱ
ἔνδον ἀπαντῶσιν ἀντὶ τῶν ὅπλων προτείνοντες[6]
ἱκετηρίας καὶ παραδιδόντες ἀμαχητὶ τὸ τεῖχος.
οὓς ἐπαινέσας ὡς τὰ κράτιστα περὶ σφῶν βεβου-

---

[1] αἱ ἄλλαι Sylburg : καὶ ἄλλη O, καὶ ἄλλαι Jacoby.
[2] εὖ κατεσκευασμένον Gelenius : ἐγκατεσκευασμένον O.
[3] οὐδὲ B : οὐ R.   [4] ἀναπαυσάμενοι B : ἀναπαυόμενοι R.

colony of the Albans. In order to terrify the inhabitants, as soon as he entered their territory he set fire to the part of the country from which the flames would most clearly be seen by them. But the Labicani, since they had well-constructed walls, neither became terrified at his invasion nor showed any sign of weakness, but made a brave resistance and often repulsed the enemy as they were attempting to scale the walls. Notwithstanding this, they were not able to resist to the end, fighting as they were few against many and without the least respite. For many attacks were made upon all parts of the city by the Volscians, who fought in shifts, those who were fatigued continually retiring and other forces that were fresh taking their place ; and the inhabitants, contending against these all day, without any respite even at night, were forced through exhaustion to abandon the walls. Marcius, having taken this city also, made slaves of the inhabitants and allowed his soldiers to divide the spoils. Thence he marched to Pedum—this also was a city of the Latins—and advancing with his army in good order, he took the town by storm as soon as he came near the walls. And having treated it in the same manner as the cities he had captured earlier, he led his forces at break of day against Corbio. When he was near its walls, the inhabitants opened their gates and came to meet him, holding out olive-branches instead of weapons and offering to surrender their walls without striking a blow. Marcius, after commending them

---

⁵ Kayser : αὐτὴ O.
⁶ ἀντὶ τῶν ὅπλων προτείνοντες (cf. xi. 17, 4 ; i. 20, 1) Jacoby : ἀντιπροτείνοντες AB (but space of one or two letters after ἀντι in B), πάντες προτείνοντες Kiessling.

λευμένους, ἐκέλευσεν ὧν ἔδει τῇ στρατιᾷ φέροντας
ἥκειν ἀργύριόν τε καὶ σῖτον, καὶ λαβὼν ὅσα προσ-
έταξεν ἀπῆγε τὴν δύναμιν ἐπὶ τὴν Κοριολανῶν[1]
πόλιν. παραδόντων δὲ κἀκείνην τῶν ἔνδον ἀμαχητὶ
καὶ μετὰ πολλῆς προθυμίας ἀγοράς τε παρασχόν-
των τῇ δυνάμει καὶ χρήματα καὶ ὅσα ἄλλα ἐπ-
ετέτακτο αὐτοῖς ἀπῆγε τὴν στρατιὰν ὡς διὰ φιλίας
5 γῆς.   πάνυ γὰρ δὴ καὶ[2] τοῦτο ἐσπούδαζεν, ὡς
μηδὲν οἱ παραδιδόντες αὐτοῖς τὰς πόλεις πάθοιεν
ὧν φιλεῖ δρᾶν ὁ πόλεμος, ἀλλὰ καὶ γῆν ἀδήωτον
ἀπολαμβάνοιεν καὶ βοσκήματα καὶ ἀνδράποδα ὅσα
κατέλιπον ἐπὶ τῶν κτήσεων κομίζοιντο, αὐλίζεσθαί
τε οὐκ εἴα τὴν δύναμιν ἐν ταῖς πόλεσιν, ἵνα μή τι
γένηται δι' ἁρπαγῆς πρὸς αὐτῶν ἢ κλοπῆς κακόν,
ἀλλὰ παρὰ τοῖς τείχεσι κατεστρατοπέδευεν.

XX. Ἀπὸ δὲ ταύτης ἀναστήσας τῆς πόλεως
ἤλαυνε τὸν στρατὸν ἐπὶ Βοίλλας,[3] ἐπιφανῆ τότε
οὖσαν καὶ ἐν ὀλίγαις πάνυ ταῖς ἡγουμέναις τοῦ
Λατίνων γένους πόλεσιν ἐξεταζομένην. οὐ προσδεξαμένων δ' αὐτὸν τῶν ἔνδον, ἀλλὰ τῷ τε ἐρύματι πιστεύοντων ἐχυρῷ γε[4] σφόδρα ὄντι καὶ τῷ
πλήθει τῶν ἀπ' αὐτοῦ μαχησομένων, παρακαλέσας
τὴν δύναμιν ἀγωνίζεσθαι προθύμως καὶ τοῖς πρώτοις ἐπιβᾶσι[5] τοῦ τείχους μεγάλας δωρεὰς ὑποσχό-
μενος ἔργου εἴχετο· καὶ γίνεται μάχη περὶ τῇ

---

[1] κοριολανῶν R : κοπιολανῶν AB, Jacoby, Καρυεντανῶν Nie-
buhr.
[2] γὰρ δὴ καὶ A : γὰρ καὶ R.
[3] Βοίλλας Gelenius : βωλάς A, βολάς B.
[4] γε B : τε R.
[5] πρώτοις ἐπιβᾶσι B : πρώτως ἐπιβαλοῦσι R.

---

[1] " The city of the Coriolani " is the reading of the later

for adopting the course that was to their best interest, ordered them to come out bringing whatever his army required, both money and corn; and having obtained what he demanded, he led his forces to Corioli.[1] When the inhabitants of this place also surrendered it without resistance and very readily supplied his army with provisions and money and everything else that he ordered, he led the army away through their territory as through a friendly land. For this too was a matter about which he always took great care—that those who surrendered their cities to him should suffer none of the ills incident to war, but should get back their lands unravaged and recover all the cattle and slaves they had left behind on their farms; and he would not permit his army to quarter itself in the cities, lest some mischief should result from their plundering or stealing, but he always encamped near the walls.

XX. Departing from this city, he led his army to Bovillae, which was then a city of note and counted as one of the very few leading cities of the Latin nation. When the inhabitants would not receive him, but trusted in their ramparts, which were very strong, and in the multitude of defenders who would fight from them, Marcius exhorted his men to fight ardently, promising great rewards to those who should first mount the walls, and then set to work; and a sharp battle took place for this city.

MSS. in place of "the city of the Copiolani," given by A and B. The latter name is certainly false. But if Coriolani is the correct form here, some other name almost certainly underlies the corrupt spelling Chorielani in chap. 36, 2. Livy (ii. 39, 2 f.) names Corioli as one of the cities taken by Coriolanus for the Volscians, but his list does not follow the same order as that of Dionysius.

2 πόλει ταύτῃ καρτερά. οὐ γὰρ μόνον ἀπὸ τοῦ
τείχους ἠμύνοντο τοὺς προσιόντας οἱ Βοϊλλανοί,
ἀλλὰ καὶ τὰς πύλας ἀνοίξαντες ἐξέθεον[1] ἀθρόοι καὶ
κατὰ τοῦ πρανοῦς ἐώθουν βίᾳ τοὺς ὑφισταμένους[2]·
φόνος τε πλεῖστος αὐτόθι τῶν Οὐολούσκων ἐγένετο
καὶ χρόνος τῆς τειχομαχίας πολὺς τοῦ τε κρατήσειν
τῆς πόλεως ἄπορος ἅπασιν ἡ ἐλπίς. ἀλλὰ τῶν
ἀπολλυμένων ἄδηλον ἐποίει τὴν ἀπουσίαν ὁ στρατηγὸς ἀντικαθιστὰς ἑτέρους, τῶν δὲ καμνόντων
παρεθάρρυνε τὴν ἀθυμίαν ἐπὶ τὸ πονοῦν μέρος τῆς
στρατιᾶς αὐτὸς ὠθούμενος. ἦν δ᾽[3] οὐχ ὁ λόγος
αὐτοῦ μόνον ἐπαγωγὸς εἰς[4] τὸ εὔψυχον, ἀλλὰ καὶ
τὰ ἔργα· πάντα γὰρ ὑφίστατο κίνδυνον καὶ οὐδεμιᾶς
3 πείρας ἀπελείφθη, ἕως[5] ἑάλω τὸ τεῖχος. κρατήσας
δὲ καὶ ταύτης σὺν χρόνῳ τῆς πόλεως καὶ τῶν ἀνθρώπων[6] τοὺς μὲν ἐν χειρῶν νόμῳ διαφθείρας, τοὺς
δ᾽ αἰχμαλώτους λαβὼν ἀπῆγε τὴν δύναμιν ἐπιφανεστάτην νίκην ἐξενεγκάμενος καὶ λάφυρα κάλλιστα
καὶ πλεῖστα ἄγων, χρήμασί τε παμπόλλοις ὧν
ἐγκρατὴς ἐγένετο (ἦν δ᾽ αὐτόθι ὅσα ἐν οὐδενὶ τῶν
ἁλόντων[7] χωρίων) πλουτίσας τὴν στρατιάν.

XXI. Μετὰ τοῦτο χώρα τε ὅσην διαπορεύοιτο
ὑποχείριος ἦν καὶ πόλις οὐδεμία ἠναντιοῦτο ἔξω
Λαουϊνίου, ἣν πρώτην τε[8] πόλιν οἱ σὺν Αἰνείᾳ
κατάραντες εἰς Ἰταλίαν Τρῶες ἔκτισαν, καὶ ἀφ᾽
ἧς τὸ Ῥωμαίων ἦν γένος, ὡς καὶ πρότερόν μοι
δεδήλωται. οἱ δ᾽ ἐν ταύτῃ κατοικοῦντες πάντα

---

[1] ἀνοίξαντες ἐξέθεον Reiske : ἐξέθεον ἀνοίξαντες B, ἐξέθεον ἀν-
οίγοντες R.
[2] Sylburg : ἐφισταμένους O.
[3] δὲ R : τε B.
[4] Kiessling : ἐπὶ O.
[5] ἕως O : τέως Jacoby.
[6] ἀνθρώπων (or ἔνδον) Cary : ἁλόντων O, Jacoby. For τῶν
ἀνθρώπων see ix. 34, 4; iii. 37, 4; for τῶν ἔνδον, the more

For the Bovillani not only repulsed the assailants from the walls, but even threw open their gates, and sallying out in a body, forcibly thrust back down hill those who opposed them. Here the Volscians suffered very heavy losses and the battle for the walls continued a long time, so that all despaired of taking the town. But the general caused the loss of those who were slain to pass unnoticed by replacing them with others, and inspired with fresh courage those who were spent with toil by pressing forward himself to that part of the army which was in distress. Thus not only his words, but his actions also were incentives to valour; for he faced every danger and was not found wanting in any attempt till the walls were taken. When at length he had made himself master of this city also and had summarily put to death some of the inhabitants and made prisoners of the rest, he withdrew his forces, having won a most glorious victory and carrying off great quantities of the finest spoils, besides enriching his army with vast amounts of money he had got possession of in this city, where it was found in greater quantity than in any of the places he had captured.

XXI. After this all the country he marched through submitted to him and no city made any resistance but Lavinium, which was the first city built by the Trojans who landed in Italy with Aeneas, and the one from which the Romans derive their origin, as I have shown earlier.[1] The inhabitants of this city thought they

[1] i. 45, 1 ; iii. 11, 2.

---

common expression, viii. 19, 1 and 4 (*bis*); 20, 1. Palaeo-graphically ἀνθρώπων is more probable. ἁλόντων may have been a marginal correction intended to apply to ἄλλων, 5 lines below, but applied here by mistake.

[7] ἁλόντων O : ἄλλων Kiessling.   [8] Reiske : γε O.

πρότερον ᾤοντο δεῖν ὑπομένειν ἢ τὸ πρὸς τοὺς
2 ἀπογόνους[1] σφῶν[2] πιστὸν ἐγκαταλιπεῖν. ἐγένοντο
μὲν οὖν καὶ τειχομαχίαι τινὲς αὐτόθι καρτεραὶ καὶ
πρὸ τῶν ἐρυμάτων ὀξεῖαι μάχαι· οὐ μὴν ἑάλω γε
τὸ τεῖχος κατὰ κράτος[3] τῇ πρώτῃ ἐφόδῳ, ἀλλ᾽
ἐδόκει χρόνου δεῖν[4] καὶ τριβῆς. ἀποστὰς οὖν τῆς
τειχομαχίας[5] ὁ Μάρκιος περιετάφρευε κύκλῳ τὴν
πόλιν καὶ ἀπεσταύρου, τὰς ὁδοὺς φυλάττων ἵνα
μήτε ἀγορὰ μήτε ἐπικουρία τις αὐτοῖς[6] ἔξωθεν
προσγένοιτο.
3   Ῥωμαῖοι δὲ τῶν τε κεκρατημένων ἤδη πόλεων
τὸν ὄλεθρον ἀκούοντες καὶ τῶν προσθεμένων τῷ
Μαρκίῳ τὴν ἀνάγκην, ταῖς τε πρεσβείαις ἐνοχλού-
μενοι ταῖς ἀφικνουμέναις ὡς αὐτοὺς ὁσημέραι παρὰ
τῶν μενουσῶν ἐν τῇ φιλίᾳ καὶ δεομένων βοηθείας,
τοῦ τε Λαουϊνίου τὸν περιτειχισμὸν ὀρρωδοῦντες
ἐν χερσὶν ὄντα, καὶ εἰ τόδε τὸ φρούριον ἁλώσεται
τὸν πόλεμον ἐπὶ σφᾶς ἥξειν εὐθὺς οἰόμενοι, μίαν
ὑπέλαβον ἔσεσθαι πάντων᾽ τῶν κακῶν λύσιν, εἰ
4 ψηφίσαιντο τῷ Μαρκίῳ τὴν κάθοδον. καὶ ὅ τε
δῆμος ἅπας ἐβόα τοῦτο[8] καὶ οἱ δήμαρχοι νόμον
εἰσφέρειν ὑπὲρ ἀκυρώσεως τῆς καταδίκης ἐβού-
λοντο· ἀλλ᾽ οἱ πατρίκιοι ἠναντιώθησαν αὐτοῖς οὐκ
ἀξιοῦντες τῶν δεδικασμένων λύειν οὐθέν. μὴ γενομένου δὲ προβουλεύματος ὑπὸ τῆς βουλῆς οὐδὲ
τοῖς δημάρχοις ἔτι προθεῖναι γνώμην εἰς τὸν δῆμον
5 ἐδόκει. ὃ καὶ θαυμάζειν ἄξιον, ἀφ᾽ ἧς δήποτε
αἰτίας ἡ βουλὴ σπουδάζουσα τὸν ἔμπροσθεν χρό-

---

[1] Sylburg : πογόνους Ba, προγόνους ABb.
[2] σφῶν R : σφῶν ῥωμαίους AB.
[3] κατὰ κράτος R : ἀπὸ κράτους AB, Jacoby.
[4] δεῖν Jacoby : δεῖν ἡ πολιορκία O, δεῖν τῇ πολιορκίᾳ Reiske.
[5] τειχομαχίας Amg : πολιορκίας O, Jacoby.

ought to suffer any extremity rather than fail to keep faith with their descendants. Here, therefore, some stubborn fighting took place upon the walls and some sharp engagements before the ramparts; nevertheless, the walls were not carried by storm at the first assault, but their capture seemed to require time and unhurried persistence. Marcius accordingly gave over the attack on the walls and undertook to construct a ditch and a palisade round the town, while guarding all the roads so that neither provisions nor reinforcements might come to the inhabitants from outside.

The Romans, being informed both of the destruction of the cities that were already taken and of the exigency which had influenced those who had joined Marcius, and importuned by the embassies which came to them daily from those who continued firm in their friendship and besought their aid, and being alarmed, moreover, by the investment of Lavinium then in progress and believing that if this stronghold should be taken the war would promptly come to their own gates, thought the only remedy for all these evils would be to pass a vote for the return of Marcius. The entire populace shouted for this and the tribunes too wished to introduce a law for the annulment of his condemnation; but the patricians opposed them, being determined not to reverse any part of the sentence which had been pronounced. And as no preliminary decree was passed by the senate, the tribunes too no longer thought fit to propose the matter to the populace. It may well excite wonder what the motive was that led the senate, which hitherto had

---

⁶ Sylburg : αὐτῶν O.   ⁷ Kiessling : ἁπάντων O.
⁸ τοῦτο B : om. R.

νον ὑπὲρ τοῦ Μαρκίου τότε βουλομένῳ τῷ δήμῳ
κατάγειν αὐτὸν ἠναντιώθη· πότερα πεῖραν αὐτοῦ
ποιουμένη τῆς γνώμης καὶ[1] τῷ μὴ συγχωρεῖν
ἑτοίμως[2] ἐπὶ τὸ μᾶλλον σπουδάζειν αὐτὸν παρορ-
μῶσα, ἢ τὰς καθ᾽[3] ἑαυτῆς ἀπολύσασθαι βουλομένη
διαβολὰς ὑπὲρ τοῦ μηθενὸς ὧν ἔπραττεν ὁ ἀνὴρ
μήτε αἰτία μήτε συνεργὸς εἶναι. χαλεπὸν γὰρ ἦν
ἀπόρρητον γενόμενον αὐτῆς τὸ βούλευμα συμβαλεῖν.

XXII. Ἀκούσας δὲ ταῦτα παρ᾽ αὐτομόλων τινῶν
ὁ Μάρκιος, ὡς εἶχεν ὀργῆς, εὐθὺς ἀναστήσας τὴν
δύναμιν ἦγεν ἐπὶ τὴν Ῥώμην, φυλακὴν τοῦ Λαουϊνίου τὴν ἀρκοῦσαν καταλιπών· καὶ αὐτίκα τῆς
πόλεως σταδίους τετταράκοντα ἀποσχὼν κατεστρατοπέδευσε περὶ τὰς καλουμένας Κλοιλίας τάφρους.
2 μαθοῦσι δὲ τὴν παρουσίαν αὐτοῦ τοῖς κατὰ τὴν
πόλιν τοσοῦτος ἐνέπεσε θόρυβος ὡς αὐτίκα τοῖς
τείχεσι τοῦ πολέμου προσάξοντος, ὥσθ᾽ οἱ μὲν ἐπὶ
τὰ τείχη τὰ ὅπλα λαβόντες ἔθεον ἄνευ παραγγέλματος, οἱ δ᾽ ἐπὶ τὰς πύλας κατὰ πλῆθος ἐφέροντο
χωρὶς ἡγεμόνος, οἱ δὲ τοὺς δούλους καθοπλίσαντες
ἐπὶ τοῖς τέγεσι[4] τῶν οἰκιῶν ἵστασαν, οἱ δὲ τήν τε
ἄκραν καὶ τὸ Καπιτώλιον καὶ τοὺς ἄλλους ἐρυμνοὺς
τόπους τῆς πόλεως κατελαμβάνοντο, γυναῖκές τε
λελυμέναι τὰς κόμας ἐπὶ τὰ τεμένη καὶ τοὺς νεὼς
ἔθεον ὀλοφυρόμεναί τε καὶ δεόμεναι τῶν θεῶν ἀπο-
3 τρέψαι[5] τῆς πόλεως τὸν ἐπιόντα φόβον. ὡς δ᾽ ἥ
τε νὺξ παρῆλθε καὶ τῆς ἐπιούσης ἡμέρας τὸ πλεῖστον, καὶ οὐδὲν ὧν ἐδεδοίκεσαν ἐγίνετο, ἀλλ᾽
ἔμενεν ὁ Μάρκιος ἐφ᾽ ἡσυχίας, συνέδραμον ἅπαντες

---

[1] καὶ Kiessling : ἢ O.
[2] ἑτοίμως B : ἑκάστῳ ἑτοίμως R.
[3] τὰς καθ᾽ R : τὰς ἴσας καθ᾽ B.

so warmly espoused the cause of Marcius, to oppose
the populace on this occasion when they wished to
recall him—whether they were sounding out the
sentiment of the populace and arousing them to
greater zeal by their own reluctance to yield to
them, or whether they wished to clear themselves of
the accusations brought against them so that they
might not be held to be either responsible for or
accomplices in any of the acts of Marcius. For as
their purpose was kept secret, it was difficult to
conjecture what it was.

XXII. Marcius,[1] being informed of these events by
some deserters, was so angry that he broke camp at
once and marched on Rome, leaving a sufficient force
to keep guard over Lavinium ; and he straightway
encamped at the place called the Cluilian Ditches,[2]
at a distance of forty stades from the city. When the
Romans heard of his presence there, such confusion
fell upon them, in their belief that the war would at
once come to their walls, that some seized their arms
and ran to the walls without orders, others went in a
body to the gates without anyone to command them,
some armed their slaves and took their stand on the
roofs of their houses, and still others seized the citadel
and the Capitol and the other strong places of
the city ; and the women, with their hair dishevelled,
ran to the sanctuaries and to the temples, lamenting
and praying to the gods to avert the danger that
threatened. But when the night had passed, as well
as most of the following day, and none of the evils
they had feared befell them, but Marcius remained

---

[1] For chaps. 22-36 *cf.* Livy ii. 39, 4-11.
[2] The fossae Cluiliae; see iii. 4, 1.

---

[4] Sylburg : τείχεσι O.   [5] Cobet : ἀποστρέψαι O.

εἰς τὴν ἀγορὰν οἱ δημοτικοὶ καὶ τοὺς πατρικίους
ἐκάλουν εἰς τὸ βουλευτήριον, καὶ εἰ μὴ προβου-
λεύσουσι τῷ ἀνδρὶ τὴν κάθοδον, αὐτοὶ βουλεύσε-
σθαι περὶ σφῶν αὐτῶν ἔφασαν ὡς προδιδόμενοι.
4 τότε δὴ συνελθόντες εἰς τὴν βουλὴν οἱ πατρίκιοι
ψηφίζονται πρεσβευτὰς πρὸς τὸν Μάρκιον ἀποστεῖλαι πέντε¹ ἄνδρας ἐκ τῶν πρεσβυτάτων, οὓς
μάλιστα ἐκεῖνος ἠσπάζετο, περὶ διαλύσεώς τε καὶ
φιλίας διαλεξομένους. ἦσαν δ' οἱ προχειρισθέντες
ἀπ' αὐτῶν ἄνδρες οἵδε, Μάρκος Μηνύκιος καὶ
Πόστομος Κομίνιος καὶ Σπόριος Λάρκιος καὶ
Πόπλιος Πινάριος καὶ Κόιντος Σολπίκιος, ἅπαντες
5 ὑπατικοί. ὡς δ' ἀφίκοντο ἐπὶ τὸ στρατόπεδον,
καὶ ἔγνω τὴν παρουσίαν αὐτῶν ὁ Μάρκιος, καθεζόμενος ἅμα τοῖς ἐπιφανεστάτοις Οὐολούσκων τε
καὶ τῶν ἄλλων συμμάχων ἔνθα πλεῖστοι ἔμελλον
ἀκούσεσθαι τῶν λεγομένων, ἐκέλευσε καλεῖν τοὺς
ἄνδρας. εἰσελθόντων δ' αὐτῶν ἤρξατο τοῦ λόγου
Μηνύκιος, ὁ πλεῖστα κατὰ τὸν τῆς ὑπατείας χρόνον
σπουδάσας ὑπὲρ αὐτοῦ καὶ μάλιστα τοῖς δημοτικοῖς ἐναντιωθείς, καὶ ἔλεξε τοιάδε·

XXIII. '' Ὅτι μὲν οὐ δίκαια πέπονθας ὑπὸ τοῦ
δήμου, ὦ Μάρκιε, μετ' αἰτίας αἰσχρᾶς ἐξελαθεὶς
ἐκ τῆς πατρίδος, ἅπαντες ἴσμεν· καὶ οὐδὲν οἰόμεθά
σε ποιεῖν θαυμαστόν, εἰ χαλεπαίνεις καὶ ἀγανακτεῖς
ἐπὶ ταῖς τύχαις. κοινὸς γὰρ δὴ τῆς ἁπάντων
φύσεως οὗτος ὁ νόμος, ἐχθρὸν εἶναι τῷ δράσαντι
2 τὸ πεπονθὸς κακῶς. ὅτι δ' οὐ μετὰ λογισμοῦ
σώφρονος ἐξετάζεις οὓς ἀμύνεσθαί τε καὶ τιμωρεῖ-
σθαί σοι προσῆκεν,² οὐδὲ μετριάζεις περὶ τὴν
ἀνάπραξιν τῆς δίκης, ἀλλ' ἐν ταὐτῷ τίθεσαι τά τε

quiet, all the plebeians flocked to the Forum and called upon the patricians[1] to assemble in the senate-house, declaring that if they would not pass the preliminary decree for the return of Marcius, they themselves, as men who were being betrayed, would take measures for their own protection. Then at last the senators met in the senate-house and voted to send to Marcius five of their oldest members who were his closest friends, to treat for reconciliation and friendship. The men chosen were Marcus Minucius, Postumus Cominius, Spurius Larcius, Publius Pinarius and Quintus Sulpicius, all ex-consuls. When they came to the camp and Marcius was informed of their arrival, he seated himself in the midst of the most important of the Volscians and their allies, where very many would hear all that was said, and then ordered the envoys to be summoned. When these came in, Minucius, who during his consulship had been most active in his favour and had distinguished himself by his opposition to the plebeians, spoke first, as follows :

XXIII. " We are all sensible, Marcius, that you have suffered injustice at the hands of the populace in having been banished from your country under a foul accusation, and we do not regard it as anything strange on your part if you feel anger and resentment at your misfortunes. For common to the nature of all men is this law—that the injured party is an enemy to the aggressor. But that you do not examine in the light of sober reason who those are whom you ought to requite and punish, nor show any moderation in exacting that punishment, but class together

---

[1] " Patricians " is here used for " senators."

[1] πέντε B : om. R.   [2] Jacoby : προσήκει O.

63

ἀναίτια τοῖς αἰτίοις καὶ τὰ φίλια τοῖς πολεμίοις,
νόμους τε κινεῖς φύσεως ἀκινήτους καὶ τὰ πρὸς
τοὺς θεοὺς συνταράττεις ὅσια, καὶ οὐδὲ σεαυτὸν
ἐξ ὧν τε καὶ ὅστις ἔφυς ἔτι μέμνησαι, τοῦτο
3 τεθαυμάκαμεν. ἥκομέν τε ἀποσταλέντες ὑπὸ τοῦ
κοινοῦ πρέσβεις οἱ προὔχοντες ἡλικίᾳ τῶν πατρικίων καὶ περὶ σὲ προθυμότατοι μεμιγμένην
φέροντες δικαιολογίαν παραιτήσει, καὶ ἐφ' οἷς
ἀξιοῦμέν σε διαλύσασθαι¹ τὴν ἔχθραν πρὸς τὸν
δῆμον ἀπαγγελοῦντες². πρὸς δὲ τούτοις, ἃ νομί-
ζομεν εἶναι κάλλιστα καὶ συμφορώτατά σοι, ταῦτα
παραινέσοντες.

XXIV. " Ἀρχέτω δ' ὁ περὶ τῶν δικαίων λόγος.
συνέστη τὸ δημοτικὸν ἐπὶ σοὶ παροξυνθὲν ὑπὸ τῶν
δημάρχων, καὶ ἦκον ὡς ἀποκτενοῦντές σε ἄκριτον,
οἷς φοβερὸς ἦσθα. τοῦτο τὸ ἔργον ἐκωλύσαμεν
ἡμεῖς οἱ ἐκ τοῦ συνεδρίου καὶ παρέσχομέν σοι
μηθὲν ὃ μὴ δίκαιον ἦν τότε παθεῖν. μετὰ τοῦτο
προὐκαλοῦντό σε οἱ κωλυθέντες ἀνελεῖν ἐπὶ δίκην,
αἰτιασάμενοι πονηροὺς κατ' αὐτῶν εἰπεῖν ἐν τῇ
2 βουλῇ λόγους. ἐνέστημεν καὶ πρὸς τοῦτο, ὡς
οἶσθα, καὶ οὐκ ἐπετρέψαμεν οὔτε γνώμης οὔτε
λόγων ὑποσχεῖν σε δίκας. ἀποτυχόντες καὶ τούτου τελευτῶντες ἦκον ἐφ' ἡμᾶς αἰτιώμενοί σε
τυραννίδι ἐπιχειρεῖν.³ ταύτην αὐτὸς ὑπέμεινας
ἀπολογήσασθαι τὴν αἰτίαν, ἐπειδὴ πάμπολυ ἀπεῖχες
αὐτῆς, καὶ παρέσχες τοῖς δημοτικοῖς περὶ σεαυτοῦ
3 τὴν ψῆφον ἀναλαβεῖν. ἡ βουλὴ δὲ καὶ τότε παρῆν
καὶ πολλὰς ἐποιεῖτο δεήσεις περὶ σοῦ. τίνος οὖν
ἡμεῖς οἱ πατρίκιοι τῶν συμβεβηκότων σοι κακῶν

¹ διαλύσασθαι R : διαλύσεσθαι Ba, Jacoby.
² ἀπαγγελοῦντες Bb : ἀπαγγελλοῦντες Ba, ἀπαγγέλλοντες R.

the innocent with the guilty and friends with enemies, and that you violate the inviolable laws of Nature, confound the duties of religion, and, even as to yourself, no longer remember from whom you are sprung and what sort of man you are—that has seemed strange to us. We have come now, the oldest of the patricians and the most zealous of your friends, sent by the commonwealth to present our defence mingled with entreaty, and to bring word upon what conditions we ask you to lay aside your enmity toward the populace; and furthermore, to advise you of the course which we believe will be most honourable and advantageous for you.

XXIV. " Let me speak first concerning the point of justice. The plebeians, inflamed by the tribunes, conspired against you and came with the intention of putting you to death without a trial, because they feared you. This attempt we of the senate prevented, and we permitted you to suffer no injustice on that occasion. Afterwards the same men who had been prevented from destroying you summoned you to trial, charging you with having uttered malicious words about them in the senate. We opposed this too, as you know, and would not permit you to be brought to trial either for your opinion or for your words. Disappointed in this also, they came to us at last, accusing you of aiming at tyranny. This charge you yourself consented to answer, since you were far from being guilty of it, and you permitted the plebeians to give their votes concerning you. The senate was present on this occasion also and made many pleas in your behalf. Of which of the misfortunes, then, that have befallen you have we

---

ᵃ ἐπιχειρεῖν Sintenis : ἐπὶ (sic) O.

γεγόναμεν αἴτιοι, καὶ διὰ τί πολεμεῖς ἡμῖν τοσαύ
την εὔνοιαν ἀποδειξαμένοις περὶ σὲ κατὰ τὸν τότε
ἀγῶνα; ἀλλὰ μὴν οὐδὲ τὸ δημοτικὸν ἅπαν ἐξ
ελαθῆναί σε βουλόμενον εὑρέθη· δυσὶ γοῦν ψήφοις
ἑάλως μόναις, ὥστε οὐδὲ τούτοις ἂν εἴης σὺν δίκῃ
πολέμιος οἵ σε ὡς οὐδὲν ἀδικοῦντα ἀπέλυσαν.
4 τίθημι δ', εἰ βούλει, πᾶσι μὲν τοῖς δημόταις δό
ξαν, ὅλῃ δὲ τῇ βουλῇ φανὲν ταύτῃ χρήσασθαί σε
τῇ συμφορᾷ, καὶ δίκαιον εἶναί σου τὸ πρὸς ἅπαν
τας ἡμᾶς μῖσος· ἀλλ' αἱ γυναῖκές σε, ὦ Μάρκιε,
τί δεινὸν εἰργάσαντο ἀνθ' ὅτου πολεμεῖς αὐταῖς;
ποίαν ἐπενέγκασαι περὶ φυγῆς ψῆφον ἢ τίνας
5 εἰποῦσαι κατὰ σοῦ πονηροὺς λόγους; τί δ' οἱ παῖ
δες ἡμῶν δράσαντες ἢ διανοηθέντες ἀδικεῖν περὶ
σοῦ κινδυνεύουσιν ὑπὲρ αἰχμαλωσίας καὶ τῶν
ἄλλων ἃ παθεῖν αὐτοὺς εἰκὸς ἐὰν ἡ πόλις ἁλῷ;
οὐ τὰ δίκαια διαιτᾷς, ὦ Μάρκιε, καὶ εἰ[1] τοῦτον
οἴει δεῖν τὸν τρόπον τὰ ὑπαίτια καὶ ἐχθρὰ μισεῖν,
ὥστε μηδὲ τῶν ἀναιτίων φείδεσθαι καὶ φιλίων, οὐκ
6 ἄρα τὰ προσήκοντα ἀνδρὶ ἀγαθῷ φρονεῖς. ἵνα δὲ
ἅπαντα ταῦτα ἀφῶ, τί ἂν ἔχοις εἰπεῖν, ὦ πρὸς
Διός, εἴ τις ἔροιτό σε, τοὺς δὲ δὴ τάφους τῶν
προγόνων τί παθὼν ὑπ' αὐτῶν[2] ἀνασκάπτεις καὶ
τιμὰς ἃς κομίζονται παρ' ἀνθρώπων ἀφαιρῇ; θεῶν
δὲ βωμοὺς καὶ τεμένη καὶ νεὼς τίνος ἀδικήματος
ὀργῇ συλᾷς καὶ κατακαίεις καὶ ἀνατρέπεις καὶ
σεβασμῶν οὐκ ἐᾷς τυγχάνειν τῶν νομίμων; τί

---

[1] καὶ εἰ Reiske : εἰ δὲ A, καὶ B.
[2] ὑπ' αὐτῶν deleted by Cobet, Jacoby.

patricians been the cause ? And why do you make
war upon us who showed so much goodwill toward
you during that contest ? But, for that matter, not
even all the plebeians were found to desire your banishment ; at any rate, you were condemned by two
votes only, so that you could not with justice be an
enemy to those plebeians, either, who acquitted you
as guilty of no wrongdoing. I will assume, however,
if you wish, that it was pursuant to the vote of all the
plebeians and the judgement of the entire senate that
you suffered this misfortune, and that your hatred
against us all is just ; but the women, Marcius, what
wrong have they done to you that you should make
war upon them ? By what vote did they condemn
you to banishment, or what malicious words did they
utter against you ? And our children, what wrong
have they done or contemplated doing that they
should be exposed to captivity and to all the other
misfortunes which they would presumably suffer if
the city should be taken ? You are not just in your
judgements, Marcius ; and if you think you ought
to hate those who are guilty and your enemies in such
a manner as not to spare even those who are innocent
and your friends, then your way of thinking is not
such as becomes a good man. But, to omit all these
considerations, what, in Heaven's name, could you
answer if anyone should ask you what injury you have
received from your ancestors to induce you to destroy
their sepulchres and to deprive them of the honours
they receive from men ? Or resentment at what
injury has led you to despoil, burn and demolish
the altars of the gods, their shrines and their temples,
and to prevent them from receiving their customary
worship ? What could you say in answer to this ?

πρὸς ταῦτα φαίης ἄν; ἐγὼ μὲν γὰρ οὐδὲν ὁρῶ.
7 ταῦτά σοι περί τε ἡμῶν αὐτῶν,[1] ὦ Μάρκιε, τῶν
ἐκ τοῦ συνεδρίου καὶ περὶ τῶν ἄλλων πολιτῶν,
οὓς ἀπολέσαι προθυμῇ κακὸν οὐδὲν ὑπ' αὐτῶν
πεπονθώς, τάφων τε καὶ ἱερῶν καὶ πόλεως τῆς
γειναμένης τε καὶ θρεψαμένης τὰ δίκαια εἰρήσθω.

XXV. '' Φέρε, εἰ δὲ δὴ[2] πάντας μὲν ἀνθρώπους
καὶ τοὺς μηδὲν ἀδικοῦντάς σε γυναιξὶν ὁμοῦ καὶ
τέκνοις δίκας σοι δοῦναι προσῆκε, πάντας δὲ θεούς
τε καὶ ἥρωας καὶ δαίμονας πόλιν τε καὶ χώραν
ἀπολαῦσαι τῆς τῶν δημάρχων ἀνοίας, καὶ μηδὲν ἐξ-
αίρετον μηδ' ἀτιμώρητον ἀφεῖσθαι μέρος ὑπὸ σοῦ,
οὐχ ἱκανὰς ἤδη παρὰ πάντων εἰσπέπραξαι δίκας
τοσοῦτον μὲν φόνον ἐργασάμενος ἀνθρώπων,[3] τοσαύτην δὲ χώραν πυρὶ καὶ σιδήρῳ λωβησάμενος,
τοσαύτας δὲ πόλεις ἐκ βάθρων ἀναστήσας, ἑορτὰς
δὲ καὶ θυσίας καὶ σεβασμοὺς θεῶν καὶ δαιμόνων ἐν
πολλοῖς τόποις ἀνεόρτους ἀναγκάσας γενέσθαι καὶ
2 ἀθύτους καὶ τιμῶν νομίμων ἀμοίρους; ἐγὼ μὲν
οὐκ[4] ἠξίουν ἂν[5] ἄνδρα ὅτῳ φροντὶς ὁποσηοῦν ἀρετῆς ἐστιν οὔτε συναναιρεῖν τοῖς ἐχθροῖς τὰ φίλια
οὔτε χαλεπὸν ὀργὴν εἶναι καὶ ἀπαραίτητον εἰς τοὺς
ἐξαμαρτάνοντάς τι περὶ αὐτόν, ἄλλως τε καὶ δίκας
3 παρ' αὐτῶν εἰληφότα πολλὰς καὶ μεγάλας. ἃ μὲν
οὖν ἀπολογεῖσθαί τε περὶ ἡμῶν αὐτῶν εἴχομεν καὶ
παραιτεῖσθαί σε περὶ τῶν δημοτικῶν, ταῦτ' ἐστίν,
ἃ δ' ὑποτίθεσθαί σοι δι' εὔνοιαν οἱ τιμιώτατοι

---

[1] αὐτῶν B : om. R.
[2] φέρε, εἰ δὲ δὴ Jacoby, ἀλλὰ φέρε εἰ δὲ δὴ Sintenis :
ἀφαιρέσει δὲ δὴ O.   [3] ἀνθρώπων B : om. R.
[4] μὲν οὐκ B : μὲν οὖν οὐκ R.   [5] ἂν added by Cary.

For my part, I see nothing that you could say. Let these considerations of justice suffice, Marcius, both in behalf of us of the senate and of the other citizens whom you are eager to destroy, even though you have suffered no wrong at their hands, and in behalf of the sepulchres, the sanctuaries and the city to which you owe both your birth and your rearing.

XXV. " Come now, even if it were fitting that all men, even those who have not wronged you at all, together with their wives and children should make atonement to you, and that all the gods, the heroes and the lesser divinities, the city and the country, should reap the benefit of the tribunes' folly, and that nothing whatever should be exempted, nothing go unrevenged by you, have you not already exacted sufficient punishment from us all by slaying so many people, ravaging so much territory by fire and sword, razing to the ground so many cities, and doing away in many places with the festivals, the sacrifices and the worship of the gods and other divinities and compelling them to go without their festivals and sacrifices and to have no part in their customary honours ? For my part, I should have refused to believe that a man who has the least regard for virtue would either destroy his friends along with his enemies or show himself harsh and inexorable in his anger toward those who offend him in any way, especially after he has already exacted from them many severe retributions. These, then, are the considerations we had to offer you by way of both clearing ourselves and asking you to be lenient toward the plebeians ; and the advice which we, your most valued friends, were ready to give you out of goodwill if you were bent on

φιλονεικοῦντι[1] καὶ ὑπισχνεῖσθαι διαλλαττομένῳ
πρὸς τὴν πατρίδα, ταυτί· ἐν ᾧ τὸ δύνασθαί σοι
μάλιστα ὑπάρχει καὶ τὸ θεῖον ἔτι συλλαμβάνει,
μετριάσαι καὶ ταμιεύεσθαι τὴν τύχην, ἐνθυμηθέντα
ὅτι μεταβολὰς ἔχει πάντα[2] τὰ πράγματα καὶ οὐδὲν ἐπὶ τῶν αὐτῶν φιλεῖ διαμένειν, νεμεσᾶταί τε
πάντα ὑπὸ θεῶν τὰ ὑπερέχοντα, ὅταν εἰς ἄκρον
ἐπιφανείας ἀφίκηται, καὶ τρέπεται πάλιν εἰς τὸ μη-
δέν. μάλιστα δὲ τοῦτο πάσχει τὰ σκληρὰ καὶ
μεγάλαυχα φρονήματα καὶ τοὺς ὅρους ἐκβαίνοντα
4 τῆς ἀνθρωπίνης φύσεως. ὑπάρχει δέ σοι νῦν ἁπάντων[3] κράτιστα καταλύσασθαι τὸν πόλεμον· ἥ τε γὰρ
βουλὴ πᾶσα ὥρμηται τὴν κάθοδον ψηφίσασθαί σοι,
καὶ ὁ δῆμος ἕτοιμός ἐστι νόμῳ κυρωθέντι λῦσαι
τὴν ἀειφυγίαν. τί οὖν ἔτι κωλύει σε τὰς ἡδίστας
καὶ τιμιωτάτας ὄψεις τῶν ἀναγκαιοτάτων σωμάτων ἀπολαβεῖν καὶ κεκομίσθαι τὴν περιμάχητον
πατρίδα ἄρχειν τε ὥσπερ σοι προσῆκε· ἀρχόντων
καὶ ἡγεῖσθαι ἡγεμόνων παισί τε καὶ ἐγγόνοις
μέγιστον αὔχημα καταλιπεῖν; τούτων μέντοι τῶν
ὑποσχέσεων ἡμεῖς ἐγγυηταὶ πασῶν ἐσμεν ὡς αὐ-
5 τίκα μάλα γενησομένων. νῦν μὲν γὰρ οὐχὶ καλῶς
εἶχε ψηφίσασθαί σοι τὴν βουλὴν ἢ τὸν δῆμον οὐθὲν
ἐπιεικὲς ἢ μέτριον, ἕως ἀντιπαρεστρατοπέδευκας
ἡμῖν καὶ τὰ πολεμίων ἔργα δρᾷς· εἰ δ' ἀποσταίης
τῶν ὅπλων, ἥξει σοι τὸ περὶ τῆς καθόδου ψήφισμα
φερόμενον ὑφ' ἡμῶν οὐκ εἰς μακράν.

XXVI. "Ἀγαθὰ μὲν δὴ ταῦτα ὑπάρξει σοι
διαλλαττομένῳ, μένοντι δ' ἐπὶ τῆς ὀργῆς καὶ μὴ

---

[1] φιλονεικοῦντι (or φίλων εἴκοντι) Kiessling : φιλονεικοῦντες
AC, φίλων ἥκοντες B, Jacoby, φίλων ἥκομεν Reiske.
[2] Kiessling : ἅπαντα O.   [3] Kiessling : πάντων O.

strife, and the promises we could make if you were ready to be reconciled to your country, are as follows: While your power is greatest and Heaven still assists you, we advise you to act with moderation and to husband your good fortune, bearing in mind that all things are subject to change and that nothing is apt to continue long in the same state. All things that wax too great, when they reach the peak of eminence, incur the displeasure of the gods and are brought to naught again. And this is the fate which comes especially to stubborn and haughty spirits and those that overstep the bounds of human nature. It is in your power now to put an end to the war on the best possible terms ; for the whole senate is eager to pass a vote for your return, and the populace is ready by a law ratifying the senate's vote to annul your sentence of perpetual banishment. What is there, then, to prevent you any longer from enjoying once more the most dear and precious sight of your nearest of kin, from recovering your fatherland that is so well worth fighting for, from ruling, as you ought, over rulers and commanding those who command others, and from bequeathing to children and descendants the greatest glory ? Moreover, we are the sureties that all these promises will be performed forthwith. For though at present it would not be well for the senate or the people to pass any mild or lenient vote in your favour while you are encamped against us and are committing hostile acts, yet if you lay down your arms, the decree for your return will soon come to you, brought by us.

XXVI. " These, then, are the advantages you will reap by becoming reconciled ; whereas, if you persist in your resentment and do not give up your

διαλυομένῳ τὸ μῖσος πρὸς ἡμᾶς πολλὰ καὶ χαλεπά, ἐξ ὧν ἐγὼ δύο τὰ μέγιστα νυνὶ καὶ φανερώτατα ἐρῶ. πρῶτον μὲν ὅτι δυσκόλου γενέσθαι, μᾶλλον δ' ἀδυνάτου, πράγματος πονηρὸν ἔρωτα ἔχεις, πόλεως τῆς Ῥωμαίων καθελεῖν τὴν ἰσχὺν καὶ ταῦτα τοῖς Οὐολούσκων ὅπλοις· ἔπειθ' ὅτι σοι κατορθώσαντί τε καὶ μὴ τυχόντι[1] πάντων ἀνθρώπων ὑπάρξει δυστυχεστάτῳ νομίζεσθαι. ἐξ ὧν δὲ ταῦτα παρίσταταί μοι περὶ σοῦ φρονεῖν, ἄκουσον, ὦ Μάρκιε, μηθὲν πρὸς τὴν ἐλευθερίαν μου τῶν λόγων τρα-
2 χυνόμενος. σκόπει δὲ πρῶτον ὑπὲρ τοῦ ἀδυνάτου. Ῥωμαίοις, ὡς οἶσθα καὶ σύ, πολλὴ μέν ἐστι νεότης ἐπιχώριος, ἧς εἰ τὸ στασιάζον ἐξαιρεθείη (γενήσεται δὲ τοῦτο κατὰ πολλὴν ἀνάγκην νυνὶ διὰ τόνδε τὸν πόλεμον· πάντα γὰρ ὑπὸ δέους κοινοῦ συνίστασθαι φιλεῖ τὰ διάφορα), οὐχ ὅτι Οὐολοῦσκοι κρατήσουσιν, ἀλλ' οὐδὲ ἄλλο τῶν κατὰ τὴν Ἰταλίαν ἐθνῶν οὐθέν· πολλὴ δ' ἡ Λατίνων καὶ τῶν ἄλλων συμμάχων τε καὶ[2] ἀποίκων τῆς πόλεως ἰσχύς, ἣν δι'[3] ὀλίγου πᾶσαν ἐπίκουρον ἥξειν προσδέχου· στρατηγοί τε οἷος σὺ καὶ πρεσβύτεροι καὶ νέοι τοσοῦτοι τὸ πλῆθος ὅσοι παρὰ πάσαις οὐκ εἰσὶ ταῖς
3 ἄλλαις πόλεσι. μεγίστη δὲ πασῶν βοήθεια καὶ τὰς ἐν τοῖς δεινοῖς ἐλπίδας οὐδέποθ' ἡμῶν ψευσαμένη συμπάσης τε ἀμείνων ἀνθρωπίνης ἰσχύος, ἡ παρὰ τῶν θεῶν εὔνοια, δι' οὓς οὐ μόνον ἐλευθέραν εἰς τόδε χρόνου τὴν πόλιν τήνδε οἰκοῦμεν ὀγδόην ἤδη τὴν νῦν γενεάν, ἀλλὰ καὶ εὐδαίμονα καὶ πολλῶν
4 ἐθνῶν ἄρχουσαν. μὴ δὲ Πεδανοῖς ἡμᾶς εἰκάσῃς

---

[1] μὴ τυχόντι ABC : ἐπιτυχόντι D, δὴ τυχόντι Jacoby.
[2] τε καὶ added by Gelenius.
[3] δι' (cf. ix. 10, 5) Kallenberg : om. O, Jacoby.

hatred toward us, many disagreeable things will befall you, of which I shall now mention two as the most important and the most obvious. The first is that you have an evil passion for a thing that is difficult of accomplishment, or rather, impossible—the overthrow of the power of Rome, and that too by the arms of the Volscians ; the second is that, alike if you succeed and if you fail, it will be your lot to be looked upon as the most unfortunate of all men. Hear now, Marcius, the reasons that induce me to entertain this opinion concerning you, and take no offence at my frankness of speech. Consider, first, the impossibility of the thing. The Romans, as you yourself know, have a numerous body of youth of their own nation, whom, if the sedition is once banished from among them—and banished it will now inevitably be by this war, since a common fear is wont to reconcile all differences—surely not the Volscians, nay, no other Italian nation either, will ever overcome. Great also is the power of the Latins and of our other allies and colonies, and that power, be assured, will soon come to our assistance. We have generals too of the same ability as yourself, both older men and young, in greater number than are to be found in any other states. But the greatest assistance of all, and one which in times of danger has never betrayed our hopes, and better too than all human strength combined, is the favour of the gods, by whom this city which we inhabit not only continues to this day to preserve her liberty for already the eighth generation, but is also flourishing and the ruler over many nations. And do not liken us to the

μηδὲ Τολερίνοις μηδὲ τοῖς ἄλλοις μικροπολίταις
ὧν κατέσχες τὰ πολίχνια· καὶ γὰρ ἥττων ἄν τίς
σου στρατηγὸς καὶ ἀπ' ἐλάττονος ἢ τοσαύτης
στρατιᾶς ὀλιγανθρωπίαν καὶ φαυλότητα ἐρυμάτων
ἐβιάσατο· ἀλλ' ἐνθυμοῦ τὸ μέγεθος τῆς πόλεως καὶ
τὴν λαμπρότητα τῶν ἐν τοῖς πολέμοις πράξεων καὶ
τὴν ἐκ τοῦ θείου παροῦσαν αὐτῇ τύχην, δι' ἣν ἐκ
5 μικρᾶς τοσαύτη γέγονε. καὶ τὴν σεαυτοῦ δύναμιν,
ἣν ἐπάγων[1] ἔργῳ τοσῷδε ἐπιχειρεῖς, μὴ νόμιζε
ἠλλάχθαι, ἀλλὰ μέμνησο ἀκριβῶς ὅτι Οὐολούσκων
τε καὶ Αἰκανῶν στρατιὰν ἐπάγεις,[2] οὓς ἡμεῖς οἶδε
οἱ νῦν ὄντες[3] ἐν πολλαῖς ἐνικῶμεν μάχαις, ὁσάκις
ἡμῖν ἐτόλμησαν εἰς πόλεμον καταστῆναι· ὥστε σὺν
τοῖς χειρσὶν ἀγωνίζεσθαι μέλλων ἴσθι πρὸς τοὺς
κρείττονας καὶ σὺν τοῖς ἡττωμένοις διὰ παντὸς πρὸς
6 τοὺς νικῶντας ἀεί. εἰ δὲ δὴ τἀναντία τούτων ἦν,
ἐκεῖνό γέ τοι θαυμάζειν ἄξιον, πῶς λέληθέ σε,
πολεμικῶν ὄντα πραγμάτων ἔμπειρον, ὅτι τὸ παρὰ
τὰ δεινὰ εὔτολμον οὐκ ἐξ ἴσου παραγίνεσθαι φιλεῖ
τοῖς τε ὑπὲρ οἰκείων ἀγαθῶν ἀγωνιζομένοις καὶ
τοῖς ἐπὶ τἀλλότρια πορευομένοις· οἱ μέν γε οὐδέν,
ἐὰν μὴ[4] κατορθώσωσι, βλάπτονται, τοῖς δ' οὐδέν,
ἐὰν πταίσωσι, καταλείπεται· καὶ τοῦ σφάλλεσθαι
τὰς μεγάλας δυνάμεις ὑπὸ τῶν ἐλαττόνων καὶ τὰς
κρείττους ὑπὸ τῶν φαυλοτέρων τοῦτ' ἐν τοῖς
μάλιστ' αἴτιον ἦν. δεινὴ γὰρ ἡ ἀνάγκη, καὶ
ὁ περὶ τῶν ἐσχάτων κίνδυνος ἱκανὸς θάρσος ἐν-
θεῖναί τινι καὶ μὴ προϋπάρχον φύσει. εἶχον ἔτι

---

[1] ἐπάγων O : ἄγων Jacoby, ἐπαγόμενος Kiessling.
[2] Kayser : ἐπάγῃ O, Jacoby.
[3] οἱ νῦν ὄντες O : οἱ νῦν παρόντες Kiessling, om. Cobet,
Jacoby.   [4] ὐδέν, ἐὰν μὴ B : ἐὰν οὐδὲν R.

Pedani, the Tolerienses, or the peoples of the other petty towns you have seized ; for a general less able than yourself and with a smaller army than this great host of yours could have reduced small garrisons and slight defences. But consider the greatness of our city, the brilliance of her achievements in war, and the good fortune that abides with her through the favour of the gods, by which she has been raised from a small beginning to her present grandeur. As for your own forces, at the head of which you are undertaking so great an enterprise, do not imagine that they have changed, but bear clearly in mind that you are leading against us an army of mere Volscians and Aequians, whom we here who are still living were wont to defeat in many battles, yes, as often as they dared to come to an engagement with us. Know, then, that you are going to fight with inferior troops against those that are superior to them, and with troops that are accustomed to defeat every time against those that are always victorious. Yet even if the contrary of this were true, it would still be a matter for wonder how you, who are experienced in warfare, could have failed to observe that courage in the face of danger is not apt to be felt in equal measure by those who fight for their own blessings and by those who set out after what belongs to others. For the latter, if they do not succeed, suffer no loss, whereas the others, if they are defeated, have nothing left. And this is the chief reason why large armies have often been beaten by smaller ones and superior forces by inferior ones. For necessity is formidable, and a struggle in which life itself is at stake is capable of inspiring boldness in a man which was not already his by nature. I had many other things to

πλείω λέγειν ὑπὲρ τοῦ ἀδυνάτου, ἀλλὰ καὶ ταῦθ᾽ ἱκανά.

XXVII. '' Εἷς ἔτι μοι καταλείπεται λόγος, ὃν εἰ μὴ μετ᾽ ὀργῆς ἀλλ᾽ ἐκ λογισμοῦ κρινεῖς, ὀρθῶς τε εἰρῆσθαι δόξει καὶ παραστήσεταί σοι μεταμέλεια τῶν πραττομένων.. τίς δ᾽ ἐστὶν οὗτος ὁ λόγος; οὐδενὶ θνητῷ φύντι θεοὶ τῶν μελλόντων ἔσεσθαι βεβαίαν ἐπιστήμην ἔδωκαν ἔχειν, οὐδ᾽ ἂν εὕροις ἐκ τοῦ παντὸς αἰῶνος ὅτῳ πάντα κατὰ νοῦν ἐχώρησε 2 τὰ πράγματα μηδὲν ἐναντιωθείσης τῆς τύχης. καὶ διὰ τοῦτο οἱ φρονήσει προὔχοντες ἑτέρων, ἣν ὁ μακρὸς βίος καὶ τὰ πολλὰ παθήματα φέρει,[1] πρὶν ἐγχειρεῖν ὁτῳδήποτε ἔργῳ, τὸ τέλος αὐτοῦ πρῶτον οἴονται δεῖν σκοπεῖν, οὐ θάτερον μόνον ὃ βούλονται γενέσθαι σφίσιν, ἀλλὰ καὶ τὸ παρὰ γνώμην ἐκβησόμενον· μάλιστα δ᾽ οἱ τῶν πολέμων ἡγεμόνες, ὅσῳ μειζόνων τε γίνονται πραγμάτων κύριοι, καὶ τὰς αἰτίας τῶν κατορθωμάτων ἢ σφαλμάτων ἅπαντες ἐπὶ τούτους ἀναφέρουσιν. ἔπειτα ἂν μὲν εὕρωσι μηδεμίαν ἐνοῦσαν ἢ μικρὰς καὶ ὀλίγας ἐν τῷ μὴ κατορθῶσαι βλάβας, ἅπτονται τῶν ἔργων, ἐὰν δὲ 3 πολλὰς καὶ μεγάλας, ἀφίστανται. τοῦτο δὴ καὶ σὺ ποίησον καὶ σκόπει πρὸ τῶν ἔργων, ἐὰν σφαλῆς κατὰ τὸν πόλεμον καὶ μὴ πάντα ὑπάρξῃ, τί συμβήσεταί σοι παθεῖν. δι᾽ αἰτίας μὲν ἔσῃ παρὰ τοῖς ὑποδεξαμένοις, μέμψῃ δὲ καὶ αὐτὸς σεαυτὸν ὡς μείζοσιν ἐπιχειρήσας πράγμασιν ἢ δυνατοῖς.[2] στρατιᾶς δ᾽ ἡμετέρας πάλιν ἐκεῖσε ἀφικομένης καὶ φθειρούσης τὴν ἐκείνων γῆν (οὐ γὰρ ἀνεξόμεθα

---

[1] παθήματα φέρει Kiessling : πάθη μεταφέρει B, μαθήματα φέρει A.
[2] ἢ δυνατοῖς A : ἢ ἀδυνάτοις B, καὶ ἀδυνάτοις Kiessling.

say concerning the impossibility of your undertaking, but this is enough.

XXVII. " I still have one argument left which, if you will judge of it by reason rather than in anger, will not only seem to you to have been well made, but will also cause you to repent of what you are doing. What is this argument? That the gods have not given it to any mortal creature to possess sure knowledge of future events, and you will not find in all past time a man for whom all his undertakings succeeded according to his plan and whom Fortune thwarted in none. For this reason those who excel others in prudence—the fruit of a long life and many lessons from experience—think that they ought, before beginning any enterprise whatever, first to consider its possible outcome—not only the one which they desire for themselves, but also the one which will be contrary to their judgement. And this is particularly true of commanders in wars, the more so because the affairs of which they have charge are of greater importance and because everybody imputes to them the responsibility for both victories and defeats. Then, if they find that no loss inheres in failure, or few and small losses, they set about their undertakings, but if the losses might be many and serious, they abandon them. Do you too, then, follow their example, and before you resort to action, consider what it will be your fate to suffer if you fail in this war and all conditions do not favour you. You will be reproached by those who have received you and you will also blame yourself for having undertaken greater things than are possible ; and when our army in turn marches into their territory and lays it waste

μὴ ἀντιτιμωρούμενοι τοὺς ἄρξαντας ἡμᾶς κακῶς
ποιεῖν) δυεῖν οὐκ ἂν ἁμάρτοις θατέρου, ἢ πρὸς
αὐτῶν ἐκείνων, οἷς αἴτιος ἔσῃ συμφορῶν μεγάλων,
αἰσχρῶς ἀναιρεθῆναι, ἢ πρὸς ἡμῶν, οὓς ἀπο-
4 κτενῶν[1] τε καὶ δουλωσόμενος ἦλθες· τάχα δ' ἂν
ἐκεῖνοι, πρὶν ἐν τῷ παθεῖν τι κακὸν γενέσθαι,
διαλύσεις ποιεῖσθαι πρὸς ἡμᾶς ἐπιχειροῦντες ἔκδοτον ἀξιώσειαν ἐπὶ τιμωρίᾳ σε παραδιδόναι ὃ
πολλοὶ βάρβαροί τε καὶ Ἕλληνες εἰς τοιαύτας
καταστάντες τύχας ἠναγκάσθησαν ὑπομεῖναι. ἆρά
γε μικρὰ καὶ οὐκ ἄξια λόγου ταῦτ' εἶναί σοι δοκεῖ
καὶ δεῖν[2] αὐτῶν ὑπεριδεῖν, ἢ κακῶν συμπάντων
ἔσχατα[3] παθεῖν;

XXVIII. " Φέρε, ἐὰν δὲ δὴ κατορθώσῃς, τί τὸ
θαυμαστὸν ἔσται[4] σοι καὶ περιμάχητον ἀγαθόν, ἢ
τίνας ἐξοίσῃ δόξας; καὶ γὰρ τοῦτο ἐξέτασον.
πρῶτον μὲν τῶν φιλτάτων τε καὶ ἀναγκαιοτάτων
ὑπάρξει σοι στέρεσθαι σωμάτων, μητρὸς ἀθλίας, ἣ
γενέσεως καὶ τροφῆς καὶ τῶν ἄλλων ὧν ἔσχεν ἐπὶ
σοὶ πόνων οὐ καλὰς ἀμοιβὰς ἀποδίδως· ἔπειτα
γαμετῆς σώφρονος, ἢ διὰ τὸν σὸν πόθον ἐν ἐρημίᾳ
καὶ χηρείᾳ κάθηται πᾶσαν ἡμέραν καὶ νύκτα τὰς
σὰς φυγὰς ὀδυρομένη· πρὸς δὲ τούτοις τέκνων
δυεῖν, οὓς ἐχρῆν ἀγαθῶν προγόνων ὄντας ἀπογόνους καρποῦσθαι τὰς ἐκείνων τιμὰς εὐδοξοῦντας
2 ἐν εὐτυχούσῃ τῇ πατρίδι. ὧν ἁπάντων οἰκτρὰς
καὶ ἀτυχεῖς ἀναγκασθήσῃ θεωρεῖν καταστροφάς,
εἰ τολμήσεις προσάγειν τοῖς τείχεσι τὸν πόλεμον·
οὐ γὰρ δὴ φείσονται τῶν σῶν οὐθενὸς οἱ περὶ τῶν

---

[1] Steph. : ἀποκτείνων ABC.   [2] Cobet : δέον O, Jacoby.
[3] ἔσχατα O : τὰ ἔσχατα Reiske, Jacoby.
[4] Sylburg : ἔστι AB.

—for we shall never submit to such injuries without avenging ourselves on our aggressors—you will not be able to avoid one of these two fates : you will be put to death in a shameful manner either by those very men, in whose eyes you will be to blame for great misfortunes, or by us, whom you came to slay and to enslave. But perhaps those others, before they become involved in any misfortune, may, in the attempt to effect an accommodation with us, think fit to deliver you up to us to be punished—a course to which many, both barbarians and Greeks, have been obliged to submit when reduced to such extremities. Do you look upon these as small matters unworthy of your consideration and believe that you ought to overlook them, or rather as the worst evils of all to suffer ?

XXVIII. "Come now, if you do succeed, what wonderful, what enviable advantage will be yours, or what glory will you gain ? For this also you must consider. In the first place, it will be your fate to be deprived of those who are dearest and nearest of kin to you—of an unhappy mother, to whom you are making no honourable return for your birth and rearing and for all the hardships she underwent on your account ; and again, of a faithful wife, who through yearning for you sits in solitude and widowhood, lamenting every day and night your banishment; and furthermore of two sons who ought, being descendants of worthy ancestors, to benefit from their honours by being held in high esteem in a flourishing fatherland. But you will be forced to behold the pitiable and unhappy deaths of all these if you dare to bring the war to our walls. For surely no mercy will be shown to any of your family by those

σφετέρων κινδυνεύοντες καὶ εἰς τὰ ὅμοια[1] κακῶς
ὑπὸ σοῦ πάσχοντες, ἀλλ' εἰς αἰκισμοὺς αὐτῶν
δεινοὺς[2] καὶ ὕβρεις ἀνηλεεῖς καὶ πᾶσαν ἄλλην ἰδέαν
προπηλακισμοῦ χωρήσουσιν ὑπὸ τῶν συμφορῶν
βιαζόμενοι· καὶ τούτων οὐχ οἱ δρῶντες, ἀλλ' ὁ τὴν
3 ἀνάγκην αὐτοῖς ἐπιτιθεὶς αἴτιος ἔσῃ σύ.[3] ἡδονὰς
μὲν δὴ τοιαύτας καρπώσῃ κατὰ γνώμην χωρή-
σαντός σοι τοῦδε τοῦ ἔργου, ἔπαινον δὲ καὶ ζῆλον
καὶ τιμάς, ὧν ὀρέγεσθαι χρὴ τοὺς ἀγαθοὺς ἄνδρας,
σκόπει ποίας τινάς[4]· μητροκτόνος κεκλήσῃ καὶ
παιδοφόνος καὶ γυναικὸς ἀλιτήριος καὶ πατρίδος
ἀλάστωρ, καὶ οὔτε θυσιῶν οὔτε σπονδῶν οὔθ'
ἑστίας, ὅποι ποτ' ἂν ἀφίκῃ, κοινωνεῖν ἐθελήσει σοι
τῶν εὐσεβῶν καὶ δικαίων οὐθείς, αὐτοῖς τε οὐκ
ἔσῃ τίμιος οἷς εὔνοιαν ἐνδεικνύμενος ταῦτα δρᾷς,
ἀλλὰ καρπωσάμενοί τινα ἕκαστος τούτων ἐκ τῶν
σῶν ἀσεβημάτων ὠφέλειαν μισήσουσι τὴν αὐθά-
4 δειαν τοῦ τρόπου. ἐῶ γὰρ λέγειν ὅτι, χωρὶς τοῦ
μίσους ὃ παρὰ τῶν ἐπιεικεστάτων ἕξεις, καὶ φθόνος ἀπαντήσεται πολὺς ἐκ τῶν ἴσων καὶ φόβος
ἐκ τῶν ἡσσόνων καὶ δι' ἄμφω ταῦτα ἐπιβουλαὶ
καὶ ἄλλα πολλὰ καὶ χαλεπά, ὅσα εἰκὸς συμπεσεῖν
ἀνδρὶ ἐρήμῳ φίλων καὶ ἐν ξένῃ ὄντι γῇ. τὰς γὰρ
δὴ παρὰ θεῶν τε καὶ δαιμόνων ἐπιπεμπομένας τοῖς
ἀνόσια καὶ δεινὰ διαπραξαμένοις ἐρινύας ἐῶ, ὑφ'
ὧν αἰκιζόμενοι ψυχάς τε καὶ σώματα κακοὺς μὲν
διαντλοῦσι βίους, οἰκτρὰς δ' ὑπομένουσι τελευτάς.

---

[1] ὅμοια O : οἰκεῖα Kiessling.   [2] δεινοὺς B : om. R.
[3] ἔσῃ σύ Reiske : ἔσῃ O, Jacoby.
[4] τινάς Jacoby, τίνας B : καὶ τίνας R.

who are in danger of losing their own and are treated
by you with the same cruelty. On the contrary, they
will proceed to inflict on them dreadful tortures,
pitiless indignities and every other kind of abuse, if
they are forced thereto by their calamities. And for
all these things it will not be those who do them that
are to blame, but you, who impose the necessity upon
them. Such will be the pleasures you will reap if
this enterprise of yours succeeds ; but as for praise
and emulation and honours, which good men ought
to strive for, consider of what nature they will be.
You will be called the slayer of your mother, the
murderer of your children, the assassin of your wife,
and the evil genius of your country ; wherever you
go, no man who is pious and just will be willing
to let you partake with him in sacrifices or liba-
tions or in the hospitality of his home ; and even
by those for whom out of friendliness you perform
these services you will not be held in honour, but
every one of them, after reaping some advantage
from your impious actions, will detest your arrogant
manner. I forbear to add that, besides the hatred
which you will encounter on the part of the most
fair-minded men, you will have to face much envy
from your equals and fear from your inferiors and, in
consequence of both the envy and the fear, plots and
many other disagreeable things which are likely to
befall a man destitute of friends and living in a foreign
land. I say nothing, indeed, of the Furies sent by
the gods and other divinities to punish those who
have been guilty of impious and dreadful deeds—
those Furies tormented by whom in both soul and
body they drag out a miserable life while awaiting
a pitiable death. Bearing these things in mind,

5 ταῦτα ἐνθυμηθείς, ὦ Μάρκιε, μετάγνωθι καὶ παῦσαι μνησικακῶν τῇ σεαυτοῦ πατρίδι· τύχην τε
πάντων αἰτίαν ἡγησάμενος ὧν πέπονθας πρὸς ἡμῶν
ἢ δέδρακας ἡμᾶς κακῶν, ἄπιθι χαίρων ἐπὶ τὰ
οἰκεῖα, καὶ κόμισαι¹ μητρός τε περιβολὰς προσ-
ηνεστάτας καὶ γυναικὸς² φιλοφροσύνας ἡδίστας
καὶ τέκνων ἀσπασμοὺς γλυκυτάτους, καὶ σεαυτὸν
ἀπόδος ὀφείλημα κάλλιστον τῇ γειναμένῃ³ σε καὶ
τηλικοῦτον ἄνδρα παιδευσαμένῃ πατρίδι."

XXIX. Τοιαῦτα διεξελθόντος τοῦ Μηνυκίου μικρὸν ἐπισχὼν ὁ Μάρκιος εἶπε·

" Σοὶ μέν, ὦ Μηνύκιε, καὶ ὑμῖν τοῖς ἅμα τούτῳ
πεμφθεῖσιν ὑπὸ τῆς βουλῆς φίλος εἰμὶ καὶ πρό-
θυμος, εἴ τι δύναμαι, ποιεῖν ἀγαθόν, ὅτι μοι καὶ
πρότερον, ὅτε πολίτης ὑμέτερος ἦν καὶ τὰ κοινὰ
ἔπραττον, ἐν πολλοῖς καὶ ἀναγκαίοις⁴ ἐγένεσθε
καιροῖς χρήσιμοι, καὶ μετὰ τὴν φυγὴν οὐκ ἀπ-
εστράφητέ με καταφρονήσει τῆς τότε τύχης, ὡς
οὔτε φίλους εὖ ποιεῖν δυνάμενον ἔτι οὔτ᾽ ἐχθροὺς
κακῶς, ἀλλὰ χρηστοὶ καὶ βέβαιοι διεμείνατε φίλοι μητρός τε τῆς ἐμῆς κηδόμενοι καὶ γυναικὸς
καὶ τέκνων, καὶ τὰς συμφορὰς αὐτοῖς κουφοτέρας
2 ποιοῦντες ταῖς ἰδίαις ἐπιμελείαις. τοῖς δ᾽ ἄλλοις
Ῥωμαίοις ἀπέχθομαί τε ὡς δύναμαι μάλιστα καὶ
πολεμῶ⁵ καὶ οὐδέποτε μισῶν αὐτοὺς παύσομαι· οἳ
με ἀντὶ πολλῶν καὶ καλῶν ἔργων, ἐφ᾽ οἷς τιμᾶσθαι προσῆκεν, ὡς τὰ μέγιστα ἐξημαρτηκότα περὶ
τὸ κοινὸν αἰσχρῶς ἐξήλασαν ἐκ τῆς πατρίδος, οὔτε
μητέρα αἰδεσθέντες τὴν⁶ ἐμὴν οὔτε παιδία ἐλεή-

---

¹ καὶ κόμισαι B : om. R.
² τε after γυναικὸς deleted by Reiske.
³ Cobet : γεννησομένῃ A, γεννησαμένῃ R.

Marcius, repent of your purpose and give up your grudge against your country; and regarding Fortune as having been the cause of all the evils you have suffered at our hands or have inflicted on us, return with joy to your family, receive a mother's most affectionate embraces, a wife's sweetest welcome, and the children's tenderest greetings, and give yourself back to your country as a most honourable repayment of the debt you owe to her for having given birth and rearing to so great a man."

XXIX. Minucius having spoken in this manner, Marcius after a short pause replied :

" To you, Minucius, and to all you others who have been sent here with him by the senate I am a friend and am ready to do you any service in my power, because not only earlier, when I was your fellow citizen and had a share in the administration of public affairs, you assisted me in many times of need, but also after my banishment you did not turn from me in contempt of my then unhappy fate, as if I were no longer able either to serve my friends or to hurt my enemies, but you continued to show yourselves good and staunch friends by taking care of my mother, my wife and my children, and alleviating their misfortune by your personal attentions. But to the rest of the Romans I am as hostile as I can be and am at war with them, and I shall never cease to hate them ; for they, in return for the many glorious achievements for which I deserved honour, drove me out of my country with ignominy, as being guilty of the most grievous crimes against the commonwealth, and showed neither respect for my mother, nor com-

---

[4] ἀναγκαίοις B : ἀγαθοῖς A.
[5] καὶ πολεμῶ O : om. Reudler, Jacoby.   [6] τὴν B : om. R.

σαντες οὔτ᾽ ἄλλο πάθος ἥμερον οὐδὲν ἐπὶ ταῖς
3 ἐμαῖς λαβόντες τύχαις. μαθόντες δὲ τοῦτο, εἰ μὲν
αὐτοὶ δεῖσθέ του παρ᾽ ἡμῶν, λέγετε μηθὲν ὀκνοῦν-
τες, ὡς οὐθενὸς ἀτυχήσοντες τῶν δυνατῶν, περὶ
δὲ φιλίας καὶ διαλλαγῶν, ἃς ἀξιοῦτέ με ποιήσασθαι πρὸς τὸν δῆμον ἐπὶ ταῖς ἐλπίσι τῆς καθόδου,
παύσασθε διαλεγόμενοι. πάνυ γὰρ ἀγαπητῶς δεξαί-
μην ἂν εἰς τοιαύτην κατελθεῖν πόλιν, ἐν ᾗ τὰ
μὲν τῆς ἀρετῆς ἆθλα ἡ κακία φέρεται, τὰς δὲ τῶν
κακούργων τιμωρίας οἱ μηδὲν ἡμαρτηκότες ὑπο-
4 μένουσιν. ἐπεί, φέρε, πρὸς θεῶν εἴπατέ μοι, τίνος
ἀδικήματος αἰτίᾳ ταύτης ἐγὼ πεπείραμαι τῆς
τύχης, ἢ ποῖον ἐπιτηδεύσας ἔργον ἀνάξιον τῶν
ἐμαυτοῦ προγόνων; πρώτην ἐστρατευσάμην ἔξοδον κομιδῇ νέος ὤν, ὅτε πρὸς τοὺς βασιλεῖς βίᾳ
κατιόντας ἠγωνιζόμεθα. ἐκ ταύτης τῆς μάχης ἀριστείοις ἀνεδούμην ὑπὸ τοῦ στρατηγοῦ στεφάνοις
πολίτην ὑπερασπίσας καὶ πολέμιον ἀποκτείνας.
5 ἔπειθ᾽ ὅσας ἄλλας ἱππικὰς καὶ πεζικὰς ἠγωνισάμην
μάχας, ἐπιφανὴς ἐν ἁπάσαις ἐγενόμην καὶ τἀρισ-
τεῖα ἐξ ἁπασῶν ἔλαβον· καὶ οὔτε πόλις ἐκ τειχομαχίας ἑάλω τις ἧς οὐκ ἐγὼ πρῶτος ἐπέβην ἢ
μόνος[1] ἢ σὺν ὀλίγοις, οὔτε φυγὴ πολεμίων ἐκ
παρατάξεως ἐγένετο ἧς οὐκ ἐμὲ αἰτιώτατον γενέσθαι πάντες οἱ παρόντες ὡμολόγουν, οὔτε ἄλλο
τῶν λαμπρῶν ἢ γενναίων ἐν πολέμοις ἔργων οὐθὲν ἄνευ τῆς ἐμῆς εἴτε εὐτολμίας εἴτε εὐτυχίας
ἐπράχθη.

XXX. "Καὶ ταυτὶ μὲν ἴσως ἂν ἔχοι τις καὶ

---

[1] ἢ μόνος Reudler, ἢ μόνοις C : om. AB.

---

[1] The *corona civica*, which bore the simple inscription

passion for my children, nor any other humane feeling in view of my misfortunes. Now that you have been informed of this, if you desire anything from me for yourselves, declare it without hesitation, in the assurance that you shall fail of naught that is in my power; but as regards friendship and a reconciliation, which you desire me to enter into with the populace in the hope that they will let me return, discuss it no more. Great indeed would be the satisfaction with which I should accept restoration to a city like this, in which vice receives the rewards of virtue and the innocent await the punishment of criminals! For come, tell me, in Heaven's name, with what crime am I charged that I should have experienced this misfortune? Or what course have I pursued that is unworthy of my ancestors? I made my first campaign when I was very young, at the time we fought against the kings who were endeavouring to bring about their restoration by force. As a result of that battle I was crowned by the general with a wreath of valour for having saved a citizen and slain an enemy.[1] After that, in every other action I was engaged in, whether of the horse or foot, I distinguished myself in all and from all received the rewards for valour. And there was neither any town taken by storm whose walls I was not the very first or among the first few to mount, nor any flight of the enemy from the field of battle where all who were present did not acknowledge that I had been the chief cause of it, nor any other signal or brave action performed in war without the assistance of either my valour or my good fortune.

XXX. " These are exploits, it is true, that some

[1] OB CIVEM SERVATVM. The slaying of the foe is not expressly mentioned, as a rule.

ἕτερος ὑπὲρ αὐτοῦ γενναῖος ἀνήρ, εἰ μὴ καὶ τοσαῦτα, λέγειν· ἀλλὰ πόλιν ὅλην τίς δύναιτ' ἂν καυχή-
σασθαι στρατηγὸς ἢ λοχαγὸς ἑλών, ὥσπερ ἐγὼ
τὴν Κοριολανῶν, καὶ τῆς αὐτῆς ἡμέρας ὁ αὐτὸς
ἀνὴρ στρατιὰν πολεμίων τρεψάμενος, ὥσπερ ἐγὼ
τὴν Ἀντιατῶν ἐπίκουρον τοῖς πολιορκουμένοις
2 ἀφικομένην; ἐῶ γὰρ λέγειν ὅτι τοιαύτας ἀρετὰς
ἀποδειξάμενος, ἐξόν μοι λαβεῖν ἐκ τῶν λαφύρων
πολὺν μὲν χρυσόν, πολὺν δ' ἄργυρον ἀνδράποδά τε
καὶ ὑποζύγια καὶ βοσκήματα καὶ γῆν πολλὴν καὶ
ἀγαθήν, οὐκ ἠξίωσα, ἀλλ' ἀνεπίφθονον ὡς μάλιστα
βουληθεὶς ἐμαυτὸν παρασχεῖν, πολεμιστὴν ἵππον
ἕνα μόνον ἐκ τῶν λαφύρων ἔλαβον καὶ τὸν ἐμαυτοῦ
ξένον ἐκ τῶν αἰχμαλώτων, τὸν δ' ἄλλον πλοῦτον
3 εἰς τὸ κοινὸν ἔθηκα φέρων. πότερον οὖν τιμωρίας
ἄξιος ἦν ἐπὶ τούτοις ὑπέχειν, ἢ τιμὰς λαμβάνειν,
καὶ πότερον ὑπὸ τοῖς κακίστοις γενέσθαι τῶν πολιτῶν, ἢ τὰ δίκαια τάττειν αὐτὸς τοῖς ἥττοσιν;
ἀλλ' οὐ διὰ ταῦτά με ἀπήλασεν ὁ δῆμος, ἀλλ' ὅτι
περὶ τὸν ἄλλον βίον ἀκόλαστος καὶ πολυτελὴς καὶ
παράνομος ἦν; καὶ τίς ἂν ἔχοι δεῖξαί τινα διὰ τὰς
ἐμὰς παρανόμους ἡδονὰς ἢ τὴν πατρίδα φεύγοντα
ἢ τὴν ἐλευθερίαν ἀπολωλεκότα ἢ χρημάτων στερό-
μενον ἢ ἄλλῃ τινὶ συμφορᾷ χρησάμενον; ἀλλ' οὐδὲ
τῶν ἐχθρῶν με οὐδεὶς πώποτε ᾐτιάσατο οὐδὲ δι-
έβαλεν ἐπ' οὐδενὶ τούτων, ἀλλ' ὑπὸ πάντων ἐμαρ-
τυρεῖτό μοι καὶ ὁ καθ' ἡμέραν ἀνεπίληπτος εἶναι
4 βίος. ' ἀλλ' ἡ προαίρεσις, νὴ Δία,' φαίη τις ἄν,
' ἡ τῶν πολιτευμάτων σου μισηθεῖσα ταύτην ἐξ-
ειργάσατό σοι τὴν συμφοράν. ἐξὸν γὰρ ἑλέσθαι τὴν

other brave man also might perhaps be able to cite in his favour, even if not so many of them ; but what general or captain could boast of capturing an entire city, as I captured Corioli, and also of putting to flight the enemy's army on that very same day, as I did that of the Antiates when it came to the assistance of the besieged ?[1] I refrain from adding that after I had given such proofs of my valour, when I might have received out of the spoils a large amount of gold and silver, as well as slaves, beasts of burden and cattle, and much fertile land, I refused, but desiring to secure myself as far as possible against envy, took only a single war-horse out of the spoils and my personal friend from among the captives, and all the rest of the wealth I brought and turned over to the state. Did I, then, for these actions deserve to suffer punishments, or to receive honours ? To become subject to the basest of the citizens, or myself to issue orders to my inferiors ? Or perhaps it was not for these reasons that the populace banished me, but rather because in my private life I was unrestrained, extravagant and lawless ? And yet who can point to anyone who because of my lawless pleasures has either been banished from his country, or lost his liberty, or been deprived of his money, or met with any other misfortune ? On the contrary, no one even of my enemies ever accused or charged me with any of these things, but all bore witness that even my daily life was irreproachable. 'But, great heavens, man,' some one may say, 'it was your political principles that aroused hatred and brought this misfortune upon you. For when you had it in your power to choose the better side, you chose the

[1] See vi. 92 ff.

κρείττω μερίδα τὴν χείρονα εἵλου καὶ διετέλεις
ἅπαντα καὶ λέγων καὶ πράττων ἐξ ὧν καταλυθή-
σεται μὲν ἡ πάτριος ἀριστοκρατία, κύριος δ' ἔσται
τῶν κοινῶν ὄχλος ἀμαθὴς καὶ πονηρός.' ἀλλ'
ἔγωγε τἀναντία ἔπραττον, ὦ Μηνύκιε, καὶ ὅπως
ἡ βουλὴ τῶν κοινῶν διὰ παντὸς ἐπιμελήσεται καὶ
ὁ πάτριος διαμενεῖ κόσμος τῆς πολιτείας προὐνοού-
5 μην. ἀντὶ τούτων μέντοι τῶν καλῶν ἐπιτηδευ-
μάτων, ἃ τοῖς προγόνοις ἡμῶν ζηλωτὰ εἶναι ἐδόκει,
τὰς εὐτυχεῖς ταύτας καὶ μακαρίας κεκόμισμαι
παρὰ τῆς πατρίδος ἀμοιβάς, οὐχ ὑπὸ τοῦ δήμου
μόνον ἐξελαθείς, ὦ Μηνύκιε, ἀλλὰ πολὺ πρότερον
ὑπὸ τῆς βουλῆς, ἣ κατ' ἀρχὰς ἐπαίρουσά με κεναῖς
ἐλπίσιν, ἡνίκα τοῖς δημάρχοις τυραννίδα περι-
βαλλομένοις ἠναντιούμην ὡς αὐτὴ παρέξουσα τὸ
ἀσφαλές, ἐπειδὴ κίνδυνόν τινα ἐκ τῶν δημοτικῶν
ὑπείδετο, ἀπέστη καὶ παρέδωκέ με τοῖς ἐχθροῖς.
6 σὺ μέντοι τότε αὐτὸς ὕπατος ἦσθα, ὦ Μηνύκιε,
ὅτε τὸ προβούλευμα τὸ περὶ τῆς δίκης ἐγένετο,
καὶ ἡνίκα Οὐαλέριος ὁ παραδιδόναι με τῷ δήμῳ
παραινῶν σφόδρα ἐπὶ τοῖς λόγοις εὐδοκίμει, κἀγὼ
δεδιὼς μὴ ψήφου δοθείσης ὑπὸ τῶν συνέδρων
ἁλῶ, συνέγνων καὶ παρέξειν ἐμαυτὸν ὑπεσχόμην
ἑκόντα[1] ἐπὶ τὴν δίκην.
XXXI. '' Ἴθι δή μοι, Μηνύκιε, ἀπόκριναι, πότερα καὶ τῇ βουλῇ τῆς τιμωρίας ἄξιος ἐφάνην
εἶναι, ὅτι τὰ κράτιστα ἐπολιτευόμην τε καὶ ἔπραττον, ἢ τῷ δήμῳ μόνῳ; εἰ μὲν γὰρ ἅπασι ταὐτὰ[2]
ἐδόκει τότε καὶ πάντες με ἀπηλάσατε, φανερὸν ὅτι
πάντες οἱ ταῦτα βουληθέντες ἀρετὴν μισεῖτε, καὶ
τόπος οὐδείς ἐστιν ἐν τῇ πόλει δεχόμενος καλο-

---

[1] Reiske : ἥξοντα O.   [2] Grasberger : ταῦτα O.

worse, and you continued to say and do everything
calculated to effect the overthrow of the established
aristocracy and to put the whole power of the
commonwealth into the hands of an ignorant and base
multitude.' But I, Minucius, pursued a course the
very reverse of that, and sought to provide that the
senate should always administer the public business
and that the established constitution should be maintained. In return, however, for these honourable
principles, which our forefathers thought worthy of
emulation, I have received this happy, this blessed
reward from my country—to have been banished, not
by the populace alone, Minucius, but, long before
that, by the senate, which encouraged me at first with
vain hopes while I was opposing the tribunes in their
efforts to establish a tyranny, promising that it would
itself provide for my security, and then, upon the first
suspicion of any danger from the plebeians, abandoned me and delivered me up to my enemies!
But you yourself were consul at the time, Minucius,
when the senate passed the preliminary decree concerning my trial and when Valerius, who advised
delivering me up to the populace, gained great
applause by his speech, and I, fearing that, if the
question were put, I should be condemned by the
senators, acquiesced and promised to appear voluntarily for trial.

XXXI. " Come, answer me, Minucius, did I seem
to the senate also to deserve punishment for having
promoted and pursued the best measures, or to the
populace only ? For if you were all of the same
opinion at that time and if all of you banished me, it
is plain that all of you who were of this mind hate
virtue and that there is no place in your city for

κἀγαθίαν· εἰ δὲ βιασθεῖσ ἡ βουλὴ συνεχώρησε
τῷ δήμῳ καὶ τὸ ἔργον αὐτῆς ἀνάγκης ἦν, οὐ
γνώμης, ὁμολογεῖτε δήπου πονηροκρατεῖσθαι καὶ
μηδενὸς εἶναι τὴν βουλὴν ὧν ἂν προέληται κυρίαν.
2 ἔπειτα εἰς τοιαύτην ἀξιοῦτέ με κατελθεῖν πόλιν, ἐν ᾗ
τὸ κρεῖττον μέρος ὑπὸ τοῦ χείρονος ἄρχεται; πολλὴν ἄρα κατεγνώκατέ μου μανίαν. φέρε, καὶ δὴ
πέπεισμαι καὶ διαλυσάμενος τὸν πόλεμον, ὥσπερ
ἀξιοῦτε, κατελήλυθα, τίς ἡ μετὰ ταῦτα ἔσται μου
διάνοια καὶ τίνα βίον ζήσομαι; πότερα τἀσφα-
λὲς καὶ ἀκίνδυνον αἱρούμενος ἀρχάς τε καὶ τιμὰς
καὶ τἆλλα ἀγαθὰ ὧν ἄξιον ἐμαυτὸν ἡγοῦμαι μετ-
ιών, θεραπεύειν ὑπομενῶ τὸν ἔχοντα τὴν τούτων ἐξουσίαν ὄχλον; πονηρὸς ἄρα ἐξ ἀγαθοῦ γενήσομαι,
καὶ οὐδὲν ἔσται μοι τῆς προτέρας ἀρετῆς ὄφελος.
3 ἀλλ' ἐν τοῖς αὐτοῖς ἤθεσι μένων καὶ τὴν αὐτὴν
προαίρεσιν τῆς πολιτείας φυλάττων ἐναντιώσομαι
τοῖς μὴ ταὐτὰ προαιρουμένοις; εἶτα οὐ πρόδηλον
ὅτι πολεμήσει μοι πάλιν ὁ δῆμος καὶ δίκας ἑτέρας
πάλιν ἀξιώσει λαμβάνειν, τοῦτ' αὐτὸ πρῶτον ἔγκλημα ποιούμενος, ὅτι τῆς καθόδου δι' ἐκείνου
τυχὼν οὐ τὰ πρὸς ἡδονὴν αὐτῷ πολιτεύομαι; οὐκ
4 ἔνεστ' ἄλλως εἰπεῖν. ἔπειτ' ἀναφανήσεταί τις ἕτερος Ἰκιλίῳ παραπλήσιος ἢ Δεκίῳ θρασὺς δημαγω-
γός, ὃς αἰτιάσεταί με διιστάναι τοὺς πολίτας ἀπ'
ἀλλήλων ἢ κατὰ τοῦ δήμου πράττειν ἐπιβουλὴν ἢ
προδιδόναι τοῖς πολεμίοις τὴν πόλιν[1] ἢ τυραννίδι,
ὥσπερ καὶ Δέκιος ᾐτιάσατο, ἐπιχειρεῖν ἢ ἄλλο
ἀδικεῖν, ὁτιδήποτε ἂν αὐτῷ φανῇ· οὐ γὰρ ἀπορήσει

---

[1] τὴν πόλιν B : om. R.

loyalty to principle. But if the senate was forced to yield to the populace and its action was the result of compulsion, not of conviction, you senators admit, I take it, that you are governed by the baser element and that the senate has not the power to act in any matter as it thinks fit. After this do you ask me to return to such a city, in which the better element is governed by the worse? Then you have judged me capable of an act of sheer madness! But come, suppose that I have been persuaded, and having put an end to the war as you desire, have returned home; what sentiments shall I entertain after this, and what manner of life shall I live? Shall I choose the safe and secure course, and, in order to obtain magistracies, honours and the other advantages of which I think myself worthy, consent to court the mob which has the power of bestowing them? In that case I shall change from a worthy to a base citizen and shall reap no benefit from my former virtue. Or, maintaining the same character and observing the same political principles, shall I oppose those who do not make the same choice? Then is it not obvious that the populace will again make war upon me and insist on exacting fresh penalties, making this very point their first charge against me, that after obtaining my return at their hands I do not humour them in the measures I pursue? You cannot deny it. Then some other bold demagogue, an Icilius or a Decius, will appear who will accuse me of setting the citizens at variance with one another, of forming a plot against the populace, of betraying the commonwealth to the enemy, or of aiming at tyranny, even as Decius charged me, or of any other crime that may occur to him; for hatred will never be at a loss to find an

5 τὸ μισοῦν αἰτίας. ἥξει τε πρὸς τοῖς ἄλλοις ἐγκλή-
μασι καὶ ταυτὶ φερόμενα οὐκ εἰς μακρὰν ὅσα ἐν
τῷ πολέμῳ πέπρακταί μοι τούτῳ, ὅτι χώραν
ὑμῶν τέτμηκα καὶ λείαν ἀπελήλακα καὶ πόλεις ἀφ-
ῄρημαι καὶ τοὺς ὑπὲρ τούτων ἀμυνομένους τοὺς
μὲν πεφόνευκα, τοὺς δὲ τοῖς πολεμίοις παραδέδωκα.
ταῦτ' ἐὰν οἱ κατήγοροι λέγωσι, τί φήσω πρὸς
αὐτοὺς ἀπολογούμενος ἢ τίνι βοηθείᾳ χρήσομαι;

XXXII. " Ἆρ' οὐ φανερὸν ὅτι καλλιλογεῖτε καὶ
εἰρωνεύεσθε, ὦ Μηνύκιε, ὄνομα καλὸν ἔργῳ περι-
θέντες ἀνοσίῳ; οὐ γὰρ δὴ κάθοδόν μοι δίδοτε,
ἀλλὰ σφάγιόν με τῷ δήμῳ κατάγετε, τάχα μὲν καὶ
βεβουλευμένοι τοῦτο πράττειν· οὐθὲν γὰρ ἔτι μοι
2 χρηστὸν ὑπὲρ ὑμῶν ἐπέρχεται φρονεῖν· εἰ δὲ βούλεσθε—τίθημι γάρ—οὐδὲν ὧν πείσομαι προορώ-
μενοι, τί οὖν ἔσται μοι τῆς ὑμετέρας ἀγνοίας ἢ
μωρίας ὄφελος, κωλύειν μὲν οὐδὲν οὐδ' ἂν οἷοι ἦτε
δυνησομένων,[1] χαρίζεσθαι δὲ καὶ τοῦτο τῷ δήμῳ
σὺν τοῖς ἄλλοις ἀναγκαζομένων· ἀλλὰ γὰρ ὅτι
μὲν[2] οὐ συνοίσει μοι πρὸς ἀσφάλειαν ἥδε, ἣν ὑμεῖς
μὲν κάθοδον καλεῖτε, ἐγὼ δὲ ταχεῖαν ὁδὸν ἐπὶ τὸν
ὄλεθρον, οὐ πολλῶν οἴομαι δεῖν ἔτι λόγων· ὅτι δ'
οὐδὲ πρὸς εὐδοξίαν ἢ τιμὴν ἢ πρὸς εὐσέβειαν—
ἐπειδὴ καὶ σὺ τούτων, ὦ Μηνύκιε, πρόνοιαν ἔχειν
με ἠξίους, εὖ ποιῶν—ἀλλ' αἴσχιστά μοι καὶ ἀν-
οσιώτατα πραχθήσεται πεισθέντι ὑμῖν, ἄκουσον ἐν
3 τῷ μέρει. ἐγὼ πολέμιος ἐγενόμην τούτοις[3] καὶ
πολλὰ ἠδίκησα αὐτοὺς ἐν τῷ πολέμῳ, τῇ πατρίδι

---

[1] οὐδ' ἂν οἷοι ἦτε δυνησομένων Sintenis : οὐδ' ἂν οἷοί τε δυνησομένων Β, οὐδ' ἂν βούλησθε οὐ δυνάμενοι Α.
[2] μὲν Β : om. R.
[3] τούτοις Kiessling, τουτοισὶ Cobet : τούτοις οὐλολύσκοις Β,
τοῖς οὐλολύσκοις Α.

accusation. And, besides the other charges, there
will also be brought up presently all the things I have
done in this war—that I have laid waste your country,
driven off booty, taken your towns, slain some of
those who defended them and delivered up others to
the enemy. If my accusers charge me with these
things, what shall I say to them in my defence, or on
what assistance shall I rely ?

XXXII. " Is it not therefore plain, Minucius, that
you envoys are indulging in fair words and dissimula-
tion, cloaking with a specious name a wicked design ?
For surely it is not my restoration that you are offering me, but you are taking me back to the populace
as a sacrificial victim, perhaps because you have
actually planned to do this (for it no longer occurs
to me to hold any good opinion of you); but if you
wish it so—I am merely assuming this—that it is
because you do not foresee any of the things that I
shall suffer, what advantage shall I gain from your
ignorance or folly, since you will not be able to prevent anything even if you are so disposed, but are
compelled to gratify the populace in this too, as in
everything else ? Now to show that from the point
of view of my safety there will be no gain to me in
this—'restoration,' as you call it, but I a quick road
to destruction, not many more words are called for,
I think ; but to prove that it will not enhance my
reputation, either, or my honour, or my piety—for
you, Minucius, asked me to take these into consideration, and rightly—but that, on the contrary, I shall
be acting in a most shameful and impious manner if
I follow your advice, pray hear in turn what I have
to say. I became an enemy to these men here
and did them many injuries during the war while I

πράττων ἡγεμονίαν καὶ ἰσχὺν καὶ κλέος. οὐκοῦν
προσῆκέ μοι τιμᾶσθαι μὲν ὑπὸ τῶν εὖ πεπονθότων,
μισεῖσθαι δ' ὑπὸ τῶν ἠδικημένων; εἰ γοῦν τι τῶν
εἰκότων ἐγένετο. ἀνέτρεψε δ'[1] ἀμφότερα ταῦτα ἡ
τύχη, καὶ εἰς τἀναντία μετέθηκε τὰς ἀξιώσεις.
ὑμεῖς μὲν γάρ, ὑπὲρ ὧν τούτοις[2] ἐχθρὸς ἦν, ἀφ-
είλεσθέ με πάντα τἀμὰ καὶ τὸ μηδὲν ποιήσαντες
ἐρρίψατε· οὗτοι δ' οἱ τὰ δεινὰ ὑπ' ἐμοῦ παθόντες,
τὸν ἄπορον καὶ ἀνέστιον καὶ ταπεινὸν καὶ ἄπολιν
4 ὑπεδέξαντό με ταῖς ἑαυτῶν πόλεσι. καὶ οὐκ ἀπέχρη αὐτοῖς τοῦτο ποιῆσαι μόνον οὕτω λαμπρὸν
καὶ μεγαλόψυχον ἔργον, ἀλλὰ καὶ πολιτείαν ἔδοσάν
μοι ἐν ἁπάσαις ταῖς ἑαυτῶν πόλεσι καὶ ἀρχὰς καὶ
τιμὰς αἳ μέγισται παρ' αὐτοῖς εἰσιν. ἐῶ τἆλλα·
ἀλλὰ νυνὶ στρατηγὸν ἀποδεδείχασί με αὐτοκράτορα
τῆς ὑπερορίου στρατιᾶς καὶ πάντα τὰ κοινὰ ἐπ'
5 ἐμοὶ πεποιήκασι μόνῳ. φέρε δή, τίνα λαβὼν καρδίαν προδοίην ἂν ἔτι τούτους, ὑφ' ὧν τηλικαύταις
κεκόσμημαι τιμαῖς, οὐθὲν οὔτε μεῖζον οὔτε ἔλαττον
ἀδικηθείς; εἰ μὴ ἄρα αἱ χάριτες αὐτῶν ἀδικοῦσί
με, ὥσπερ ὑμᾶς αἱ ἐμαί· καλήν γε δόξαν οἴσει μοι
παρὰ πᾶσιν ἀνθρώποις γνωσθεῖσα ἡ παλιμπρο-
δοσία.[3] τίς δ' οὐκ[4] ἂν ἐπαινέσειέ με ἀκούσας ὅτι
τοὺς μὲν φίλους, ὑφ' ὧν εὖ πάσχειν μοι προσῆκε,
πολεμίους εὑρών, τοὺς δ' ἐχθρούς, ὑφ' ὧν ἐχρῆν
με ἀπολωλέναι, φίλους, ἀντὶ τοῦ μισεῖν μὲν τὰ
μισοῦντα φιλεῖν δὲ τὰ φιλοῦντα, τὴν ἐναντίαν
γνώμην ἔσχον;

XXXIII. "Ἴθι δὴ σκόπει καὶ τὰ παρὰ θεῶν,

---

[1] ἀνέτρεψεν Bb : καὶ ἂν ἔστρεψεν A, ἀλλ' ἀνέστρεψεν Reiske,
ἀντέστρεψε δ' Cobet.
[2] τούτοις B : om. R.   [3] Sylburg : πάλιν προδοσία O.

was acquiring sovereignty, power and glory for my country. Was it not fitting, therefore, that I should be honoured by those I had benefited and hated by those I had injured? Certainly, if what one could reasonably expect had happened. But Fortune upset both these expectations and reversed the two principles. For you Romans, on whose account I was an enemy to these men, deprived me of all my possessions, and making a nobody of me, cast me off; while they, who had suffered those dire evils at my hands, received me into their cities, the resourceless, homeless, humbled outcast. And not content with doing this only, an action so splendid and magnanimous, they also conferred on me citizenship in all their cities, as well as the magistracies and honours that in their country are highest. To omit the rest, they have now appointed me supreme commander of their expeditionary force and have committed to me alone all the interests of their state. Look you, with what heart would I now betray these men by whom I have been decked with such honours, when I have suffered no injury, great or small, at their hands? Unless, indeed, their favours are injurious to me, as mine are to you! A fine reputation forsooth, throughout all the world will such double treachery bring me, when it shall be known! Who would not praise me on hearing that when I found my friends, from whom I had the right to expect kindness, to be my enemies, and my foes, by whom I should have been put to death, to be my friends, instead of hating those who hate me and loving those who love me, I took the opposite view!

XXXIII. "Come now, Minucius, consider next

---

⁴ οὐκ O : om. Sylburg, Jacoby.

Μηνύκιε, οἷά μοι νῦν τε ἀπήντηται καί, ἐὰν ἄρα
πεισθεὶς ὑμῖν προδῶ τὴν τούτων πίστιν, οἷα τὸν
λοιπὸν ὑπάρξει μοι βίον. νῦν μέν γε πάσης πράξεως ἧς ἂν ἅψωμαι καθ' ὑμῶν συλλαμβάνουσί μοι,
2 καὶ οὐδεμιᾶς πείρας ἀποτυγχάνω. καὶ τοῦτο πη-
λίκον οἴεσθε εἶναι τεκμήριον εὐσεβείας τῆς ἐμῆς;
εἰ γὰρ δὴ[1] κατὰ τῆς πατρίδος οὐχ ὅσιον ἐγὼ
πόλεμον ἐνεστησάμην, ἅπαντα χρῆν[2] ἐναντία μοι
γίνεσθαι τὰ[3] παρὰ θεῶν· ὁπότε δ' οὐρίῳ πνεούσῃ
κέχρημαι τῇ περὶ τοὺς πολέμους τύχῃ, καὶ ὁπόσοις
ἂν ἐπιβάλωμαι πράγμασι κατ' ὀρθὸν ἅπαντά μοι
χωρεῖ, δῆλον ὅτι εὐσεβής εἰμι ἀνὴρ καὶ πράξεις
3 προῄρημαι καλάς. τί οὖν, ἐὰν μεταβάλωμαι καὶ
τὰ μὲν ὑμέτερα αὔξειν, τὰ δὲ τούτων ταπεινὰ
ποιεῖν ζητῶ, γενήσεταί μοι; ἆρ' οὐχὶ τἀναντία,
καὶ πονηρὰν νέμεσιν ἔξω παρὰ τοῦ δαιμονίου τοῖς
ἠδικημένοις τιμωρόν, καὶ ὥσπερ ἐκ ταπεινοῦ μέγας
διὰ τοὺς θεοὺς ἐγενόμην, οὕτως αὖθις ἐκ μεγάλου
ταπεινὸς γενήσομαι, καὶ τἀμὰ παθήματα παιδεύ-
4 ματα γενήσεται τοῖς ἄλλοις; ἐμοὶ μὲν ταῦτα παρ-
ίσταται περὶ τοῦ δαιμονίου φρονεῖν, καὶ πείθομαί
γε τὰς ἐρινύας ἐκείνας τὰς φοβερὰς καὶ ἀπαραιτή-
τους τοῖς ἀνόσιόν τι διαπραξαμένοις, ὧν καὶ σὺ
ἐμνήσθης, ὦ Μηνύκιε, τότε μοι παρακολουθή-
σειν ψυχήν τε καὶ σῶμα αἰκιζομένας, ὅταν ἐγκατα-
λίπω καὶ προδῶ τοὺς σώσαντάς με ἀπολωλότα
ὑφ' ὑμῶν καὶ μετὰ τοῦ σῶσαι πολλὰς καὶ καλὰς
προσθέντας εὐεργεσίας, οἷς ἐγγυητὰς ἔδωκα θεούς,
ὡς ἐπ' οὐδενὶ κακῷ τὴν ἄφιξιν ποιησάμενος καὶ

---

[1] δὴ Cobet : αὖ O.　　　　[2] Jacoby : ἐχρῆν O.
[3] τὰ B : om. R.

the matter of the gods' treatment of me, what it has
shown itself to be at present and, if I do let you
persuade me to betray the trust reposed in me by
these people, what it will be for the rest of my life.
At present they assist me in every enterprise I
undertake against you and in no attempt am I unsuccessful. And how weighty a testimony to my
piety do you consider that? For surely, if I had
undertaken an impious war against my country, the
gods ought to have opposed me in everything; but
since I enjoy the favouring breeze of Fortune in
the wars I wage and everything that I attempt
goes steadily forward for me, it is evident that I
am a pious man and that my choice of conduct
has been honourable. What, then, will be my fate
if I change my course and endeavour to increase
your power and humble theirs? Will it not be
just the reverse, and shall I not incur the dire
wrath of Heaven which avenges the injured, and
just as by the help of the gods I from a low
estate have become great, shall I not in turn from
a great be brought again to a low estate, and my
sufferings become lessons to the rest of the world?
These are the thoughts that occur to me concerning
the gods; and I am persuaded that those Furies
you mentioned, Minucius, so frightful and inexorable
toward those who have committed any impious deed,
will dog my steps and torment both my soul and body
only when I abandon and betray those who preserved
me after you had ruined me, and, at the same time
as they preserved me, conferred upon me many fine
marks of their favour, and to whom I gave the gods
as guarantors of my pledge that I had not come among
them with the purpose of doing them any injury and

φυλάξων[1] τὴν εἰς τόδε χρόνου καθαρὰν καὶ ἀμίαντον συνοῦσάν μοι πίστιν.

XXXIV. "Ὅταν δὲ φίλους ἔτι καλῇς, ὦ Μηνύκιε, τοὺς ἐξελάσαντάς με καὶ πατρίδα τὴν ἀπαρνησαμένην, φύσεώς τε νόμους ἀνακαλῇ καὶ περὶ τῶν ὁσίων διαλέγῃ, φαίνῃ μοι τὰ κοινότατα καὶ ὑπὸ μηδενὸς ἀγνοούμενα μόνος ἀγνοεῖν· ὅτι τὸ φίλιον ἢ πολέμιον οὔτε ὄψεως ὁρίζει χαρακτὴρ οὔτε ὀνόματος θέσις, ἀλλὰ ταῖς χρείαις καὶ τοῖς ἔργοις δηλοῦται τούτων ἑκάτερον, φιλοῦμέν τε πάντες τὰ ὠφελοῦντα καὶ μισοῦμεν τὰ βλάπτοντα, οὐκ ἀνθρώπων τινῶν ἡμῖν τόνδε θεμένων τὸν νόμον, οὐδὲ ἀνελούντων[2] ποτὲ αὐτόν, ἐὰν τἀναντία αὐτοῖς δοκῇ, ἀλλ' ὑπὸ τῆς κοινῆς φύσεως ἐξ ἅπαντος τοῦ[3] χρόνου πᾶσι τοῖς αἰσθήσεως μετειληφόσι κείμενον καὶ
2 εἰς ἀεὶ διαμενοῦντα παραλαβόντες· καὶ διὰ τοῦτο φίλους τε ἀπαρνούμεθα ὅταν ἀδικήσωσι, καὶ ἐχθροὺς φίλους ποιούμεθα[4] ὅταν τις ἡμῖν παρ' αὐτῶν ὑπάρξῃ χάρις, πόλιν τε τὴν γειναμένην ἡμᾶς, ὅταν μὲν ὠφελῇ, στέργομεν, ὅταν δὲ βλάπτῃ, καταλείπομεν, οὐ διὰ τὸν τόπον ἀγαπῶντες αὐτήν, ἀλλὰ
3 διὰ τὸ συμφέρον. καὶ οὐχὶ τοῖς μὲν ἰδιώταις οὕτως[5] ἐπέρχεται καθ' ἕνα φρονεῖν, οὐχὶ δὲ καὶ πόλεσιν ὅλαις καὶ ἔθνεσιν, ὥστε ὁ ταύτῃ τῇ γνώμῃ χρώμενος οὐδὲν ἔξω τῶν θείων ἀξιοῖ νομίμων, οὐδὲ παρὰ τὴν κοινὴν ἁπάντων ἀνθρώπων ποιεῖ δικαίωσιν. ἐγὼ μὲν δὴ ταῦτα[6] πράττοντα ἐμαυτὸν τά τε δίκαια ἡγοῦμαι πράττειν καὶ τὰ συμφέροντα καὶ τὰ καλὰ

---

[1] φυλάξων ACmg : om. R.
[2] ἀνελούντων B : ἀνελόντων R.   [3] τοῦ B : om. R.
[4] φίλους ποιούμεθα ACmg : φιλοποιούμεθα BC.
[5] οὕτως B (?), Sylburg : om. AC.
[6] ταῦτα B : om. R.

that I would keep with them the faith which I have hitherto preserved pure and untarnished.

XXXIV. "When you call those still my friends, Minucius, who banished me and that nation my country which has renounced me, when you appeal to the laws of Nature and discuss the obligations of religion, you seem to me to be ignorant of the most common facts, of which no one but you is ignorant—namely, that a friend or an enemy is not determined either by the lineaments of a face or by the giving of a name, but both are made manifest by their services and by their deeds, and that we all love those who do us good and hate those who do us harm. No men laid down this law for us nor will men ever annul it if the opposite course seems to them better; on the contrary, it has been enacted from the beginning of time by the universal Nature for all creatures endowed with sense, a heritage of man to remain in force forever. For this reason we renounce our friends when they injure us and make friends of our enemies when some kindly service is done for us by them; and we cherish the country that gave us birth when it helps us, but abandon it when it harms us, since our affection is based, not on the place, but on the benefit it confers. These are the sentiments not merely of individual persons in private life, but of whole cities and nations. Consequently, whoever applies this principle demands nothing not sanctioned by religious usage and does nothing that contravenes the common judgement of all mankind. I, therefore, consider that in doing these things I am doing what is just, advantageous

99

καὶ ἅμα καὶ[1] τὰ πρὸς τοὺς θεοὺς ὁσιώτατα· καὶ οὐ
δέομαι δικαστὰς ὑπὲρ αὐτῶν λαβεῖν τοὺς εἰκασμῷ
καὶ δόξῃ τεκμαιρομένους τὴν ἀλήθειαν ἀνθρώπους,
ἐπειδὴ θεοῖς ἀρέσκοντα πράττω. οὐ γὰρ ἀδυνάτοις
ἐπιχειρεῖν ὑπολαμβάνω πράγμασι θεοὺς ἔχων αὐτῶν
ἡγεμόνας, εἴγε δεῖ τεκμαίρεσθαι τοῖς γεγονόσιν
ἤδη τὰ μέλλοντα.

XXXV. " Περὶ δὲ τῆς μετριότητος, ἐφ' ἣν
παρακαλεῖτέ με, καὶ τοῦ μὴ πρόρριζον ἀνελεῖν τὸ
Ῥωμαίων γένος μηδ' ἐκ βάθρων ὅλην ἀναστῆσαι
τὴν πόλιν, εἶχον μέν,[2] ὦ Μηνύκιε, λέγειν ὅτι οὐκ
ἐγὼ τούτου κύριος οὐδὲ πρὸς ἐμὲ ὁ περὶ τούτων
ἐστὶ λόγος, ἀλλ' ἐγὼ μὲν[3] στρατηγός εἰμι τῆς
δυνάμεως, πολέμου δὲ[4] καὶ εἰρήνης οὗτοι κύριοι·
ὥστε παρὰ τούτων αἰτεῖσθέ γε ἀνοχὰς ἐπὶ δι-
2 αλλαγαῖς,[5] ἀλλὰ μὴ παρ' ἐμοῦ. οὐ μὴν[6] ἀλλὰ καὶ
θεοὺς σέβων τοὺς πατρῴους καὶ τάφους αἰδούμενος
προγόνων καὶ γῆν ἐξ ἧς ἔφυν, γυναῖκάς τε καὶ
παῖδας ὑμῶν ἐλεῶν, οἷς οὐκ ἐπιτηδείοις οὖσι τὰ
πατέρων καὶ ἀνδρῶν ἥξει[7] σφάλματα, καὶ οὐχ ἥκιστα
τῶν ἄλλων καὶ δι' ὑμᾶς, ὦ Μηνύκιε, τοὺς προ-
χειρισθέντας ὑπὸ τῆς πόλεως,[8] τάδε ἀποκρίνομαι·
ἐὰν ἀποδῶσι[9] Ῥωμαῖοι Οὐολούσκοις χώραν τε
ὅσην αὐτοὺς ἀφῄρηνται καὶ πόλεις ὅσας κατέχουσιν
ἀνακαλεσάμενοι τοὺς ἐποίκους,[10] φιλίαν τε ποιήσωνται πρὸς αὐτοὺς εἰς τὸν ἀεὶ χρόνον καὶ ἰσοπολι-

---

[1] καὶ ἅμα καὶ Cary : καὶ ἅμα ταῦτα καὶ O, Jacoby.
[2] μέν B : οὖν AC, ἄν Sylburg.
[3] μὲν added by Reiske.　　　　[4] δὲ B : om. R.
[5] αἰτεῖσθε γε ἀνοχὰς ἐπὶ διαλλαγαῖς B : αἰτεῖσθε εἴτε ἀνοχὰς
εἴτε διαλλαγὰς R.
[6] After οὐ μὴν the MSS. have ταύτην γε δίδωμι τὴν ἀπόκρισιν, which Reiske deleted.

and honourable, and at the same time what is most
holy in the eyes of the gods ; and I do not care to
take as judges of my conduct mere men who infer the
truth from guesswork and opinion, since the gods are
pleased with what I do. Nor do I agree that I am
undertaking impossible things when I have the gods
as my guides therein—not, at least, if one is to judge
of the future by the past.

XXXV. " As regards the moderation which you
recommend to me and your plea that I should not
utterly destroy the Roman race or overthrow the city
from its foundations, I might answer, Minucius, that
this is not in my power to decide, nor should your
plea be addressed to me. No, I am general of the
army, but as to war and peace these men here have
the decision ; so apply to them for a truce as a step
toward reconciliation, and not to me. Nevertheless,
because I revere the gods of my fathers and respect
the sepulchres of my ancestors and the land which
gave me birth, and feel compassion for your wives
and children, on whom, though undeserving, will fall
the errors of their fathers and husbands, and, not
least of all, on account of you men, Minucius, who
have been chosen envoys by the commonwealth,[1] I
answer as follows : If the Romans will return to the
Volscians the land they have taken from them and
the cities they hold, first recalling their colonists, and
if they will enter into a league of perpetual friendship
with them and give them equal rights of citizenship,

---

[1] Or, following Kiessling's emendation, " by the senate."

[7] ἥξει BC : ἥξειν Cmg, ἔξειν A.
[8] πόλεως O : βουλῆς Kiessling.
[9] Jacoby : ἀποδιδῶσι O.
[20] ἐποίκους ABa : ἀποίκους Bb.

τείας μεταδῶσιν[1] ὥσπερ Λατίνοις ὅρκους καὶ ἀρὰς
κατὰ τῶν παραβαινόντων τὰ συγκείμενα ποιησάμενοι, διαλύσομαι πρὸς αὐτοὺς τὸν πόλεμον, πρότερον
3 δὲ οὔ.[2]   ταῦτ' οὖν[3] ἀπαγγέλλετε αὐτοῖς, καὶ τὸν
αὐτὸν τρόπον ὅνπερ πρὸς ἐμὲ καὶ πρὸς ἐκείνους
περὶ τοῦ δικαίου πάνυ ἐπιστρεφῶς ταῦτα δια-
λέγεσθε· καλόν τοι τὰς ἰδίας ἕκαστον ἔχοντα κτήσεις ἐν εἰρήνῃ ζῆν, καὶ πολλοῦ ἄξιον τὸ μηθένα
δεδοικέναι μήτ' ἐχθρὸν μήτε καιρόν, αἰσχρὸν δὲ
τῶν ἀλλοτρίων περιεχομένους οὐκ ἀναγκαῖον πόλεμον ὑπομένειν, ἐν ᾧ καὶ[4] περὶ τῶν ἰδίων ἁπάντων
κινδυνεύσουσιν ἀγαθῶν· τά τε ἆθλα ἐπιδείκνυτε
αὐτοῖς οὐκ ἴσα[5] κατορθοῦσί τε καὶ μὴ τυχοῦσι
γινόμενα γῆς ἀλλοτρίας γλιχομένοις· εἰ δὲ βούλεσθε, προστίθετε καὶ τὰς πόλεις τῶν ἠδικημένων
προσλαβεῖν βουλομένοις, ἐὰν μὴ κρατῶσι, καὶ τὴν
ἑαυτῶν γῆν τε καὶ πόλιν ἀφαιρεθῆναι, καὶ ἔτι πρὸς
τούτῳ γυναῖκας ἐπιδεῖν τὰ[6] αἴσχιστα πασχούσας
καὶ παῖδας εἰς ὕβριν ἀγομένους καὶ γονεῖς δούλους
4 ἀντ' ἐλευθέρων ἐπὶ γήρως ὁδῷ[7] γινομένους.   καὶ
ἅμα διδάσκετε τὴν βουλὴν ὅτι τούτων τῶν κακῶν
οὐκ ἂν ἔχοιεν αἰτιάσασθαι Μάρκιον, ἀλλὰ τὴν
ἑαυτῶν ἀφροσύνην.   παρὸν γὰρ αὐτοῖς τὰ δίκαια
ποιεῖν καὶ μηδενὶ δεινῷ περιπεσεῖν τὸν ὑπὲρ τῶν
ἐσχάτων κίνδυνον ἀναιρήσονται μέχρι παντὸς φιλο-
χωροῦντες τοῖς[8] ἀλλοτρίοις.
5   '' Ἔχετε τὰς ἀποκρίσεις· τούτων οὐθὲν ἂν εὕ-

---

[1] μεταδῶσιν A : μεταδιδῶσιν R.
[2] οὔ Kiessling : om. O, but in B one or two letters erased
after δέ.
[3] ταῦτ' οὖν Jacoby, ταῦτα δὴ Kiessling : ταῦτα O, but in B
three (?) letters erased after ταῦτα.
[4] καὶ B : δὴ καὶ R.

as they have done in the case of the Latins, confirming
their covenant by oaths and by imprecations against
those who may violate it, I will put an end to the war
against them, and not until then. So carry this
report back to them, and discuss very earnestly with
them also, in the same way as you have with me,
these considerations of justice—how fine a thing it is
for everyone to enjoy his own possessions and to live
in peace, how important to have no enemy and no
crisis to fear, but how disgraceful it is for a people,
by clinging to the possessions of others, to expose
themselves to an unnecessary war, in which they will
run the hazard of losing even all their own blessings.
Point out to them also how unequal are the prizes
that reward success and failure when men covet the
territory of others. Add too, if you please, that
people who desire to seize the cities of those they
have wronged, if they do not overcome them, are
deprived of both their own territory and city, and
in addition to this see their wives suffer the greatest
indignities, their children led away to contumely,
and their parents upon the threshold of old age
become slaves instead of free men. And at the same
time point out to the senators that they would not be
able to impute the blame for these evils to Marcius,
but to their own folly ; for though they have it in
their power to practise justice and to incur no disaster,
they will hazard their all by their continual fondness
for the possessions of others.

" You have my answer, and you will get nothing

---

⁵ ἴσα Hudson : εἰς ἃ O.
⁶ τὰ added by Grasberger.
⁷ Reiske : ὁδοῦ A, ὀδοῦ B.
⁸ ἐν before τοῖς deleted by Jacoby.

ροισθε παρ' ἐμοῦ πλέον, ἀλλ' ἄπιτε καὶ σκοπεῖτε
ὅ τι πρακτέον ὑμῖν· ἕως δὲ βουλεύσησθε,[1] δίδωμι
χρόνον ὑμῖν ἡμερῶν τριάκοντα. ἐν δὲ τῷ μεταξὺ
χρόνῳ σήν τε χάριν, ὦ Μηνύκιε, καὶ τῶν ἄλλων
ὑμῶν ἕνεκα τὴν στρατιὰν ἐκ τῆς χώρας ἀπάξω·
μεγάλα γὰρ ἂν βλάπτοισθε μενούσης αὐτῆς ἐνθάδε.
τῇ δὲ τριακοστῇ προσδέχεσθέ με ἡμέρᾳ τὰς ἀποκρίσεις ληψόμενον.''

XXXVI. Ταῦτ' εἰπὼν ἀνέστη καὶ διέλυσε τὸν
σύλλογον. τῇ δ' ἐπιούσῃ νυκτὶ περὶ τὴν τελευταίαν φυλακὴν ἀναστήσας τὴν στρατιὰν ἦγεν ἐπὶ
τὰς λοιπὰς τῶν Λατίνων πόλεις, εἴτε κατ' ἀλήθειαν
πεπυσμένος ὅτι μέλλοι τις ἐκεῖθεν ἐπικουρία Ῥωμαίοις ἀφίξεσθαι,[2] ὡς τότε δημηγορῶν ἔφησεν, εἴτε
αὐτὸς πλασάμενος τὸν λόγον, ἵνα[3] μὴ δόξειε χαρι-
ζόμενος τοῖς ἐχθροῖς καταλελοιπέναι τὸν πόλεμον.
2 ἐπιβαλὼν δὲ τῇ καλουμένῃ Λογγόλᾳ[4] καὶ δίχα
πόνου γενόμενος αὐτῆς ἐγκρατὴς καὶ τὸν αὐτὸν
τρόπον ὅνπερ τὰς ἑτέρας ἐξανδραποδισάμενός τε
καὶ διαρπάσας ἐπὶ τὴν Σατρικανῶν ἤλαυνε πόλιν.
ἑλὼν δὲ καὶ ταύτην ὀλίγον ἀντισχόντων τῶν ἐν
αὐτῇ χρόνον, καὶ τὰς ἐξ αὐτῶν ἀμφοτέρων[5] ὠφελείας μέρει τῆς στρατιᾶς κελεύσας ἀπάγειν εἰς
Ἐχέτραν, τὴν λοιπὴν ἀναλαβὼν δύναμιν ἦγεν ἐπὶ
πόλιν ἄλλην τὴν καλουμένην Κετίαν.[6] γενόμενος
δὲ καὶ ταύτης ἐγκρατὴς καὶ διαρπάσας εἰς τὴν
Πολυσκανῶν χώραν ἐνέβαλεν. οὐ δυνηθέντων δ'
ἀντισχεῖν τῶν Πολυσκανῶν κατὰ κράτος ἑλὼν καὶ

---

[1] βουλεύσησθε B : βουλεύσεσθε A, βουλεύσασθε CD.
[2] Naber : ἀφικέσθαι O, Jacoby.
[3] ἵνα B : ἢ ἵνα R. [4] Sylburg : λογγάδι O.

further from me. Depart, then, and consider what you must do. I will allow you thirty days for your deliberation. In the meantime, to show my regard for you, Minucius, as well as for the rest of you envoys, I will withdraw my army from your territory, since it would cause you great injury if it remained here. And on the thirtieth day expect my return in order to receive your answer."

XXXVI. Having thus spoken, Marcius rose up and dismissed the conference; and the following night he broke camp about the last watch and led his army against the rest of the Latin cities, either having actually learned that some reinforcements were to come from them to the Romans, as he declared at the time in his harangue to the troops, or having invented the report himself, in order that he might not seem to have given up the war to gratify the enemy. And attacking the place called Longula, he gained possession of it without any difficulty, and treated it in the same manner as he had treated the others, by making slaves of the inhabitants and plundering the town. Then he marched to the city of Satricum, and having taken this also, after a short resistance by the towns-people, and ordered a detachment of his army to convey the booty taken in these two towns to Ecetra, he marched with the rest of his forces to another town, called Cetia.[1] After gaining possession of this place also and pillaging it, he made an irruption into the territory of the Poluscini; and when these were unable to withstand him, he took their city also by

---

[1] A name otherwise unknown.

---

[5] αὐτῶν ἀμφοτέρων Jacoby : αὐτῶν ἀμφοτέρων τῶν πόλεων O, ἀμφοτέρων τῶν πόλεων Portus.

[6] κετίαν O : Κοτίαν Lapus, Σητίαν Gelenius.

τούτους ἐπὶ τὰς ἑξῆς ἐχώρει. Ἀλβίητας[1] μὲν οὖν
καὶ Μογιλλανούς[2] ἐκ τειχομαχίας αἱρεῖ, Χωριελα-
3 νούς[3] δὲ καθ' ὁμολογίας παραλαμβάνει. γενόμενος
δ' ἐν ἡμέραις τριάκοντα πόλεων ἑπτὰ κύριος ἧκεν
ἐπὶ τὴν Ῥώμην ἄγων πολὺ πλείω στρατιὰν τῆς
προτέρας καὶ σταδίους ἀποσχὼν τῆς πόλεως ὀλίγῳ
πλείους τῶν τριάκοντα παρὰ τὴν ἐπὶ Τυσκλανοὺς
φέρουσαν ὁδὸν κατεστρατοπέδευσεν.

Ἐν ᾧ δὲ τὰς Λατίνων ἐξῄρει τε καὶ προσήγετο
πόλεις, Ῥωμαίοις πρὸς τὰς ἐπιταγὰς αὐτοῦ πολλὰ
βουλευσαμένοις ἔδοξε μηδὲν ἀνάξιον ποιεῖν τῆς
πόλεως, ἀλλ' ἐὰν μὲν ἀπέλθωσιν αὐτῶν ἐκ τῆς
χώρας Οὐολοῦσκοι καὶ τῆς τῶν συμμάχων τε καὶ
ὑπηκόων[4] καὶ[5] καταλυσάμενοι τὸν πόλεμον πρέσβεις
ἀποστείλωσι τοὺς διαλεξομένους περὶ φιλίας, προ-
βουλεῦσαι τὸ συνέδριον ἐφ' οἷς ἔσονται δικαίοις
φίλοι, καὶ τὰ βουλευθέντα εἰς τὸν δῆμον ἐξενεγ-
κεῖν· ἕως δ' ἂν ἐν τῇ χώρᾳ μένοντες αὐτῶν καὶ
τῶν συμμάχων ἔργα πράττωσι πολεμίων, μη-
4 θὲν αὐτοῖς ψηφίζεσθαι φιλάνθρωπον. πολὺς
γὰρ δὴ Ῥωμαίοις ἀεὶ λόγος τοῦ μηθὲν δρᾶσαί ποτε
ἐξ ἐπιτάγματος μηδὲ φόβῳ πολεμίων εἴξαντας,
σπεισαμένοις δὲ τοῖς διαφόροις καὶ παρασχοῦσιν
ἑαυτοὺς ὑπηκόους χαρίζεσθαί τε καὶ ἐπιτρέπειν

---

[1] ἀλβίητας AB : Λαβινιάτας Sylburg.
[2] Kiessling : μογιλαινοὺς BC, μοσεγιλαίνους A.
[3] χωριελανοὺς O : Κοριολανοὺς Steph.
[4] γῆς after ὑπηκόων deleted by Reudler.
[5] καὶ added by Portus.

---

[1] At least two of these names are corrupt. For the strange
form ΑΛΒΙΗΤΑΣ (Albietes or Albietae) Sylburg proposed
to read ΛΑΒΙΝΙΑΤΑΣ (Lavinienses), an emendation that is

storm, and then proceeded against the others in order : the Albietes and the Mugillani he took by assault and the Chorielani by capitulation.[1] Having thus made himself master of seven cities in thirty days, he returned toward Rome with an army much larger· than his former force, and encamped at a distance of a little more than thirty stades from the city, on the road that leads to Tusculum.

While Marcius was capturing or conciliating the cities of the Latins, the Romans, after long deliberation over his demands, resolved to do nothing unworthy of the commonwealth, but if the Volscians would depart from their territory and from that of their allies and subjects and, putting an end to the war, send ambassadors to treat for friendship, the senate would pass a preliminary vote fixing the terms on which they should become friends and would lay its resolution before the people ; but as long as the Volscians remained in their territory and in that of their allies committing hostile acts they would pass no friendly vote. For the Romans always made it a great point never to do anything at the dictation of an enemy or to yield to fear of him, but when once their adversaries had made peace and acknowledged themselves their subjects, to gratify them and con-

very attractive both palaeographically and also because Lavinium has already been mentioned as undergoing siege (chap. 21) and Livy names it among the cities taken by Coriolanus. The form Chorielani at once suggests Coriolani; but that name seems to have been used already in chap. 19. Mugilla is not otherwise known to us, though the Roman cognomen Mugillanus may well be derived from a place name. Gronovius on the basis of our passage substituted *Mugillam* for the adjective *novella(m)* in Livy's list of captured cities (ii. 39, 3), but some recent editors have not followed him in this.

ὅτου δέοιντο τῶν μετρίων. καὶ τοῦτο τὸ φρόνημα
ἐν[1] πολλοῖς καὶ μεγάλοις κινδύνοις φυλάττουσα ἡ
πόλις κατά τε τοὺς ὀθνείους καὶ τοὺς ἐμφυλίους
πολέμους μέχρι τοῦ καθ᾽ ἡμᾶς χρόνου διατετέλεκε.
XXXVII. Ταῦτα ψηφισαμένης τῆς βουλῆς καὶ
πρεσβευτὰς ἑτέρους ἑλομένης δέκα ἄνδρας ἐκ τῶν
ὑπατικῶν τοὺς ἀξιώσοντας τὸν ἄνδρα μηθὲν ἐκφέρειν ἐπίταγμα βαρὺ μηδ᾽ ἀνάξιον τῆς πόλεως, ἀλλὰ
καταλύσαντα τὴν ἔχθραν καὶ ἀναστήσαντα τὴν
δύναμιν ἐκ τῆς χώρας πειθοῖ καὶ διὰ λόγων συμ-
βατηρίων ταῦτα πειρᾶσθαι πράττειν, εἰ βούλεται
βεβαίους τε καὶ εἰς ἀεὶ διαμενούσας ποιήσασθαι
τὰς ὁμολογίας τῶν πόλεων, ὡς τῶν γε ὑπ᾽ ἀνάγκης
τινὸς ἢ καιροῦ συγχωρουμένων καὶ ἰδιώταις καὶ
πόλεσιν ἅμα τῷ μεταπεσεῖν τοὺς καιροὺς ἢ τὰς
ἀνάγκας εὐθὺς διαλυομένων· οἱ μὲν ἀποδειχθέντες
ὑπ᾽ αὐτῆς πρέσβεις ἅμα τῷ πυθέσθαι τὴν παρουσίαν τοῦ Μαρκίου πορευθέντες ὡς αὐτὸν πολλὰ
ἐπαγωγὰ διελέγοντο φυλάττοντες καὶ ἐν τοῖς λόγοις
2 τὸ ἀξίωμα τῆς πόλεως. ὁ δὲ Μάρκιος ἄλλο μὲν
οὐδὲν αὐτοῖς[2] ἀπεκρίνατο, συνεβούλευε δὲ κρεῖττόν
τι βουλευσαμένους ἥκειν τριῶν ἐντὸς ἡμερῶν· ταύτας γὰρ αὐτοῖς ἔσεσθαι μόνας ἀνοχὰς τοῦ πολέμου.
βουλομένων δέ τι πρὸς ταῦτα λέγειν τῶν ἀνδρῶν
οὐκ ἐπέτρεψεν, ἀλλ᾽ ἀπιέναι τὴν ταχίστην ἐκέλευσεν
ἐκ τοῦ χάρακος, ἀπειλήσας, εἰ[3] μὴ ποιήσουσιν, ὡς
κατασκόποις χρήσεσθαι[4]· κἀκεῖνοι σιωπῇ ἀπιόντες
3 εὐθὺς ᾤχοντο. μαθόντες δ᾽ οἱ βουλευταὶ παρὰ τῶν
πρέσβεων τὰς αὐθάδεις ἀποκρίσεις τε καὶ ἀπειλὰς

[1] ἐν B : ἐν τοῖς R.   [2] αὐτοῖς B : om. R.
[3] εἰ Cary : ὡς εἰ O, Jacoby, οὕτως εἰ Hertlein.
[4] Hertlein : χρήσεται O, Jacoby.

cede anything in reason that they asked. And this proud spirit the commonwealth has continued to preserve down to our own time amid many great dangers in both their foreign and their domestic wars.

XXXVII. The senate,[1] having passed this decree, chose ten other men from among the ex-consuls as envoys to ask Marcius not to make any demand that was severe or unworthy of the commonwealth, but laying aside his resentment and withdrawing his forces from their territory, to endeavour to obtain his demands by persuasion and conciliatory language, if he wished to make the compact between the two states firm and enduring, since all concessions made either to individuals or to states under compulsion of some necessity or crisis become void at once when the crisis or the necessity changes. The envoys appointed by the senate, as soon as they were informed of the arrival of Marcius, repaired to him and used many tempting arguments, preserving also in their discussions, however, the dignity of the commonwealth. But Marcius gave them no answer except to advise them to reach some better decision and then return within three days; for they should have a truce from war for that period only. And when the envoys desired to make some answer to this, he would not permit it, but ordered them to quit the camp immediately, threatening, if they refused, to treat them as spies. Thereupon they at once withdrew in silence. The senators, upon being informed by the envoys of the haughty answer and

---

[1] For chaps. 37 f. cf. Livy ii. 39, 12.

τοῦ Μαρκίου στρατιὰν μὲν ὑπερόριον ἐξάγειν οὐδὲ
τότε ἐψηφίσαντο, εἴτε τὸ ἀπειροπόλεμον τῶν σφετέρων στρατιωτῶν (νεοσύλλεκτοι γὰρ οἱ πλείους
ἦσαν αὐτῶν) εὐλαβηθέντες, εἴτε τὴν ἀτολμίαν τῶν
ὑπάτων (ἥκιστα γὰρ ἐν αὐτοῖς τὸ δραστήριον ἦν)
σφαλερὰν ἡγησάμενοι τηλικοῦτον ἀναιρεῖσθαι ἀγῶνα, εἴτε ἄρα καὶ τοῦ δαιμονίου σφίσιν ἐναντιου-
μένου πρὸς τὴν ἔξοδον δι' οἰωνῶν[1] ἢ χρησμῶν
Σιβυλλείων ἢ τινος ὀττείας πατρίου, ὧν οὐκ ἠξίουν
οἱ τότε ἄνθρωποι καθάπερ οἱ νῦν ὑπερορᾶν· φυλάττειν δὲ τὴν πόλιν ἐπιμελεστέρᾳ φυλακῇ καὶ ἀπὸ
τῶν ἐρυμάτων τοὺς ἐπιόντας ἀμύνεσθαι διέγνωσαν.

XXXVIII. Ταῦτα δὲ πράττοντες καὶ παρασκευαζόμενοι τῆς τε ἐλπίδος οὔπω τε ἀφιστάμενοι ὡς
δυνατὸν ὑπάρχον ἔτι μεταπεισθῆναι τὸν Μάρκιον,
εἰ μείζονι καὶ τιμιωτέρᾳ πρεσβείᾳ δεηθεῖεν αὐτοῦ,
ψηφίζονται τούς τε ἱεροφάντας καὶ τοὺς οἰωνο-
σκόπους καὶ τοὺς ἄλλους ὅσαπαντας ὅσοι τιμήν τινα
ἱερὰν ἢ λειτουργίαν περὶ τὰ θεῖα δημοτελῆ
λαβόντες εἶχον (εἰσὶ δὲ παρ' αὐτοῖς ἱερεῖς καὶ
θεραπευταὶ θεῶν πάνυ πολλοὶ καὶ αὐτοὶ οὗτοι
διαφανέστατοι τῶν ἄλλων κατά τε οἴκους πατέρων
καὶ ἀρετῆς οἰκείας ἀξίωσιν) ἔχοντας ἅμ' αὐτοῖς
τῶν ὀργιαζομένων τε καὶ θεραπευομένων θεῶν τὰ
σύμβολα καὶ τὰς ἱερὰς ἀμπεχομένους ἐσθῆτας
ἀθρόους ἐπὶ τὸν χάρακα τῶν πολεμίων πορεύεσθαι
2 τοὺς αὐτοὺς φέροντας τοῖς προτέροις λόγους. ὡς
δ' ἀφίκοντο οἱ ἄνδρες καὶ ἔλεξαν ὅσα ἡ βουλὴ
αὐτοῖς ἐπέστελλεν, οὐδὲ τούτοις ἔδωκεν ὁ Μάρκιος
ἀπόκρισιν ὑπὲρ ὧν ἠξίουν, ἀλλ' ἢ τὰ κελευόμενα

---

[1] δι' οἰωνῶν Reiske : οἰωνῶν B, οἶον A.

threats of Marcius, did not even then vote to send out
an expeditionary force, either because they feared
the inexperience of their troops, most of whom were
new recruits, or because they regarded the timidity
of the consuls—there was indeed no boldness for
action in them at all—as a serious risk in undertaking
so great a struggle, or perhaps too because Heaven opposed their expedition by means of auspices, Sibyl-
line oracles, or some traditional religious scruple—
warnings which the men of that age did not think
fit to neglect as do those of to-day. However, they
resolved to guard the city with greater diligence and
to repel from their ramparts any who should attack
them.

XXXVIII. While they were so engaged and were
making their preparations, and were not yet ready
to give up all hope, believing that Marcius could still
be persuaded to relent if they sent a larger and more
dignified embassy to intercede with him, they voted
to send the pontiffs, the augurs, and all the others
who were invested with any sacred dignity or public
ministry relating to divine worship (there are among
them large numbers of priests and ministers of religion, these also being distinguished beyond their
fellows not only for their ancestry, but for their
reputation for personal merit as well), and that these,
carrying with them the symbols of the gods whose
rites and worship they performed, and wearing their
priestly robes, should go in a body to the enemy's
camp bearing the same message as the former envoys.
When they arrived and delivered the message with
which the senate had charged them, Marcius returned
no other answer even to them concerning their
demands, but advised them either to depart and do

ποιεῖν συνεβούλευεν ἀπιόντας, εἰ θέλουσιν εἰρήνην
ἄγειν, ἢ προσδέχεσθαι τὸν πόλεμον ἥξοντα πρὸς
τὴν πόλιν, καὶ τὸ λοιπὸν ἀπεῖπε μὴ διαλέγεσθαι
3 πρὸς αὐτόν. ὡς δὲ καὶ ταύτης ἀπέτυχον τῆς πείρας οἱ Ῥωμαῖοι, πᾶσαν ἐλπίδα διαλλαγῆς ἀπογνόντες ὡς πολιορκησόμενοι παρεσκευάζοντο τοὺς
μὲν ἀκμαιοτάτους ἐπὶ[1] τῇ τάφρῳ καὶ παρὰ ταῖς
πύλαις τάξαντες, τοὺς δ᾽ ἀφειμένους ἤδη στρατείας,
οἷς ἔτι τὰ σώματα ἱκανὰ ἦν κακοπαθεῖν, ἐπὶ τοῖς
τείχεσιν.

XXXIX. Αἱ δὲ γυναῖκες αὐτῶν, ὡς ἐγγὺς ὄντος
ἤδη τοῦ δεινοῦ, καταλιποῦσαι τῆς οἴκοι μονῆς τὸ
εὐπρεπὲς ἔθεον ἐπὶ τὰ τεμένη τῶν θεῶν ὀλοφυρόμεναί τε καὶ προκυλιόμεναι τῶν ξοάνων· καὶ ἦν
ἅπας μὲν ἱερὸς τόπος οἰμωγῆς τε καὶ ἱκετείας
γυναικῶν ἀνάπλεως, μάλιστα δὲ τὸ τοῦ Καπιτω-
2 λίου Διὸς ἱερόν. ἔνθα δή τις αὐτῶν γένει τε καὶ
ἀξιώματι προὔχουσα καὶ ἡλικίας ἐν τῷ κρατίστῳ
τότ᾽ οὖσα καὶ φρονῆσαι τὰ δέοντα ἱκανωτάτη,
Οὐαλερία μὲν ὄνομα, Ποπλικόλα δὲ τοῦ συνελευ-
θερώσαντος ἀπὸ τῶν βασιλέων τὴν πόλιν ἀδελφή,
θείῳ τινὶ παραστήματι κινηθεῖσα ἐπὶ τῆς ἀνωτάτω
κρηπῖδος ἔστη τοῦ νεὼ καὶ προσκαλεσαμένη τὰς
ἄλλας γυναῖκας πρῶτον μὲν παρεμυθήσατο καὶ
παρεθάρρυνεν ἀξιοῦσα μὴ καταπεπλῆχθαι τὸ δεινόν·
ἔπειτα ὑπέσχετο μίαν εἶναι σωτηρίας ἐλπίδα τῇ
πόλει, ταύτην δ᾽ ἐν αὐταῖς εἶναι μόναις καταλειπο-
3 μένην, ἐὰν ἐθελήσωσι πράττειν ἃ δεῖ. καί τις
εἶπεν ἐξ αὐτῶν· "Καὶ τί πράττουσαι ἂν ἡμεῖς αἱ
γυναῖκες διασῶσαι δυνηθείημεν τὴν πατρίδα τῶν
ἀνδρῶν ἀπειρηκότων; τίς ἡ τοσαύτη περὶ ἡμᾶς τὰς

[1] Sintenis : ὑπὸ O, Jacoby.

as he commanded, if they wished to have peace, or to expect the war to come to their very gates ; and he forbade them to attempt any negotiations with him for the future. When the Romans failed in this attempt also, they gave up all hope of reconciliation and prepared for a siege, disposing the ablest of their men beside the moat and at the gates, and stationing upon the walls those who had been discharged from military service but whose bodies were still capable of enduring hardships.

XXXIX. In the meantime their wives,[1] seeing the danger now at hand and abandoning the sense of propriety that kept them in the seclusion of their homes, ran to the shrines of the gods with lamentations and threw themselves at the feet of their statues. And every holy place, particularly the temple of Jupiter Capitolinus, was filled with the cries and supplications of women. Then it was that one of them, a matron distinguished in birth and rank, who was then in the vigour of life and quite capable of discreet judgement, Valeria by name and sister to Publicola, one of the men who had freed the commonwealth from the kings, moved by some divine inspiration, took her stand upon the topmost step of the temple, and calling the rest of the women to her, first comforted and encouraged them, bidding them not to be alarmed at the danger that threatened. Then she assured them that there was just one hope of safety for the commonwealth and that this hope rested in them alone, if they would do what required to be done. Upon this one of them asked : " And what can we women do to save our country, when the men have given it up for lost ? What strength so

---

[1] For chaps. 39-54 cf. Livy ii. 40, 1-10.

ἀσθενεῖς καὶ ταλαιπώρους ἐστὶν ἰσχύς;" "Οὐχὶ[1]
ὅπλων," ἔφησεν ἡ Οὐαλερία, "καὶ χειρῶν δεομένη,[2]
τούτων μὲν γὰρ ἀπολέλυκεν ἡμᾶς ἡ φύσις, ἀλλ'
εὐνοίας καὶ λόγου." βοῆς δὲ μετὰ τοῦτο γενομένης
καὶ δεομένων ἁπασῶν φανερὸν[3] ποιεῖν ἥτις ἐστὶν
4 ἡ ἐπικουρία, λέγει πρὸς αὐτάς· "Ταύτην ἔχουσαι
τὴν πιναράν τε καὶ ἄκοσμον ἐσθῆτα καὶ τὰς ἄλλας
παραλαβοῦσαι γυναῖκας καὶ τὰ τέκνα ἐπαγόμεναι
βαδίζωμεν ἐπὶ τὴν Οὐετουρίας τῆς Μαρκίου μητρὸς
οἰκίαν· καὶ πρὸ τῶν γονάτων αὐτῆς τὰ τέκνα
θεῖσαι, δεώμεθα μετὰ δακρύων ἡμᾶς τε οἰκτείρασαν
τὰς μηθενὸς κακοῦ αἰτίας καὶ τὴν ἐν ἐσχάτοις
κινδύνοις οὖσαν πατρίδα προελθεῖν ἐπὶ τὸν χάρακα
τῶν πολεμίων, ἄγουσαν τούς τε υἱωνοὺς καὶ τὴν
μητέρα αὐτῶν καὶ ἡμᾶς ἁπάσας· ἀκολουθῶμεν
γὰρ αὐτῇ τὰ παιδία ἐπαγόμεναι· ἔπειτα ἱκέτιν
γενομένην τοῦ τέκνου, ἀξιοῦν καὶ δεῖσθαι μηδὲν
5 ἀνήκεστον κατὰ τῆς πατρίδος ἐξεργάσασθαι. ὀλο-
φυρομένης γὰρ αὐτῆς καὶ ἀντιβολούσης οἶκτός τις
εἰσελεύσεται τὸν ἄνδρα καὶ λογισμὸς ἥμερος. οὐχ
οὕτω στερρὰν καὶ ἄτρωτον ἔχει καρδίαν ὥστε
ἀνασχέσθαι μητέρα πρὸς τοῖς ἑαυτοῦ γόνασι
κυλιομένην."

XL. Ὡς δ' ἐπῄνεσαν αἱ παροῦσαι τὸν λόγον,
εὐξαμένη τοῖς θεοῖς πειθὼ καὶ χάριν αὐτῶν περι-
θεῖναι τῇ δεήσει προῆλθεν ἐκ τοῦ τεμένους, αἱ δ'
ἠκολούθουν. καὶ μετὰ τοῦτο παραλαβοῦσαι τὰς
ἄλλας γυναῖκας ἐπορεύοντο ἐπὶ τὴν οἰκίαν τῆς
Μαρκίου μητρὸς ἀθρόαι. ἰδοῦσα δ' αὐτὰς προσ-
ιούσας ἡ τοῦ Μαρκίου γυνὴ Οὐολουμνία πλησίον
καθημένη τῆς ἑκυρᾶς ἐθαύμασέ τε καὶ εἶπε· "Τίνος

[1] οὐχὶ A : οὐχ R.

great do we weak and miserable women possess ? "
" A strength," replied Valeria, " that calls, not for
weapons or hands—for Nature has excused us from
the use of these—but for goodwill and speech." And
when all cried out and begged of her to explain what
this assistance was, Valeria said : " Wearing this
squalid and shabby garb and taking with us the rest
of the women and our children, let us go to the house
of Veturia, the mother of Marcius ; and placing the
children at her knees, let us entreat her with tears to
have compassion both upon us, who have given her no
cause for grief, and upon our country, now in the
direst peril, and beg of her to go to the enemy's camp,
taking along her grandchildren and their mother and
all of us—for we must attend her with our children—
and becoming the suppliant of her son, to ask and
implore him not to inflict any irreparable mischief on
his country. For while she is lamenting and entreating, a feeling of compassion and a tender reasonableness will come over the man. His heart is not so
hard and invulnerable that he can hold out against a
mother who grovels at his knees."

XL. This advice having been approved of by all
the women who were present, she prayed to the gods
to invest their plea with persuasion and charm, and
then set out from the sanctuary, followed by the
others. Afterwards, taking with them the rest of the
women, they went in a body to the house of Marcius'
mother. His wife Volumnia saw them approaching
as she sat near her mother-in-law, and being surprised
at their coming, asked : " What is it you want,

---

² Sintenis : δεόμεναι O, δεόμεθα Grasberger.
³ Grasberger : φανεράν O.

115

δεόμεναι, γυναῖκες, ἐληλύθατε κατὰ πλῆθος εἰς
οἰκίαν δύστηνον καὶ ταπεινήν; " καὶ ἡ Οὐαλερία
2 ἔλεξεν· " Ἐν ἐσχάτοις οὖσαι κινδύνοις καὶ αὐταὶ
καὶ τὰ νήπια ταῦτα καταπεφεύγαμεν ἱκέτιδες ἐπὶ
σέ, ὦ Οὐετουρία, τὴν μόνην καὶ μίαν βοήθειαν,
ἀξιοῦσαί σε πρῶτον μὲν οἰκτεῖραι τὴν κοινὴν
πατρίδα, ἣν οὐθενὶ πώποτε γενομένην ὑποχείριον
μὴ περιίδῃς ἀφαιρεθεῖσαν ὑπὸ Οὐολούσκων τὴν
ἐλευθερίαν, εἰ δὴ καὶ φείσονται αὐτῆς κρατήσαντες,
ἀλλ' οὐ πρόρριζον ἐπιχειρήσουσιν ἀνελεῖν· ἔπειτα
ὑπὲρ ἡμῶν αὐτῶν ἀντιβολοῦσαι καὶ τῶν δυστή-
νων παιδίων τούτων, ἵνα μὴ πέσωμεν εἰς ἐχθρῶν
ὕβριν οὐθενὸς οὖσαι τῶν συμβεβηκότων ὑμῖν κα-
3 κῶν αἴτιαι. εἴ τίς ἐστιν ἐν σοὶ ψυχῆς ἡμέρου καὶ
φιλανθρώπου καταλειπομένη μερίς, ἐλέησον, ὦ Οὐετουρία, γυνὴ γυναῖκας κοινωνήσασα ἱερῶν ποτε
καὶ ὁσίων, καὶ παραλαβοῦσα μετὰ σεαυτῆς Οὐολουμνίαν τε τὴν ἀγαθὴν γυναῖκα καὶ τοὺς παῖδας αὐτῆς καὶ τὰς ἱκέτιδας ἡμᾶς φερούσας τὰ
νήπια ταυτί, καὶ αὐτὰς γενναίας,[1] ἴθι πρὸς τὸν υἱὸν
καὶ πεῖθε καὶ λιπάρει καὶ μὴ ἀνῇς δεομένη, μίαν
ἀντὶ πολλῶν χάριν αἰτοῦσα παρ' αὐτοῦ σπείσα-
σθαι πρὸς τοὺς ἑαυτοῦ πολίτας καὶ κατελθεῖν εἰς
τὴν δεομένην ἀπολαβεῖν αὐτὸν πατρίδα· πείσεις
γάρ, εὖ ἴσθι, καὶ οὐ περιόψεταί σε ἐρριμμένην
4 παρὰ τοῖς ἑαυτοῦ ποσὶν ἀνὴρ εὐσεβής. κατ-
αγαγοῦσα δὲ τὸν υἱὸν εἰς τὴν πόλιν αὐτή τε
ἀθάνατον ἕξεις κλέος ὥσπερ εἰκὸς ἐκ τηλικούτου
κινδύνου καὶ φόβου ῥυσαμένη τὴν πατρίδα, καὶ
ἡμῖν τιμῆς τινος αἰτία παρὰ τοῖς ἀνδράσιν ἔσῃ,

---

[1] τὰ νήπια ταυτὶ καὶ αὐτὰς γενναίας Jacoby, τὰ νήπια καὶ
ταῦτα ἱκέτας γενναίους Post : τὰ νήπια καὶ ταυτὶ τὰς γενναίας O.

women, that so many of you have come to a household that is distressed and in humiliation?" Then Valeria replied: "Because we are in the direst peril, both we ourselves and these children have turned as suppliants to you, Veturia, our one and only succour, entreating you, first, to take compassion on our common country and not to permit this land, which has never fallen under any man's hand, to be robbed of its freedom by the Volscians—even supposing that they will spare it after subduing it and not endeavour to destroy it utterly; and next, imploring you in our own behalf and in behalf of these unfortunate children that we may not be exposed to the insolence of the enemy, since we are the cause of none of the evils that have befallen your family. If there remains in you any portion of a gentle and humane spirit, do you, Veturia, as a woman, have mercy on women who once shared with you the same sacrifices and rites, and taking with you Volumnia, the good wife of Marcius, and her children, and us suppliant women—ourselves too of noble birth—carrying in our arms these infants, go to your son and try to persuade him, implore him, and cease not to entreat him, asking of him this one favour in return for many—to make peace with his fellow citizens and return to his country that longs to get him back. For you will persuade him, be assured; a man of his piety will not permit you to lie prostrate at his feet. And when you have brought your son back to Rome, not only will you yourself most likely gain immortal glory for having rescued your country from so great a danger and terror, but you will be the cause to us also of some honour in the eyes of our

ὅτι τὸν οὐ δυνηθέντα ὑπ' ἐκείνων διασκεδασθῆναι
πόλεμον αὐταὶ διελύσαμεν· ἐκείνων τε ἀληθῶς[1]
ἔγγονοι[2] τῶν γυναικῶν φανησόμεθα αἳ τὸν συ-
στάντα 'Ρωμύλῳ πρὸς Σαβίνους πόλεμον αὐταὶ
πρεσβευσάμεναι διελύσαντο καὶ συναγαγοῦσαι
τούς τε ἡγεμόνας καὶ τὰ ἔθνη μεγάλην ἐκ μικρᾶς
5 ἐποίησαν τὴν πόλιν. καλὸς ὁ κίνδυνος, ὦ Οὐετουρία, τὸν υἱὸν κομίσασθαι, ἐλευθερῶσαι τὴν
πατρίδα, σῶσαι τὰς ἑαυτῆς πολίτιδας, κλέος
ἀρετῆς ἀθάνατον τοῖς[3] ἐσομένοις καταλιπεῖν. δὸς
ἡμῖν ἑκοῦσα καὶ μετὰ προθυμίας τὴν χάριν καὶ
σπεῦσον, ὦ Οὐετουρία· βουλὴν γὰρ ἢ χρόνον ὁ
κίνδυνος ὀξὺς ὢν οὐκ ἐπιδέχεται."

XLI. Ἡ μὲν δὴ ταῦτα εἰποῦσα καὶ πολλὰ προ-
εμένη δάκρυα ἐσίγησεν· ὀδυρομένων δὲ καὶ τῶν
ἄλλων γυναικῶν καὶ πολλὰς δεήσεις ποιουμένων
μικρὸν ἐπισχοῦσα ἡ Οὐετουρία καὶ δακρύσασα
εἶπεν·

" Εἰς ἀσθενῆ καὶ λεπτὴν ἐλπίδα καταπεφεύγατε,
ὦ Οὐαλερία, τὴν ἐξ ἡμῶν τῶν ἀθλίων γυναικῶν
βοήθειαν, αἷς ἡ μὲν εὔνοια ἡ πρὸς τὴν πατρίδα
πάρεστι καὶ τὸ θέλειν σώζεσθαι τοὺς πολίτας, οἷοί
ποτέ εἰσιν, ἡ δ' ἰσχὺς καὶ τὸ δύνασθαι ποιεῖν ἃ
2 θέλομεν ἄπεστιν. ἀπέστραπται γὰρ ἡμᾶς, ὦ Οὐαλερία, Μάρκιος, ἐξ οὗ τὴν πικρὰν ἐκείνην ὁ
δῆμος αὐτοῦ κατέγνω δίκην, καὶ μεμίσηκε τὴν οἰκίαν ὅλην ἅμα τῇ πατρίδι· τοῦτο δ' ὑμῖν οὐ παρ'
ἄλλου τινός, ἀλλὰ παρ' αὐτοῦ Μαρκίου μαθοῦσαι
λέγειν[4] ἔχομεν. ὅτε γὰρ ἁλοὺς τὴν δίκην ἦλθεν
εἰς τὴν οἰκίαν προπεμπόμενος ὑπὸ τῶν ἑταίρων,
καταλαβὼν ἡμᾶς καθημένας[5] ἐν πενθίμοις τρύ-

[1] ἀληθῶς B : om. R.   [2] ἔγγονοι Ba : ἔκγονοι ABC.

husbands for having ourselves put an end to a war which they had been unable to stop ; and we shall show ourselves to be the true descendants of those women who by their own intercession put an end to the war that had arisen between Romulus and the Sabines and by bringing together both the commanders and the nations made this city great from a small beginning. It is a glorious venture, Veturia, to recover your son, to free your native land, to save your countrywomen, and to leave to posterity an imperishable reputation for virtue. Grant us this favour willingly and cheerfully, and make haste, Veturia ; for the danger is acute and admits of no deliberation or delay."

XLI. Having said this and shed many tears, she became silent. And when the other women also lamented and added many entreaties, Veturia, after pausing a short time and weeping, said :

" It is a weak and slender hope, Valeria, to which you have turned for refuge—the assistance of us wretched women who feel indeed affection for our country and a desire for the preservation of the citizens, no matter what their character, but lack the strength and power to do what we wish. For Marcius has turned away from us, Valeria, ever since the people passed that bitter sentence against him, and has hated his whole family together with his country. This we can tell you as a thing we learned from the lips of none other than Marcius himself. For when, after his condemnation, he came home, escorted by his friends, and found us sitting there in garments of mourning,

---

³ τοῖς B : ἐγγόνοις τοῖς R.
⁴ μαθοῦσαι λέγειν B : om. R.
⁵ τὴν δίκην Ba (?) : τῇ δίκῃ ABb.   ⁶ καθημένας B : om. R.

χεσι, ταπεινάς, κρατούσας ἐν τοῖς γόνασι τὰ τέκνα
αὐτοῦ στενούσας τε οἷα εἰκὸς καὶ ἀνακλαιομένας[1]
τὴν καθέξουσαν ἡμᾶς τύχην στερομένας ἐκείνου,
στὰς μικρὸν ἄπωθεν ἡμῶν ἄδακρυς ὥσπερ λίθος καὶ
3 ἀτενής· ' Οἴχεται,' φησίν, ' ὑμῖν Μάρκιος, ὦ μῆτερ
ἅμα καὶ σύ, ὦ Οὐολουμνία, κρατίστη γυναικῶν,
ἐξελαθεὶς ὑπὸ τῶν πολιτῶν, ὅτι γενναῖος ἦν καὶ
φιλόπολις καὶ πολλοὺς ὑπέμεινεν ὑπὲρ τῆς πατρίδος
ἀγῶνας. ἀλλ' ὡς πρέπει γυναιξὶν ἀγαθαῖς, οὕτω
φέρετε τὰς συμφορὰς μηδὲν ἄσχημον ποιοῦσαι μηδὲ
ἀγεννές, καὶ τὰ παιδία ταῦτα παραμύθια τῆς ἐμῆς
ἐρημίας ἔχουσαι τρέφετε ἀξίως ὑμῶν[2] τε καὶ τοῦ
γένους· οἷς θεοὶ δοῖεν εἰς ἄνδρας ἐλθοῦσι τύχην μὲν
κρείσσονα τοῦ πατρός, ἀρετὴν δὲ μὴ χείρονα· χαίρετε. ἀπέρχομαι γὰρ ἤδη καταλιπὼν τὴν οὐκέτι χωροῦσαν ἄνδρας ἀγαθοὺς πόλιν. καὶ ὑμεῖς,
ὦ θεοὶ κτήσιοι καὶ ἑστία πατρῴα καὶ δαίμονες οἱ
4 κατέχοντες τοῦτον τὸν τόπον, χαίρετε.' ὡς δὲ
ταῦτ' εἶπεν, ἡμεῖς μὲν αἱ δυστυχεῖς ἃς τὸ πάθος
ἀπῄτει φωνὰς ἀναβοῶσαι καὶ παίουσαι τὰ στήθη
περιεχύθημεν αὐτῷ τοὺς ἐσχάτους ἀσπασμοὺς κομι-
ούμεναι· τῶν δὲ παιδίων τούτων ἐγὼ μὲν τὸ
πρεσβύτερον ἦγον, ἡ δὲ μήτηρ τὸ νεώτερον εἶχεν
ἐπὶ τῆς ἀγκάλης· ὁ δ' ἀποστραφεὶς καὶ παρωσά-
μενος ἡμᾶς εἶπεν· ' Οὔτε σὸς υἱὸς ἔτι, μῆτερ, ἔσται
τὸν ἀπὸ τοῦδε χρόνον Μάρκιος, ἀλλ' ἀφῄρηταί σε
τὸν γηροβοσκὸν ἡ πατρίς, οὔτε σὸς ἀνὴρ ἀπὸ ταύτης, ὦ Οὐολουμνία, τῆς ἡμέρας, ἀλλ' εὐτυχοίης
ἕτερον ἄνδρα λαβοῦσα εὐδαιμονέστερον ἐμοῦ, οὔθ'
ὑμῶν, ὦ τέκνα φίλτατα, πατήρ, ἀλλ' ὀρφανοὶ καὶ
ἔρημοι παρὰ ταύταις, ἕως εἰς ἄνδρας ἔλθητε, τραφή-

---

[1] Portus : ἀνακαλουμένας O.   [2] Gelenius : ἡμῶν O.

abased, clasping his children upon our knees, uttering such lamentations as one would expect in the
circumstances and bewailing the unhappy fate which
would come upon us when bereft of him, he stood
at a little distance from us, tearless as a stone and
unmoved, and said : ' Marcius is lost to you, mother,
and to you also, Volumnia, best of wives, having
been exiled by his fellow citizens because he was a
brave man and a lover of his country and undertook many struggles for her sake. But bear this
calamity as befits good women, doing nothing unseemly or ignoble, and with these children as a
consolation for my absence, rear them in a manner
worthy both of yourselves and of their lineage ; and
when they have come to manhood, may the gods
grant them a fate better than their father's and
valour not inferior to his. Farewell. I am departing
now and leaving this city in which there is no longer
any room for good men. And ye too, my household
gods and hearth of my fathers, and ye other divinities
who preside over this place, farewell.' When he had
thus spoken, we unhappy women, uttering the cries
which our plight called for, and beating our breasts,
clung to him to receive his last embraces. I led the
elder of these his sons by the hand, and the younger
his mother carried in her arms. But he turned away,
and thrusting us back, said : ' No longer shall Marcius
be your son henceforth, mother, but our country has
deprived you of the support of your old age ; nor
shall he be your husband, Volumnia, from this day,
but may you be happy with another husband more
fortunate than I ; nor shall he be your father, dearest
children, but, orphans and forsaken, you will be
reared by these women till you come to manhood.'

5 σεσθε.' ταῦτ' εἰπών, ἄλλο δ'[1] οὐθὲν οὔτε διοικη-
σάμενος οὔτ' ἐπιστείλας οὔθ' ὅποι πορεύεται φράσας
ἀπῆλθεν ἐκ τῆς οἰκίας μόνος, ὦ γυναῖκες, ἄδουλος,
ἄπορος, οὐδὲ τὴν ἐφήμερον ὁ δύστηνος ἐκ τῶν
ἑαυτοῦ χρημάτων τροφὴν ἐπαγόμενος. καὶ τέταρτον ἐνιαυτὸν ἤδη τοῦτον, ἐξ οὗ φεύγει τὴν πατρίδα,
πάντας ἡμᾶς ἀλλοτρίους ἑαυτοῦ νενόμικεν, οὐ
γράφων οὐθέν, οὐκ ἐπιστέλλων, οὐ τὰ περὶ ἡμᾶς
6 εἰδέναι βουλόμενος. πρὸς δὴ τοιαύτην ψυχὴν οὕτω
σκληρὰν καὶ ἄτρωτον, ὦ Οὐαλερία, τίνα ἰσχὺν
ἕξουσιν αἱ παρ' ἡμῶν δεήσεις, αἷς οὔτε ἀσπασμῶν
μετέδωκεν οὔτε φιλημάτων οὔτε ἄλλης φιλοφροσύ-
νης οὐδεμιᾶς τὴν τελευταίαν πορευόμενος ἐκ τῆς
οἰκίας ὁδόν;

XLII. " Ἀλλ' εἰ καὶ τούτου δεῖσθε ὑμεῖς, ὦ
γυναῖκες, καὶ πάντως θέλετε ἀσχημονούσας ἡμᾶς
ἰδεῖν, ὑπολάβετε παρεῖναι πρὸς αὐτὸν κἀμὲ καὶ
Οὐολουμνίαν ἀγούσας τὰ παιδία· τίνας ἐρῶ πρῶτον
ἡ μήτηρ ἐγὼ πρὸς αὐτὸν λόγους, καὶ τίνα δέησιν
ποιήσομαι τοῦ υἱοῦ; λέγετε καὶ διδάσκετέ με.
φείσασθαι παρακαλῶ τῶν ἑαυτοῦ πολιτῶν, ὑφ' ὧν
ἐκ τῆς πατρίδος ἐξελήλαται καὶ[2] μηθὲν ἀδικῶν;
οἰκτίρμονα δὲ καὶ συμπαθῆ πρὸς τοὺς δημοτικοὺς
γενέσθαι, παρ' ὧν οὔτ' ἐλέου μετέσχεν οὔτε συμ-
παθείας; ἐγκαταλιπεῖν δ' ἄρα καὶ προδοῦναι τοὺς
ὑποδεξαμένους αὐτοῦ τὴν φυγήν, οἳ πολλὰ καὶ δεινὰ
πεπονθότες ὑπ' αὐτοῦ πρότερον, οὐ πολεμίων μῖσος,
ἀλλὰ φίλων καὶ συγγενῶν εὔνοιαν εἰς αὐτὸν[3] ἀπ-
2 εδείξαντο; τίνα ψυχὴν λαβοῦσα ἀξιώσω τὸν υἱὸν
τὰ μὲν ἀπολέσαντα φιλεῖν, τὰ δὲ σώσαντα ἀδικεῖν;
οὐκ εἰσὶν οὗτοι μητρὸς ὑγιαινούσης λόγοι πρὸς υἱὸν

---

[1] ἄλλο δ' O : ἀλλ' Jacoby.

With these words and nothing else—without arranging any of his affairs, sending any messages, or saying whither he was going—he went out of the house alone, women, without a servant, without means, and without taking from his own stores, wretched man, even a day's supply of food. And for the fourth year now, ever since he was banished from the country, he has looked upon us all as strangers to him, neither writing anything nor sending any messages nor caring to have news of us. On such a mind, so hard and invulnerable, Valeria, what force will the entreaties of us women have, to whom he gave neither embraces nor kisses nor any other mark of affection when he left his house for the last time?

XLII. " But if you desire it so, women, and firmly wish to see us act an unbecoming part, just imagine that I and Volumnia with these children have come into his presence. What words shall I, his mother, first address to him and what request shall I make of my son? Tell me and instruct me. Shall I exhort him to spare his fellow citizens, by whom he was exiled from his country though guilty of no crime? To be merciful and compassionate to the plebeians, from whom he received neither mercy nor compassion? Or perhaps to abandon and betray those who received him when an exile and, notwithstanding the many calamities he had previously inflicted on them, showed to him, not the hatred of enemies, but the affection of friends and relations? What courage can I pluck up to ask my son to love those who have ruined him and to injure those who have preserved him? These are not the words of a sane mother to her son nor of

---

² καὶ O : καὶ ταῦτα Reiske, om. Cobet.
³ εἰς αὐτὸν B : om. R.

οὐδὲ γυναικὸς ἃ δεῖ λογιζομένης πρὸς ἄνδρα· μηδ'
ὑμεῖς βιάζεσθε, γυναῖκες, ἃ μήτε πρὸς ἀνθρώπους
δίκαιά ἐστι μήτε πρὸς θεοὺς ὅσια, ταῦτα ἡμᾶς
αἰτεῖσθαι παρ' αὐτοῦ, ἀλλ' ἄφετε τὰς ἐλεεινάς, ὡς
πεπτώκαμεν ὑπὸ τῆς τύχης, κεῖσθαι ταπεινὰς μηθὲν
ἔτι πλέον ἀσχημονούσας."

XLIII. Παυσαμένης δ' αὐτῆς τοσοῦτος ὀδυρμὸς
ἐκ τῶν παρουσῶν[1] γυναικῶν ἐγένετο, καὶ τηλικαύτη
κατέσχε τὸν οἶκον οἰμωγή, ὥστ' ἐπὶ πολὺ μέρος[2]
ἐξακουσθῆναι τῆς πόλεως τὴν βοὴν καὶ μεστοὺς
γενέσθαι τοὺς ἐγγὺς τῆς οἰκίας στενωποὺς ὄχλου.
2 ἔπειτα ἥ τε Οὐαλερία πάλιν ἑτέρας ἐξέτεινε μακρὰς
καὶ συμπαθεῖς δεήσεις, αἵ τε ἄλλαι γυναῖκες αἱ
κατὰ φιλίαν ἢ συγγένειαν ἑκατέρᾳ τῶν γυναικῶν
προσήκουσαι[3] παρέμενον λιπαροῦσαί τε καὶ γονάτων ἁπτόμεναι, ὥστε οὐκ ἔχουσα ὅ τι πάθῃ πρὸς
τοὺς ὀδυρμοὺς αὐτῶν καὶ τὰς πολλὰς δεήσεις, εἶξεν
ἡ Οὐετουρία καὶ τελέσειν τὴν πρεσβείαν ὑπὲρ τῆς
πατρίδος ὑπέσχετο[4] τήν τε γυναῖκα τοῦ Μαρκίου
παραλαβοῦσα καὶ τὰ τέκνα καὶ τῶν ἄλλων πολι-
3 τίδων τὰς βουλομένας. αἱ μὲν δὴ περιχαρεῖς
γενόμεναι καὶ τοὺς θεοὺς ἐπικαλεσάμεναι συλλαβέσθαι σφίσι τῆς ἐλπίδος ἀπῄεσαν ἐκ τῆς οἰκίας καὶ
προσήγγειλαν τὰ γενόμενα τοῖς ὑπάτοις· οἱ δὲ τὴν
προθυμίαν αὐτῶν ἐπαινέσαντες συνεκάλουν τὴν βουλὴν καὶ περὶ τῆς ἐξόδου τῶν γυναικῶν, εἰ συγ-
χωρητέον αὐταῖς, γνωμηδὸν ἐπυνθάνοντο.[5] πολλοὶ
μὲν οὖν ἐλέχθησαν καὶ παρὰ πολλῶν λόγοι, καὶ
μέχρι τῆς ἑσπέρας διετέλεσαν ὅ τι χρὴ ποιεῖν βου-

___

[1] παρουσῶν B : om. R.   [2] μέρος deleted by Jacoby.

a wife who reasons as she should to her husband ; nor ought you either, women, to compel us to ask of him things that are neither just in the sight of men nor right in the eyes of the gods, but permit us miserable women to lie abased as we have been cast down by Fortune, committing no further unseemly act."

XLIII. After she had done speaking there was so great lamentation on the part of the women present and such wailing pervaded the household that their cries were heard over a great part of the city and the streets near the house were crowded with people. Then Valeria again indulged in fresh entreaties that were long and affecting, and all the rest of the women who were connected by friendship or kindred with either of them remained there, beseeching her and embracing her knees, till Veturia, not seeing how she could help herself in view of their lamentations and their many entreaties, yielded and promised to perform the mission in behalf of her country, taking with her the wife of Marcius and his children and as many matrons as wished to join them. The women rejoiced exceedingly at this and invoked the gods to aid in the accomplishment of their hopes ; then, departing from the house, they informed the consuls of what had passed. These, having commended their zeal, assembled the senate and called upon the members to deliver their opinions one after the other whether they ought to permit the women to go out on this mission. Many speeches were made by many senators, and they continued debating till

---

³ προσήκουσαι Post : προσήκουσαι καὶ O, Jacoby.

⁴ καὶ τελέσειν . . . ὑπέσχετο B : καὶ τέλος ἀπῆει τὴν πρεσβείαν ὑπὲρ τῆς πατρίδος ποιησομένη ἣν ὑπέσχετο R.

⁵ γνωμηδὸν ἐπυνθάνοντο O : γνώμας διεπυνθάνοντο Cobet.

4 λευόμενοι.[1] οἱ μὲν γὰρ οὐ μικρὸν ἀπέφαινον εἶναι
τῇ πόλει κινδύνευμα γυναῖκας ἅμα τέκνοις εἰς
πολεμίων στρατόπεδον πορευομένας ἐᾶσαι· εἰ γὰρ
αὐτοῖς ὑπεριδοῦσα τῶν νενομισμένων ὁσίων περί
τε πρεσβείας καὶ ἱκεσίας δόξειε μηκέτι προΐεσθαι
τὰς γυναῖκας, ἀμαχητὶ σφῶν ἁλώσεσθαι τὴν πόλιν·
ἠξίουν τε αὐτὰς μόνον ἐᾶσαι τὰς προσηκούσας τῷ
Μαρκίῳ γυναῖκας ἅμα τοῖς τέκνοις αὐτοῦ πορευομένας. ἕτεροι δ᾽ οὐδὲ ταύταις ᾤοντο δεῖν ἐπιτρέπειν τὴν ἔξοδον, ἐπιμελῶς δὲ καὶ ταύτας παρῄνουν φυλάττειν, ὅμηρα νομίσαντας ἔχειν παρὰ τῶν
πολεμίων ἐχέγγυα τοῦ μηδὲν τὴν πόλιν ἀνήκεστον
5 ὑπ᾽ αὐτῶν παθεῖν. οἱ δὲ πάσαις συνεβούλευον συγ-
χωρῆσαι ταῖς βουλομέναις γυναιξὶ τὴν ἔξοδον, ἵνα
σὺν μείζονι ἀξιώματι αἱ τῷ Μαρκίῳ προσήκουσαι
ποιήσωνται τὴν ὑπὲρ τῆς πατρίδος δέησιν. τοῦ δὲ
μηθὲν αὐταῖς συμβήσεσθαι δεινὸν ἐγγυητὰς ἀπέφαινον ἐσομένους θεοὺς μὲν πρῶτον οἷς καθοσιω-
θεῖσαι τὰς ἱκεσίας ποιήσονται· ἔπειτα τὸν ἄνδρα
αὐτὸν πρὸς ὃν ἔμελλον πορεύεσθαι, πάσης ἀδίκου
τε καὶ ἀνοσίου πράξεως καθαρὸν καὶ ἀμίαντον
6 ἐσχηκότα τὸν βίον. ἐνίκα δ᾽ ὅμως ἡ συγχωροῦσα
γνώμη ταῖς γυναιξὶ τὴν ἔξοδον, μέγιστον ἀμφοῖν
ἐγκώμιον ἔχουσα, τῆς μὲν βουλῆς τοῦ φρονίμου,
ὅτι κράτιστα τὰ[2] γενησόμενα προείδετο οὐδὲν ὑπὸ
τοῦ κινδύνου τηλικούδε ὄντος ἐπιταραχθεῖσα, τοῦ
δὲ Μαρκίου τῆς εὐσεβείας, ὅτι πολέμιος ὢν ἐπι-
στεύετο μηδὲν ἀσεβήσειν εἰς τὸ ἀσθενέστατον τῆς
7 πόλεως μέρος κύριος αὐτοῦ καταστάς. ὡς δὲ τὸ

---

[1] ὅ τι χρὴ ποιεῖν βουλευόμενοι ACb : ἀποροῦντες ὅτι χρὴ
ποιεῖν R (?).

126

the evening what they ought to do. For some argued
that it was no small risk to the commonwealth to
permit the women with the children to go to the
enemy's camp ; for if the Volscians, in contempt of
the recognized rights of ambassadors and suppliants,
should decide not to let them go afterwards, their
city would be taken without a blow. These men,
therefore, advised permitting only the women who
were related to Marcius to go, accompanied by his
children. Others believed that not even these should
be allowed to go out, and advised that they too
should be carefully guarded, considering that in them
they had hostages from the enemy, to secure the city
from suffering any irreparable injury at their hands.
Still others advised giving leave to all the women to
go who so desired, in order that the kinswomen of
Marcius might intercede more impressively for their
country ; and to insure that no harm should befall
them, they said they would have as sureties, first,
the gods, to whom the women would be consecrated
before making their petition, and next, the man
himself to whom they were going, who had kept his
life pure and unstained by any act of injustice or
impiety. However, the proposal to allow the women
to go prevailed, implying a great compliment to both
parties—to the senate for its wisdom, in that it perceived best what was going to happen, without being
disquieted at all by the danger, though it was so great,
and to Marcius for his piety, inasmuch as it was not
believed that he would, even though an enemy, do
anything impious toward the weakest element of the
state when he should have them in his power. After

---

[2] κράτιστα τὰ Sintenis : κράτιστα καὶ B, τὰ κράτιστα καὶ A,
Jacoby.

προβούλευμα ἐγράφη, προελθόντες οἱ ὕπατοι εἰς
τὴν ἀγορὰν καὶ συναγαγόντες ἐκκλησίαν σκότους
ὄντος ἤδη τὰ δόξαντα τῷ συνεδρίῳ διεσάφησαν καὶ
προεῖπον ἥκειν ἅπαντας ἕωθεν ἐπὶ τὰς πύλας
προπέμψοντας ἐξιούσας τὰς γυναῖκας· αὐτοὶ δὲ τῶν
κατεπειγόντων ἔλεγον ἐπιμελήσεσθαι.

XLIV. Ὅτε δ' ἤδη περὶ τὸν ὄρθρον ἦν, αἱ μὲν
γυναῖκες ἄγουσαι τὰ παιδία μετὰ λαμπάδων ἦκον
ἐπὶ τὴν οἰκίαν καὶ παραλαβοῦσαι τὴν Οὐετουρίαν
προῆγον ἐπὶ τὰς πύλας· οἱ δ' ὕπατοι ζεύγη τε
ὁρικὰ καὶ ἁμάξας καὶ τἆλλα πορεῖα[1] ὡς πλεῖστα
παρασκευασάμενοι καθεζομένας αὐτὰς προὔπεμπον
ἄχρι πολλοῦ. παρηκολούθουν δ' αὐταῖς οἵ τε ἐκ
τοῦ συνεδρίου καὶ τῶν ἄλλων πολιτῶν συχνοὶ σὺν
εὐχαῖς καὶ ἐπαίνοις καὶ δεήσεσι[2] τὴν ἔξοδον ἐπι-
2 φανεστέραν αὐταῖς ποιοῦντες. ὡς δ' εὐσύνοπτοι
πόρρωθεν ἔτι προσιοῦσαι τοῖς ἐκ τοῦ χάρακος αἱ
γυναῖκες ἐγένοντο, πέμπει τῶν ἱππέων τινὰς ὁ
Μάρκιος κελεύσας μαθεῖν τίς ἐστιν ὁ προσιὼν ὄχλος
ἐκ τῆς πόλεως, καὶ ἐπὶ τί παραγένοιντο. μαθὼν δὲ
παρ' αὐτῶν ὅτι Ῥωμαίων αἱ γυναῖκες ἥκουσιν
ἐπαγόμεναι παιδία, προηγεῖται δ' αὐτῶν ἥ τε μήτηρ
καὶ ἡ γυνὴ αὐτοῦ καὶ τὰ τέκνα, πρῶτον μὲν ἐθαύμα-
σε τῆς τόλμης τὰς γυναῖκας, εἰ γνώμην ἔσχον
εἰς χάρακα πολεμίων ἄτερ ἀνδρῶν φυλακῆς ἐλθεῖν
ἄγουσαι τὰ τέκνα, οὔτε αἰδοῦς ἔτι τῆς ἁρμοττούσης
γυναιξὶν ἐλευθέραις καὶ σώφροσι προνοούμεναι τὸ[3]
μὴ ἐν ἀνδράσιν ἀσυνήθεσιν ὁρᾶσθαι, οὔτε κινδύνων
λαβοῦσαι δέος οὓς ἀναρριπτεῖν ἔμελλον, εἰ τὰ
συμφέροντα πρὸ τῶν δικαίων ἑλομένοις σφίσι

---

[1] Cobet : φορεῖα O, Jacoby.
[2] Reiske : δεήσει O.

the decree had been drawn up, the consuls proceeded to the Forum, and summoning an assembly when it was already dark, announced the senate's decision and gave notice that all should come early the next morning to the gates to accompany the women when they went out ; and they said that they themselves would attend to all urgent business.

XLIV. When it was now break of day, the women, leading the children, went with torches to the house of Veturia, and taking her with them, proceeded to the gates. In the meantime the consuls, having got ready spans of mules, carts, and a great many other conveyances, seated the women in them and accompanied them for a long distance. The women were attended by the senators and many other citizens, who by their vows, commendations and entreaties lent distinction to their mission. As soon as the women, while still approaching at a distance, could be clearly seen by those in the camp, Marcius sent some horsemen with orders to learn what multitude it was that advanced from the city and what was the occasion of their coming. And being informed that the wives of the Romans together with their children had come to him and that they were led by his mother, his wife and his sons, he was at first astonished at the assurance of the women in resolving to come with their children into an enemy's camp without a guard of men, neither showing regard any longer for the modesty becoming to free-born and virtuous women, which forbids them to be seen by men who are strangers, nor becoming alarmed at the dangers which they would run if his soldiers, preferring their

---

³ τὸ O : τοῦ Sylburg. Naber would reject τὸ μὴ . . . ὁρᾶσθαι as a gloss.

δόξειε κέρδος αὐτὰς ποιήσασθαι καὶ ὠφέλειαν.
3 ἐπεὶ δ' ἀγχοῦ ἦσαν, ὑπαντᾶν τῇ μητρὶ προελθὼν
ἐκ τοῦ χάρακος ἔγνω σὺν ὀλίγοις, τούς τε πελέκεις,
οὓς προηγεῖσθαι τῶν στρατηγῶν ἔθος ἦν, ἀποθέσθαι κελεύσας τοῖς ὑπηρέταις, καὶ τὰς ῥάβδους,
ὅταν ἐγγὺς τῆς μητρὸς γένηται, καταστεῖλαι.
4 ταῦτα δὲ Ῥωμαίοις ἐστὶ ποιεῖν ἔθος ὅταν ὑπαντῶσι
ταῖς μείζοσιν ἀρχαῖς οἱ τὰς ἐλάττους ἀρχὰς ἔχοντες,
ὡς καὶ[1] μέχρι τοῦ καθ' ἡμᾶς χρόνου γίνεται· ἦν δὴ
τότε συνήθειαν φυλάττων ὁ Μάρκιος, ὡς ἐξουσίᾳ
μείζονι μέλλων εἰς ταὐτὸ ἥξειν, πάντα ἀπέθετο τὰ
τῆς ἰδίας παράσημα ἀρχῆς. τοσαύτη περὶ αὐτὸν
ἦν αἰδὼς καὶ πρόνοια τῆς πρὸς τὸ γένος εὐσεβείας.

XLV. Ἐπεὶ δὲ σύνεγγυς ἀλλήλων ἐγένοντο,
πρώτη μὲν αὐτῷ δεξιωσομένη προσῆλθεν ἡ μήτηρ
πένθιμά τε ἠμφιεσμένη τρύχη καὶ τὰς ὁράσεις
ἐκτετηκυῖα ὑπὸ τῶν δακρύων, ἐλεεινὴ σφόδρα. ἦν
ὁ Μάρκιος ἰδών, ἄτεγκτος τέως καὶ στερρός, οἷος
ἅπασι τοῖς ἀνιαροῖς ἀντέχειν, οὐθὲν ἔτι τῶν λελογισ-
μένων φυλάττειν ἱκανὸς ἦν, ἀλλ' ᾤχετο φερόμενος
ὑπὸ τῶν παθῶν ἐπὶ τὸ ἀνθρώπινον, καὶ περιβαλὼν
αὐτὴν ἠσπάζετο καὶ ταῖς ἡδίσταις φωναῖς ἀνεκάλει
καὶ μέχρι πολλοῦ κλαίων τε καὶ περιέπων κατεῖχεν
ἐκλελυμένην καὶ ῥέουσαν ἐπὶ τὴν γῆν. ὡς δὲ τῶν
ἀσπασμῶν τῆς μητρὸς ἅλις εἶχε, τὴν γυναῖκα
προσελθοῦσαν[2] δεξιωσάμενος ἅμα τοῖς τέκνοις εἶ-
2 πεν· '' Ἀγαθῆς γυναικὸς ἔργον ἐποίησας, ὦ Οὐολουμνία, μείνασα παρὰ τῇ μητρί μου καὶ οὐκ
ἐγκαταλιποῦσα τὴν ἐρημίαν αὐτῆς, ἐμοί τε[3] πασῶν
ἡδίστην κεχάρισαι δωρεάν.'' μετὰ ταῦτα τῶν παι-

---

[1] καὶ added by Reiske.   [2] προσελθοῦσαν B : om. R.
[3] ἐμοί τε Kiessling : ἔμοιγε O, Jacoby.

own interests to justice, should think fit to make a profit and advantage of them. But when they were near, he resolved to go out of the camp with a few of his men and to meet his mother, after first ordering his lictors to lay aside the axes which were customarily carried before generals, and when he should come near his mother, to lower the rods. This is a custom observed by the Romans when inferior magistrates meet those who are their superiors, which continues even to our time ; and it was in observance of this custom that Marcius, as if he were going to meet a superior power, now laid aside all the insignia of his own office. So great was his reverence and his concern to show his veneration for the tie of kinship.

XLV. When they came near to one another, his mother was the first to advance toward him to greet him, clad in rent garments of mourning and with her eyes melting in tears, an object of great compassion. Upon seeing her, Marcius, who till then had been hard-hearted and stern enough to cope with any distressing situation, could no longer keep any of his resolutions, but was carried away by his emotions into human kindness, and embracing and kissing her, he called her by the most endearing terms, and supported her for a long time, weeping and caressing her as her strength failed and she sank to the ground. After he had had enough of caressing his mother, he greeted his wife when with their children she approached him, and said : " You have acted the part of a good wife, Volumnia, in living with my mother and not abandoning her in her solitude, and to me you have thereby done the dearest of all favours." After this, drawing each of his children to him, he

δίων ἑκάτερον προσαγόμενος καὶ τοὺς προσήκοντας
ἀσπασμοὺς ἀποδούς, ἐπέστρεψεν αὖθις πρὸς τὴν
μητέρα καὶ λέγειν ἐκέλευσε τίνος δεομένη πάρεστιν.
ἡ δὲ πάντων ἀκουόντων ἔφησεν ἐρεῖν, οὐθενὸς γὰρ
ἀνοσίου δεήσεσθαι, παρεκάλει τε αὐτόν, ἐν ᾧ
καθεζόμενος εἰώθει χωρίῳ δικάζειν τοῖς ὄχλοις, ἐν
3 τούτῳ καθίσαι. καὶ ὁ Μάρκιος ἀσμένως τὸ ῥηθὲν
ἐδέξατο ὡς δὴ περιουσίᾳ τε πολλῇ[1] τῶν δικαίων
πρὸς τὴν ἔντευξιν αὐτῆς χρησόμενος καὶ ἐν καλῷ
ποιησόμενος[2] τοῖς ὄχλοις τὴν ἀπόκρισιν. ἐλθὼν δ᾽
ἐπὶ τὸ στρατηγικὸν βῆμα πρῶτον μὲν ἐκέλευσε τοῖς
ὑπηρέταις καθελεῖν ἀπ᾽ αὐτοῦ τὸν δίφρον καὶ θεῖναι
χαμαί, μητρὸς ὑψηλότερον οὐκ οἰόμενος δεῖν τόπον
ἔχειν οὐδ᾽ ἐξουσίᾳ χρῆσθαι κατ᾽ ἐκείνης οὐδεμιᾷ·
ἔπειτα παρακαθισάμενος τοὺς ἐπιφανεστάτους τῶν
τε ἡγεμόνων καὶ λοχαγῶν, καὶ τῶν ἄλλων ἐάσας
παρεῖναι τὸν βουλόμενον, ἐκέλευσε τὴν μητέρα
λέγειν.

XLVI. Καὶ ἡ Οὐετουρία παραστησαμένη τήν τε
γυναῖκα τοῦ Μαρκίου καὶ τὰ τέκνα καὶ τὰς ἐπι-
φανεστάτας τῶν ἐν Ῥώμῃ γυναικῶν πρῶτον μὲν
ἔκλαιεν εἰς τὴν γῆν ὁρῶσα μέχρι πολλοῦ, καὶ πολὺν
ἐκίνησεν ἐκ τῶν παρόντων ἔλεον. ἔπειτα ἀνα-
2 λαβοῦσα αὑτὴν ἔλεξεν· " Αἱ γυναῖκες, ὦ Μάρκιε
τέκνον,[3] τὰς ὕβρεις ἐνθυμούμεναι καὶ τὰς ἄλλας
συμφορὰς τὰς συμβησομένας αὐταῖς ἐὰν ἡ πόλις
ἡμῶν ὑπὸ τοῖς πολεμίοις γένηται, πᾶσαν ἄλλην
ἀπογνοῦσαι βοήθειαν, ἐπειδὴ τοῖς ἀνδράσιν αὐτῶν
ἀξιοῦσι διαλύσασθαι τὸν πόλεμον αὐθάδεις καὶ

---

[1] πολλῇ B : om. R.

gave them a father's caresses, and then, turning again to his mother, begged her to state what she had come to ask of him. She answered that she would speak out in the presence of all, since she had no impious request to make of him, and bade him be seated where he was wont to sit when administering justice to his troops. Marcius willingly agreed to her proposal, thinking, naturally, that he should have a great abundance of just arguments to use in combating his mother's intercession and that he should be giving his answer where it was convenient for the troops to hear. When he came to the general's tribunal, he first ordered the lictors to remove the seat that stood there and to place it on the ground, since he thought he ought not to occupy a higher position than his mother or use against her any official authority. Then, causing the most prominent of the commanders and captains to sit by him and permitting any others to be present who wished, he bade his mother speak.

XLVI. Thereupon Veturia, having placed the wife of Marcius with his children and the most prominent of the Roman matrons near her, first wept, fixing her eyes on the ground for a long time, and roused great compassion in all who were present. Then, recovering herself, she said : " These women, Marcius, my son, mindful of the outrages and other calamities which will come upon them if our city falls into the power of the enemy, and despairing of all other assistance, since you gave haughty and harsh answers to their husbands when they asked you to end the

---

² Casaubon : ποιούμενος O, Jacoby.
³ ὦ Μάρκιε τέκνον (or ὦ τέκνον) Kiessling : ὦ τέκνον Μάρκιε O.

σκληρὰς ἔδωκας ἀποκρίσεις, ἄγουσαι τὰ τέκνα καὶ
τοῖς πενθίμοις τούτοις ἠμφιεσμέναι τρύχεσι κατέφυγον ἐπ' ἐμέ, τὴν σὴν μητέρα, καὶ Οὐολουμνίαν,
τὴν σὴν γυναῖκα, δεόμεναι μὴ περιιδεῖν αὐτὰς τὰ
μέγιστα τῶν ἐν ἀνθρώποις κακῶν ὑπὸ σοῦ παθού-
σας, οὐθὲν μὲν οὔτε μεῖζον οὔτ' ἔλαττον εἰς ἡμᾶς
ἐξαμαρτούσαι, πολλὴν δὲ καί, ὅτ' εὐτυχοῦμεν,
εὔνοιαν ἔτι παρασχόμεναι, καί, ὅτ' ἐπταίσαμεν,
3 συμπάθειαν. ἔχομεν γὰρ αὐταῖς μαρτυρεῖν, ἐξ οὗ
σὺ ἀπῆρας ἐκ τῆς πατρίδος, ἡμεῖς δ' ἔρημοι καὶ
τὸ μηθὲν ἔτι οὖσαι κατελειπόμεθα, συνεχῶς τε
παραγινομέναις πρὸς ἡμᾶς καὶ παραμυθουμέναις
τὰς συμφορὰς[1] ἡμῶν καὶ συναλγούσαις.[2] τούτων
δὴ λαμβάνουσαι μνήμην ἐγώ τε καὶ ἡ σὴ γυνὴ ἡ[3]
συνοικουροῦσα μετ' ἐμοῦ τὰς ἱκεσίας αὐτῶν οὐκ
ἀπεστράφημεν, ἀλλ' ὑπεμείναμεν, ὡς ἠξίουν ἡμᾶς,
ἐλθεῖν ἐπὶ σὲ καὶ τὰς ὑπὲρ τῆς πατρίδος ποιήσασθαι δεήσεις.''

XLVII. Ἔτι δ' αὐτῆς λεγούσης ὑπολαβὼν ὁ
Μάρκιος εἶπεν· ''Ἀδυνάτων δεομένη, μῆτερ,
ἐλήλυθας ἀξιοῦσα προδοῦναί με τοῖς ἐκβαλοῦσι
τοὺς ὑποδεξαμένους, καὶ τοῖς ἅπαντά με ἀφελο-
μένοις τὰ ἐμαυτοῦ τοὺς χαρισαμένους τὰ μέγιστα
τῶν ἐν ἀνθρώποις ἀγαθῶν· οἷς ἐγὼ τὴν ἀρχὴν
τήνδε παραλαμβάνων θεούς τε καὶ δαίμονας ἐγγυητὰς ἔδωκα μήτε προδώσειν τὸ κοινὸν αὐτῶν μήτε
προκαταλύσεσθαι τὸν πόλεμον ἐὰν μὴ Οὐολούσκοις
2 ἅπασι δοκῇ. θεούς τε δὴ σεβόμενος οὓς ὤμοσα, καὶ
ἀνθρώπους αἰδούμενος οἷς τὰς πίστεις ἔδωκα,
πολεμήσω Ῥωμαίοις ἄχρι τέλους. ἐὰν δ' ἀποδιδῶσι

---

[1] παραγινομέναις πρὸς ἡμᾶς καὶ παραμυθουμέναις τὰς συμφορὰς A : παραγινομέναις ταῖς συμφοραῖς B.

war, took their children, and clad in these rent garments of mourning, turned for refuge to me, your mother, and to Volumnia, your wife, begging us not to permit them to suffer the greatest of all human evils at your hands, as they have never done us any injury, great or slight, but showed much affection for us while we were still prosperous, and compassion when we met with adversity. For we can bear them witness that since you withdrew from your country and we were left desolate and no longer of any account, they constantly visited us, alleviated our misfortunes, and condoled with us. So, remembering all this, neither I nor your wife, who lives with me, rejected their entreaties, but brought ourselves to come to you, as they asked, and to make our supplications in behalf of our country.''

XLVII. While she was yet speaking Marcius interrupted her and said : '' You have come demanding the impossible, mother, when you ask me to betray to those who have cast me out those who have received me, and to those who have deprived me of all my possessions those who have conferred on me the greatest of human blessings—men to whom, when I accepted this command, I gave the gods and other divinities as sureties that I would neither betray their state nor end the war unless all the Volscians agreed to do so. Both out of reverence, then, for the gods by whom I swore and out of respect for the men to whom I gave my pledges I shall continue to make war upon the Romans to the last. But if they will

---

[2] καὶ τὰς συμφορὰς ἡμῶν συναλγούσαις C, καὶ ταῖς συμφοραῖς ἡμῶν συναλγούσαις Cobet.   [3] ἡ added by Reiske.

τὴν χώραν Οὐολούσκοις ἣν κατέχουσιν αὐτῶν βίᾳ,
καὶ φίλους αὐτοὺς[1] ποιήσωνται πάντων αὐτοῖς
μεταδιδόντες τῶν ἴσων ὥσπερ Λατίνοις, διαλύσο
3 μαι τὸν πρὸς αὐτοὺς πόλεμον, ἄλλως δ' οὔ. ὑμεῖς
μὲν οὖν, ὦ γυναῖκες, ἄπιτε καὶ λέγετε τοῖς ἀνδράσι
ταῦτα καὶ πείθετε αὐτοὺς μὴ φιλοχωρεῖν τοῖς
ἀλλοτρίοις ἀδίκως, ἀλλ' ἀγαπᾶν ἐὰν τὰ ἑαυτῶν
ἔχειν τις αὐτοὺς[1] ἐᾷ, μηδ', ὅτι πολέμῳ λαβόντες
ἔχουσι τὰ Οὐολούσκων, περιμένειν ἕως πολέμῳ
πάλιν αὐτὰ ὑπὸ τούτων ἀφαιρεθῶσιν. οὐ γὰρ ἀπο
χρήσει τοῖς κρατοῦσι τὰ ἑαυτῶν μόνον ἀπολαβεῖν,
ἀλλὰ καὶ τὰ τῶν κρατηθέντων ἴδια ἀξιώσουσιν
ἔχειν. ἐὰν δὲ περιεχόμενοι τῶν μηθὲν αὐτοῖς προσ
ηκόντων πᾶν ὁτιοῦν πάσχειν ὑπομένωσι φυλάτ
τοντες τὸ αὔθαδες, ἐκείνους αἰτιάσεσθε[2] τῶν κατα
ληψομένων κακῶν, οὐ Μάρκιον οὐδὲ Οὐολούσκους
4 οὐδ' ἄλλον[3] ἀνθρώπων οὐδένα. σοῦ δέ, ὦ μῆτερ,
ἐν μέρει πάλιν υἱὸς ὢν ἐγὼ δέομαι μή με[4] παρα
καλεῖν εἰς ἀνοσίους πράξεις καὶ ἀδίκους, μηδὲ
μετὰ τῶν ἐχθίστων ἐμοί τε καὶ σεαυτῇ τεταγμένην
πολεμίους ἡγεῖσθαι τοὺς ἀναγκαιοτάτους· ἀλλὰ
παρ' ἐμοὶ γενομένην, ὥσπερ ἐστὶ δίκαιον, πατρίδα
τε νέμειν ἣν ἐγὼ νέμω, καὶ οἶκον[5] ὃν ἐγὼ κέκτημαι,
τιμάς τε καρποῦσθαι τὰς ἐμὰς καὶ δόξης ἀπολαύειν
τῆς ἐμῆς, τοὺς αὐτοὺς ἡγουμένην φίλους τε καὶ
πολεμίους[6] οὕσπερ ἐγώ· ἀποθέσθαι τε ἤδη τὸ
πένθος ὃ διὰ τὰς ἐμὰς ὑπέμεινας, ὦ ταλαίπωρε,

<hr />

[1] αὐτοὺς B : om. R.
[2] Cobet, Jacoby : αἰτιᾶσθε O.
[3] οὐδ' ἄλλον Ba : οὐδ' ἄλλων ABb, οὐδὲ τῶν ἄλλων Cobet,
Jacoby.   [4] με added by Kiessling.

restore to the Volscians the lands of theirs which they
hold by force, and will make them their friends,
giving them an equal share in all privileges as they
have to the Latins, I will put an end to the war
against them, otherwise not. As for you women,
then, depart and carry this word to your husbands ;
and persuade them to cease their unjust fondness for
the possessions of others and to be content if they are
permitted to keep what is their own, and not, just
because they now hold the possessions of the Volscians which they took in war, to wait till they are in
turn deprived of them in war by the Volscians. For
the conquerors will not be satisfied with merely recovering their own possessions, but will think themselves
entitled also to those that belong to the conquered.
And if, by clinging to what is not theirs at all, the
Romans persist in their arrogance and are willing to
suffer anything whatever, you will impute to them,
rather than to Marcius, the Volscians or anyone else,
the blame for the miseries that shall befall them. And
of you, mother, I, who am your son, beg in my turn
that you will not urge me to wicked and unjust
actions, nor, ranging yourself on the side of those
who are the bitterest foes both to me and to yourself,
regard as enemies your nearest of kin, but that,
taking your place at my side, as is right, you will
make the land where I dwell your fatherland, and
your home the house I have acquired, and that you
will enjoy my honours and share in my glory, looking
upon my friends and enemies as your own ; also that
you will lay aside at last the mourning which, un-

---

⁵ Reiske proposed to add κεκτῆσθαι after οἶκον. Capps
would read οἶκον οἰκεῖν.

⁶ καὶ πολεμίους B : καὶ συγγενεῖς καὶ πολεμίους R.

φυγάς, καὶ παύσασθαι τιμωρουμένην με τῷ σχή-
5 ματι τούτῳ. ἐμοὶ γὰρ τὰ μὲν ἄλλα, ὦ μῆτερ,
ἀγαθὰ κρείττονα ἐλπίδων καὶ μείζονα εὐχῆς παρὰ
θεῶν τε καὶ ἀνθρώπων ἀπήντηται, ἡ δὲ περὶ σοῦ
φροντίς, ᾗ τὰς γηροβοσκοὺς οὐκ ἀπέδωκα χάριτας,
ἐντετηκυῖα τοῖς σπλάγχνοις πικρὸν πεποίηκε¹ καὶ
ἀνόνητον ἁπάντων τῶν ἀγαθῶν τὸν βίον. εἰ δὲ
σὺν ἐμοὶ τάξεις σεαυτὴν καὶ τῶν ἐμῶν κοινωνεῖν
ἐθελήσεις ἁπάντων, οὐθενός ἔτι μοι δεήσει τῶν
ἀνθρωπίνων ἀγαθῶν.''

XLVIII. Παυσαμένου δ' αὐτοῦ μικρὸν ἡ Οὐετουρία ἐπισχοῦσα χρόνον, ἕως ὁ τῶν περιεστηκότων
ἔπαινος ἐπαύσατο πολύς τε καὶ μέχρι πολλοῦ
γενόμενος, λέγει πρὸς αὐτόν·
''Ἀλλ' ἔγωγέ σε, ὦ Μάρκιε τέκνον, οὔτε προδότην Οὐολούσκων γενέσθαι ἀξιῶ, οἵ σε φεύγοντα
ὑποδεξάμενοι τοῖς τε ἄλλοις ἐτίμησαν καὶ τὴν ἑαυτῶν ἡγεμονίαν ἐπίστευσαν, οὔτε παρὰ τὰς ὁμολογίας καὶ τοὺς ὅρκους οὓς ἔδωκας αὐτοῖς ὅτε τὰς
δυνάμεις παρελάμβανες, ἄνευ κοινῆς γνώμης ἰδίᾳ
καταλύσασθαι τὴν ἔχθραν βούλομαι· μηδ' ὑπολάβῃς
τὴν σεαυτοῦ μητέρα τοσαύτης ἀναπεπλῆσθαι θεο-
βλαβείας, ὥστε τὸν ἀγαπητὸν καὶ μόνον υἱὸν εἰς
2 αἰσχρὰς καὶ ἀνοσίους πράξεις παρακαλεῖν. ἀλλὰ
μετὰ κοινῆς γνώμης ἀποστῆναί σε ἀξιῶ τοῦ πολέμου, πείσαντα τοὺς Οὐολούσκους μετριάσαι περὶ
τὰς διαλλαγὰς καὶ ποιήσασθαι τὴν εἰρήνην ἀμφοτέροις τοῖς ἔθνεσι καλὴν καὶ πρέπουσαν. τοῦτο δὲ
γένοιτ' ἄν, εἰ νῦν μὲν ἀναστήσας τὴν στρατιὰν
ἀπαγάγοις ἐνιαυσίους ποιησάμενος ἀνοχάς, ἐν δὲ
τῷ μεταξὺ χρόνῳ πρέσβεις ἀποστέλλων τε καὶ

¹ Post : ἐποίει O, Jacoby.

happy woman, you have endured because of my banishment, and cease to avenge yourself upon me by this garb. For though all other blessings, mother, have been conferred on me both by the gods and men above my hopes and beyond my prayers, yet the concern I have felt for you, whose old age I have not cherished in return for all your pains, has so sunk into my inmost being as to render my life bitter and incapable of enjoying all my blessings. But if you will take your place by my side and consent to share all I possess, no longer will any of the blessings which fall to the lot of man be lacking to me."

XLVIII. When he had ended, Veturia, after waiting a short time till the great and long-continued applause of the bystanders ceased, spoke to him as follows :

"But I, Marcius, my son, neither ask you to become a traitor to the Volscians who received you when an exile and, among other honours, entrusted you with the command of their army, nor do I desire that, contrary to the agreements and to the sworn pledges you gave them when you took command of their forces, you should arbitrarily, without the general consent, put an end to enmity. And do not imagine that your mother has been filled with such fatuousness as to urge her dear and only son to shameful and wicked actions. On the contrary, I ask you to withdraw from the war only with the general consent of the Volscians, after you have persuaded them to use moderation with regard to an accommodation and to make such a peace as shall be honourable and seemly for both nations. This may be done if you will now withdraw your forces, first making a truce for a year, and will in the meantime, by sending and receiving

δεχόμενος ἀληθῆ φιλίαν πράττοις καὶ διαλλαγὰς
3 βεβαίας. καὶ εὖ ἴσθι· Ῥωμαῖοι μέν, ὅσα μήτε τὸ
ἀδύνατον μήτε ἄλλη τις ἀδοξία προσοῦσα[1] κωλύσει,
πάντα ὑπομενοῦσι πράττειν λόγῳ καὶ παρακλήσει
πειθόμενοι, ἀναγκαζόμενοι δ᾽, ὥσπερ σὺ νῦν ἀξιοῖς,
οὐθὲν ἂν πώποτε χαρίσαιντο ὑμῖν οὔτε μεῖζον οὔτ᾽
ἔλαττον, ὡς ἐξ ἄλλων τε πολλῶν πάρεστί σοι
καταμαθεῖν καὶ τὰ τελευταῖα ἐξ ὧν Λατίνοις
συνεχώρησαν ἀποστᾶσιν ἀπὸ τῶν ὅπλων. Οὐολοῦσκοι δὲ πολὺ τὸ αὔθαδες ἔχουσιν, ὃ συμβαίνει
4 τοῖς μεγάλα εὐτυχήσασιν· ἐὰν δὲ[2] διδάσκῃς αὐτοὺς
ὅτι πᾶσα μὲν εἰρήνη παντός ἐστι πολέμου κρείττων,
σύμβασις δὲ φίλων κατὰ τὸν ἑκούσιον γινομένη
τρόπον τῶν ὑπ᾽ ἀνάγκης συγχωρηθέντων βεβαιο-
τέρα, καὶ ὅτι σωφρόνων ἐστὶν ἀνθρώπων, ὅταν μὲν
εὖ πράττειν δοκῶσι, ταμιεύεσθαι τὰς τύχας, ὅταν
δ᾽ εἰς ταπεινὰς καὶ φαύλας ἔλθωσι, μηθὲν ὑπομένειν
ἀγεννές, καὶ τἆλλα ὅσα εἰς ἡμερότητα καὶ ἐπι-
είκειαν ἐπαγωγὰ παιδεύματα εὕρηται λόγων, οὓς
ὑμεῖς οἱ τὰ πολιτικὰ πράττοντες μάλιστ᾽ ἐπίστασθε,[3] εὖ ἴσθ᾽[4] ὅτι τοῦ τε αὐχήματος ἐφ᾽ οὗ νῦν
εἰσιν ἑκόντες ὑποβήσονται, καὶ ποιήσουσιν ἐξουσίαν
σοι τοῦ πράττειν ὅ τι ἂν αὐτοῖς ὑπολαμβάνῃς
5 συνοίσειν. ἐὰν δ᾽ ἀντιπράττωσί σοι καὶ τοὺς λόγους μὴ προσδέχωνται, ταῖς διὰ σὲ καὶ διὰ τὴν

[1] προσοῦσα B : προσπεσοῦσα AC.
[2] δὲ added by Sylburg.
[3] ἐπίστασθε added by Jacoby, προχείρους ἔχετε by Reiske,
ἔχετε διὰ στόμα by Capps, σπουδάζετε (or ἀσκεῖτε) by Sintenis.
[4] εὖ ἴσθ᾽ (ἴσθι) Reiske, ἴσθι Sintenis : ἴστε O, Jacoby.

[1] The verb of this relative clause is wanting in the MSS.:

ambassadors, work to bring about a genuine friendship and a firm reconciliation. And be well assured of this : the Romans, in so far as no impossible condition or any dishonour attaching to the terms prevents, will consent to perform them all if won over by persuasion and exhortation, but if compulsion is attempted, as you now think proper, they will never make any concession, great or small, to please you, as you may learn from many other instances and particularly from the concessions they recently made to the Latins after these had laid down their arms. As to the Volscians, on the other hand, their arrogance is now great, as happens to all who have met with signal success ; but if you point out to them that ' any peace is preferable to any war,' that ' a voluntary agreement between friends is more secure than concessions extorted by necessity,' and that ' it is the part of wise men, when they seem to be prosperous, to husband their good fortune, but when their fortunes become low and paltry, to submit to nothing that is ignoble,' and if you make use of such other instructive maxims conducive to moderation and reasonableness as have been devised, maxims with which you politicians in particular are familiar,[1] be assured that they will voluntarily recede from their present boastfulness and give you authority to do anything you believe will be to their advantage. But if they oppose you and refuse to accept your proposals, being elated by the successes they have

see the critical note. The translation follows Jacoby's emendation—literally, " which you politicians more than anyone understand." The proposal of Reiske means " which you . . . have ready at hand " ; that of Capps, " which you . . . have at your tongues' end " ; that of Sintenis, " which you . . . cultivate (or practise)."

ἡγεμονίαν τὴν σὴν γενομέναις περὶ αὐτοὺς τύχαις
ὡς ἀεὶ διαμενούσαις ἐπαιρόμενοι, τῆς στρατηγίας
αὐτοῖς ἀφίστασο φανερῶς, καὶ μήτε προδότης γίνου
τῶν πεπιστευκότων μήτε πολέμιος τῶν ἀναγκαιο-
τάτων· ἀσεβὲς γὰρ ἑκάτερον. ταῦτα ἥκω δεομένη
σου γενέσθαι μοι παρὰ σοῦ, Μάρκιε τέκνον, οὔτε
ἀδύνατα, ὡς σὺ φῄς, πάσης τε ἀδίκου καὶ ἀνοσίου
συνειδήσεως καθαρά.

XLIX. " Φέρε, ἀλλὰ δόξαν αἰσχρὰν οἴσεσθαι
δέδοικας, ἐὰν ἃ παρακαλῶ σε πράττῃς, ὡς ἀχάρισ-
τος εἰς τοὺς εὐεργέτας ἐξελεγχθησόμενος, οἵ σε
πολέμιον ὄντα ὑποδεξάμενοι πάντων μετέδωκαν ὧν
τοῖς φύσει πολίταις μέτεστιν ἀγαθῶν· ταῦτα γάρ
2 ἐστιν ἃ μεγάλα ποιεῖς τοῖς λόγοις ἀεί. οὐκ ἀπο-
δέδωκας οὖν αὐτοῖς πολλὰς καὶ καλὰς ἀμοιβὰς καὶ
νενίκηκας ἀπείρῳ δή τινι μεγέθει καὶ πλήθει[1] χαρί-
των τὰς ἐξ ἐκείνων εὐεργεσίας; οὓς ἀγαπητὸν
ἡγουμένους καὶ πάντων μέγιστον ἀγαθῶν,[2] ἐὰν
ἐλευθέρας οἰκῶσι τὰς πατρίδας, οὐ μόνον ἑαυτῶν
κυρίους εἶναι βεβαίως παρεσκεύακας, ἀλλὰ καὶ[3]
πεποίηκας ἤδη σκοπεῖν πότερα καταλῦσαι τὴν
'Ρωμαίων ἀρχὴν αὐτοῖς[4] ἄμεινον ἢ μετέχειν αὐτῆς
3 ἐξ ἴσου κοινὴν καταστησαμένους πολιτείαν. ἐῶ
γὰρ λέγειν ὅσοις κεκόσμηκας ἐκ τοῦ πολέμου
λαφύροις τὰς πόλεις αὐτῶν καὶ πηλίκους κεχάρισαι
τοῖς συστρατευσαμένοις πλούτους. τοὺς δὴ τοσούτους διὰ σὲ γενομένους καὶ ἐπὶ τηλικαύτης βεβη-

---

[1] καὶ πλήθει B : om. R. [2] ἀγαθῶν B : ἀγαθόν R.
[3] καὶ added by Reiske.
[4] ἀρχὴν αὐτοῖς Reiske : αὐτοῖς ἀρχὴν B, ἀρχὴν R.

gained through you and your leadership, as if these
would always continue, resign publicly the command
of their army and make yourself neither a traitor to
those who have trusted you nor an enemy to those
who are nearest to you ; for to do either is impious.
These are the favours I have come begging you to
grant me, Marcius, my son, and they are not only
not impossible to grant, as you assert, but are free
from any consciousness on my part of an unjust or
impious intent.

XLIX. " But come, you are afraid perhaps that if
you do what I urge you will incur a shameful reputation, believing that you will stand convicted of in-
gratitude to your benefactors, who received you, an
enemy, and shared with you all the advantages to
which their native-born citizens are entitled ; for
these are the things you constantly stress in your
remarks. Have you not, then, made them many
fine returns, and have you not by the favours you
have bestowed, well nigh limitless in magnitude and
number, surpassed the kindnesses received from
them ? Though they regarded it as enough and as
the greatest of all blessings if they could continue to
live as freemen in their native cities, you have not
only made them securely their own masters, but have
also brought it about that they are already considering whether it is better for them to destroy the
dominion of the Romans or to have an equal share in
it by forming a joint commonwealth. I say nothing
of all the spoils of war with which you have adorned
their cities nor of the great riches you have bestowed
upon those who accompanied you on your expeditions.
Do you believe that those who through your aid have
become so great and have entered upon such pros-

κότας εὐτυχίας οὐ δοκεῖς ἀγαπήσειν οἷς ἔχουσιν
ἀγαθοῖς, ἀλλ' ὀργιεῖσθαί σοι καὶ ἀγανακτήσειν, ἐὰν
μὴ καὶ τὸ τῆς πατρίδος αἷμα ταῖς χερσὶν αὐτῶν
4 ἐπισπείσῃς; ἐγὼ μὲν οὐκ οἴομαι. εἰς[1] ἔτι μοι
καταλείπεται λόγος, ἰσχυρὸς μέν, ἐὰν λογισμῷ
κρίνῃς αὐτόν, ἀσθενὴς δ', ἐὰν μετ' ὀργῆς, ὁ περὶ
τῆς οὐ δικαίως μισουμένης ὑπὸ σοῦ πατρίδος.
οὔτε γὰρ ὑγιαίνουσα καὶ τῷ πατρίῳ κόσμῳ πολι-
τευομένη τὴν οὐ δικαίαν κατὰ σοῦ κρίσιν ἐξήνεγκεν,
ἀλλὰ νοσοῦσα καὶ ἐν πολλῷ κλύδωνι σαλευομένη,
οὔτε ἅπασα ταύτην τὴν[2] γνώμην τότε ἔσχεν, ἀλλὰ
τὸ κάκιον ἐν αὐτῇ μέρος πονηροῖς προστάταις
5 χρησάμενον. εἰ δὲ δὴ μὴ τοῖς κακίστοις μόνον,
ἀλλὰ καὶ τοῖς ἄλλοις ἅπασιν ἐδόκει ταῦτα, καὶ ὡς
οὐ τὰ κράτιστα πολιτευόμενος ἀπηλάθης ὑπ' αὐτῶν, οὐδ' οὕτω σοι προσῆκε μνησικακεῖν πρὸς τὴν
σεαυτοῦ πατρίδα. πολλοῖς γὰρ δὴ καὶ ἄλλοις τῶν
ἀπὸ τοῦ βελτίστου πολιτευομένων τὰ παραπλήσια
συνέβη παθεῖν· καὶ σπάνιοι δή τινές εἰσιν οἷς οὐκ
ἀντέπνευσε πρὸς τὴν δοκοῦσαν ἀρετὴν φθόνος ἐκ
6 τῶν συμπολιτευομένων ἄδικος.[3] ἀλλ' ἀνθρωπίνως,
ὦ Μάρκιε, φέρουσι καὶ μετρίως ἅπαντες οἱ γενναῖοι
τὰς συμφοράς, καὶ πόλεις μεταλαμβάνουσιν ἐν αἷς
οἰκήσαντες οὐθὲν λυπήσουσι τὰς πατρίδας· ὥσπερ
καὶ Ταρκύνιος ἐποίησεν ὁ Κολλατῖνος ἐπικαλού-
μενος (ἱκανὸν ἓν παράδειγμα καὶ οἰκεῖον),[4] ὃς
συνελευθερώσας ἀπὸ τῶν τυράννων τοὺς πολίτας,

---

[1] εἰς added by Kiessling.
[2] ταύτην τὴν Kiessling : τὴν αὐτὴν O, Jacoby.
[3] ἄδικος B : ἀδίκως R.
[4] This parenthesis rejected by Cobet as spurious; καὶ
omitted in B.

perity will not be content with the blessings they
have, but will be angry with you and indignant if
you do not also spill by their hands your country's
blood? For my part, I do not believe so. I have
still one point left to speak of—a strong one if you
judge of it by reason, but weak if you judge by passion.
I refer to the unjust hatred you bear toward your
country. For the commonwealth was neither in a
state of health nor governed according to the established constitution when she pronounced that unjust
sentence against you, but was diseased and tossed in
a violent tempest; nor did the state as a whole entertain this opinion at that time, but only the baser
element in it, which had followed evil leaders. Yet
supposing not only the worst of the citizens, but all the
rest as well had been of this mind, and you had been
banished by them as not acting for the best interests
of the state, not even in that case did it become you
to bear any resentment against your country. For
it has fallen to the lot of many others, you know,
of those whose policies were prompted by the best
motives, to have the same experience, and few indeed
are those who have not, because of their reputation
for virtue, felt the breath of unjust envy on the part
of their political rivals. But all who are high-minded,
Marcius, bear their misfortunes like men and with
moderation, and remove to other cities in which they
can dwell without causing harm to their fatherland.
This was the case with Tarquinius, surnamed Col-
latinus. (A single instance and one from our own
history will suffice.) [1] He had assisted in freeing his
fellow citizens from the tyrants, but was later accused

---

[1] This parenthetical remark is perhaps due to a scribe.

ἔπειτα διαβληθεὶς πρὸς αὐτοὺς ὡς συμπράττων
πάλιν τοῖς τυράννοις τὴν κάθοδον, καὶ διὰ τοῦτο
ἐξελαθεὶς αὐτὸς ἐκ τῆς πατρίδος, οὐκ ἐμνησικάκει
πρὸς τοὺς ἐκβαλόντας αὐτόν, οὐδ' ἐπεστράτευε τῇ
πόλει τοὺς τυράννους ἐπαγόμενος, οὐδ' ἐποίει
τεκμήρια τῶν διαβολῶν τὰ ἔργα, ἀλλ' εἰς τὴν
μητρόπολιν ἡμῶν Λαουίνιον ἀπελθὼν ἐκεῖ πάντα
τὸν λοιπὸν ἐβίω χρόνον εὔνους ὢν τῇ πατρίδι καὶ
φίλος.

L. " Ἔστω δ' οὖν ὅμως, καὶ δεδόσθω τοῖς τὰ
δεινὰ παθοῦσι μὴ διακρίνειν εἴτε φίλιον εἴη τὸ
κακῶς δεδρακὸς εἴτε ἀλλότριον, ἀλλ' ἴσην πρὸς
ἅπαντας ὀργὴν ἔχειν· ἔπειτα οὐχ ἱκανὰς εἰσπέπραξαι παρὰ τῶν ὑβρισάντων σε δίκας γῆν τε αὐτῶν
τὴν ἀρίστην πεποιηκὼς μηλόβοτον καὶ πόλεις
διαπεπορθηκὼς συμμαχίδας, ἃς πολλοῖς πόνοις
κτησάμενοι κατέσχον,[1] καὶ τρίτον ἤδη τοῦτ' ἔτος
εἰς πολλὴν τῶν ἀναγκαίων κατακεκλεικὼς αὐτοὺς[2]
ἀπορίαν; ἀλλὰ καὶ μέχρι[3] ἀνδραποδισμοῦ τῆς
πόλεως αὐτῶν καὶ κατασκαφῆς τὴν ἀγριαίνουσαν
2 καὶ μαινομένην ὀργὴν προάγεις[4]· καὶ οὐδὲ τοὺς
πεμφθέντας ὑπὸ τῆς βουλῆς πρέσβεις φέροντάς
σοι τῶν τε ἐγκλημάτων ἄφεσιν καὶ κάθοδον ἐπὶ
τὰ οἰκεῖα φίλους καὶ ἀγαθοὺς ἄνδρας ἐλθόντας
ἐνετράπης, οὐδὲ τοὺς ἱερεῖς οὓς τὸ τελευταῖον
ἔπεμψεν ἡ πόλις, γηραιοὺς ἄνδρας[5] ἱερὰ στέμματα
θεῶν προτείνοντας,[6] ἀλλὰ καὶ τούτους ἀπήλασας,
αὐθάδεις καὶ δεσποτικὰς ὡς κεκρατημένοις ἀπο-

[1] κτησάμενοι κατέσχον Sylburg : κτησαμένη κατέσχε O,
Jacoby.
[2] αὐτοὺς added by Schenkl.
[3] μέχρι Reiske, πόρρω Jacoby : περὶ O.

146

before them of attempting in turn to restore these tyrants and for that reason was himself banished from his country ; yet he retained no resentment against those who had exiled him, nor would he march against his country bringing with him the tyrants nor commit acts that would substantiate the charges made against him, but retiring to Lavinium, our mother-city, he spent the remainder of his life there, continuing loyal to his country and its friend.

L. " Conceding the point nevertheless, and granting the right to all who have suffered grievously not to distinguish whether those who have injured them are friends or aliens but to direct their anger against all impartially, even so have you not taken a sufficient revenge on such as abused you, now that you have turned their best land into a sheep-walk, have utterly destroyed the cities of their allies, which they had acquired and held at the cost of many hardships, and have reduced them now for the third year to a great scarcity of provisions ? But you carry your wild and mad resentment even to the point of enslaving them and razing their city ; and you showed no regard even for the envoys sent to you by the senate, men of worth and your friends, who came to offer you a dismissal of the charges and leave to return home, nor yet for the priests whom the commonwealth sent at the last to you, old men holding before them the holy garlands of the gods ; but these also you drove away, giving a haughty and imperious answer to them as

---

⁴ προάγεις Ba : προσάγεις ABb.

⁵ γηραιοὺς ἄνδρας placed here by Portus : after ἱερὰ στέμματα θεῶν ἔχοντας by O ; Jacoby deleted.

⁶ προτείνοντας Capps : ἔχοντας γηραιοὺς ἄνδρας προτείνοντας ABD, ἔχοντας καὶ προτείνοντας Portus, Jacoby.

3 κρίσεις δούς. ἐγὼ μὲν οὐκ ἔχω πῶς ἐπαινέσω
ταῦτα τὰ σκληρὰ καὶ ὑπέραυχα καὶ τὴν θνητὴν
φύσιν ἐκβεβηκότα δικαιώματα, ὁρῶσα καταφυγὰς
εὑρημένας ἅπασιν ἀνθρώποις καὶ παραιτήσεις ὧν
ἂν ἐξαμαρτάνωσι περὶ ἀλλήλους ἱκετηρίας καὶ
λιτάς,[1] ὑφ' ὧν μαραίνεται πᾶσα ὀργὴ καὶ ἀντὶ τοῦ
μισεῖν τὸν ἐχθρὸν ἐλεεῖ· τοὺς δ' αὐθαδείᾳ χρησαμένους καὶ λιτὰς ἱκετῶν ὑβρίσαντας ἅπαντας
νεμεσωμένους ὑπὸ θεῶν καὶ εἰς συμφορὰς κατα-
4 στρέφοντας οὐκ εὐτυχεῖς. αὐτοὶ γὰρ δὴ πρῶτον οἱ
ταῦτα καταστησάμενοι[2] καὶ παραδόντες ἡμῖν θεοὶ
συγγνώμονες τοῖς ἀνθρωπίνοις εἰσὶν ἁμαρτήμασι καὶ
εὐδιάλλακτοι, καὶ πολλοὶ ἤδη μεγάλα εἰς αὐτοὺς
ἐξαμαρτάνοντες[3] εὐχαῖς καὶ θυσίαις τὸν χόλον ἐξ-
ιλάσαντο· εἰ μὴ σύ, ὦ Μάρκιε, ἀξιοῖς τὰς μὲν τῶν
θεῶν ὀργὰς θνητὰς εἶναι, τὰς δὲ τῶν ἀνθρώπων
ἀθανάτους. δίκαια μὲν οὖν ποιήσεις καὶ σεαυτῷ
πρέπονται καὶ τῇ πατρίδι, ἀφεὶς αὐτῇ[4] τὰ ἐγκλήματα
μετανοούσῃ γε καὶ διαλλαττομένῃ καὶ ὅσα πρότερον
ἀφείλετό σοι νῦν ἀποδιδούσῃ.

LI. " Εἰ δ' ἄρα πρὸς ἐκείνην ἀδιαλλάκτως ἔχεις,
ἐμοὶ ταύτην δός, ὦ τέκνον, τὴν τιμὴν καὶ χάριν,
παρ' ἧς οὐ τὰ ἐλαχίστου ἄξια ἔχεις οὐδ' ὧν ἀντι-
ποιήσαιτ' ἄν τις καὶ ἕτερος, ἀλλὰ τὰ μέγιστα καὶ
τιμιώτατα καὶ οἷς ἅπαντα τὰ λοιπὰ κέκτησαι, τὸ
σῶμα καὶ τὴν ψυχήν. δανείσματα γὰρ ἔχεις ταῦτα

---

[1] After λιτάς the MSS. all add : καὶ τὸ καταφυγεῖν ἐπὶ τοὺς
ἠδικημένους τὸ ἀδικοῦν ταπεινόν, θεῶν ἡμῖν ταῦτα τὰ ἔθη κατα-
στησαμένων. Jacoby deleted.

[2] Portus (and B, according to Jacoby) : παραστησάμενοι R.

to men who had been conquered. For my part, I
cannot commend these harsh and overbearing claims,
which overstep the bounds of human nature, when I
observe that a refuge for all men and the means of
securing forgiveness for their offences one against
another have been devised in the form of suppliant
boughs and prayers, by which all anger is softened
and instead of hating one's enemy one pities him; and
when I observe also that those who act arrogantly
and treat with insolence the prayers of suppliants all
incur the indignation of the gods and in the end come
to a miserable state. For the gods themselves, who
in the first place instituted and delivered to us these
customs, are disposed to forgive the offences of men
and are easily reconciled; and many have there been
ere now who, though greatly sinning against them,
have appeased their anger by prayers and sacrifices.
Unless you think it fitting, Marcius, that the anger
of the gods should be mortal, but that of men immortal! You will be doing, then, what is just and
becoming both to yourself and to your country if you
forgive her her offences, seeing that she is repentant
and ready to be reconciled and to restore to you now
everything that she took away from you before.

LI. " But if you are indeed irreconcilable to her,
grant, my son, this honour and favour to me, at least,
from whom you have received, not the boons that are
of least value nor those to which another also might
lay claim, but rather those that are the greatest and
most precious and have enabled you to acquire everything else you possess—namely, your body and your
soul. These are loans you have from me, and neither

---

³ ἐξαμαρτάνοντες O : ἐξαμαρτόντες Portus, Jacoby.
⁴ ἀφεὶς αὐτῇ Kiessling : αὐτῇ, ἀφεὶς O, Jacoby.

ἐμά, καὶ οὐκ ἀφαιρήσεταί με ταῦτα οὐθεὶς οὔτε
τόπος οὔτε καιρός, οὐδέ γε αἱ Οὐολούσκων οὐδὲ
·τῶν ἄλλων ἀνθρώπων εὐεργεσίαι συμπάντων καὶ
χάριτες τοσοῦτον ἰσχύσουσιν[1] οὐδ' ἂν οὐρανομήκεις
γένωνται, ὥστε τὰ τῆς φύσεως ἐξαλείψαι καὶ παρελθεῖν δίκαια· ἀλλ' ἐμὸς ἅπαντα τὸν χρόνον ἔσῃ
καὶ πρώτῃ πάντων τὰς τοῦ βίου χάριτας ὀφειλήσεις
ἐμοί,[2] καὶ ὧν ἂν δέωμαι δίχα προφάσεως ὑπουργή-
2 σεις.   τοῦτο γὰρ ὁ τῆς φύσεως νόμος ὥρισεν ἅπασι
τοῖς αἰσθήσεως καὶ λόγου μετειληφόσι τὸ δίκαιον,
ᾧ πιστεύουσα, Μάρκιε τέκνον, κἀγὼ δέομαί σου μὴ
ἐπάγειν πόλεμον τῇ πατρίδι, καὶ ἐμποδὼν ἵσταμαί
σοι βιαζομένῳ.   ἢ προτέραν οὖν ἐμὲ τὴν ἐναντιου-
μένην σοι μητέρα ταῖς ἐρινύσι προθυσάμενος αὐτοχειρίᾳ τότε τοῦ κατὰ τῆς πατρίδος ἅπτου πολέμου,
ἢ τὸ μητροκτόνον ἄγος αἰδούμενος εἶξον τῇ σεαυτοῦ
3 μητρὶ καὶ δός, ὦ τέκνον, τὴν χάριν ἑκών.   νόμον
μὲν οὖν[3] τόνδε, ὃν οὐθεὶς πώποτε ἀνελεῖ[4] χρόνος,
τιμωρὸν καὶ σύμμαχον ἔχουσα οὐκ ἀξιῶ, Μάρκιε,
μόνη τιμῶν ἃς οὗτός μοι δίδωσιν ἄμοιρος ἐκ σοῦ
γενέσθαι· ἔργων δὲ χρηστῶν ὑπομνήσεις, ἵν' ἀφῶ
τὸν νόμον, σκόπει πάλιν ὡς πολλὰς καὶ μεγάλας·
ἥτις ὀρφανὸν ὑπὸ τοῦ πατρὸς καταλειφθέντα σε[5]
παραλαβοῦσα νήπιον διέμεινα ἐπὶ σοὶ χήρα καὶ
τοὺς ἐπὶ τῆς παιδοτροφίας ἀνήντλησα πόνους, οὐ
μήτηρ μόνον, ἀλλὰ καὶ πατὴρ[6] καὶ τροφὸς καὶ
4 ἀδελφὴ καὶ πάντα τὰ φίλτατά σοι γενομένη.   ἐπειδὴ
δ' εἰς ἄνδρας ἦλθες, ἐξόν μοι τότε ἀπηλλάχθαι τῶν
φροντίδων ἑτέρῳ γημαμένη καὶ ἕτερα τέκνα ἐπι-
θρέψαι καὶ πολλὰς γηροβοσκοὺς ἐλπίδας ἐμαυτῇ

[1] Steph. : ἰσχύσωσιν AB, Jacoby.
[2] Kiessling : μοι O.   [3] οὖν added by Reiske.

place nor time will ever deprive me of them, nor will the benefactions and favours of the Volscians or of all the rest of mankind together, even if they should reach the heavens in magnitude, avail to efface and surpass the rights of Nature; but you will be mine forever, and to me before all others you will owe gratitude for your life, and you will oblige me in everything I ask without alleging any excuse. For this is a right which the law of Nature has prescribed for all who partake of sense and reason; and putting my trust in this law, Marcius, my son, I too beg of you not to make war upon your country, and I stand in your way if you resort to violence. Either, therefore, first sacrifice with your own hand to the Furies your mother who opposes you and then begin the war against your country, or, if you shrink from the guilt of matricide, yield to your mother, my son, and grant this favour willingly. Having this law, then, which no lapse of time will ever repeal, to avenge my wrongs and be my ally, I cannot consent, Marcius, to be alone deprived by you of honours to which it entitles me. But leaving this law aside, consider in turn the reminders I have to give you of the good offices you have received from me, how many and how great they are. When you were left an orphan by your father, I took you as an infant, and for your sake I remained a widow and underwent the labours of rearing you, showing myself not only a mother to you, but also a father, a nurse, a sister, and everything that is dearest. When you reached manhood and it was in my power to be freed from these cares by marrying again, to rear other children, and lay up many hopes

---

⁴ Cobet : ἀνεῖλε O. ⁵ σε B : om. R.
⁶ πατήρ B : πατήρ καὶ ἀδελφὸς R.

καταβαλεῖν,[1] οὐκ ἠβουλήθην, ἀλλ᾽ ἔμεινα ἐπὶ τῆς
αὐτῆς ἑστίας καὶ τὸν αὐτὸν ἔστερξα βίον, ἐν σοὶ
μόνῳ πάσας τιθεῖσα τὰς ἐμαυτῆς ἡδονάς τε καὶ
ὠφελείας· ὧν ἐψεύσας με τὰ μὲν ἄκων, τὰ δ᾽ ἑκών,
καὶ πασῶν ἀτυχεστάτην ἐποίησας μητέρων. ποῖον
γὰρ χρόνον, ἀφ᾽ οὗ σε εἰς ἄνδρας ἤγαγον, ἄνευ
λύπης ἢ φόβου διετέλεσα, ἢ πότε ἱλαρὰν ἔσχον ἐπὶ
σοὶ τὴν ψυχὴν πολέμους ἐπὶ πολέμοις στέλλοντα
ὁρῶσά σε καὶ μάχας ἐπὶ μάχαις ἀναιρούμενον καὶ
τραύματα ἐπὶ τραύμασι λαμβάνοντα;

LII. "᾽Αλλ᾽ ἐξ οὗ[2] ἐπολιτεύου καὶ τὰ κοινὰ
ἔπραττες, ἡδονήν τινα ἐκαρπωσάμην ἡ μήτηρ ἐγὼ
διὰ σέ; τότε μὲν οὖν τὰ μάλιστα ἠτύχουν στάσεως
πολιτικῆς μέσον ὁρῶσά σε κείμενον. ἐν οἷς γὰρ
ἀνθεῖν ἐδόκεις πολιτεύμασι καὶ πολὺς ἔπνεις ἐναντι-
ούμενος ὑπὲρ τῆς ἀριστοκρατίας τοῖς δημοτικοῖς,
ταῦτ᾽ ἐμοὶ φόβου μεστὰ ἦν ἐνθυμουμένῃ τὸν ἀνθρώπινον βίον, ὡς ἐπὶ μικρᾶς αἰωρεῖται ῥοπῆς, καὶ
ἐκ πολλῶν ἀκουσμάτων τε καὶ παθημάτων μαθούσῃ
ὅτι τοῖς ἐπισήμοις ἀνδράσι θεία τις ἐναντιοῦται νέ-
μεσις ἢ φθόνος τις ἀνθρώπινος πολεμεῖ· καὶ ἦν ἄρα
μάντις ἀληθής, ὡς μήποτε ὤφελον,[3] τῶν ἐκβησο-
μένων. κατηγωνίσατό γε οὖν σε πολὺς ἐπιρράξας
ὁ πολιτικὸς φθόνος καὶ ἀνήρπασεν ἐκ τῆς πατρίδος·
ὁ δὲ μετὰ ταῦτά μου βίος, εἰ δὴ καὶ βίον αὐτὸν δεῖ
καλεῖν, ἀφ᾽ οὗ με καταλιπὼν ἔρημον ἐπὶ τοῖς παι-
δίοις τούτοις ἀπῆλθες, ἐν τούτῳ δεδαπάνηται τῷ
2 ῥύπῳ καὶ ἐν τοῖς πενθίμοις τρύχεσι τούτοις. ἀνθ᾽

---

[1] Capps : καταλιπεῖν O, Jacoby.
[2] ἐξ οὗ Gelenius : ἐξ ὧν O.
[3] Jacoby : ὄφελον O.

to support me in my old age, I would not do so, but
remained at the same hearth and put up with the
same kind of life, placing all my pleasures and all my
advantages in you alone. Of these you have disappointed me, partly against your will and partly
of your own accord, and have made me the most
wretched of all mothers. For what time, since I
brought you up to manhood, have I passed free from
grief or fear? Or when have I possessed a spirit
cheerful on your account, seeing you always undertaking wars upon wars, engaged in battles upon
battles, and receiving wounds upon wounds?

LII. " But from the time when you took up the life
of a statesman and engaged in public affairs have I,
your mother, enjoyed any pleasure on your account?
Nay, it was then that I was most unhappy, seeing you
placed in the midst of civil strife. For those very
measures which seemed to make you flourish and
blow strong in popularity as you opposed the plebeians
in behalf of the aristocracy filled me with fear, as
I called to mind what the life of man is, how it
hangs nicely suspended as in a balance, and had
learned from many instances which I had heard
and experienced that a kind of divine vengeance
opposes men of prominence or a certain envy of men
makes war upon them; and I proved a true prophet
of what was to be—would to Heaven I had not! At
any rate, you were overpowered by the ill-will of
your fellow citizens, which burst upon you violently
and snatched you away from your country; and my
life thereafter—if, indeed I ought to call it life since
you departed leaving me and these children, too,
desolate—has been spent in this squalor and in these
rent garments of mourning. In return for all this I,

ὧν ἁπάντων ταύτην ἀπαιτῶ σε χάριν, μηδέποτέ σοι
βαρεῖα γενομένη μηδ᾽ εἰς τὸν λοιπὸν ἐσομένη
χρόνον, ἕως ἂν ζῶ, διαλλαγῆναι πρὸς τοὺς σεαυτοῦ
πολίτας ἤδη ποτὲ καὶ παύσασθαι τὸν ἀμείλικτον
χόλον φυλάσσοντα κατὰ τῆς πατρίδος, κοινὸν
ἀγαθὸν ἀμφοτέροις ἡμῖν ἀξιοῦσα λαβεῖν καὶ οὐκ
3 ἐμαυτῆς ἴδιον μόνης. σοί τε γάρ, ἐὰν πεισθῇς καὶ
μηθὲν ἀνήκεστον ἐξεργάσῃ, καθαρὰν καὶ ἀμίαντον
ἔχειν συμβήσεται τὴν ψυχὴν ἀπὸ παντὸς χόλου καὶ
ταράγματος δαιμονίου· ἐμοί τε ἡ παρὰ τῶν πολιτῶν
τε καὶ πολιτίδων τιμὴ ζώσῃ τε παρακολουθοῦσα
τὸν[1] βίον εὐδαίμονα ποιήσει καὶ μετὰ τὴν τελευτὴν
ἀποδιδομένη καθάπερ εἰκὸς εὔκλειαν ἀθάνατον
4 οἴσει. καὶ εἴ τις ἄρα τὰς ἀνθρωπίνους ψυχὰς ἀπο-
λυθείσας τοῦ σώματος ὑποδέξεται τόπος, οὐχ ὁ
καταχθόνιος καὶ ἀφεγγὴς ὑποδέξεται τὴν ἐμήν, ἐν
ᾧ φασι τοὺς κακοδαίμονας οἰκεῖν, οὐδὲ τὸ λεγόμενον τῆς Λήθης[1] πεδίον, ἀλλ᾽ ὁ μετέωρος καὶ
καθαρὸς αἰθήρ, ἐν ᾧ τοὺς ἐκ θεῶν φύντας οἰκεῖν
λόγος εὐδαίμονα καὶ μακάριον ἔχοντας βίον· οἷς
διαγγέλλουσα τὸ σὸν εὐσεβὲς καὶ τὰς σὰς χάριτας,
αἷς αὐτὴν ἐκόσμησας, ἀεί τινας αἰτήσεταί σοι παρὰ
θεῶν ἀμοιβὰς καλάς.

LIII. ''Ἐὰν δὲ προπηλακίσῃς τὴν σεαυτοῦ μητέρα καὶ ἄτιμον ἀπολύσῃς, ὅ τι μὲν αὐτῷ σοι
συμβήσεται διὰ ταῦτα παθεῖν, οὐκ ἔχω λέγειν,
μαντεύομαι δ᾽ οὐδὲν εὐτυχές. ὅτι δ᾽ ἐὰν καὶ τἆλλα
πάντα εὐδαιμονῇς, ἔστω γάρ, ἡ δι᾽ ἐμὲ καὶ τὰς
ἐμὰς συμφορὰς παρακολουθήσουσά σοι καὶ οὐδέποτε ἀνήσουσα τὴν ψυχὴν ὀδύνη πάντων ἀγαθῶν

---

[1] τὸν added by Kiessling, Jacoby.

---

[1] Forgetfulness.

who was never a burden to you nor ever shall be as
long as I live, ask this favour of you—that you will
at last be reconciled to your fellow citizens and cease
nursing that implacable anger against your country.
In doing this I am but asking to receive what will be
a boon common to us both, and not mine alone. For
you, if you hearken to me and commit no irreparable
deed, will have a mind free and unvexed by any
heaven-sent wrath and disquiet, while as for me, the
honour I shall receive from the men and women of
the city, attending me while I live, will make my life
happy, and being paid to my memory after my death,
as I may well expect, will bring me everlasting fame.
And if there is in very truth a place which will receive
men's souls when released from the body, it is not
that subterranean and gloomy place where, men say,
the unhappy dwell, that will receive mine, nor the
region called the Plain of Lethe,[1] but the pure ether
high up in the heavens, where, as report has it, those
who are sprung from the gods dwell, enjoying a happy
and a blessed life ; and to them my soul will relate
your piety and the acts of kindness with which you
honoured her, and will ever ask the gods to requite
you with glorious rewards.

LIII. " If, however, you treat your mother with
indignity and send her away unhonoured, what you
yourself will have to suffer for this I cannot say,
though I presage no happiness. But even if you
should be fortunate in all other respects—for let that
be assumed—yet your compunction because of me
and my afflictions, haunting you and never giving
respite to your soul, will rob your life of the enjoy-

2 σοι ἀνόνητον ποιήσει τὸν βίον, εὖ οἶδα. οὐ γὰρ
ἀνέξεται Οὐετουρία τὴν δεινὴν καὶ ἀνήκεστον ὕβριν
ἐν τοσούτοις μάρτυσιν ὑβρισθεῖσα τὸν ἐλάχιστον
βιῶναι χρόνον, ἀλλ᾽ ἐν τοῖς ἁπάντων ὑμῶν φίλων
τε καὶ ἐχθρῶν ὄμμασιν ἐμαυτὴν διαχρήσομαι,
βαρεῖαν ἀρὰν καὶ δεινὰς ἐρινύας ἀντ᾽ ἐμαυτῆς
3 καταλιποῦσά σοι τιμωρούς. ὧν μὴ δεήσειεν, ὦ
θεοὶ τῆς Ῥωμαίων φύλακες ἡγεμονίας, ἀλλ᾽ εὐ-
σεβεῖς καὶ καλοὺς δοίητε Μαρκίῳ λογισμούς· καὶ
ὥσπερ ἄρτι προσιούσῃ μοι τούς τε πελέκεις ἀπέθετο καὶ τὰς ῥάβδους ἔκλινε καὶ τὸν δίφρον ἀπὸ
τοῦ βήματος ἔθηκε χαμαὶ καὶ[1] πάντα τἆλλα οἷς
κοσμεῖσθαι τὰς αὐτοκράτορας ἀρχὰς νόμος, τὰ μὲν
ἐμείωσε, τὰ δ᾽ ἐκποδὼν εἰς τέλος ἐποίησε,[1] δῆλον
ἅπασι βουλόμενος ποιῆσαι ὅτι τῶν μὲν ἄλλων
ἄρχειν αὐτῷ προσῆκεν, ὑπὸ δὲ τῆς μητρὸς ἄρχεσθαι, οὕτω καὶ νῦν τιμίαν καὶ περίβλεπτόν με
ποιήσειε, καὶ χαρισάμενος τὴν κοινὴν πατρίδα ἀντὶ
κακοδαιμονεστάτης εὐδαιμονεστάτην ἀποδείξειέ με
4 πασῶν γυναικῶν. εἰ δὲ ὅσιόν[2] ἐστι καὶ θεμιτὸν
υἱοῦ γόνασι μητέρα προσκυλίεσθαι, καὶ τοῦτο καὶ
πᾶν ἄλλο ταπεινὸν σχῆμα καὶ λειτούργημα ὑπομενῶ σωτηρίας ἕνεκα τῆς πατρίδος.''

LIV. Ταῦτ᾽ εἰποῦσα ἔρριψεν ἑαυτὴν χαμαὶ καὶ
περιπλέξασα ταῖς χερσὶν ἀμφοτέραις τοὺς πόδας
τοῦ Μαρκίου κατεφίλησε. πεσούσης δ᾽ αὐτῆς αἱ
μὲν γυναῖκες ἀνεβόησαν ἅμα πᾶσαι κωκυτὸν ὀξὺν
καὶ μακρόν, οἱ δ᾽ ἐν τῷ συνεδρίῳ παρόντες Οὐε-

---

[1] καὶ πάντα . . . εἰς τέλος ἐποίησε rejected as a gloss by
Garrer, Jacoby.   [2] Sylburg : αἴσιον O.

ment of all its blessings; this I do know full well.
Veturia, for one thing, after this cruel and irreparable
ignominy received before so many witnesses, will not
bear to live a moment; nay, I will kill myself before
the eyes of all of you, both friends and enemies,
leaving to you in my stead a grievous curse and dire
furies to be my avengers. May there be no occasion
for this, O gods who guard the empire of the Romans,
but inspire Marcius with sentiments of piety and
honour; and just as a little while ago at my approach
he ordered the axes to be laid aside, the rods to be
lowered, and his chair to be taken from the tribunal
and placed on the ground, and as for all the other
observances by which it is the custom to honour
supreme magistrates, he moderated some and did
away with others altogether,[1] desiring to make it
clear to all that though it was fitting that he should
rule all others, by his mother he should be ruled, even
so may he now also make me honoured and conspicuous, and by giving me back our common country
as a favour, render me, instead of the most ill-starred,
the most fortunate of all women. And if it is right
and lawful for a mother to grovel at the feet of her
son, even to this and every other posture and office of
humility will I submit in order to save my country."

LIV. With these words she threw herself upon the
ground, and embracing the feet of Marcius with both
her hands, she kissed them. As soon as she fell
prostrate, all the women cried out together, raising
a loud and prolonged wailing; and the Volscians who

---

[1] The words " and, as for all the other observances . . .
and did away with others altogether " were rejected by
Garrer and Jacoby as an interpolation. There is nothing
corresponding to these words in chap. 44, 3 and 45, 3, where
the actual circumstances are related.

λούσκων οὐκ ἠνέσχοντο τὴν ἀήθειαν[1] τῆς ὄψεως,
ἀλλ' ἀπεστράφησαν. αὐτὸς δ' ὁ Μάρκιος ἀναλό-
μενος ἐκ τοῦ δίφρου καὶ περιπεσὼν τῇ μητρὶ
ἀνίστησιν αὐτὴν ἀπὸ τῆς γῆς ὀλίγον ἐμπνέουσαν,
καὶ περιβαλὼν[2] καὶ πολλὰ ἐκχέας δάκρυα εἶπε·
" Νικᾷς, ὦ μῆτερ, οὐκ εὐτυχῆ νίκην οὔτε σεαυτῇ
οὔτ' ἐμοί· τὴν μὲν γὰρ πατρίδα σέσωκας, ἐμὲ δὲ
τὸν εὐσεβῆ καὶ φιλόστοργον υἱὸν ἀπολώλεκας."
2 ταῦτα εἰπὼν ἐπὶ τὴν σκηνὴν ἀπῄει κελεύσας
ἀκολουθεῖν τήν τε μητέρα καὶ τὴν γυναῖκα καὶ τὰ
παιδία, ἔνθα τὸν λοιπὸν τῆς ἡμέρας χρόνον σκοπού-
μενος σὺν αὐταῖς ὅ τι χρὴ πράττειν διετέλεσεν. ἦν
δὲ τὰ δόξαντα αὐτοῖς τοιάδε· περὶ μὲν τῆς καθόδου
μήτε τὴν βουλὴν τέλος μηθὲν ἐκφέρειν εἰς τὸν
δῆμον μήτ' ἐκεῖνον ἐπιψηφίζειν, πρὶν ἂν τοῖς
Οὐολούσκοις εὐτρεπῆ γένηται τὰ περὶ φιλίας καὶ
καταλύσεως τοῦ πολέμου· αὐτὸν δὲ τὴν στρατιὰν
ἀναστήσαντα ὡς διὰ φιλίας γῆς ἀπάγειν· ὑπο-
σχόντα δὲ τῆς ἀρχῆς λόγον καὶ τὰς εὐεργεσίας
ἀποδειξάμενον ἀξιοῦν τοὺς ἐπιτρέψαντας αὐτῷ τὴν
στρατιάν, μάλιστα μὲν φιλίᾳ δέχεσθαι τοὺς πολεμίους καὶ συνθήκας ποιήσασθαι δικαίας, αὐτῷ τὴν
ἰσότητα καὶ τὸ μὴ σφαλῆναι περὶ τὰς ὁμολογίας
3 ἐπιτρέψαντας. εἰ δ' ἐπὶ τοῖς κατωρθωμένοις σφίσιν αὐθαδείας ἀναπιμπλάμενοι μὴ δέχοιντο τὰς
διαλλαγάς, ἀφίστασθαι τῆς ἀρχῆς αὐτοῖς. ἢ γὰρ
οὐχ ὑπομενεῖν αὐτοὺς ἄλλον τινὰ αἱρεῖσθαι στρατηγὸν δι' ἀπορίαν ἀγαθοῦ ἡγεμόνος, ἢ παρακινδυνεύ-
σαντας ὅτῳδήτινι παραδοῦναι τὰς δυνάμεις σὺν
μεγάλῃ διδαχθήσεσθαι βλάβῃ τὴν τοῦ συμφέροντος

_____
[1] ἀήθειαν B : ἀλήθειαν R.
[2] περιβαλὼν B : περιλαβὼν R.

were present at the assembly could not bear the
unusual sight, but turned away their eyes. Marcius
himself, leaping up from his seat, took his mother in
his arms, and raising her up from the ground scarcely
breathing, embraced her, and shedding many tears,
said : " Yours is the victory, mother, but a victory
which will be happy for neither you nor me. For
though you have saved your country, you have ruined
me, your dutiful and affectionate son." After saying
this, he retired to his tent, bidding his mother, his wife,
and his children follow him ; and there he passed the
rest of the day in considering with them what should
be done. The decisions they reached were as follows :
That the senate should lay no proposal before the
people providing for his return nor should the latter
pass any vote till the Volscians should be ready to consider friendship and the termination of the war; that
Marcius should break camp and lead his army away
as through friendly territory ; and that after he had
given an accounting to the Volscians of his conduct in
the command of their army and recounted the services he had done them, he should ask those who had
entrusted him with the army, preferably to admit
their enemies into friendship and to conclude a just
treaty with them, commissioning him to see that the
terms of the agreement were fair and free from
guile ; but if, becoming puffed up with arrogance
over their successes, they should reject an accommodation, he should resign the command they had
given him. For they thought that the Volscians
would either not bring themselves to choose another
commander, for want of a good general, or, if they
did run the hazard of handing over their forces to any
chance person, they would learn through heavy losses

αἵρεσιν. τὰ μὲν δὴ βουλευθέντα αὐτοῖς καὶ δόξαντα
δίκαιά τε καὶ ὅσια εἶναι, φήμης τε ἀγαθῆς, ἐφ᾽ ᾗ
μάλιστα ὁ ἀνὴρ ἐσπούδαζε, παρὰ πᾶσι τευξόμενα,
4 τοιάδε ἦν. ἐτάραττε δέ τις αὐτοὺς ὑποψία δέος
ἔχουσα, μή ποτε ἀλόγιστος ὄχλος ἐν ἐλπίδι τοῦ
καταπεπολεμηκέναι τὸ ἀντίπαλον ἤδη ὢν δι᾽ ὀργῆς
ἀκράτου λάβῃ τὴν ἀποτυχίαν κἄπειτα ὡς προδότην
αὐτὸν οὐδὲ λόγου μεταδοὺς αὐτοχειρίᾳ φθάσῃ δι-
ολέσας. ἐδόκει οὖν αὐτοῖς καὶ τοῦτο καὶ εἴ τι ἄλλο
δεινότερον εἴη κινδύνευμα σὺν ἀρετῇ σῴζουσι τὴν
5 πίστιν ὑπομένειν. ἐπεὶ δὲ περὶ δύσιν ἡλίου ἦν[1]
ἤδη, ἀσπασάμενοι ἀλλήλους ἐξῄεσαν ἐκ τῆς σκηνῆς·
ἔπειθ᾽ αἱ μὲν γυναῖκες εἰς τὴν πόλιν ἀπῇεσαν, ὁ
δὲ Μάρκιος ἐν ἐκκλησίᾳ τὰς αἰτίας ἀποδοὺς τοῖς
παροῦσι δι᾽ ἃς ἔμελλε λύειν τὸν πόλεμον, καὶ πολλὰ
τῶν στρατιωτῶν δεηθεὶς συγγνῶναί τε αὐτῷ καί,
ἐπειδὰν οἴκαδε ἀφίκωνται, μεμνημένους ὧν ἔπαθον
εὖ[2] τοῦ μηθὲν ὑπὸ τῶν ἄλλων ἀνήκεστον παθεῖν
συναγωνιστὰς γενέσθαι, καὶ ἄλλα πολλὰ καὶ ἐπαγωγὰ διαλεχθεὶς παρασκευάζεσθαι ἐκέλευσεν ὡς
τῇ ἐπιούσῃ νυκτὶ ἀναστρατοπεδεύσοντας.

LV. Ῥωμαῖοι δ᾽ ὡς ἔμαθον ὅτι λέλυται σφῶν ὁ
κίνδυνος (ἔφθασε γὰρ τῶν γυναικῶν τὴν παρουσίαν
προλαβοῦσα ἡ φήμη), σὺν πολλῇ χαρᾷ καταλιπόντες
τὴν πόλιν ἔθεον ἔξω καὶ ὑπήντων ταῖς γυναιξὶν
ἀσπασμοὺς καὶ παιᾶνας καὶ πάνθ᾽ ὅσα ἐκ μεγάλων
κινδύνων εἰς ἀδόκητον εὐτυχίαν ἄνθρωπο καταστάντες πράττουσί τε καὶ λέγουσιν ὑπὸ χαρᾶς, τὰ
μὲν ἀθρόοι, τὰ δὲ καθ᾽ ἕνα ἕκαστον ἀποδεικνύμενοι.

---

[1] ἦν Steph. : om. AB. [2] εὖ B : om. R.

to choose what was advantageous. Such were the subjects of their deliberation and such were the decisions they reached as just and right and calculated to win the good opinion of all men—a thing which Marcius had most at heart. But they were troubled by a suspicion, not unmixed with fear, that an unreasoning mob, now buoyed up with the hope that they had completely crushed their foe, might take their disappointment with uncontrolled anger and as a result put Marcius to death with their own hands as a traitor without even granting him a hearing. However, they determined to submit even to this or to any other danger still more formidable which they might incur in honourably keeping faith. When it was now near sunset, they embraced one another and left the tent, after which the women returned to the city. Then Marcius in an assembly of the troops laid before those present the reasons why he intended to put an end to the war ; and after earnestly beseeching the soldiers both to forgive him and, when they returned home, to remember the benefits they had received from him and to strive with him to prevent his suffering any irreparable injury at the hands of the other citizens, and after saying many other things calculated to win their support, he ordered them to make ready to break camp the following night.

LV. When the Romans heard that their peril was over—for the report of it was brought before the arrival of the women—they left the city with great joy, and running out to meet them, embraced them, sang songs of triumph, and now all together and now one by one showed all the signs of joy which men who emerge out of great dangers into unexpected good fortune exhibit in both their words and actions. That

2 ἐκείνην μὲν οὖν τὴν νύκτα ἐν θαλείαις τε καὶ
εὐπαθείαις διετέλεσαν, τῇ δ' ἑξῆς ἡμέρᾳ συν-
αχθεῖσα ὑπὸ τῶν ὑπάτων ἡ βουλὴ περὶ μὲν τοῦ
Μαρκίου γνώμην ἀπεδείξαντο εἰς ἑτέρους ἀναβάλ-
λεσθαι καιροὺς ἐπιτηδειοτέρους τὰς δοθησομένας
αὐτῷ τιμάς· ταῖς δὲ γυναιξὶν ἔπαινόν τε ἀποδεδόσθαι τῆς προθυμίας ἕνεκα[1] δημοσίᾳ γραφῇ μνήμην
οἴσοντα ἐκ τῶν ἐπιγινομένων αἰώνιον, καὶ γέρας,
ὅ τι ἂν αὐταῖς λαβούσαις ἥδιστόν τε καὶ τιμιώτατον
3 ἔσεσθαι μέλλῃ· καὶ ὁ δῆμος ἐπεκύρωσε ταῦτα.[2] ταῖς
δὲ γυναιξὶ βουλευσαμέναις εἰσῆλθεν[3] ἐπιφθόνου μὲν
δωρεᾶς μηδεμιᾶς δεῖσθαι, ἀξιοῦν δ' ἐπιτρέψαι σφίσι
τὴν βουλὴν Τύχης[4] γυναικῶν ἱδρύσασθαι ἱερὸν ἐν
ᾧ τὰς περὶ τῆς πόλεως ἐποιήσαντο λιτὰς χωρίῳ,
θυσίας τε καθ' ἕκαστον ἔτος αὐτῇ συνιούσας ἐπιτελεῖν ἐν ᾗ τὸν πόλεμον ἔλυσαν ἡμέρᾳ. ἡ μέντοι
βουλὴ καὶ ὁ δῆμος ἀπὸ τῶν κοινῶν ἐψηφίσαντο
χρημάτων τέμενός τε ὠνηθὲν καθιερωθῆναι τῇ θεῷ,
καὶ ἐν αὐτῷ νεὼν καὶ βωμόν, ὡς ἂν οἱ ἱερο-
μνήμονες ἐξηγῶνται, συντελεσθῆναι, θυσίας τε

---

[1] ἕνεκα (or αὐτίκα or αὐτίκα μάλα) Cary; πάλαι O, πάλιν
Sintenis, παλαιᾷ Jacoby; Kiessling proposed στήλης δημοσίας
ἐπιγραφῇ.
[2] καὶ ὁ δῆμος ἐπεκύρωσε ταῦτα R (?) : om. B.
[3] εἰσῆλθε B : εἰσελθεῖν C, ἐδόκει ACmg.
[4] ἐπὶ before Τύχης deleted by Reiske.

---

[1] For chap. 55, 2-5 cf. Livy ii. 40, 11 f.
[2] From this point the clause is packed with difficulties.
(1) πάλαι (" long ago "), the reading of the MSS., is almost
certainly corrupt. ἕνεκα, while probably not really necessary
here after the genitive, does at least give the construction
normally found in laudatory decrees. On the other hand,
we rather expect an adverb or adverbial phrase meaning
" at once," and the early translators rendered πάλαι by

night, then, they passed in festivities and merry-making. The next day the senate, having been assembled by the consuls, resolved, in the case of Marcius, to postpone to a more suitable occasion such honours as were to be given to him, but as for the women,[1] that not only praise should be bestowed upon them for their zeal,[2] the same to be expressed by a public decree which should gain for them eternal remembrance on the part of future generations, but also a gift of honour, whatever to those receiving it would be most pleasing and most highly prized; and the people ratified this resolution. It occurred to the women after some deliberation to ask for no invidious gift, but to request of the senate permission to found a temple to Fortuna Muliebris on the spot where they had interceded for their country, and to assemble and perform annual sacrifices to her on the day on which they had put an end to the war. However, the senate and people decreed that from the public funds a precinct should be purchased and consecrated to the goddess, and a temple and altar erected upon it, in such manner as the pontiffs should direct, and that sacrifices should be performed

---

quam primum; either αὐτίκα or αὐτίκα μάλα would be quite in accord with Dionysius' usage. (2) The phrase δημοσίᾳ γραφῇ is suspicious. γραφή has generally been interpreted here as " inscription "; but Dionysius normally uses ἐπιγραφή when he means " inscription," and γραφή in the sense of " writing." If the text is correct, he probably means by a " public writing," a publicly displayed decree of the senate and people. (3) ἐκ τῶν ἐπιγινομένων, in place of εἰς τοὺς ἐπιγινομένους, is a surprising construction, if οἴσοντα be taken in the sense of " carry," " transmit." But in this context it probably means " win " as a prize, " gain "; *cf.* vi. 68, 2, where remembrance on the part of future generations is also mentioned; also viii. 52, 3.

προσάγεσθαι δημοτελεῖς καταρχομένης τῶν ἱερῶν
γυναικός, ἣν ἂν ἀποδείξωσιν αὐταὶ[1] λειτουργὸν τῶν
4 ἱερῶν. ταῦτα τῆς βουλῆς ψηφισαμένης ἱέρεια μὲν
ὑπὸ τῶν γυναικῶν ἀπεδείχθη τότε πρῶτον ἡ τὴν
γνώμην αὐταῖς εἰσηγησαμένη περὶ τῆς πρεσβείας
Οὐαλερία καὶ τὴν μητέρα τοῦ Μαρκίου πείσασα
συλλαβέσθαι σφίσι τῆς ἐξόδου. θυσίαν δὲ πρώτην
αἱ γυναῖκες ἔθυσαν ὑπὲρ τοῦ δήμου καταρχομένης
τῶν ἱερῶν τῆς Οὐαλερίας ἐπὶ τοῦ κατασκευασ-
θέντος ἐν τῷ τεμένει βωμοῦ, πρὶν ἢ τὸν νεὼν καὶ
τὸ ξόανον ἀνασταθῆναι, μηνὶ Δεκεμβρίῳ τοῦ κατόπιν ἐνιαυτοῦ, τῇ νέᾳ σελήνῃ, ἣν Ἕλληνες μὲν
νουμηνίαν, Ῥωμαῖοι δὲ καλάνδας καλοῦσιν· αὕτη
5 γὰρ ἦν ἡ λύσασα τὸν πόλεμον ἡμέρα. ἐνιαυτῷ δ᾽
ὕστερον δευτέρῳ[2] μετὰ τὴν πρώτην θυσίαν ὁ κατασκευασθεὶς ἐκ τῶν δημοσίων χρημάτων νεὼς συν-
ετελέσθη τε καὶ καθιερώθη Κοϊντιλίου μηνὸς ἑβδόμῃ
μάλιστα κατὰ σελήνην· αὕτη δὲ κατὰ Ῥωμαίους
ἐστὶν ἡ προηγουμένη τῶν Κοϊντιλίων νωνῶν ἡμέρα.
ὁ δὲ καθιερώσας αὐτὸν ἦν Πρόκλος Οὐεργίνιος
ἅτερος τῶν ὑπάτων.

LVI. Εἴη δ᾽ ἂν ἁρμόττον ἱστορίας σχήματι καὶ
ἐπανορθώσεως ἕνεκα τῶν οἰομένων μήτ᾽ ἐπὶ ταῖς
τιμαῖς ταῖς παρ᾽ ἀνθρώπων χαίρειν τοὺς θεοὺς μήτ᾽
ἐπὶ ταῖς ἀνοσίοις καὶ ἀδίκοις πράξεσιν ἀγανακτεῖν,
τὸ δηλῶσαι τὴν γενομένην ἐπιφάνειαν τῆς θεοῦ
κατ᾽ ἐκεῖνον τὸν χρόνον οὐχ ἅπαξ, ἀλλὰ καὶ δίς,
ὡς αἱ τῶν ἱεροφαντῶν περιέχουσι γραφαί, ἵνα τοῖς

---

[1] Sylburg : αὗται O.
[2] δευτέρῳ Kiessling : ἑτέρῳ O, Jacoby.

---

[1] *Nouménia* and *calendae* were the names given to the first

at the public expense, the initial ceremonies to be conducted by a woman, whichever one the women themselves should choose to officiate at the rites. The senate having passed this decree, the woman then chosen by the others to be priestess for the first time was Valeria, who had proposed to them the embassy and had persuaded the mother of Marcius to join the others in going out of the city. The first sacrifice was performed on behalf of the people by the women, Valeria beginning the rites, upon the altar raised in the sacred precinct, before the temple and the statue were erected, in the month of December of the following year, on the day of the new moon, which the Greeks call *nouménia* and the Romans calends[1]; for this was the day which had put an end to the war. The year after the first sacrifice the temple built at public expense was finished and dedicated about the seventh day of the month Quintilis, reckoning by the course of the moon ; this, according to the Romans' calendar, is the day before the nones of Quintilis.[2] The man who dedicated the temple was Proculus Verginius, one of the consuls.

LVI. It would be in harmony with a formal history and in the interest of correcting those who think that the gods are neither pleased with the honours they receive from men nor displeased with impious and unjust actions, to make known the epiphany of the goddess at that time, not once, but twice, as it is recorded in the books of the pontiffs, to the end that

day of the month, but the new moon fell on that day only so long as the calendar followed the lunar months.

[2] There is an error somewhere in this sentence, since the nones fell on the seventh day of the month Quintilis (later Iulius). Glareanus proposed to read " sixth " in place of " seventh " just above.

μὲν εὐλαβεστέροις περὶ τὸ συνέχειν ἃς παρὰ τῶν
προγόνων δόξας ὑπὲρ τοῦ δαιμονίου παρέλαβον
ἀμεταμέλητος ἡ τοιαύτη προαίρεσις καὶ βεβαία
διαμένῃ, τοῖς δ' ὑπερορῶσι τῶν πατρίων ἐθισμῶν
καὶ μηθενὸς ποιοῦσι τὸ δαιμόνιον τῶν ἀνθρωπίνων
λογισμῶν κύριον μάλιστα μὲν ἀναθέσθαι ταύτην
τὴν δόξαν,¹ εἰ δ' ἀνιάτως ἔχουσιν, ἔτι μᾶλλον αὐ-
τοῖς² ἀπεχθάνεσθαι καὶ κακοδαιμονεστέροις εἶναι.
2 ἱστορεῖται τοίνυν ὅτι τῆς βουλῆς ψηφισαμένης ἐκ
τοῦ δημοσίου πάσας ἐπιχορηγηθῆναι τὰς εἰς τὸν
νεών τε καὶ τὸ ξόανον δαπάνας, ἕτερον δ' ἄγαλμα
κατασκευασαμένων τῶν γυναικῶν ἀφ' ὧν αὐταὶ³
συνήνεγκαν χρημάτων, ἀνατεθέντων τε αὐτῶν
ἀμφοτέρων ἅμα ἐν τῇ πρώτῃ τῆς ἀνιερώσεως
ἡμέρᾳ, θάτερον τῶν ἀφιδρυμάτων, ὃ κατεσκευά-
σαντο⁴ αἱ γυναῖκες, ἐφθέγξατο πολλῶν παρουσῶν
γλώττῃ Λατίνῃ φωνὴν εὐσύνετόν τε καὶ γεγωνόν·
ἧς ἐστι φωνῆς ἐξερμηνευόμενος ὁ νοῦς εἰς τὴν
Ἑλλάδα διάλεκτον τοιόσδε· " Ὁσίῳ πόλεως νόμῳ
3 γυναῖκες γαμεταί, δεδώκατέ με." οἷα δὲ φιλεῖ
γίνεσθαι περὶ τὰς παραδόξους φωνάς τε καὶ ὄψεις,
πολλὴ ταῖς παρούσαις ἐνέπιπτεν ἀπιστία, μή ποτ'
οὐ τὸ ξόανον εἴη τὸ φθεγξάμενον, ἀνθρωπίνη δέ τις
φωνή· μάλιστα δ' ὅσαι πρὸς ἄλλῳ τινὶ τὸν νοῦν
ἔχουσαι τηνικαῦτα ἔτυχον, οὐκ ἰδοῦσαι τὸ φθεγγό-
μενον, ὅ τι ποτ' ἦν, ταύτην εἶχον τὴν πρὸς τὰς
ἰδούσας ἀπιστίαν. ἔπειτ' αὖθις πληθύοντος τοῦ

¹ Unless we assume an anacoluthon, a subjunctive is required in this clause corresponding to διαμένῃ just above.
Reiske supplied ᾖ, Kiessling περιῇ, after ἀναθέσθαι. Capps
would add δοκῇ after δόξαν.

by those who are more scrupulous about preserving
the opinions concerning the gods which they have
received from their ancestors such belief may be
maintained firm and undisturbed by misgivings, and
that those who, despising the customs of their forefathers, hold that the gods have no power over man's
reason, may, preferably, retract their opinion, or, if
they are incurable, that they may become still more
odious to the gods and more wretched. It is related,
then, that when the senate had ordered that the whole
expense both of the temple and of the statue should
be defrayed from the public treasury, and the women
had caused another statue to be made with the money
they themselves had contributed, and both statues
had been set up together on the first day of the
dedication of the temple, one of them, the one which
the women had provided, uttered some words in
Latin in a voice both distinct and loud, when many
were present. The meaning of the words when
translated is as follows : " You have conformed to the
holy law of the city, matrons, in dedicating me." [1]
The women who were present were very incredulous,
as usually happens in the case of unusual voices and
sights, believing that it was not the statue that had
spoken, but some human voice ; and those particularly who happened at the moment to have their
mind on something else and did not see what it was
that spoke, showed this incredulity toward those who
had seen it. Later, on a second occasion, when the

[1] According to Valerius Maximus (i. 8, 4) the words uttered were : *Rite me, matronae, dedistis riteque dedicastis.*

[2] αὐτοῖς O : αὖ τοῖς θεοῖς Post.
[3] Sylburg : αὖται O.
[4] Kiessling : κατεσκεύασαν O.

νεὼ καὶ σιωπῆς πλείστης κατὰ δαίμονα γενομένης
ἐν μείζονι φωνῇ ταὐτὸ ξόανον ἐφθέγξατο τὴν αὐτὴν
4 λέξιν, ὥστε μηδὲν ἔτι εἶναι τὸ ἀμφίλογον. ἡ μὲν
οὖν βουλὴ ὡς ταῦτ' ἔμαθεν ἐψηφίσατο θυσίας
ἄλλας καὶ σεβασμούς, οὓς ἂν οἱ τῶν ἱερῶν ἐξηγηταὶ παραδῶσι, καθ' ἕκαστον ἔτος ἐπιτελεῖν. αἱ
δὲ γυναῖκες ἐν ἔθει κατεστήσαντο, τῇ τῆς ἱερείας
χρησάμεναι γνώμῃ, τῷ ξοάνῳ τούτῳ μήτε στεφάνους ἐπιτιθέναι[1] μήτε χεῖρας προσφέρειν γυναῖκας
ὅσαι δευτέρων ἐπειράθησαν γάμων, τὴν δὲ τιμὴν
καὶ θεραπείαν αὐτοῦ πᾶσαν ἀποδεδόσθαι ταῖς νεο-
γάμοις. ἀλλὰ περὶ μὲν τούτων οὔτε παρελθεῖν τὴν
ἐπιχώριον ἱστορίαν καλῶς εἶχεν οὔτε πλείονα περὶ
αὐτῆς ποιεῖσθαι λόγον. ἐπάνειμι δ' ὅθεν εἰς
τοῦτον ἐξέβην τὸν λόγον.

LVII. Μετὰ τὴν ἐκ τοῦ χάρακος ἀπαλλαγὴν τῶν
γυναικῶν ὁ Μάρκιος περὶ τὸν ὄρθρον ἀναστήσας
τὴν στρατιὰν ἀπῆγεν ὡς διὰ φιλίας, καὶ ἐπειδὴ
ἐν τῇ Οὐολούσκων ἐγένετο, πάντα ὅσα ἐκ τῶν
λαφύρων ἔλαβε δωρησάμενος τοῖς στρατιώταις,
ἑαυτῷ δ' οὐδ' ὁτιοῦν ὑπολιπόμενος[2] ἀπέλυσεν ἐπὶ
τὰ οἰκεῖα. ἡ μὲν οὖν κοινωνήσασα τῶν ἀγώνων
αὐτῷ στρατιὰ πλούτῳ βαρεῖ[3] ἀφικομένη τήν τε
ἀνάπαυλαν οὐκ ἀηδῶς ἐδέξατο τοῦ πολέμου καὶ δι'
εὐνοίας εἶχε τὸν ἄνδρα, συγγνώμης τε ἄξιον ἡγεῖτο,
εἰ μὴ τέλος ἐπέθηκε τῷ πολέμῳ μητρὸς οἴκτους
2 καὶ λιτὰς ἐντραπείς. ἡ δ' ἐν ταῖς πόλεσιν ὑπο-
μείνασα νεότης φθονοῦσα μὲν τοῖς ἐπὶ στρατοπέδου
γενομένοις τῶν πολλῶν ὠφελειῶν, διημαρτηκυῖα δ'
ὧν ἤλπισεν εἰ καθαιρεθείη τὸ Ῥωμαίων φρόνημα

---

[1] Hudson : ἐπιτεθῆναι O.   [2] Sylburg : ὑπολειπόμενος O.
[3] Jacoby : βαρεῖ O, but one letter deleted in B after ι.

temple was full and there chanced to be a profound silence, the same statue pronounced the same words in a louder voice, so that there was no longer any doubt about it. The senate, upon hearing what had passed, ordered other sacrifices and rites to be performed every year, such as the interpreters of religious rites should direct. And the women upon the advice of their priestess established it as a custom that no women who had been married a second time should crown this statue with garlands or touch it with their hands, but that all the honour and worship paid to it should be committed to the newly-married women. But concerning these matters it was fitting that I should neither omit the native account nor dwell too long upon it. I now return to the point from which I digressed.

LVII. After the departure of the women from the camp [1] Marcius roused his army about daybreak and led it away as through a friendly country ; and when he came into the territory of the Volscians, he divided among the soldiers all the booty he had taken, without reserving the least thing for himself, and then dismissed them to their homes. The army, accordingly, which had shared in the battles with him, returning loaded with riches, was not displeased with the respite from war and felt well disposed toward him and thought he deserved to be forgiven for not having brought the war to a successful end out of regard for the lamentations and entreaties of his mother. But the young men who had remained at home, envying those who had seen active service the great booty they had won, and being disappointed in their hopes of seeing the pride of the Romans humbled by

[1] For chaps. 57-59 cf. Livy ii. 40, 10 f.

τῆς πόλεως ἁλούσης, ἐτραχύνετο πρὸς τὸν ἡγεμόνα
καὶ πικρὰ σφόδρα ἦν· καὶ τελευτῶσα, ἐπειδὴ τοῦ
μίσους ἡγεμόνας ἔλαβε τοὺς πλεῖστον ἐν τῷ ἔθνει
δυναμένους, ἐξηγριώθη τε καὶ ἔργον ἔδρασεν ἀν-
3 όσιον. ἦν δὲ Τύλλος Ἄττιος ὁ τὰς ὀργὰς αὐτῶν
παραθήξας ἔχων περὶ αὐτὸν ἑταιρίαν ἐξ ἁπάσης
πόλεως οὐκ ὀλίγην. τούτῳ δ᾿ ἄρα ἐδέδοκτο παλαίτερον ἔτι τὸν φθόνον οὐ δυναμένῳ κατέχειν, εἰ
μὲν εὖ πράξας ὁ Μάρκιος καὶ τὴν Ῥωμαίων πόλιν
διαφθείρας εἰς Οὐολούσκους[1] ἔλθοι, κρύφα καὶ σὺν
δόλῳ αὐτὸν ἀνελεῖν, εἰ δὲ διαμαρτὼν τῆς πείρας
ἀτελὴς τοῦ ἔργου ἀναστρέψειεν, ὡς προδότην παρα-
4 δόντα τῇ περὶ αὐτὸν ἑταιρίᾳ ἀποκτεῖναι· ὅπερ
ἐποίει τότε, καὶ συναγαγὼν χεῖρα οὐκ ὀλίγην
κατηγόρει τοῦ ἀνδρὸς ψευδῆ τεκμαιρόμενος ἀλη-
θέσι καὶ οὐ γενησόμενα εἰκάζων γεγενημένοις·[2]
ἐκέλευέ τε ἀποθέμενον αὐτὸν τὴν ἀρχὴν λόγον
ὑπέχειν τῆς στρατηγίας. ἦν δὲ τῆς ὑπομενούσης
στρατιᾶς ἐν ταῖς πόλεσιν ἡγεμών,[3] ὡς καὶ πρότερον
εἴρηταί μοι, κύριος τοῦ τε συναγαγεῖν ἐκκλησίαν
καὶ τοῦ καλεῖν ὃν βούλοιτο ἐπὶ δίκην.

LVIII. Ὁ δὲ Μάρκιος ἀντιλέγειν μὲν πρὸς οὐ-
δέτερον τούτων ἐδικαίου, περὶ δὲ τῆς τάξεως
αὐτῶν διεφέρετο λόγον ἀξιῶν ἀποδοῦναι πρότερον
τῶν πεπραγμένων αὐτῷ κατὰ τὸν πόλεμον, ἔπειτα,
ἐὰν ἅπασι δόξῃ Οὐολούσκοις, ἀποθήσεσθαι τὴν
ἀρχήν. τούτων δ᾿ οὐ μίαν ᾤετο πόλιν δεῖν, ἐν ᾗ
τὸ πλεῖον ὑπὸ τοῦ Τύλλου διέφθαρτο μέρος, γενέ-

---

[1] διαφθείρας εἰς οὐολούσκους B : διαφθείρας εἰς οὐολούσκους
ὑποτάξας R.
[2] γεγενημένοις (or γενομένοις) Steph.[2] : γενησομένοις O.
[3] ἡγεμών B : om. R.

the capture of their city, were incensed against the
general and very bitter ; and at last, when they
found as leaders of their hatred the men of the
greatest power in the nation, they grew wild with
rage and committed an impious deed. The one who
in particular whetted their anger against Marcius
was Tullus Attius, who had about him a large faction
collected out of every city. This man had, in fact,
long since resolved, being unable to control his
jealousy, that if Marcius succeeded and returned to
the Volscians after destroying Rome, he would make
away with him secretly and by guile, or if, failing in
his attempt, he came back leaving the task unfinished,
he would deliver him over to his faction as a traitor
and have him put to death—a plan which he now proceeded to carry out. And getting together a considerable band, he brought charges against him,
drawing false inferences from things that were true
and, from what had happened, surmising things that
were not going to happen ; and he kept bidding him
resign his command and give an account of his conduct. For, as I said before,[1] Tullus was general of
the forces which had been left in the cities, and had
authority both to call an assembly and to summon
to trial any man he pleased.

LVIII. Marcius did not think proper to oppose
either of these demands, but objected to their order,
insisting that he ought first to give an account of his
conduct in the war, after which he would resign his
command if all the Volscians should so decide. But
he thought that no single city in which the greater
part of the citizens had been corrupted by Tullus

[1] In chap. 13

σθαι κυρίαν, ἀλλὰ τὸ ἔθνος ἅπαν εἰς τὴν ἔννομον
ἀγορὰν συναχθέν, εἰς ἣν ἔθος ἦν αὐτοῖς ὅτε περὶ
τῶν μεγίστων βουλεύεσθαι μέλλοιεν, ἐξ ἁπάσης
2 πόλεως προβούλους ἀποστέλλειν. ὁ δὲ Τύλλος
ἀντέλεγε πρὸς ταῦτα καλῶς εἰδὼς ὅτι δεινὸς εἰπεῖν
ἀνὴρ[1] πολλῶν καὶ καλῶν ἔργων λόγον ἀποδιδοὺς
ἐν ἡγεμονικῷ ἀξιώματι μένων πείσει τὸ πλῆθος,
καὶ τοσούτου δεήσει τιμωρίαν προδοτῶν ὑποσχεῖν
ὥστε καὶ λαμπρότερος ἔτι καὶ τιμιώτερος ὑπ'
αὐτῶν ἔσται, τόν τε πόλεμον ὅπως ἂν βούληται
καταλύσασθαι συγχωρησάντων ἁπάντων γενήσεται
3 κύριος. καὶ ἦν μέχρι πολλοῦ λόγων τε καὶ
ἀντιμαχήσεων τῶν ἐπ' ἀλλήλοις γινομένων καθ'
ἑκάστην ἡμέραν ἐν ταῖς ἐκκλησίαις καὶ κατὰ τὴν
ἀγορὰν πολὺς ἀγών· ἔργῳ γὰρ οὐχ οἷόν τε ἦν οὐδ-
ετέρῳ βιάσασθαι τὸν ἕτερον τῆς ἰσοτίμου ἀρχῆς
4 ἀξιώσει κρατυνόμενον. ὡς δ' οὐδὲν τῆς φιλονεικίας
ἐγίνετο πέρας, ἡμέραν προειπὼν ὁ Τύλλος ἐν ᾗ τὸν
Μάρκιον ἐκέλευσεν ἥκειν τὴν ἀρχὴν ἀποθησόμενον
καὶ δίκην ὑφέξοντα τῆς προδοσίας, θρασυτάτους
τε ἄνδρας εὐεργεσιῶν ἐλπίσιν ἐπάρας ἀρχηγοὺς ἀνοσίου ἔργου γενέσθαι, παρῆν εἰς τὴν ἀποδειχθεῖσαν
ἀγορὰν καὶ προελθὼν[2] ἐπὶ τὸ βῆμα πολλῇ κατ-
ηγορίᾳ ἐχρήσατο τοῦ Μαρκίου, καί, εἰ μὴ βούλοιτο
ἀποθέσθαι τὴν ἀρχὴν ἑκών, τῷ δήμῳ παρεκελεύετο
παύειν[3] αὐτὸν ἁπάσῃ δυνάμει.

LIX. Ἀναβάντος δὲ τοῦ ἀνδρὸς ἐπὶ τὴν ἀπολογίαν βοή τε πολλὴ κωλύουσα τοὺς λόγους ἐκ τῆς
ἑταιρίας τῆς περὶ τὸν Τύλλον ἐγίνετο· καὶ μετὰ

---

[1] ἀνὴρ Kiessling, ὁ ἀνὴρ Christian : ἀνὴρ O.
[2] προελθὼν O : παρελθὼν Sylburg, Jacoby.
[3] Sylburg : παύσειν O.

ought to be given sole authority in the matter, but rather the whole nation meeting in their lawful assembly, to which it was the custom for them to send deputies from every city when they were to deliberate upon affairs of the greatest importance. This Tullus opposed, well knowing that Marcius, eloquent as he was, when he came to give an account of the many splendid actions he had performed, if he still retained a general's prestige, would persuade the multitude, and would be so far from suffering the punishment of a traitor that he would actually become still more illustrious and be more highly honoured by them, and would be authorized by general consent to put an end to the war in such manner as he pleased. And for a long time there was great strife as they daily engaged in arguing and wrangling with one another in the assemblies and the forum ; for it was not possible for either of them to employ force against the other, since both were protected by the prestige of an equal command. But when there was no end to their contention, Tullus appointed a day on which he commanded Marcius to appear for the purpose of laying down his office and standing trial for treason ; and having encouraged some of the most daring, by hopes of rewards, to be the ringleaders in an impious deed, he appeared at the assembly on the day appointed, and coming forward to the tribunal, inveighed at length against Marcius and exhorted the people to use all the force at their command to depose him if he would not voluntarily resign his power.

LIX. When Marcius had ascended the tribunal in order to make his defence, a great clamour arose from the faction of Tullus, hindering him from speaking ;

ταῦτα " Παῖε " καὶ " Βάλλε " φωνοῦντες περι-
ίστανται αὐτὸν οἱ θρασύτατοι καὶ συναράττοντες
τοῖς λίθοις ἀποκτιννύουσιν. ἐρριμμένου δ' αὐτοῦ
χαμαί[1] κατὰ τὴν ἀγορὰν οἵ τε παραγενόμενοι τῷ
πάθει καὶ οἱ μετὰ ταῦτα ἤδη νεκροῦ ὄντος ἀφικόμενοι τόν τε ἄνδρα τῆς τύχης ὠδύροντο ὡς οὐ καλὰς
εἰληφότα παρὰ σφῶν ἀμοιβάς, ἐπιλεγόμενοι πάντα
ὅσα τὸ κοινὸν ὠφέλησε, καὶ τοὺς δράσαντας τὸν
φόνον ἐπόθουν λαβεῖν ὡς ἀνόμου ἔργου καὶ ἀσυμ-
φόρου ταῖς πόλεσιν ἄρξαντας, ἄνευ δίκης ἐν χειρῶν
2 νόμῳ τινὰ ἀποκτεῖναι καὶ ταῦτα ἡγεμόνα. μάλιστα
δ' ἠγανάκτουν οἱ ταῖς στρατείαις αὐτοῦ παραγενόμενοι, καὶ ἐπειδὴ ζῶντι αὐτῷ οὐχ ἱκανοὶ ἐγένοντο
κωλυταὶ τῆς συμφορᾶς, τὰς μετὰ τὸν θάνατον
ὀφειλομένας ἔγνωσαν ἀποδιδόναι χάριτας, συμ-
φέροντες εἰς τὴν ἀγορὰν ὅσων ἔδει τοῖς ἀγαθοῖς
3 ἀνδράσιν εἰς τὴν ἀναγκαίαν τιμήν. ἐπειδὴ δὲ πάντα
εὐτρέπιστο, θέντες ἐπὶ στρωμνῆς ἐκπρεπεστάτῳ[2]
ἠσκημένης κόσμῳ τὴν αὐτοκρατορικὴν ἔχοντα
ἐσθῆτα, καὶ πρὸ τῆς κλίνης αὐτοῦ φέρεσθαι
κελεύσαντες λάφυρά τε καὶ σκῦλα καὶ στεφάνους
καὶ μνήμας ὧν εἷλε πόλεων, ἤραντο τὴν κλίνην οἱ
λαμπρότατοι τῶν νέων ἐν τοῖς κατὰ πολέμους
ἔργοις· καὶ κομίσαντες εἰς τὸ προάστειον ὃ μάλιστα ἦν ἐπιφανές, ἔθεσαν ἐπὶ τὴν παρεσκευασμένην
πυράν, συμπροπεμπούσης τὸ σῶμα τῆς πόλεως
4 ὅλης μετ' οἰμωγῆς τε καὶ δακρύων. ἔπειτα κατα-
σφάξαντες τ' αὐτῷ πολλὰ[3] βοσκήματα καὶ τῶν
ἄλλων ἀπαρξάμενοι πάντων ὅσων ἄνθρωποι βασι-
λεῦσιν ἢ στρατιᾶς ἡγεμόσιν ἐπὶ πυραῖς ἀπάρχον-
ται, παρέμειναν οἱ μάλιστα τὸν ἄνδρα ἀσπαζόμενοι

[1] χαμαί B : om. R.   [2] Steph. : ἐκπρεπεστάτης ABC.

then, with cries of " Hit him," " Stone him," the
most daring surrounded him and stoned him to death.
While he lay where he had been hurled upon the
ground in the forum, both those who had been present
at the tragedy and those who came there after he was
dead bewailed the misfortune of the man who had
found so ill a return from them, recounting all the
services he had rendered to their state, and they
longed to apprehend the murderers for having set the
example of a deed that was lawless and prejudicial
to their cities, in killing a man, and him a general,
by an act of violence without a trial. But most
indignant were the men who had taken part in his
campaigns ; and since they had been unable, while
he was living, to prevent his misfortune, they resolved
to show fitting gratitude after his death by bringing
into the forum everything that was necessary for the
honour owed to brave men. When all was ready,
they laid him, dressed in the garb of a supreme commander, on a couch adorned in a most sumptuous
manner, and ordered the booty, the spoils and the
crowns, together with the representations of the
cities he had taken, to be carried before his bier ;
and the young men who were the most distinguished
for their military achievements took up the bier, and
carrying it to the most conspicuous suburb, placed it
on the funeral pile that had been prepared, the whole
population of the city accompanying the body with
lamentations and tears. Then, when they had slain
a large number of victims in his honour and offered
up all the first-offerings that people make at the
funeral piles of kings and commanders of armies,
those who had been most closely attached to him

---

³ πολλὰ B : om. R.

μέχρι τοῦ μαρανθῆναι τὴν φλόγα, κἄπειτα συναγαγόντες τὰ λείψανα ἔθαψαν ἐν τῷ αὐτῷ χωρίῳ
χώματι ὑψηλῷ διὰ πολυχειρίας χωσθέντι[1] μνῆμα
ἐπίσημον ἐργασάμενοι.

LX. Μάρκιος μὲν δὴ τοιαύτης καταστροφῆς
ἔτυχεν, ἀνὴρ καὶ[2] τὰ πολέμια ἄριστος τῶν καθ᾽
ἡλικίαν καὶ πρὸς ἁπάσας τὰς ἡδονὰς ὅσαι ἄρχουσι
νέων ἐγκρατής, τά τε δίκαια οὐκ ἀπὸ νόμου μᾶλλον
ἀνάγκης διὰ τιμωριῶν δέος ἀκούσιος ἀποδιδούς,
ἀλλ᾽ ἑκών τε καὶ πεφυκὼς πρὸς αὐτὰ εὖ, καὶ οὐδ᾽
ἐν ἀρετῆς μοίρᾳ τὸ μηθὲν ἀδικεῖν τιθέμενος, οὐ
μόνον τε αὐτὸς ἁγνεύειν ἀπὸ πάσης κακίας προ-
θυμούμενος, ἀλλὰ καὶ τοὺς ἄλλους προσαναγκάζειν
2 δικαιῶν· μεγαλόφρων τε καὶ δωρηματικὸς καὶ εἰς
ἐπανόρθωσιν ὧν ἑκάστῳ δέοι τῶν φίλων, ὁπότε
γνοίη, προχειρότατος, τά τε πολιτικὰ πράττειν
οὐδενὸς χείρων τῶν ἀριστοκρατικῶν· καὶ εἰ μὴ τὸ
στασιάζον τῆς πόλεως ἐμποδὼν αὐτοῦ τοῖς πολι-
τεύμασιν ἐγένετο, μεγίστην ἂν ἡ Ῥωμαίων πόλις
ἐπίδοσιν εἰς ἡγεμονίαν ἐκ τῶν ἐκείνου πολιτευμάτων ἔλαβεν. ἀλλ᾽ οὐ γὰρ ἐν δυνατῷ ἦν ἅμα[3]
πάσας τὰς ἀρετὰς ἐν ἀνθρώπου γενέσθαι φύσει,
οὐδὲ φύσεταί τις ἀπὸ θνητῶν καὶ ἐπικήρων σπερ-
μάτων περὶ πάντα ἀγαθός.

LXI. Ἐκείνῳ γε οὖν ταύτας ὁ δαίμων τὰς ἀρετὰς χαρισάμενος ἑτέρας οὐκ εὐτυχεῖς κῆράς τε καὶ
ἄτας προσῆψε. τὸ γὰρ πρᾷῦ[4] καὶ φαιδρὸν οὐκ ἐνῆν[5]
αὐτοῦ τοῖς τρόποις, οὐδὲ τὸ θεραπευτικὸν τῶν
πέλας ἔν τε ἀσπασμοῖς καὶ προσαγορεύσεσιν,[6] οὐδὲ

---

[1] χωσθέντι Cary : ἐργασθέντι O, Jacoby.
[2] καὶ B : om. R.
[3] ἅμα Kiessling : ἄρα O.

remained there till the flames died down, after which they gathered together his remains and buried them in that very place, constructing an imposing monument by heaping up a high mound with the assistance of many hands.

LX. Such was the end of Marcius, who was not only the greatest general of his age, but was superior to all the pleasures that dominate young men, and practised justice, not so much through compulsion of the law with its threat of punishment and against his will, but voluntarily and from a natural propensity to it. He did not regard it as a virtue to do no injustice, and not only was eager to abstain from all vice himself, but thought it his duty to compel others to do so too. He was both high-minded and open-handed and most ready to relieve the wants of his friends as soon as he was informed of them. In his talent for public affairs he was inferior to none of the aristocratic party, and if the seditious element of the city had not hindered his measures, the Roman commonwealth would have received the greatest accession of power from those measures. But it was impossible that all the virtues should be found together in a human being's nature, nor will anyone ever be created by Nature from mortal and perishable seed who is good in all respects.

LXI. In any case the divinity who bestowed these virtues upon him added to them unfortunate blemishes and fatal flaws. For there was no mildness or cheerfulness in his character, no affability in greeting and addressing people that would win those whom he

---

⁴ πρᾳὺ O : πρᾷον Cobet.
⁵ Kiessling : ἐπῆν O, Jacoby.
⁶ προσαγορεύσεσιν A : προσαγορεύσει R.

177

δὴ τὸ εὐδιάλλακτον καὶ μετριοπαθές, ὁπότε δι'
ὀργῆς τῳ γένοιτο, οὐδὲ ἡ πάντα τὰ ἀνθρώπινα
ἐπικοσμοῦσα χάρις· ἀλλ' ἀεὶ πικρὸς καὶ χαλεπὸς
2 ἦν. ταῦτά τε δὴ αὐτὸν ἐν πολλοῖς[1] ἔβλαψε, καὶ
πάντων μάλιστα ἡ περὶ τὰ δίκαια καὶ τὴν φυλακὴν
τῶν νόμων ἄκρατός τε καὶ ἀπαράπειστος καὶ οὐθὲν
τῷ ἐπιεικεῖ διδοῦσα ἀποτομία· ἔοικέ τε ἀληθὲς
εἶναι τὸ ὑπὸ τῶν ἀρχαίων λεγόμενον φιλοσόφων,
ὅτι μεσότητές εἰσιν ἀλλ' οὐκ ἀκρότητες αἱ τῶν
ἠθῶν ἀρεταί, μάλιστα δ' ἡ δικαιοσύνη. οὐ γὰρ
μόνον ἐλλείπουσα τοῦ μετρίου πέφυκεν, ἀλλὰ καὶ
ὑπερβάλλουσα, αὐτοῖς τε οὐ λυσιτελής, ἀλλ' ἔστιν
ὅτε αἰτία μεγάλων συμφορῶν, καὶ εἰς θανάτους
οἰκτροὺς καὶ λύμας ἀνηκέστους καταστρέφουσα.
3 Μάρκιόν γε[2] οὐδὲν ἦν ἕτερον ἄρα ὃ τῆς πατρίδος
ἐξήλασε καὶ τῶν ἄλλων ἀγαθῶν ἀνόνητον ἐποίησεν
ἢ τὸ ἀκριβὲς καὶ ἄκρον δίκαιον. τοῖς τε γὰρ
δημόταις εἴκειν τὰ μέτρια δέον καὶ ἐφιέναι τι ταῖς
ἐπιθυμίαις καὶ τὰ πρῶτα φέρεσθαι παρ' αὐτοῖς, οὐκ
ἠβουλήθη, ἀλλὰ πρὸς ἅπαντα τὰ μὴ δίκαια ἀντι-
λέγων μῖσος ἤγειρε καὶ ἐξηλάθη πρὸς αὐτῶν· τῆς
τε Οὐολούσκων στρατηγίας εὐθὺς ἅμα τῷ διαλῦσαι
τὸν πόλεμον ἀπαλλαγῆναι παρὸν καὶ μετενέγκασθαι
τὴν οἴκησιν ἑτέρωσέ ποι, ἕως[3] ἂν ἡ κάθοδος αὐτῷ
δοθῇ[4] ὑπὸ τῆς πατρίδος, καὶ μὴ παρασχεῖν αὐτὸν
ἐχθρῶν ἐπιβουλαῖς καὶ ὄχλων ἀμαθίαις σκοπόν,
οὐκ ἠξίωσεν, ἀλλ' ὑπεύθυνον οἰόμενος δεῖν τὸ σῶμα

---

[1] πολλοῖς B : πολλοῖς πολέμοις AC.   [2] γε B : δὲ R.
[3] ἕως R : τέως Ba (?), Cod. Peirescianus, Jacoby.
[4] δοθῇ Cod. Peiresc., Kiessling : δοθείη O.

met, nor yet any disposition to conciliate or placate others when he was angry with them, nor that charm which adorns all human actions ; but he was always harsh and severe.   And it was not alone these qualities that hurt him in the minds of many, but, most of all, his immoderate and inexorable sternness in the matter of justice and the observance of the laws, and a strictness which would make no concessions to reasonableness.   Indeed, the dictum of the ancient philosophers seems to be true, that the moral virtues are means and not extremes,[1] particularly in the case of justice.[2]   For by its nature it not only may fall short of the mean, but also may go beyond it, and is not profitable to its possessors, but is sometimes the cause of great calamities and leads to miserable deaths and irreparable disasters.   In the case of Marcius, at any rate, it was nothing else but his passion for exact and extreme justice that drove him from his country and deprived him of the enjoyment of all his other blessings.   For when he ought to have made reasonable concessions to the plebeians, and by yielding somewhat to their desires to have gained the foremost place among them, he would not do so, but by opposing them in everything that was not just he incurred their hatred and was banished by them.   And when it was in his power to resign the command of the Volscian army the moment he had put an end to the war, and to remove his habitation to some other place till his country had granted him leave to return, instead of offering himself as a target for the plotting of his enemies and the folly of the masses, he did not think fit to do so ; but regarding it as his duty to put his

---

[1] *Cf.* Aristotle, *Nic. Eth.* 1106 b 27.
[2] *Ibid.* 1133 b 32.

παρασχεῖν τοῖς πεπιστευκόσι τὴν ἀρχὴν καὶ λόγον
ἀποδοὺς ὧν ἔπραξε κατὰ τὴν ἡγεμονίαν, εἴ τι φαί-
νοιτο ἀδικῶν, τὴν κατὰ νόμους ὑποσχεῖν δίκην, τῆς
ἄκρας δικαιοσύνης οὐ καλοὺς ἀπέλαβε μισθούς.

LXII. Εἰ μὲν οὖν ἅμα τοῖς σώμασι διαλυομένοις
καὶ τὸ τῆς ψυχῆς, ὁτιδήποτ' ἐστὶν ἐκεῖνο, συνδια-
λύεται, καὶ οὐδαμῇ οὐθὲν ἔτι ἐστίν, οὐκ οἶδ' ὅπως
μακαρίους ὑπολάβω τοὺς μηθὲν μὲν ἀπολαύσαντας
τῆς ἀρετῆς ἀγαθόν, δι' αὐτὴν δὲ ταύτην ἀπολο-
μένους. εἰ δ' ἄφθαρτοι μέχρι τοῦ παντὸς αἱ ψυχαὶ
τυγχάνουσιν ἡμῶν οὖσαι, καθάπερ οἴονταί τινες, ἢ
χρόνον τινὰ[1] μετὰ τὴν ἀπαλλαγὴν τῶν σωμάτων
ἐπιδιαμένουσι,[2] μήκιστον μὲν αἱ τῶν ἀγαθῶν ἀνδρῶν, ἐλάχιστον δ' αἱ τῶν κακῶν, ἀποχρῶσα τιμὴ
φαίνοιτ' ἄν, οἷς ἀρετὴν ἀσκοῦσιν ἠναντιώθη τὰ ἐκ
τῆς τύχης, ἡ παρὰ τῶν ζώντων εὐλογία καὶ μνήμη
μέχρι πλείστου παραμείνασα χρόνου· ὃ καὶ τῷ
2 ἀνδρὶ ἐκείνῳ συνέβη. οὐ γὰρ μόνον Οὐολοῦσκοι
τὸν θάνατον ἐπένθησαν αὐτοῦ καὶ ὡς τῶν ἀρίστων
γενόμενον ἐν τιμῇ ἔχουσιν, ἀλλὰ καὶ Ῥωμαῖοι,
ἐπειδὴ τὸ πάθος ἐγνώσθη, μεγάλην συμφορὰν
ὑπολαβόντες εἶναι τῆς πόλεως, πένθος ἐποιήσαντο
ἰδίᾳ καὶ δημοσίᾳ· καὶ αἱ[3] γυναῖκες αὐτῶν, ἃ νόμος
ἐστὶν αὐταῖς ἐπὶ τοῖς ἰδίοις τε καὶ ἀναγκαίοις
ποιεῖν κήδεσιν, ἀποθέμεναι χρυσόν τε καὶ πορφύραν
καὶ τὸν ἄλλον ἅπαντα κόσμον μέλασιν ἀμφιεσμοῖς
3 χρώμεναι τὸν ἐνιαύσιον ἐπένθησαν χρόνον. ἐτῶν
δὲ μετὰ τὸ πάθος ὁμοῦ τι πεντακοσίων ἤδη δια-
γεγονότων εἰς τόνδε τὸν χρόνον οὐ γέγονεν ἐξίτηλος

---

[1] τινὰ placed here by Sylburg : after ἀπαλλαγὴν by O.
[2] ἐπιδιαμένουσι Cobet, ἔτι διαμένουσι Sintenis, Jacoby :
ἐνδιαμένουσι O. [3] αἱ added by Reiske.

person at the disposal of those who had entrusted him with the command and after giving an account of his conduct during his generalship, if he were found guilty of any misconduct, to undergo the punishment ordained by the laws, he received a sorry reward for his extreme justice.

LXII. Now if when the body perishes the soul also, whatever that is, perishes together with it and no longer exists anywhere, I do not see how I can conceive those to be happy who have received no advantage from their virtue but, on the contrary, have been undone by this very quality. Whereas, if our souls are perchance forever imperishable, as some think, or if they continue on for a time after their separation from the body, those of good men for a very long time and those of the wicked for a very short period, a sufficient reward for those who, though they have practised virtue, have suffered the enmity of Fortune, would seem to be the praise of the living and the continuance of their memory for the longest period of time. And that was the case with this man. For not only the Volscians mourned his death and still hold him in honour as having proved himself one of the best of men, but the Romans also, when they were informed of his fate, looked upon it as a great calamity to the commonwealth and mourned for him both in private and in public ; and their wives, as it is their custom to do at the loss of those who are nearest and dearest to them, laid aside their gold and purple and all their other adornment, and dressing themselves in black, mourned for him for the full period of a year. And though nearly five hundred years have already elapsed since his death down to the present time, his memory has not be-

ἡ τοῦ ἀνδρὸς μνήμη, ἀλλ' ᾄδεται καὶ ὑμνεῖται πρὸς πάντων ὡς εὐσεβὴς καὶ δίκαιος ἀνήρ.

Ὁ μὲν δὴ κατασχὼν Ῥωμαίους κίνδυνος ἐκ τῆς Οὐολούσκων τε καὶ Αἰκανῶν ἐπιστρατείας Μάρκιον λαβούσης ἡγεμόνα, μέγιστος τῶν πρὸ αὐτοῦ γενόμενος καὶ μικρὸν ἀποσχὼν τοῦ πᾶσαν τὴν πόλιν ἀνελεῖν ἐκ βάθρων, τοιούτου τέλους ἔτυχεν.

LXIII. Ἡμέραις δ' ὀλίγαις ὕστερον ἐξελθόντες εἰς τὴν ὕπαιθρον Ῥωμαῖοι πολλῇ στρατιᾷ τῶν ὑπάτων ἀγόντων ἀμφοτέρων, καὶ προελθόντες ἄχρι τῶν ὅρων τῆς σφετέρας κατεστρατοπέδευσαν ἐπὶ λόφοις δυσίν, ἴδιον ἑκατέρου τῶν ὑπάτων στρατόπεδον ἐπὶ τοῖς ἐρυμνοτάτοις καταστησαμένου.[1] οὐ μὴν ἔδρασάν γε οὐδὲν οὔτε μεῖζον οὔτ' ἔλαττον,[2] ἀλλ' ἀνέστρεψαν ἄπρακτοι, καίτοι καλὰς ἀφορμὰς δόντων αὐτοῖς τῶν πολεμίων δρᾶσαί τι γενναῖον.
2 πρότεροι γὰρ ἔτι τούτων Οὐολοῦσκοί τε καὶ Αἰκανοὶ στρατὸν ἐπὶ τὴν Ῥωμαίων γῆν ἤγαγον γνώμην ποιησάμενοι μὴ ἀνεῖναι τὸν καιρόν, ἀλλ', ἕως ἔτι καταπεπλῆχθαι τὸ ἀντίπαλον ἐδόκουν, χωρεῖν ἐπ' αὐτό, ὡς καὶ ἑκούσιον διὰ δέος παραστησόμενον. στασιάσαντες δὲ περὶ τῆς ἡγεμονίας κατ' ἀλλήλων τὰ ὅπλα ἥρπασαν καὶ συμπεσόντες ἐμάχοντο, οὔτε κατὰ τάξιν οὔτε ἐκ παραγγέλματος, ἀλλὰ φύρδην καὶ ἀναμίξ, ὥστε πολὺν ἐξ ἀμφοῖν γενέσθαι φόνον· καὶ εἰ μὴ δὺς ὁ ἥλιος ἔφθασεν, ἅπασαι ἂν αὐτῶν αἱ δυνάμεις διεφθάρησαν. τῇ δὲ νυκτὶ λυούσῃ τὸ νεῖκος ἀκούσιοι εἴξαντες διεκρίθη-

---

[1] κατεστρατοπέδευσαν added by Kiessling.   Reiske added ἔχοντος before ἴδιον.
[2] οὐδὲν οὔτε μεῖζον οὔτε ἔλαττον Sylburg : οὐδὲν μεῖζον AC, μεῖζον οὐδὲν B.

come extinct, but he is still praised and celebrated by all as a pious and just man.

Thus ended the danger with which the Romans had been threatened by the expedition of the Volscians and Aequians under the command of Marcius, a danger that was greater than any to which they had ever been exposed before and came very near destroying the whole commonwealth from its foundations.

LXIII. A few days later [1] the Romans took the field with a large army commanded by both consuls, and advancing to the confines of their own territory, encamped on two hills, each of the consuls placing his camp in the strongest position. Nevertheless, they accomplished nothing, either great or little, but returned unsuccessful, though excellent opportunities had been afforded them by the enemy for performing some gallant action. It seems that even before their expedition the Volscians and the Aequians had led an army against the Roman territory, having resolved not to let the opportunity slip, but to attack their adversaries while they seemed to be still panic-stricken ; for they thought that in their fear they would surrender of their own accord. But quarrelling among themselves over the command, they rushed to arms, and falling upon one another, fought without keeping their ranks or receiving orders, but in confusion and disorder, so that many were killed on both sides; and if the sun had not set in time to prevent it, all their forces would have been utterly destroyed. But yielding reluctantly to the night which put an

---

[1] *Cf.* Livy ii. 40, 12 f.

σάν τε ἀπ' ἀλλήλων καὶ ἐπὶ τοὺς ἰδίους χάρακας
ἀπηλλάγησαν· ἔωθεν δ' ἀναστήσαντες τὰς δυνάμεις
3 ἀπῄεσαν ἑκάτεροι ἐπὶ τὰ σφέτερα. οἱ δ' ὕπατοι
παρά τε αὐτομόλων καὶ αἰχμαλώτων, οἳ παρ' αὐτὸ
τὸ ἔργον ἀπέδρασαν, ἀκούσαντες οἷα κατέσχε
λύσσα καὶ θεοβλάβεια τὰ πολέμια, οὔτε συνεπ-
έθεντο τῷ κατ' εὐχὴν δοθέντι καιρῷ τριάκοντα
σταδίων οὐ πλεῖον ἀπέχοντες, οὔτε ἀπιόντας ἐδίω-
ξαν, ἐν ᾧ κεκμηκότας καὶ τραυματίας καὶ ὀλίγους
ἐκ πολλῶν καὶ[1] ἀτάκτους χωροῦντας ἀκραιφνεῖς
αὐτοὶ καὶ σὺν κόσμῳ ἑπόμενοι ῥᾳδίως ἂν διέφθειραν
4 πασσυδί. λύσαντες δὲ καὶ αὐτοὶ τοὺς χάρακας
ἀπῄεσαν εἰς τὴν πόλιν, εἴτε ἀρκούμενοι τῷ παρὰ
τῆς τύχης δοθέντι ἀγαθῷ, εἴτε οὐ πιστεύοντες
ἀνασκήτῳ στρατιᾷ τῇ σφετέρᾳ, εἴτε περὶ πολλοῦ
ποιούμενοι τὸ μηδ' ὀλίγους τῶν σφετέρων ἀπο-
βαλεῖν. ἀφικόμενοι δ' εἰς τὴν πόλιν ἐν αἰσχύνῃ
πολλῇ ἦσαν δειλίας δόξαν ἐπὶ τῷ ἔργῳ φερόμενοι·
καὶ οὐδεμίαν ἔξοδον ἔτι ποιησάμενοι παρέδοσαν
τοῖς μεθ' ἑαυτοὺς ὑπάτοις τὴν ἀρχήν.

LXIV. Τῷ δ' ἑξῆς ἐνιαυτῷ Γάιος μὲν Ἀκύλλιος
καὶ Τίτος Σίκκιος, ἄνδρες ἔμπειροι πολέμων, τὴν
ὑπατείαν παρειλήφεσαν. ἡ δὲ βουλὴ προθέντων
λόγον περὶ τοῦ πολέμου τῶν ὑπάτων πρῶτον
ἐψηφίσατο πρεσβείαν πέμψαι πρὸς Ἕρνικας αἰτή-
σουσαν ὡς παρὰ φίλων τε καὶ ἐνσπόνδων δίκας
νομίμους· ἠδίκητο γὰρ ἡ πόλις ὑπ' αὐτῶν κατὰ τὴν
Οὐολούσκων τε καὶ Αἰκανῶν ἐπιστρατείαν λῃστεί-

---

[1] καὶ added by Reiske.

end to the quarrel, they separated and retired to their own camps ; and rousing their forces at dawn, both sides returned home. The consuls, though they learned both from deserters and from prisoners who had escaped during the action itself what fury and madness had possessed the enemy, neither embraced an opportunity so desirable when it offered, though they were no more than thirty stades distant, nor pursued them in their retreat—a situation in which their own troops, being fresh and following in good order, might easily have destroyed to a man those of the enemy, who were fatigued, wounded, reduced from a large to a small number, and were retiring in disorder. But they too broke camp and returned to Rome, either being contented with the advantage Fortune had given them, or having no confidence in their troops, who were undisciplined, or considering it very important not to lose even a few of their own men. When they got back to Rome, however, they found themselves in great disgrace and had to bear the stigma of cowardice for their behaviour. And without undertaking any other expedition they surrendered their magistracy to their successors.

LXIV. The next year Gaius Aquilius and Titus Siccius,[1] men experienced in war, succeeded to the consulship. The senate, when the consuls had brought up the war for consideration, voted, first, to send an embassy to the Hernicans to demand, as from friends and allies, the customary satisfaction ; for the commonwealth had suffered wrongs at their hands at the time of the attack of the Volscians and Aequians through brigandage and incursions into the part of

---

[1] For chaps. 64-67 cf. Livy ii. 40. 14. Our MSS. of Livy give the name as T. Sicinius, but Cassiodorus read Siccius.

αἰς τε καὶ καταδρομαῖς τῆς ὁμορούσης αὐτοῖς
γῆς· ἕως δ' ἂν τὰς παρ' ἐκείνων λάβωσιν ἀποκρίσεις, στρατιὰν ὅσην δύνανται πλείστην καταγράφειν
τοὺς ὑπάτους καὶ τοὺς συμμάχους πρεσβειῶν
ἀποστολαῖς παρακαλεῖν σῖτόν τε καὶ ὅπλα καὶ
χρήματα καὶ τἆλλα ὅσων ἔδει τῷ πολέμῳ διὰ
2 πολυχειρίας παρασκευάσασθαι καὶ ἐν τάχει. ὡς δ'
ἀπήγγειλαν αὐτοῖς ἀναστρέψαντες οἱ πρέσβεις ἃς
παρὰ τῶν Ἑρνίκων ἔλαβον ἀποκρίσεις, ὅτι συνθήκας μὲν οὔ φασιν αὐτοῖς εἶναι πρὸς Ῥωμαίους
κοινῇ γενομένας οὐδέποτε, τὰς δὲ πρὸς βασιλέα
Ταρκύνιον ὁμολογίας αἰτιῶνται λελύσθαι τήν τε
ἀρχὴν ἀφαιρεθέντος ἐκείνου καὶ τεθνηκότος ἐπὶ τῆς
ξένης· εἰ δέ τινες ἁρπαγαὶ καὶ καταδρομαὶ τῆς
χώρας ἐγένοντο διὰ λῃστηρίων, οὐκ ἀπὸ κοινῆς
γνώμης γεγονέναι λέγουσιν, ἀλλ' ἰδιωτῶν ἀδική-
ματα μετιόντων τὰ ἴδια, καὶ οὐδὲ τοὺς ταῦτα
δράσαντας παρέχειν οἷοί τ' εἰσὶν ἐπὶ δίκην, ἕτερα
καὶ αὐτοὶ τοιαῦτα πεπονθέναι λέγοντες καὶ ἀντεγ-
καλοῦντες, ἄσμενοί τε δέχονται[1] τὸν πόλεμον·
3 ταῦτα ἡ βουλὴ μαθοῦσα ἐψηφίσατο νείμασθαι τὴν
καταγραφεῖσαν ἐκ τῶν νεωτέρων στρατιὰν τριχῇ·
τούτων δὲ τὴν μὲν μίαν ἄγοντα Γάιον Ἀκύλλιον
τὸν ὕπατον ὁμόσε τῇ Ἑρνίκων στρατιᾷ χωρεῖν (καὶ
γὰρ ἐκεῖνοι ἤδη ἦσαν ἐν τοῖς ὅπλοις), τὴν δ' ἑτέραν
Τίτον Σίκκιον ἐπὶ Οὐολούσκους ἄγειν, τὸν ἕτερον
τῶν ὑπάτων, τὴν δὲ λοιπὴν τρίτην μερίδα παρα-
λαβόντα Σπόριον Λάρκιον, ὃς ἦν ἀποδεδειγμένος
ὑπὸ τῶν ὑπάτων ἔπαρχος τὴν ἔγγιστα τῆς πόλεως

---

[1] δέχονται Cary, ἐκδέχεσθαι Post : εἰσι δέχεσθαι O, Jacoby.

the Roman territory that bordered on their own; and they voted further that while waiting to receive their answer the consuls should enrol all the forces they could, summon the allies by sending out embassies, and get ready corn, arms, money, and all the other things necessary for the war, by employing a large number of men and using haste. When the ambassadors returned from the Hernicans, they reported to the senate the answer they had received from them, to the following effect: They denied that there had ever been a treaty between them and the Romans by act of the public, and they charged that the compact they had made with King Tarquinius had been dissolved both by his expulsion from power and by his death in a foreign land; but if any depredations had been committed or incursions made into the territory of the Romans by bands of robbers, they said these had not been made by the general consent of their nation, but were the misdeeds of individuals pursuing their private ends, and that they were unable to deliver up to justice even the men who had done these things, since they claimed that they themselves had also suffered similar wrongs and had the same complaints to make; and they said that they cheerfully accepted the war. The senate, upon hearing this, voted that the youth already enrolled should be divided into three bodies, and that with one of these the consul Gaius Aquilius should march against the army of the Hernicans (for these were already in arms), that Titus Siccius, the other consul, should lead the second against the Volscians, and that Spurius Larcius, who had been appointed prefect of the city by the consuls, should with the remaining third part defend the portion of the country that lay

χώραν φυλάττειν· τοὺς δ' ὑπὲρ τὸν στρατιωτικὸν
κατάλογον, ὅσοι δύναμιν εἶχον ἔτι βαστάζειν ὅπλα,
ταχθέντας ὑπὸ σημείαις τάς τε ἄκρας φρουρεῖν τῆς
πόλεως καὶ τὰ τείχη, μή τις αἰφνίδιος πολεμίων
γένηται ἔφοδος ἐξεστρατευμένης τῆς νεότητος
ἀθρόας· ἡγεῖσθαι δὲ τῆς δυνάμεως ταύτης Αὖλον
Σεμπρώνιον Ἀτρατῖνον, ἄνδρα τῶν ὑπατικῶν.
ἐγίνετο δὲ ταῦτα οὐ διὰ μακροῦ.

LXV. Ἀκύλλιος μὲν οὖν ἅτερος τῶν ὑπάτων ἐν
τῇ Πραινεστίνων χώρᾳ τὸν Ἑρνίκων στρατὸν
ὑπομένοντα καταλαβὼν ἀντικατεστρατοπέδευσεν ὡς
ἐδύνατο μάλιστα ἀγχοτάτω σταδίους ἀπὸ τῆς
Ῥώμης ἀποσχὼν ὀλίγῳ πλείους διακοσίων· τρίτῃ
δ' ἀφ' ἧς κατεστρατοπέδευσεν ἡμέρᾳ προελθόντων
ἐκ τοῦ χάρακος τῶν Ἑρνίκων εἰς τὸ πεδίον ἐν τάξει
καὶ τὰ σημεῖα ἀράντων τῆς μάχης, ἀντεξῆγε καὶ
αὐτὸς τὴν δύναμιν ἐν κόσμῳ τε καὶ κατὰ τέλη.
2 ἐπεὶ δ' ἀγχοῦ ἐγένοντο ἀλλήλων ἔθεον ἀλαλάξαντες
ὁμόσε, πρῶτον μὲν οἱ ψιλοὶ σαυνίων τε βολαῖς καὶ
τοξεύμασι καὶ λίθοις ἀπὸ σφενδόνης μαχόμενοι, καὶ[1]
πολλὰ τραύματα ἔδοσαν ἀλλήλοις· ἔπειτα ἱππεῖς
ἱππεῦσι συρράττουσι κατ' ἴλας ἐλαύνοντες καὶ τὸ
πεζὸν τῷ πεζῷ κατὰ σπείρας μαχόμενον. ἔνθα δὴ
καλὸς ἀγὼν ἦν ἐκθύμως ἀμφοτέρων ἀγωνιζομένων,
καὶ μέχρι πολλοῦ διέμενον οὐδέτεροι τοῖς ἑτέροις
τοῦ χωρίου ἐν ᾧ ἐτάχθησαν εἴκοντες. ἔπειτα ἡ
Ῥωμαίων ἤρξατο κάμνειν φάλαγξ, οἷα διὰ πολλοῦ
τοῦ μεταξὺ χρόνου τότε πρῶτον ἠναγκασμένη ὁμι-
3 λεῖν πολέμῳ. τοῦτο συνιδὼν Ἀκύλλιος ἐκέλευσε
τοὺς ἀκμῆτας ἔτι καὶ εἰς αὐτὸ τοῦτο φυλαττο-

---

[1] καὶ placed before πρῶτον (one line above) by Sylburg.

nearest to the city; that those who were above the military age but were still capable of bearing arms should be arrayed under their standards and guard the citadels of the city and the walls, to prevent any sudden attack by the enemy while all the youth were in the field, and that Aulus Sempronius Atratinus, one of the ex-consuls, should have the command of this force. These orders were presently carried out.

LXV. Aquilius, one of the consuls, finding the army of the Hernicans waiting for him in the country of the Praenestines, encamped as near to them as he could, at a distance of a little more than two hundred stades from Rome. The second[1] day after he had pitched his camp the Hernicans came out of their camp into the plain in order of battle and gave the signal for combat; whereupon Aquilius also marched out to meet them with his army duly drawn up and disposed in their several divisions. When they drew near to one another, they uttered their war-cries and ran to the encounter; and first to engage were the light-armed men, who, fighting with javelins, arrows, and stones from their slings, gave one another many wounds. Next, horsemen clashed with horsemen, charging in troops, and infantry with infantry, fighting by cohorts. Then there was a glorious struggle as both armies fought stubbornly; and for a long time they stood firm, neither side yielding to the other the ground where they were posted. At length the Romans' line began to be in distress, this being the first occasion in a long time that they had been forced to engage in war. Aquilius, observing this, ordered that the troops which were still fresh and were being reserved for this very purpose should

---

[1] Literally "third," reckoning inclusively.

μένους ὑπὸ τὰ κάμνοντα τῆς φάλαγγος ὑπελθεῖν
μέρη, τοὺς δὲ τραυματίας καὶ τοὺς ἀπειρηκότας
ὀπίσω τῆς φάλαγγος ἀπιέναι. οἱ δ' Ἕρνικες ὡς
ἔμαθον κινουμένους αὐτῶν τοὺς λόχους, φυγῆς τε
ἄρχειν τοὺς Ῥωμαίους ὑπέλαβον, καὶ παρακελευ-
σάμενοι ἀλλήλοις ἐμβάλλουσι πυκνοῖς τοῖς λόχοις
εἰς τὰ κινούμενα τῶν πολεμίων μέρη, καὶ οἱ ἀ-
κραιφνεῖς τῶν Ῥωμαίων ἐπιόντας αὐτοὺς δέχονται·
καὶ ἦν αὖθις ἐξ ὑπαρχῆς ἀμφοτέρων ἐκθύμως
ἀγωνιζομένων μάχη καρτερά· καὶ γὰρ¹ οἱ τῶι
Ἑρνίκων ἐξεπληροῦντο λόχοι τοῖς ἀκμῆσιν ὑπο-
πεμπομένοις εἰς τὰ κάμνοντα ὑπὸ τῶν ἡγεμόνων.
4 ἐπειδὴ δὲ περὶ δείλην ὀψίαν ἦν ἤδη, παρακαλέσας
τοὺς ἱππεῖς ὁ ὕπατος νυνί γ'² ἄνδρας ἀγαθοὺς
γενέσθαι, ἐμβάλλει τοῖς πολεμίοις κατὰ τὸ δεξιὸν
κέρας αὐτὸς ἡγούμενος τῆς ἴλης. οἱ δ' ὀλίγον
τινὰ δεξάμενοι χρόνον αὐτοὺς ἐγκλίνουσι, καὶ
γίνεται φόνος ἐνταῦθα πολύς. τὸ μὲν οὖν δεξιὸν
τῶν Ἑρνίκων κέρας ἐπόνει τε ἤδη καὶ ἐξέλειπε τὴν
τάξιν, τὸ δ' εὐώνυμον ἔτι ἀντεῖχε καὶ περιῆν τοῦ
Ῥωμαίων³ δεξιοῦ· μετ' ὀλίγον μέντοι καὶ τοῦτο
5 ἐνέδωκεν. ὁ γὰρ Ἀκύλλιος τοὺς ἀρίστους τῶν
νέων ἐπαγόμενος παρεβοήθει κἀκεῖ παραθαρρύνων
τε καὶ ἐξ ὀνόματος ἀνακαλῶν τοὺς εἰωθότας ἐν
ταῖς πρὶν ἀριστεύειν μάχαις, τά τε σημεῖα τῶν
λόχων ὅσοι μὴ ἐρρωμένως ἐδόκουν ἀμύνεσθαι παρὰ
τῶν σημειοφόρων ἁρπάζων εἰς μέσους ἐρρίπτει
τοὺς πολεμίους, ἵνα τὸ δέος αὐτοὺς τῆς ἐννόμου
τιμωρίας, εἰ μὴ ἀνασώσαιντο τὰς σημείας, ἄνδρας
ἀγαθοὺς εἶναι ἀναγκάσῃ· τῷ τε κάμνοντι αὐτὸς

---

¹ καὶ γὰρ Ο : καὶ γὰρ καὶ Reiske, Jacoby.
² γε added by Sylburg.

come up to reinforce the parts of the line that were in distress and that the men who were wounded and exhausted should retire to the rear. The Hernicans, learning that their troops were being shifted, imagined that the Romans were beginning flight; and encouraging one another and closing their ranks, they fell upon those parts of the enemy's army that were in motion, and the fresh troops of the Romans received their onset. Thus once more, as both sides fought stubbornly, there was a strenuous battle all over again; for the ranks of the Hernicans were also continually reinforced with fresh troops sent up by their generals to the parts of the line that were in distress. At length, late in the afternoon, the consul, encouraging the horsemen now at least to acquit themselves as brave men, led the squadron in a charge against the enemy's right wing. This, after resisting them for a short time, fell back, and a great slaughter ensued. While the Hernicans' right wing was now in difficulties and no longer keeping its ranks, their left still held out and was superior to the Romans' right; but in a short time this too gave way. For Aquilius, taking with him the best of the youth, hastened to the rescue there also, and exhorting his men and calling by name upon those who had been wont to distinguish themselves in former battles, and seizing from their bearers the standards of any centuries that did not seem to be fighting resolutely, he hurled them into the midst of the enemy, in order that their fear of the punishment prescribed by the laws in the case of failure to recover the standards might compel them to be brave men; and he himself continually came to

---

³ Sylburg : Ῥωμαίου O.

παρεβοήθει μέρει ἀεί, ἕως[1] ἐξέωσε τῆς στάσεως
καὶ θάτερον κέρας.[2] ψιλωθέντων δὲ τῶν ἄκρων
6 οὐδὲ τὰ μέσα παρέμεινε. φυγὴ δὴ τῶν Ἑρνίκων
τὸ μετὰ τοῦτο ἐγίνετο ἐπὶ τὸν χάρακα τεταραγμένη
τε καὶ ἄκοσμος, καὶ οἱ Ῥωμαῖοι αὐτοῖς κτείνοντες
ἠκολούθουν. τοσαύτη δ' ἄρα προθυμία παρὰ τὸν
τότε ἀγῶνα τῇ Ῥωμαίων στρατιᾷ ἐνέπεσεν ὥστε
καὶ τοῦ χάρακος τῶν πολεμίων πειρᾶσθαί τινας
ἐπιβαίνειν ὡς ἐξ ἐφόδου χειρωσομένους· ὧν οὐκ
ἀσφαλῆ τὴν προθυμίαν οὐδ' ἐν τῷ συμφέροντι
γιγνομένην ὁρῶν ὁ ὕπατος, σημαίνειν κελεύσας τὸ
ἀνακλητικὸν κατεβίβασε τοὺς ὁμόσε χωροῦντας
ἄκοντας ἀπὸ τῶν ἐρυμάτων, δείσας μὴ ἐξ ὑπερδεξίων βαλλόμενοι σὺν αἰσχύνῃ τε καὶ μετὰ
μεγάλης βλάβης ἀναγκασθῶσιν ὑποχωρεῖν, ἔπειτα
καὶ τὴν ἐκ τῆς προτέρας νίκης εὔκλειαν ἀφανί-
σωσι. τότε μὲν οὖν—ἤδη γὰρ[3] ἦν περὶ δύσιν ἡλίου
—χαίροντές τε καὶ παιανίζοντες οἱ Ῥωμαῖοι κατεστρατοπέδευσαν.

LXVI. Τῇ δ' ἐπιούσῃ νυκτὶ ψόφος τε ἠκούετο
πολὺς ἐκ τοῦ χάρακος τῶν Ἑρνίκων καὶ βοή, καὶ
πολλὰ ἐφαίνετο σέλα λαμπάδων. ἀπογνόντες γὰρ
ἔτι ἀνθέξειν ἑτέρᾳ μάχῃ καταλιπεῖν τὸν χάρακα
ἔγνωσαν αὐτοκέλευστοι· καὶ τὸ ποιῆσαν αὐτῶν
τὴν ἀταξίαν καὶ βοὴν τοῦτο ἦν. ὡς γὰρ ἕκαστοι
δυνάμεως εἶχον καὶ τάχους ἔφευγον ἐπιβοῶντές τε
ἀλλήλους καὶ ἐπιβοώμενοι, τῶν δ' ὑπολειπομένων
διὰ τραύματα ἢ νόσους οἰμωγὰς καὶ λιτανείας ἐν
2 οὐδενὶ λόγῳ τιθέμενοι. τοῦτο ἀγνοοῦντες οἱ
Ῥωμαῖοι, πεπυσμένοι δὲ παρὰ τῶν αἰχμαλώτων

[1] ἕως R : τέως Ba, Jacoby.
[2] κέρας Sylburg : μέρος O.
[3] γὰρ Reiske : καὶ γὰρ O.

the relief of any part that was in distress, till he dislodged the other wing also from its position. Their flanks being now exposed, even the centre did not stand its ground. It became a flight then for the Hernicans, a flight back to their camp in confusion and disorder; and the Romans pursued, cutting them down. Such ardour, indeed, came upon the Roman army in that struggle that some of the men endeavoured even to mount the ramparts of the enemy's camp in the hope of taking it by storm. But the consul, perceiving that their ardour was hazardous and detrimental, ordered the signal for a retreat to be sounded and thus brought down from the ramparts against their will those who were coming to blows with the enemy; for he feared that they would be forced by the missiles hurled down upon them from above to retire with shame and great loss and would thus efface the glory of their earlier victory. On that occasion, then, it being now near sunset, the Romans made their camp rejoicing and singing songs of triumph.

LXVI. The following night there was much noise and shouting heard in the camp of the Hernicans, and the lights of many torches were seen. For the enemy, despairing of being able to hold their own in another engagement, had resolved to leave their camp of their own accord; and this was the cause of the disorder and shouting. For they were fleeing with all the strength and speed which each man was capable of, calling to and being called by one another, without showing the least regard for the lamentations and entreaties of those who were being left behind on account of their wounds and sickness. The Romans, who knew nothing of this but had been

πρότερον ὅτι δύναμις Ἑρνίκων ἑτέρα μέλλοι βοη-
θὸς ἥξειν τοῖς σφετέροις, καὶ τὴν βοήν τε καὶ
ταραχὴν ἐπὶ τῇ ἐκείνων ἀφίξει γεγονέναι νομίζον-
τες, τά τε ὅπλα ἀνέλαβον καὶ τὸν χάρακα περι-
στεφανώσαντες, μή τις ἔφοδος αὐτοῖς γένοιτο
νύκτωρ, τοτὲ μὲν ὅπλων κτύπον ἐποίουν ἀθρόοι,
τοτὲ δ' ὥσπερ εἰς μάχην ὁρμώμενοι θαμινὰ ἐπ-
ηλάλαζον. τοῖς δ' Ἕρνιξι καὶ ταῦτα δέος μέγα
παρεῖχε, καὶ ὡς διωκόμενοι πρὸς τῶν πολεμίων
3 σποράδες ἄλλοι κατ' ἄλλας ὁδοὺς ἔθεον.[1] ἡμέρας
δὲ γενομένης, ἐπειδὴ ἀπήγγειλαν αὐτοῖς οἱ πεμφ-
θέντες ἐπὶ τὴν κατασκοπὴν ἱππεῖς ὡς οὔτε δύναμις
ἑτέρα παρῄει[2] σύμμαχος τοῖς πολεμίοις, οἵ τε τῇ
προτέρᾳ παραταξάμενοι μάχῃ πεφεύγασιν, ἐξαγαγὼν τὴν δύναμιν ὁ Ἀκύλλιος τόν τε χάρακα
τῶν πολεμίων αἱρεῖ μεστὸν ὄντα ὑποζυγίων τε καὶ
ἀγορᾶς καὶ ὅπλων, καὶ τοὺς τραυματίας αὐτῶν οὐκ
ἐλάττους ὄντας τῶν πεφευγότων λαμβάνει, τήν τε
ἵππον ἐκπέμψας ἐπὶ τοὺς ἐσκεδασμένους ἀνὰ τὰς
ὁδούς τε καὶ τὰς ὕλας πολλῶν γίνεται σωμάτων
ἐγκρατής· καὶ τὸ λοιπὸν ἤδη τὴν Ἑρνίκων γῆν
ἐπῄει λεηλατῶν ἀδεῶς, οὐδενὸς ἔτι ὑπομένοντος εἰς
χεῖρας ἰέναι. ταῦτα μὲν Ἀκύλλιος ἔδρασεν.

LXVII. Ὁ δ' ἕτερος τῶν ὑπάτων Τίτος Σίκκιος,
ὁ πεμφθεὶς ἐπὶ Οὐολούσκους, ὅσον ἦν κράτιστον
τῆς δυνάμεως μέρος ἀναλαβὼν[3] εἰς τὴν Οὐελι-
τρανῶν χώραν εἰσέβαλεν. ἐνταῦθα γὰρ ἦν Τύλλος
Ἄττιος ὁ τῶν Οὐολούσκων ἡγεμὼν τὴν ἀκμαιο-
τάτην συσκευασάμενος στρατιάν, γνώμην ἔχων τὰ

---

[1] ἔθεον B : om. R.
[2] παρῄει B : παρῆν A, παρείη Reiske.
[3] ἀναλαβὼν B (?) : λαβὼν Cb, om. R.

informed earlier by the prisoners that another army
of Hernicans was intending to come to the aid of
their countrymen, imagined that this shouting and
tumult had been occasioned by the arrival of those
reinforcements, and they accordingly took up their
arms once more, and forming a circle about their
entrenchments, for fear some attack might be made
upon them in the night, they would now make a din
by all clashing their weapons together at the same
time and now raise their war-cry repeatedly as if
they were going into battle. The Hernicans were
greatly alarmed at this also, and believing themselves
pursued by the enemy, dispersed and fled, some by
one road and some by another. When day came and
the horse sent out to reconnoitre had reported to the
Romans that not only was there no fresh force coming
to the enemy's assistance, but that even those who
had been arrayed in battle the day before had fled,
Aquilius marched out with his army and seized the
enemy's camp, which was full of beasts of burden,
provisions, and arms, and also took captive their
wounded, not fewer in number than those who had
fled; and sending the horse in pursuit of such as were
scattered along the roads and in the woods, he captured many of them. Thereafter he overran the
Hernicans' territory and laid it waste with impunity,
no one any longer daring to encounter him. These
were the exploits of Aquilius.

LXVII. The other consul, Titus Siccius, who had
been sent against the Volscians, took with him the
flower of the army and made an irruption into the
territory of Velitrae. For Tullus Attius, the Volscian
general, was there with the most vigorous part of the
army, which he had assembled with the intention of

συμμαχικὰ Ῥωμαίων κακῶσαι πρῶτον, ὥσπερ ὁ
Μάρκιος ἔδρασεν ὅτ' ἤρχετο τοῦ πολέμου, δόξας
ἐν τῷ αὐτῷ φόβῳ Ῥωμαίους ἔτι διαμένειν καὶ
μηδεμίαν τοῖς ὑπὲρ αὐτῶν κινδυνεύουσι πέμπειν
ἐπικουρίαν. ὡς δ' ὤφθησάν τε καὶ εἶδον ἀλλήλας
αἱ δυνάμεις, οὐδὲν ἔτι ἀναβαλόμεναι συνῄεσαν εἰς
2 τὸ αὐτό. ἦν δ' ὁ χῶρος ὁ μεταξὺ τῶν στρατοπέδων, ἐν ᾧ τὴν μάχην ἔδει γενέσθαι, λόφος πετρώδης
πολλαχῇ περικατεαγώς, ἔνθα οὐδετέροις ἡ ἵππος
ἔμελλεν ἔσεσθαι χρησίμη. μαθόντες δὲ τοῦτο οἱ
τῶν Ῥωμαίων ἱππεῖς καὶ ἐν αἰσχύνῃ θέμενοι εἰ
παρόντες τῷ ἀγῶνι μηδὲν προσωφελήσουσιν, ἐδέ-
οντο τοῦ ὑπάτου προσελθόντες ἀθρόοι ἐᾶσαι σφᾶς
καταβάντας ἀπὸ τῶν ἵππων μάχεσθαι πεζούς, εἰ
3 τοῦτο αὐτῷ δοκεῖ κράτιστον εἶναι. κἀκεῖνος πολλὰ
ἐπαινέσας αὐτοὺς καταβιβάζει τε ἀπὸ τῶν ἵππων,
καὶ σὺν ἑαυτῷ τεταγμένους εἶχεν ἐπισκόπους τε
καὶ ἐπανορθωτὰς τοῦ κάμνοντος ἐσομένους· καὶ
ἐγένοντο τῆς τότε νίκης λαμπρᾶς σφόδρα γενο-
μένης¹ οὗτοι Ῥωμαίοις αἴτιοι. τὸ μὲν γὰρ πεζὸν
ἀμφοτέρων πλήθει τε ἀνθρώπων² ὡς μάλιστα ἦν
καὶ ὁπλισμοῖς ὁμοιότροπον, τάξεώς τε κόσμῳ καὶ
μάχης ἐμπειρίᾳ κατά τε ἐπαγωγὰς καὶ ὑποχωρή-
σεις πληγάς τε αὖ καὶ φυλακὰς παραπλήσιον.
4 μετέμαθον γὰρ οἱ Οὐολοῦσκοι πάντα τὰ πολέμια
ἐξ οὗ Μάρκιον ἔσχον ἡγεμόνα, καὶ εἰς τὰ Ῥωμαίων προσεχώρησαν ἔθη.

Διέμενον οὖν ἐπὶ πλεῖστον χρόνον τῆς ἡμέρας
ἀγχωμάλως αἱ φάλαγγες ἀγωνιζόμεναι, καὶ ἡ τοῦ
χωρίου φύσις ἀνώμαλος οὖσα ἑκατέροις πολλὰ εἰς
τὸ πλεονεκτεῖν κατ' ἀλλήλων παρείχετο. οἱ δ'

¹ γενομένης AmgC : ἐσομένης AB.

first harassing the Romans' allies as Marcius had done when he began the war, thinking that the Romans still continued in the same state of fear and would not send any assistance to those who were incurring danger for their sake. As soon as the two armies were seen by and saw each other, they engaged without delay. The ground between their camps on which the battle would have to take place was a rocky hill broken away in many parts of its circuit, where the horse could be of no use to either side. The Roman cavalry, observing this, thought it would be a shame for them to be present at the action without assisting in it ; and coming to the consul in a body, they begged him to permit them to quit their horses and fight on foot, if this seemed best to him. He commended them heartily, and ordering them to dismount, drew them up and kept them with him to observe any part of the line that might be hard pressed and to go to its relief ; and they proved to be the cause of the very brilliant victory which the Romans then gained. For the foot on both sides were remarkably alike both in numbers and in arma-ment, and were very similar in the tactical formation of their lines and in their experience in fighting, whether in attacking or retreating, or again in dealing blows or in warding them off. For the Volscians had changed all their military tactics after securing Marcius as their commander, and had adopted the customs of the Romans.

Accordingly, the legionaries of the two armies con-tinued fighting the greater part of the day with equal success ; and the unevenness of the terrain afforded each side many advantages against the other. The

---

² ἀνθρώπων ἰσάριθμον Reiske.

ἱππεῖς τῶν Ῥωμαίων διχῇ νείμαντες ἑαυτούς, οἱ
μὲν κατὰ τὰ πλάγια τῶν πολεμίων ἀπὸ τοῦ δεξιοῦ
κέρως ἐμβάλλουσιν, οἱ δὲ περιελθόντες διὰ[1] τοῦ
5 λόφου τοῖς κατόπιν ἐπιρράττουσιν. ἔπειθ' οἱ μὲν
εἰσακοντίζοντες τὰς λόγχας, οἱ δὲ τοὺς ὁμόσε
χωροῦντας τοῖς ἱππικοῖς ξίφεσι μακροτέροις οὖσι
κατὰ βραχιόνων παίοντες καὶ παρὰ τὰς ἀγκύλας
καταφέροντες, πολλῶν μὲν τὰς[2] χεῖρας αὐτοῖς σκε-
πάσμασί τε καὶ ἀμυντηρίοις ἀπέκοπτον, πολλοὺς
δὲ γονάτων τε καὶ ἀστραγάλων πληγαῖς βαθείαις
6 ἀπὸ κρατίστης βάσεως ἐρρίπτουν ἡμιθανεῖς. περιειστήκει τε πάντοθεν τοῖς Οὐολούσκοις τὸ δεινόν·
ἐκ μὲν γὰρ τῶν κατὰ πρόσωπον οἱ πεζοὶ αὐτοῖς
ἐνέκειντο, ἐκ δὲ τῶν πλαγίων τε καὶ τῶν κατόπιν
οἱ ἱππεῖς, ὥστε ὑπὲρ δύναμιν ἀγαθοὶ γενόμενοι καὶ
πολλὰ ἔργα τόλμης τε καὶ ἐμπειρίας ἀποδειξάμενοι,
μικροῦ δεῖν πάντες εἰς τὸ δεξιὸν κέρας ἔχοντες
κατεκόπησαν. οἱ δ' ἐν μέσῃ τε τῇ φάλαγγι τεταγμένοι καὶ ἐπὶ τοῦ ἑτέρου κέρως ἐπειδὴ τὸ δεξιόν τε
παρερρηγμένον εἶδον καὶ τὸν αὐτὸν τρόπον ἐπιόντας
σφίσι τοὺς τῶν Ῥωμαίων ἱππεῖς, ἐξελίξαντες τοὺς
λόχους βάδην ἀπεχώρουν ἐπὶ τὸν χάρακα, καὶ οἱ
τῶν Ῥωμαίων ἱππεῖς ἐν[3] τάξει ἠκολούθουν.

7 Ἐπεὶ δὲ πρὸς τῷ ἐρύματι ἦσαν, ἑτέρα γίνεται
μάχη τῶν ἱππέων ἐπιβαινόντων τοῖς περισταυρώ-
μασι κατὰ πολλὰ μέρη τοῦ χάρακος ὀξεῖα καὶ
παλίντροπος. πονουμένων δὲ τῶν Ῥωμαίων ὁ
ὕπατος κελεύσας τοῖς πεζοῖς ὕλην προσενέγκαντας
ἀποχῶσαι τὰς τάφρους, πρῶτος ἐχώρει κατὰ τὸ
ἐπιβατὸν ἔχων τοὺς ἀρίστους τῶν ἱππέων ἐπὶ τὰς

<hr>

[1] διὰ B : ἀπὸ R.

Roman horsemen having divided themselves into two
bodies, one of these attacked the enemy's right wing
in flank, while the other, going round the hill, stormed
across it against their rear. Thereupon some of them
hurled their spears at the Volscians, and others with
their cavalry swords, which are longer than those of
the infantry, struck all whom they encountered on the
arms and slashed them down to the elbows, cutting
off the forearms of many together with the clothing
that covered them and their weapons of defence, and
by inflicting deep wounds on the knees and ankles of
many others, hurled them, no matter how firmly they
had stood, half dead upon the ground. And now
danger encompassed the Volscians on every side, the
foot pressing them in front and the horse on their
flank and in the rear ; so that, after having displayed
bravery beyond their strength and given many proofs
of hardihood and experience, nearly all who held the
right wing were cut down. When those arrayed in
the centre and on the other wing saw their right wing
broken and the Roman horse charging them in the
same manner, they caused their files to countermarch
and retired slowly to their camp ; and the Roman
horse followed, keeping their ranks.

When they were near the ramparts, there ensued
another battle, as the horsemen endeavoured to sur-
mount the breastworks of the camp in many different
places—a battle that was sharp and of shifting fortunes. When the Romans found themselves hard
pressed, the consul ordered the foot to bring brush-
wood and fill up the ditches ; then, putting himself
at the head of the bravest horsemen, he advanced

---

[2] ἀμυνομένας ἢ σκεπούσας τὰ σώματα after τὰς deleted by
Reiske.   [3] ἐν added by Steph.[1]

ἐχυρωτάτας τοῦ χάρακος πύλας· ἀναστείλας δὲ
τοὺς πρὸ αὐτῶν μαχομένους καὶ τοὺς καταρράκτας
τῶν πυλῶν διακόψας ἐντὸς ἐγεγόνει τῶν ἐρυμάτων,
καὶ τοὺς ἐπιόντας τῶν σφετέρων πεζῶν ἐδέχετο.
8 Τύλλος δ' Ἄττιος ἔχων τοὺς ἐρρωμενεστάτους καὶ
εὐτολμοτάτους Οὐολούσκων ὁμόσε αὐτῷ χωρεῖ καὶ
πολλὰ ἔργα γενναῖα ἀποδειξάμενος (ἦν γὰρ ἀγω-
νιστὴς μὲν πολέμων σφόδρα ἄλκιμος, στρατηγῆσαι
δ' οὐχ ἱκανός) ὑπὸ κόπου τε καὶ πλήθους τραυμάτων καταπονηθεὶς ἀποθνήσκει. τῶν δ' ἄλλων
Οὐολούσκων, ἐπειδὴ ὁ χάραξ ἡλίσκετο, οἱ μὲν
ἀγωνιζόμενοι κατεκόπησαν, οἱ δὲ τὰ ὅπλα ῥίψαντες
πρὸς ἱκεσίας τῶν κεκρατηκότων ἐτράποντο, ὀλίγοι
δέ τινες ἐπὶ τὰ οἰκεῖα φεύγοντες ἀπεσώθησαν.
9 Ἀφικομένων δ' εἰς τὴν Ῥώμην ἀγγέλων, οὓς
ἀπέστειλαν οἱ ὕπατοι, μεγίστη χαρὰ τὸν δῆμον
κατέσχε, καὶ αὐτίκα τοῖς μὲν θεοῖς χαριστηρίους
ἐψηφίσαντο θυσίας, τοῖς δ' ὑπάτοις τὴν τῶν θρι-
άμβων τιμὴν προσέθεσαν, οὐ μέντοι τὴν αὐτήν γε
ἀμφοτέροις· ἀλλὰ Σικκίῳ μέν, ἐπειδὴ φόβου μείζο-
νος ἠλευθερωκέναι ἐδόκει τὴν πόλιν τὸν Οὐολούσκων ὑβριστὴν καθελὼν στρατὸν καὶ τὸν ἡγεμόνα
αὐτῶν ἀποκτείνας τὴν μείζονα πομπὴν ἐψηφίσαντο·
καὶ εἰσήλασεν ὁ ἀνὴρ ἄγων τὰ λάφυρα καὶ τοὺς
αἰχμαλώτους καὶ τὴν συναγωνισαμένην δύναμιν
ἅρματι παρεμβεβηκὼς χρυσοχαλίνων ἵππων τὴν
βασιλικὴν ἠμφιεσμένος ἐσθῆτα, ὡς περὶ[1] τοὺς
10 μείζονας θριάμβους νόμος. Ἀκυλλίῳ δὲ τὸν ἐλάτ-
τονα θρίαμβον ἀπέδοσαν, ὃν αὐτοὶ καλοῦσιν οὐαστ-
τήν[2]· δεδήλωται δέ μοι διὰ τῶν προτέρων ἣν ἔχει

---

[1] ὡς περὶ Reiske : ὥσπερ O.
[2] Casaubon : εὐάστην A, ὠάν R.

over the passage they had made to the strongest gate
of the camp, and having driven back the defenders
in front of it and cut asunder the portcullis, he got
inside the ramparts and let in those of his foot who
followed. Here Tullus Attius encountered him with
the sturdiest and most daring of the Volscians, and
after performing many gallant deeds—for he was
a very valiant warrior, though not competent as a
general—at last, overcome by weariness and the
many wounds he had received, he fell dead. As
for the other Volscians, as soon as their camp was
being taken, some were slain while fighting, others
threw down their arms and turned to supplicating
the conquerors, while some few took to flight and
got safely home.

When the couriers sent by the consuls arrived in
Rome, the people were filled with the greatest joy,
and they immediately voted sacrifices of thanksgiving
for the gods and decreed the honour of a triumph to
the consuls, though not the same to both. For as
Siccius was thought to have freed the state from the
greater fear by destroying the insolent army of the
Volscians and killing their general, they granted to
him the greater triumph. He accordingly drove into
the city with the spoils, the prisoners, and the army
that had fought under him, he himself riding in a
chariot drawn by horses with golden bridles and being
arrayed in the royal robes, as is the custom in the
greater triumphs. To Aquilius they decreed the
lesser triumph, which they call an ovation (I have
earlier [1] shown the difference between this and the

[1] v. 47.

διαφορὰν οὗτος πρὸς τὸν μείζονα· καὶ εἰσῆλθεν ὁ
ἀνὴρ πεζὸς τὰ λοιπὰ τῆς πομπῆς ἐπαγόμενος. καὶ
τὸ ἔτος τοῦτο ἐτελεύτα.

LXVIII. Οἱ δὲ παρὰ τούτων τὴν ὑπατείαν παραλαβόντες Πρόκλος[1] Οὐεργίνιος καὶ Σπόριος Κάσσιος τρίτον[2] τότε ἀποδειχθεὶς ὕπατος, τάς τε
πολιτικὰς καὶ τὰς συμμαχικὰς ἀναλαβόντες δυνάμεις ἐξῆγον εἰς τὴν ὕπαιθρον, Οὐεργίνιος μὲν ἐπὶ
τὰς Αἰκανῶν πόλεις, Κάσσιος δ' ἐπὶ τὰς Ἑρνίκων
τε καὶ Οὐολούσκων, κλήρῳ διαλαχόντες τὰς ἐξόδους. Αἰκανοὶ μὲν οὖν ὀχυρώσαντες τὰς πόλεις καὶ
τὰ πλείστου ἄξια ἐκ τῶν ἀγρῶν ἀνασκευασάμενοι
τήν τε γῆν περιεώρων δῃουμένην καὶ τὰς αὐλὰς
ἐμπιπραμένας, ὥστε κατὰ πολλὴν εὐπέτειαν ὁ
Οὐεργίνιος ὅσην ἐδύνατο πλείστην αὐτῶν γῆν κεί-
ρας τε καὶ λωβησάμενος, ἐπειδὴ οὐδεὶς ὑπὲρ αὐτῆς
2 ἐξῄει μαχούμενος[3] ἀπῆγε τὴν στρατιάν. Οὐολοῦσκοι δὲ καὶ Ἕρνικες, ἐφ' οὓς ὁ Κάσσιος ἐστράτευσε, γνώμην μὲν ἐποιήσαντο δῃουμένης τῆς
χώρας περιορᾶν καὶ συνέφυγον εἰς τὰς πόλεις[4]· οὐ
μὴν ἔμεινάν γε ἐν τοῖς ἐγνωσμένοις, χώρας τε
ἀγαθῆς κειρομένης, ἣν οὐ ῥᾳδίως ἀνακτήσεσθαι[5]
ἔτι ἤλπισαν, οἴκτῳ ὑπαχθέντες, καὶ τοῖς ἐρύμασιν,
οὐ σφόδρα ἐχυροῖς οὖσιν, εἰς ἃ κατεπεφεύγεσαν[6]
ἀπιστοῦντες, ἀλλὰ πρέσβεις[7] ἀπέστειλαν πρὸς τὸν
ὕπατον ὑπὲρ καταλύσεως τοῦ πολέμου δεησομέ-
νους[8]· Οὐολοῦσκοι μὲν πρότεροι, καὶ θᾶττον οὗτοι
τῆς εἰρήνης ἔτυχον ἀργύριόν τε δόντες ὅσον αὐτοῖς

---

[1] Sigonius : πόπλιος O.   [2] τὸ τρίτον Reiske.
[3] μαχούμενος B : μαχόμενος R.
[4] τὰς πόλεις Portus : τὴν πόλιν O.
[5] Sylburg : ἀνακτήσασθαι O.

greater triumph); and he entered the city on foot, bringing up the remainder of the procession. Thus that year ended.

LXVIII. These consuls [1] were succeeded by Proculus Verginius and Spurius Cassius (the latter being then chosen consul for the third time), who took the field with both the citizen forces and those of the allies. It fell to the lot of Verginius to lead his army against the Aequians and to that of Cassius to march against the Hernicans and the Volscians. The Aequians, having fortified their cities and removed thither out of the country everything that was most valuable, permitted their land to be laid waste and their country-houses to be set on fire, so that Verginius with great ease ravaged and ruined as much of their country as he could, since no one came out to defend it, and then led his army home. The Volscians and the Hernicans, against whom Cassius took the field, had resolved to permit their land to be laid waste and had taken refuge in their cities. Nevertheless, they did not persist in their resolution, being overcome with regret at seeing the desolation of a fertile country which they could not expect to restore easily to its former condition, and at the same time distrusting the defences in which they had taken refuge, as these were not very strong ; but they sent ambassadors to the consul to sue for a termination of the war. The Volscians were the first to send envoys and they obtained peace the sooner by giving as

[1] For chaps. 68-76 cf. Livy ii. 41, 1-9.

[6] Sylburg : καταπεφεύγασιν O.
[7] Cobet : πρεσβείας O.
[8] Cobet : δεησόμενοι O (but letter erased after οι in B), δεησομένας added above line in C.

ὁ ὕπατος ἔταξε, καὶ τἆλλα ὅσων ἔδει τῇ στρατιᾷ
πάντα ὑπηρετήσαντες· καὶ οὗτοι μὲν ὑπήκοοι
Ῥωμαίοις ἔσεσθαι ὡμολόγησαν οὐθενὸς ἔτι μετα-
3 ποιούμενοι τῶν ἴσων· Ἕρνικες δ' ὕστεροι, ἐπειδὴ
μεμονωμένους ἑαυτοὺς εἶδον, ὑπὲρ εἰρήνης τε καὶ
φιλίας διελέγοντο πρὸς τὸν ὕπατον. ὁ δὲ Κάσσιος
πολλὴν κατηγορίαν πρὸς τοὺς πρέσβεις κατ' αὐτῶν
διαθέμενος πρῶτον ἔφη δεῖν αὐτοὺς τὰ τῶν κεκρατημένων τε καὶ ὑπηκόων ποιήσαντας, τότε
διαλέγεσθαι περὶ φιλίας· τῶν δὲ πρεσβευτῶν ὁμολογούντων[1] ποιήσειν τὰ δυνατὰ καὶ μέτρια ἐκέλευσεν
αὐτοῖς ἀργύριόν τε ὃ κατ' ἄνδρα τοῖς στρατιώταις εἰς ὀψωνιασμὸν ἔθος ἦν ἐξ[2] μηνῶν δίδοσθαι
4 καὶ διμήνου[3] τροφὰς ἀποφέρειν. ἕως δ' ἂν ταῦτα
εὐπορήσωσι,[4] τάξας τινὰ χρόνον ἡμερῶν ἀνοχὰς
αὐτοῖς ἐδίδου τοῦ πολέμου. ὑπηρετησάντων δ'
αὐτοῖς ἅπαντα τῶν Ἑρνίκων διὰ τάχους καὶ μετὰ
προθυμίας, καὶ τοὺς περὶ τῆς[5] φιλίας διαλεξομένους
ἀποστειλάντων αὖθις, ἐπαινέσας αὐτοὺς ὁ Κάσσιος
ἀνέπεμψεν ἐπὶ τὴν βουλήν. τοῖς δ' ἐκ τοῦ συνεδρίου πολλὰ βουλευσαμένοις ἔδοξε δέχεσθαι μὲν
τοὺς ἄνδρας εἰς φιλίαν, ἐφ' οἷς δὲ γενήσονται δικαίοις αἱ πρὸς αὐτοὺς συνθῆκαι, Κάσσιον τὸν ὕπατον
γνῶναί τε καὶ καταστήσασθαι,[6] ὅ τι δ' ἂν ἐκείνῳ
δόξῃ, τοῦτ' εἶναι σφίσι κύριον.

LXIX. Ταῦτα τῆς βουλῆς ψηφισαμένης ἀνα-
στρέψας εἰς τὴν πόλιν ὁ Κάσσιος θρίαμβον κατάγειν
ἠξίου δεύτερον ὡς τὰ μέγιστα τῶν ἐθνῶν κεχειρω-
μένος, χάριτι μᾶλλον ἁρπάζων τὸ τίμιον ἢ τῷ

---

[1] ὁμολογούντων Cary, εἰπόντων Cobet, Jacoby : χάριν A,
om. R (but D has λεγόντων after μέτρια).
[2] ἐξ added by Sylburg.

204

much money as the consul ordered and furnishing everything else the army needed; and they agreed to become subject to the Romans without making any further claims to equality. After them the Hernicans, seeing themselves isolated, treated with the consul for peace and friendship. But Cassius made many accusations against them to their ambassadors, and said that they ought first to act like men conquered and subjects and then treat for friendship. When the ambassadors agreed to do everything that was possible and reasonable, he ordered them to furnish the amount of money it was customary to give each soldier as pay for six months, as well as provisions for two months; and in order that they might raise these supplies he granted them a truce, appointing a definite number of days for it to run. When the Hernicans, after supplying them with everything promptly and eagerly, sent ambassadors again to treat for friendship, Cassius commended them and referred them to the senate. The senators after much deliberation resolved to receive this people into their friendship, but as to the terms on which the treaty with them should be made, they voted that Cassius the consul should decide and settle these, and that whatever he approved of should have their sanction.

LXIX. The senate having passed this vote, Cassius returned to Rome and demanded a second triumph, as if he had subdued the greatest nations, thus attempting to seize the honour as a favour rather than

---

³ διμήνου Kiessling : διὰ μηνὸς O, Jacoby.
⁴ εὐπορήσωσι O (but erasure of 2-3 letters before εὐ in B) : εἰσευπορήσωσι Naber, συμπορίσωσι Kiessling.
⁵ τῆς B : om. R.　　⁶ Reiske : στῆσαι O, Jacoby.

δικαίῳ λαμβάνων, ὃς οὔτε πόλεις κατὰ κράτος
ἑλὼν ἐκ τειχομαχίας οὔτ᾽ ἐν ὑπαίθρῳ μάχῃ στρατιὰν πολεμίων τρεψάμενος αἰχμάλωτα καὶ σκῦλα,
οἷς κοσμεῖται θρίαμβος, ἔμελλε κατάγειν. τοιγάρ-
τοι δόξαν αὐθαδείας καὶ τοῦ μηδὲν ἔτι τῶν ὁμοίων
τοῖς ἄλλοις φρονεῖν τοῦτο τὸ ἔργον αὐτῷ πρῶτον¹
2 ἤνεγκε. διαπραξάμενος δὲ τὸν θρίαμβον αὑτῷ
δοθῆναι τὰς πρὸς Ἕρνικας ἐξήνεγκεν ὁμολογίας·
αὗται δ᾽ ἦσαν ἀντίγραφοι τῶν πρὸς Λατίνους γενομένων, ἐφ᾽ αἷς πάνυ ἤχθοντο οἱ πρεσβύτατοί τε καὶ
τιμιώτατοι καὶ δι᾽ ὑποψίας αὐτὸν ἐλάμβανον, οὐκ
ἀξιοῦντες τῆς ἴσης τιμῆς τοῖς συγγενέσι Λατίνοις
τοὺς ἀλλοεθνεῖς Ἕρνικας τυγχάνειν, οὐδὲ τοῖς πολλὰ
εὐνοίας ἔργα ἐπιδειξαμένοις τοὺς μηδ᾽ ὁτιοῦν ἀγαθὸν δεδρακότας τῶν αὐτῶν φιλανθρώπων μετέχειν,
τῇ τε ὑπεροψίᾳ² τοῦ ἀνδρὸς ἀχθόμενοι, ὃς ὑπὸ τῆς
βουλῆς τιμηθεὶς οὐκ ἀντετίμησεν αὐτὴν τοῖς ἴσοις,
οὐδὲ μετὰ κοινῆς γνώμης τῶν συνέδρων ἀλλ᾽ ὡς
3 αὐτῷ ἐδόκει γράψας ἐξήνεγκε τὰς ὁμολογίας. ἦν
τε ἄρα τὸ ἐν πολλοῖς εὐτυχεῖν σφαλερὸν ἀνθρώπῳ
χρῆμα καὶ ἀσύμφορον· αὐχήματός τε γὰρ ἀνοήτου
πολλοῖς αἴτιον γενόμενον λανθάνει καὶ ἐπιθυμιῶν
ἀρχηγὸν ἐκβαινουσῶν τὴν ἀνθρωπίνην φύσιν· ὃ καὶ
τῷ ἀνδρὶ ἐκείνῳ συνέβη. τρισὶ γὰρ ὑπατείαις καὶ
δυσὶ θριάμβοις μόνος τῶν τότε ἀνθρώπων ὑπὸ τῆς
πόλεως τετιμημένος σεμνότερον ἑαυτὸν ἦγε καὶ μον-
αρχικῆς ἐξουσίας ἐλάμβανε πόθον· ἐνθυμούμενος
δ᾽ ὅτι τοῖς βασιλείας ἢ τυραννίδος ἐφιεμένοις
ῥάστη τε καὶ ἀσφαλεστάτη πασῶν ἐστιν ὁδὸς ἡ

---

¹ φθόνον after πρῶτον deleted by Kiessling.
² τῇ τε ὑπεροψίᾳ Cb, Reiske : τῆς τε ὑπεροψίας O.

to receive it as a right, since, though he had neither taken any cities by storm nor put to rout an army of enemies in the field, he was to lead home captives and spoils, the adornments of a triumph. Accordingly, this action first brought him a reputation for presumption and for no longer entertaining thoughts like those of his fellow citizens. Then, when he had secured for himself the granting of the triumph, he produced the treaty he had made with the Hernicans, which was a copy of the one that had been made with the Latins. At this the oldest and most honoured of the senators were very indignant and regarded him with suspicion; for they were unwilling that the Hernicans, an alien race, should obtain the same honour as their kinsmen, the Latins, and that those who had not done them the least service should be treated with the same kindness as those who had shown them many instances of their goodwill. They were also displeased at the arrogance of the man, who, after being honoured by the senate, had not shown equal honour to that body, but had produced a treaty drawn up according to his own pleasure and not with the general approval of the senate. But it seems that to be successful in many undertakings is a dangerous and prejudicial thing for a man; for to many it is the hidden source of senseless pride and the secret author of desires that are too ambitious for our human nature. And so it was with Cassius. For, being the only man at that time who had been honoured by his country with three consulships and two triumphs, he now conducted himself in a more pompous manner and conceived a desire for monarchical power. And bearing in mind that the easiest and safest way of all for those who aim at

τὸ πλῆθος εὐεργεσίαις τισὶν ὑπαγομένη καὶ ἐκ τῶν
χειρῶν τοῦ διδόντος τὰ κοινὰ σιτεῖσθαι ἐθίζουσα,
ταύτην ἐτράπετο· καὶ αὐτίκα οὐθενὶ προειπών, ἦν
γάρ τις χώρα δημοσία πολλὴ παρημελημένη τε καὶ
ὑπὸ τῶν εὐπορωτάτων κατεχομένη, ταύτην ἔγνω
4 τῷ δήμῳ διανέμειν. καὶ εἰ μὲν ἄχρι τοῦδε ἐλθὼν ἠρκέσθη, τάχ᾽ ἂν αὐτῷ κατὰ νοῦν τὸ ἔργον
ἐχώρησε· νῦν δὲ πλειόνων ὀρεγόμενος στάσιν οὐ
μικρὰν ἤγειρεν, ἐξ ἧς οὐκ εὐτυχὲς τὸ τέλος αὐτῷ
συνέβη. Λατίνους τε γὰρ ἠξίου τῇ καταγραφῇ τῆς
χώρας συμπεριλαμβάνων καὶ τοὺς νεωστὶ προσ-
ληφθέντας εἰς τὴν πολιτείαν Ἕρνικας οἰκεῖα ἑαυτῷ
παρασκευάσαι[1] τὰ ἔθνη.

LXX. Ταῦτα διανοηθεὶς τῇ μετὰ τὸν θρίαμβον
ἡμέρᾳ συνεκάλεσε τὸ πλῆθος εἰς ἐκκλησίαν· καὶ
παρελθὼν ἐπὶ τὸ βῆμα, ὡς ἔθος ἐστὶ ποιεῖν τοῖς
τεθριαμβευκόσι, πρῶτον μὲν ἀπέδωκε[2] τὸν ὑπὲρ
τῶν πραχθέντων αὐτῷ λόγον, οὗ κεφάλαια ἦν
2 ταῦτα· ὅτι τῆς μὲν πρώτης ὑπατείας τυχὼν τὸ
Σαβίνων ἔθνος ἀντιποιούμενον τῆς ἡγεμονίας μάχῃ
νικήσας ὑπήκοον ἠνάγκασε Ῥωμαίοις γενέσθαι·
ἀποδειχθεὶς δὲ τὸ δεύτερον ὕπατος τὴν ἐμφύλιον
ἔπαυσε τῆς πόλεως στάσιν καὶ κατήγαγε τὸν δῆμον εἰς τὴν πατρίδα, Λατίνους δὲ συγγενεῖς μὲν
ὄντας τῆς Ῥωμαίων πόλεως, ἀεὶ δὲ τῆς ἡγεμονίας

---

[1] συμπεριλαμβάνων ... παρασκευάσαι Sintenis, συμπεριλαμβάνειν ... παρασκευάσαι Jacoby : συμπεριλαμβάνειν ... παρα-
σκευάσας Ο (but Cmg adds βουλόμενος after τὰ ἔθνη). Cobet
supplied καὶ οὕτως before παρασκευάσαι.
[2] Sintenis : ἀποδέδωκε Ο.

---

[1] Cf. Aristotle, Athen. Pol. 27, 4, διδόναι τοῖς πολλοῖς τὰ
αὑτῶν, the demagogic principle which Pericles is said to have
adopted in introducing pay for jury duty.

monarchy or tyranny is to draw the multitude to oneself by sundry gratifications and to accustom them to feed themselves out of the hands of the one who distributes the possessions of the public,[1] he took that course ; and at once, without communicating his intention to anyone, he determined to divide among the people a certain large tract of land belonging to the state which had been neglected and was then in the possession of the richest men. Now if he had been content to stop there, the business might perhaps have gone according to his wish ; but as it was, by grasping for more, he raised a violent sedition, the outcome of which proved anything but fortunate for him. For he thought fit in assigning the land to include not only the Latins, but also the Hernicans, who had only recently been admitted to citizenship, and thus to attach these nations to himself.

LXX. Having formed this plan, the day after his triumph he called the multitude together in assembly, and coming forward to the tribunal, according to the custom of those who have triumphed, he first gave his account of his achievements, the sum of which was as follows : that in his first consulship he had defeated in battle the Sabines, who were laying claim to the supremacy, and compelled them to become subject to the Romans ; that upon being chosen consul for the second time he had appeased the sedition in the state and restored the populace to the fatherland,[2] and had caused the Latins, who, though kinsmen of the Romans, had always envied them their supremacy

---

[2] After their withdrawal to the Sacred Mount. But there is nothing in Dionysius' lengthy account of the secession (vi. 45-90) to indicate that Cassius deserved any special credit for the return of the plebeians.

καὶ τῆς δόξης αὐτῇ φθονοῦντας, εἰς φιλότητα συν
ήγαγε τῆς ἰσοπολιτείας μεταδούς, ὥστε μηκέτι
3 ἀντίπαλον ἀλλὰ πατρίδα τὴν Ῥώμην νομίζειν· τρί
τον¹ δὲ καταστὰς ἐπὶ τὴν αὐτὴν ἀρχὴν Οὐολούσκους
τε ἠνάγκασε φίλους ἀντὶ πολεμίων γενέσθαι καὶ τὸ
Ἑρνίκων ἔθνος μέγα τε καὶ ἄλκιμον καὶ πλησίον
σφῶν κείμενον βλάπτειν τε καὶ ὠφελεῖν τὰ μέγιστα
4 ἱκανώτατον ἑκούσιον ὑπηγάγετο. ταῦτά τε δὴ καὶ
τὰ ὅμοια τούτοις διεξελθὼν ἠξίου τὸν δῆμον ἑαυτῷ
προσέχειν τὸν νοῦν, ὡς παρὰ πάντας τοὺς ἄλλους
πρόνοιαν ἔχοντι τοῦ κοινοῦ καὶ εἰς τὸν λοιπὸν
ἕξοντι χρόνον. τελευτῶν δὲ τοῦ λόγου τοσαῦτα
ἔφη καὶ τηλικαῦτα ἀγαθὰ ποιήσειν τὸν δῆμον ὥστε
ἅπαντας ὑπερβαλέσθαι τοὺς ἐπαινουμένους ἐπὶ τῷ
φιλεῖν καὶ σώζειν τὸ δημοτικόν· καὶ ταῦτα ἔφη
5 ποιήσειν οὐκ εἰς μακράν. διαλύσας δὲ τὴν ἐκκλη
σίαν καὶ χρόνον οὐδὲ ἀκαριαῖον διαλιπὼν τῇ κατ
όπιν ἡμέρᾳ συνεκάλει τὴν βουλὴν εἰς τὸ συνέδριον,
ὀρθὴν καὶ περίφοβον οὖσαν ἐπὶ τοῖς ῥηθεῖσιν ὑπ'
αὐτοῦ λόγοις· καὶ πρὶν ἑτέρου τινὸς ἄρξασθαι λόγου
τὴν ἀπόρρητον ἐν τῷ δήμῳ φυλαχθεῖσαν γνώμην
εἰς μέσον ἔφερεν, ἀξιῶν τοὺς βουλευτάς, ἐπειδὴ
πολλὰ ὁ δῆμος τῇ πόλει χρήσιμος γέγονε τὰ μὲν
εἰς τὴν ἐλευθερίαν, τὰ δ' εἰς τὸ ἑτέρων ἄρχειν
συλλαβόμενος, πρόνοιαν αὐτοῦ ποιήσασθαι, τήν τε
χώραν αὐτῷ νείμαντας ὅση πολέμῳ κρατηθεῖσα
λόγῳ μὲν ἦν δημοσία, ἔργῳ δὲ τῶν ἀναιδεστά
των τε καὶ σὺν οὐδενὶ δικαίῳ κατεσχηκότων πατρι
κίων, καὶ τῆς ὑπὸ Γέλωνος τοῦ Σικελίας τυράννου

¹ τὸ τρίτον Cobet.

and glory, to become their friends by conferring upon them equal rights of citizenship, so that they looked upon Rome no longer as a rival, but as their fatherland; that being for the third time invested with the same magistracy, he had not only compelled the Volscians to become their friends instead of enemies, but had also brought about the voluntary submission of the Hernicans, a great and warlike nation situated near them and quite capable of doing them either the greatest mischief or the greatest service. After recounting these and similar achievements he asked the populace to pay good heed to him, as to one who then had and always would have a greater concern for the commonwealth than any others. He concluded his speech by saying that he would confer upon the populace so many benefits and so great as to surpass all those who were commended for befriending and saving the plebeians; and these things he said he would soon accomplish. He then dismissed the assembly, and without even the slightest delay called a meeting the next day of the senate, which was already in suspense and terrified at his words. And before taking up any other subject he proceeded to lay before them openly the purpose which he had kept concealed in the popular assembly, asking of the senators that, inasmuch as the populace had rendered the commonwealth great service by aiding it, not only to retain its liberty, but also to rule over other peoples, they should show their concern for them by dividing among them the land conquered in war, which, though nominally the property of the state, was in reality possessed by the most shameless patricians, who had occupied it without any legal claim; and that the price paid for the corn sent

πεμφθείσης σφίσι δωρεᾶς σιτικῆς, ἣν προῖκα
δέον ἅπαντας διανείμασθαι τοὺς πολίτας ὠνητὴν
ἐλάμβανον οἱ πένητες, ἀποδοθῆναι τὰς τιμὰς τοῖς
ὠνησαμένοις ἐξ ὧν εἶχε τὸ κοινὸν χρημάτων.

LXXI. Εὐθὺς μὲν οὖν ἔτι λέγοντος αὐτοῦ θόρυβος ἦν πολύς, ἀχθομένων ἁπάντων καὶ οὐχ ὑπο-
μενόντων τὸν λόγον. ἐπειδὴ δ᾽ ἐπαύσατο ὅ τε
συνύπατος αὐτοῦ Οὐεργίνιος πολλὴν ἐποιήσατο
κατηγορίαν ὡς στάσιν εἰσάγοντος, καὶ τῶν ἄλλων
βουλευτῶν οἱ πρεσβύτατοί τε καὶ τιμιώτατοι,
μάλιστα δ᾽ Ἄππιος Κλαύδιος· καὶ μέχρι πολλῆς
ὥρας ἠγριωμένοι τε καὶ τὰ ἔσχατα[1] κατ᾽ ἀλλήλων
2 ὀνείδη λέγοντες οὗτοι διετέλεσαν. ταῖς δὲ κατόπιν
ἡμέραις ὁ μὲν Κάσσιος ἐκκλησίας συνεχεῖς ποιούμενος ἐξεδημαγώγει τὸ πλῆθος, καὶ τοὺς ὑπὲρ τῆς
κληρουχίας λόγους εἰσέφερε, καὶ πολὺς ἦν ἐν ταῖς
κατηγορίαις τῶν ἀντιπραττόντων. ὁ δὲ Οὐεργίνιος
τὴν βουλὴν ὁσημέραι συνάγων μετὰ κοινῆς γνώμης
τῶν πατρικίων ἀντιπαρεσκευάζετο φυλακάς τε καὶ
3 κωλύσεις νομίμους. καὶ ἦν στῖφος ἑκατέρῳ τῶν
παρακολουθούντων τε καὶ φυλακὴν τῷ σώματι
παρεχόντων πολύ, τὸ μὲν ἄπορον καὶ ῥυπαρὸν καὶ
πάντα τολμᾶν πρόχειρον ὑπὸ τῷ Κασσίῳ τεταγ-
μένον, τὸ δ᾽ εὐγενέστατόν τε καὶ καθαρώτατον ὑπὸ
4 τῷ Οὐεργινίῳ.[2] τέως μὲν οὖν τὸ χεῖρον ἐν ταῖς
ἐκκλησίαις ἐπεκράτει μακρῷ θατέρου προὖχον,
ἔπειτα ἰσόρροπον ἐγένετο προσνειμάντων ἑαυτοὺς
τῶν δημάρχων τῇ κρείττονι μοίρᾳ, τάχα μὲν καὶ
διὰ τὸ μὴ δοκεῖν ἄμεινον εἶναι τῇ πόλει δεκασμοῖς

---

[1] ἔσχατα O : αἴσχιστα Sylburg, Jacoby.
[2] οὐεργινίῳ B : οὐεργινίῳ τιθέμενον R.

them by Gelon, the tyrant of Sicily, as a present, which, though it ought to have been divided among all the citizens as a free gift, the poor had got by purchase, should be repaid to the purchasers from the funds held in the public treasury.

LXXI. At once, while he was still speaking, a great tumult arose, the senators to a man disliking his proposal and refusing to countenance it. And when he had done, not only his colleague Verginius, but the oldest and the most honoured of the senators as well, particularly Appius Claudius, inveighed against him vehemently for attempting to stir up a sedition; and until a late hour these men continued to be beside themselves with rage and to utter the severest reproaches against one another. During the following days Cassius assembled the populace continually and attempted to win them over by his harangues, introducing the arguments in favour of the allotment of the land and laying himself out in invectives against his opponents. Verginius, for his part, assembled the senate every day and in concert with the patricians prepared legal safeguards and hindrances against the other's designs. Each of the consuls had a strong body of men attending him and guarding his person; the needy and the unwashed and such as were prepared for any daring enterprise were ranged under Cassius, and those of the noblest birth and the most immaculate under Verginius. For some time the baser element prevailed in the assemblies, being far more numerous than the others; then they became evenly balanced when the tribunes joined the better element. This change of front on the part of the tribunes was due perhaps to their feeling that it was not best for the commonwealth

τε ἀργυρίου καὶ διανομαῖς τῶν δημοσίων διαφθειρό-
μενον τὸ πλῆθος ἀργὸν καὶ πονηρὸν εἶναι, τάχα
δὲ καὶ διὰ τὸν φθόνον, ὅτι τῆς φιλανθρωπίας ταύτης
οὐκ αὐτοὶ ἦρξαν οἱ τοῦ δήμου προεστηκότες, ἀλλ᾿[1]
ἕτερος· οὐθὲν δὲ κωλύει καὶ[1] διὰ τὸ δέος[2] ὃ πρὸς
τὴν αὔξησιν τοῦ ἀνδρὸς ἐλάμβανον μείζονα γενο-
5 μένην[3] ἢ τῇ πόλει συνέφερεν. ἀντέλεγον γοῦν[4] ἤδη
κατὰ κράτος ἐν ταῖς ἐκκλησίαις οὗτοι πρὸς τοὺς
εἰσφερομένους ὑπὸ τοῦ Κασσίου νόμους, διδάσκοντες τὸν δῆμον ὡς οὐκ εἴη δίκαιον, ἃ διὰ πολλῶν
ἐκτήσατο πολέμων,[5] ταῦτα μὴ Ῥωμαίους νείμασθαι μόνους, ἀλλὰ καὶ Λατίνους αὐτοῖς ἰσομοιρεῖν
τοὺς μὴ παραγενομένους τοῖς πολέμοις, καὶ τοὺς
νεωστὶ προσελθόντας πρὸς τὴν φιλίαν Ἕρνικας, οἷς
ἀγαπητὸν ἦν πολέμῳ προσαχθεῖσι τὸ μὴ τὴν ἑαυ-
6 τῶν ἀφαιρεθῆναι χώραν. ὁ δὲ δῆμος ἀκούων τοτὲ
μὲν τοῖς τῶν δημάρχων προσετίθετο λόγοις, ἐνθυμούμενος ὅτι μικρόν τι καὶ οὐκ ἄξιον ἔσται λόγου
τὸ ἐκ τῆς δημοσίας γῆς ἐσόμενον ἑκάστῳ λάχος,
εἰ μεθ᾿ Ἑρνίκων τε καὶ Λατίνων αὐτὴν νεμήσονται,
τοτὲ δ᾿ ὑπὸ τοῦ Κασσίου μετεπείθετο δημαγωγοῦν-
τος ὡς προδιδόντων αὐτοὺς τοῖς πατρικίοις τῶν
δημάρχων καὶ πρόφασιν ποιουμένων τῆς κωλύσεως
εὐπρεπῆ τὴν Ἑρνίκων τε καὶ Λατίνων ἰσομοιρίαν,

---

[1] καὶ added by Reiske.
[2] τὸ δέος Reiske : τοῦτο τὸ δέος O, Jacoby.
[3] Kiessling : γινομένην B, γενέσθαι A.
[4] Capps : οὖν O, μὲν οὖν Garrer.
[5] πολέμων O : πόνων Cobet.

that the multitude should be corrupted by bribes of
money and distributions of the public lands and so be
idle and depraved, and perhaps also to envy, since it
was not they themselves, the leaders of the populace,
who had been the authors of this liberality, but someone else ; however, there is no reason why their action
was not due also to the fear they felt at the increase
in Cassius' power, which had grown greater than was
to the interest of the commonwealth.   At any rate,
these men in the meetings of the assembly now began
to oppose with all their power the laws which Cassius
was introducing, showing the people that it was not
fair if the possessions which they had acquired in
the course of many wars [1] were not to be distributed
was not due also to the fear they felt at the increase
among the Romans alone, but were to be shared
equally not only by the Latins, who had not been
present in those wars, but also by the Hernicans, who
had but lately entered into friendship with them, and
having been brought to it by war, would be content not to be deprived of their own territory.   The
people, as they listened, would now assent to the
representations of the tribunes, when they recalled
that the portion of the public land which would fall
to the lot of each man would be small and inconsider-
able if they shared it with the Hernicans and the
Latins, and again would change their minds as Cassius
in his harangues charged that the tribunes were
betraying them to the patricians and using his proposal to give an equal share of the land to the Hernicans and the Latins as a specious pretence for their
opposition ; whereas, he said, he had included these

---

[1] Or, following Cobet's emendation, " through many hardships "—a favourite expression with Dionysius.

ἦν αὐτὸς ἔφη νόμῳ περιλαβεῖν ἰσχύος τῶν πενήτων
ἕνεκα καί, εἴ τις ἀφαιρεῖσθαί ποτε αὐτοὺς ἀξιώσαι
τὰ δοθέντα, κωλύσεως,[1] κρεῖττον ἡγούμενος εἶναι
καὶ ἀσφαλέστερον τοῖς πολλοῖς μικρὰ λαβοῦσιν
ὁμοίως ἔχειν ἢ πολλὰ ἐλπίσασιν ἁπάντων ἀπο-
τυχεῖν.

LXXII. Τούτοις δὴ τοῖς λόγοις τοῦ Κασσίου
θαμινὰ μεταπείθοντος ἐν ταῖς ἐκκλησίαις τὸν ὄχλον
παρελθὼν εἷς τῶν δημάρχων, Γάιος Ῥαβολήιος,
ἀνὴρ οὐκ ἄφρων, τήν τε διχοστασίαν τῶν ὑπάτων
ὑπέσχετο παύσειν οὐκ εἰς μακράν, καὶ τῷ δήμῳ
ποιήσειν φανερὸν ὅ τι χρὴ ποιεῖν. ἐπισημασίας δὲ
γενομένης αὐτῷ μεγάλης καὶ μετὰ τοῦτο σιωπῆς,
" Οὐχὶ ταῦτα," εἶπεν, " ὦ Κάσσιε, καὶ σὺ Οὐεργίνιε, τὰ κεφάλαιά ἐστι τοῦ νόμου, ἓν μέν, εἰ χρὴ
τὴν δημοσίαν γῆν κατ' ἄνδρα διανεμηθῆναι, ἕτερον
δ', εἰ χρὴ καὶ Λατίνους καὶ Ἕρνικας μέρος αὐτῆς
2 λαβεῖν[2];" ὁμολογησάντων δ' αὐτῶν· " Εἶεν δή·
σὺ μέν," εἶπεν, " ὦ Κάσσιε, ἀμφότερα ταῦτ' ἐπιψηφίζειν ἀξιοῖς τὸν δῆμον, σὺ δὲ δὴ πρὸς θεῶν, ὦ
Οὐεργίνιε, λέξον ἡμῖν, πότερα θάτερον[3] ἀκυροῖς τῆς
Κασσίου γνώμης μέρος τὸ κατὰ τοὺς συμμάχους
οὐκ οἰόμενος δεῖν ἰσομοίρους ἡμῖν Ἕρνικάς τε καὶ
Λατίνους ποιεῖν, ἢ καὶ θάτερον ἀκυροῖς ἀξιῶν
οὐδὲ ἡμῖν αὐτοῖς διανέμειν τὰ κοινά; ταυτὶ γὰρ
3 ἀπόκριναί μοι μηθὲν ἀποκρυψάμενος." εἰπόντος
δὲ τοῦ Οὐεργινίου τῇ Λατίνων τε καὶ Ἑρνίκων

---

[1] κωλύσεως Ba : κωλῦσαι ABb.
[2] λαβεῖν (or λαβόντας ἔχειν) Sylburg, λαβόντας ἔχειν Jacoby :
λαβόντας O.
[3] θάτερον O : θάτερον μόνον Reiske. Jacoby in accepting
Reiske's emendation, inadvertently added μόνον after the
second θάτερον, three lines below, instead of here.

peoples in his law with a view to adding strength to
the poor and of hindering any attempt that might
thereafter be made to deprive them of what had been
once granted to them, since he regarded it as better
and safer for the masses to get little, but to keep that
little undiminished, than to expect a great deal and
to be disappointed of everything.

LXXII. While Cassius by these arguments frequently changed the minds of the multitude in the
meetings of the assembly, one of the tribunes, Gaius
Rabuleius, a man not lacking in intelligence, came
forward and promised that he would soon put an end
to the dissension between the consuls and would also
make it clear to the populace what they ought to do.
And when a great demonstration of approval followed,
and then silence, he said : " Are not these, Cassius
and Verginius, the chief issues of this law—first,
whether the public land should be distributed with
an equal portion for everyone, and second, whether
the Latins and the Hernicans should receive a share
of it ? " And when they assented, he continued :
" Very well. You, Cassius, ask the people to vote
for both provisions. But as for you, Verginius, tell us,
for Heaven's sake, whether you oppose that part of
Cassius' proposal which relates to the allies, believing
that we ought not to make the Hernicans and the
Latins equal sharers with us, or whether you oppose
the other also, holding that we should not distribute
the property of the state even among ourselves. Just
answer these questions for me without concealing
anything." When Verginius said that he opposed
giving an equal share of the land to the Hernicans

ἀντιλέγειν ἰσομοιρίᾳ, τὸ δὲ κατὰ τοὺς πολίτας, εἰ
πᾶσι δόξειε, διανέμεσθαι συγχωρεῖν, ἐπιστρέψας ὁ
δήμαρχος εἰς τὸν ὄχλον εἶπεν· '' Ἐπεὶ τοίνυν τὸ
μὲν ἕτερον τῆς γνώμης μέρος ἀμφοτέροις τοῖς
ὑπάτοις συνδοκεῖ, τὸ δ' ἕτερον ἀντιλέγεται πρὸς
θατέρου, ἰσότιμοι δ' ἀμφότεροι, καὶ οὐχ οἷόν τε
βιάσασθαι θατέρῳ τὸν ἕτερον, ὃ μὲν δίδοται παρ'
ἀμφοτέρων, ἤδη λάβωμεν, ὑπὲρ οὗ δ' ἀμφισβητοῦ-
4 σιν, ἀναβαλώμεθα.'' ἐπισημήναντος δὲ τοῦ πλήθους ὡς τὰ κράτιστα ὑποθεμένῳ καὶ καταλύειν ἐκ
τοῦ νόμου τὸ ποιοῦν διχοστασίαν μέρος ἀξιοῦντος,
ἀπορῶν ὅ τι χρὴ πράττειν ὁ Κάσσιος καὶ οὔτε
ἀναθέσθαι τὴν γνώμην προαιρούμενος οὔτε μένειν
ἐπ' αὐτῆς ἀντιπραττόντων τῶν δημάρχων δυνά-
μενος, τότε μὲν διέλυσε τὴν ἐκκλησίαν, ταῖς δ'
ἑξῆς ἡμέραις ἀρρωστίαν σκηπτόμενος οὐκέτι κατ-
έβαινεν εἰς τὴν ἀγοράν, ἀλλ' ὑπομένων ἔνδον ἐπραγ-
ματεύετο βίᾳ καὶ χειροκρασίᾳ κυρῶσαι τὸν νόμον·
καὶ μετεπέμπετο Λατίνων τε καὶ Ἑρνίκων ὅσους
5 ἐδύνατο πλείστους ἐπὶ τὴν ψηφοφορίαν. οἱ δὲ
συνῄεσαν ἀθρόοι, καὶ δι' ὀλίγου μεστὴ ξένων ἦν
ἡ πόλις. ταῦτα μαθὼν ὁ Οὐεργίνιος κηρύττειν
ἐκέλευσε κατὰ τοὺς στενωποὺς ἀπιέναι τοὺς μὴ
κατοικοῦντας ἐν τῇ πόλει, χρόνον ὁρίσας οὐ πολύν.
ὁ δὲ Κάσσιος τἀναντία ἐκέλευσε κηρύττειν παρα-
μένειν τοὺς μετέχοντας τῆς ἰσοπολιτείας ἕως ἂν
ἐπικυρωθῇ ὁ νόμος.

LXXIII. Ὡς δ' οὐδὲν ἐγίνετο πέρας, δείσαντες
οἱ πατρίκιοι μὴ ψήφων τε ἁρπαγαὶ καὶ χειρῶν
ἐπιβολαὶ γένωνται καὶ τἄλλα[1] ὅσα φιλεῖ βίαια
συμβαίνειν ἐν ταῖς στασιαζούσαις ἐκκλησίαις εἰσ-

---

[1] Capps : ἄλλα O, Jacoby.

and the Latins, but consented to its being divided among the Roman citizens, if all were of that opinion, the tribune, turning to the multitude, said : " Since, then, one part of the proposed measure is approved of by both consuls and the other is opposed by one of them, and as both men are equal in rank and neither can use compulsion on the other, let us accept now the part which both are ready to grant us, and postpone the other, concerning which they differ." The multitude signified by their acclamations that his advice was most excellent and demanded that he strike out of the law that part which gave occasion for discord ; whereupon Cassius was at a loss what to do, and being neither willing to withdraw his proposal nor able to adhere to it while the tribunes opposed him, he dismissed the assembly for that time. During the following days he feigned illness and no longer went down to the Forum ; but remaining at home, he set about getting the law passed by force and violence, and sent for as many of the Latins and Hernicans as he could to come and vote for it. These assembled in great numbers and presently the city was full of strangers. Verginius, being informed of this, ordered proclamation to be made in the streets that all who were not residents of the city should depart ; and he set an early time limit. But Cassius ordered the contrary to be proclaimed—that all who possessed the rights of citizens should remain till the law was passed.

LXXIII. There being no end of these contests, the patricians, fearing that when the law came to be proposed there would be stealing of votes, recourse to violence, and all the other forcible means that are wont to be employed in factious assemblies, met in

φερομένου τοῦ νόμου, συνῆλθον εἰς τὸ συνέδριον
2 ὡς ὑπὲρ ἁπάντων ἅπαξ βουλευσόμενοι. Ἄππιος
μὲν οὖν πρῶτος ἐρωτηθεὶς γνώμην οὐκ εἴα συγχωρεῖν τῷ δήμῳ τὴν διανομήν, διδάσκων ὡς χαλεπὸς ἔσται καὶ ἀλυσιτελὴς σύνοικος ὄχλος ἀργὸς
ἐθισθεὶς τὰ δημόσια λιχνεύειν, καὶ οὐθὲν ἐάσει ποτὲ
τῶν κοινῶν οὔτε κτημάτων οὔτε χρημάτων ἔτι κοινὸν μένειν· αἰσχύνης τε ἄξιον πρᾶγμα εἶναι λέγων, εἰ
Κασσίου κατηγοροῦντες ὡς πονηρὰ καὶ ἀσύμφορα
πολιτευομένου καὶ τὸν δῆμον διαφθείροντος, ἔπειτ'
αὐτοὶ κοινῇ γνώμῃ ταῦτ' ἐπικυρώσουσιν ὡς δίκαια
καὶ συμφέροντα· ἐνθυμεῖσθαί τε αὐτοὺς ἀξιῶν, ὡς
οὐδ' ἡ χάρις ἡ παρὰ τῶν πενήτων, εἰ τὰ κοινὰ
διανείμαιντο, τοῖς συγχωρήσασι καὶ ἐπιψηφισα-
μένοις ὑπάρξει,[1] ἀλλ' ἑνὶ[2] τῷ προθέντι τὴν γνώμην Κασσίῳ καὶ δόξαντι ἠναγκακέναι τὴν βουλὴν
3 ἄκουσαν ἐπικυρῶσαι. προειπὼν δὴ ταῦτα καὶ
παραπλήσια τούτοις ἕτερα τελευτῶν τάδε συνεβού-
λευσεν· ἄνδρας ἐκ τῶν ἐντιμοτάτων βουλευτῶν
ἑλέσθαι δέκα[3] οἵτινες ἐπελθόντες τὴν δημοσίαν γῆν
ἀφοριοῦσι, καὶ εἴ τινα ἐξ αὐτῆς κλέπτοντες ἢ
βιαζόμενοί τινες ἰδιῶται κατανέμουσιν ἢ ἐπεργάζον-
ται διαγνόντες ἀποδώσουσι τῷ δημοσίῳ. τὴν
δ' ὁρισθεῖσαν ὑπ' ἐκείνων γῆν διαιρεθεῖσαν εἰς
κλήρους ὅσους δή τινας καὶ στήλαις εὐκόσμοις
διαγραφεῖσαν τὴν μὲν ἀπεμπολῆθῆναι παρῄνει καὶ
μάλιστα περὶ ἧς ἀμφίλογόν τι πρὸς ἰδιώτας ἦν,

---

[1] Sylburg : ὑπάρχει O.　　　　[2] ἑνὶ Reiske : ἐπὶ O.
[3] δέκα added by Cobet.

---

[1] "Ten" is omitted here by the MSS.; but the next refer-

the senate-house to deliberate concerning all these matters once and for all. Appius, upon being asked his opinion first, refused to grant the distribution of land to the people, pointing out that an idle multitude accustomed to devour the public stores would prove troublesome and unprofitable fellow citizens and would never allow any of the common possessions, whether property or money, to continue to be held in common. He declared that it would be a shameful thing if the senators, who had been accusing Cassius of introducing mischievous and disadvantageous measures and of corrupting the populace, should then themselves by common consent ratify these measures as just and advantageous. He asked them also to bear in mind that even the gratitude of the poor, if they should divide up among themselves the public possessions, would not be shown to those who gave their consent and sanction to this law, but to Cassius alone, who had proposed it and was believed to have compelled the senators to ratify it against their will. After saying this and other things to the same purport, he ended by giving them this advice—to choose ten [1] of the most distinguished senators to go over the public land and fix its bounds, and if they found that any private persons were by fraud or force grazing or tilling any part of it, to take cognizance of this abuse and restore the land to the state. And he further advised that when the land thus delimited by them had been divided into allotments, of whatever number, and marked off by pillars duly inscribed, one part of it should be sold, particularly the part about which there was any dispute with private persons, so

ence (chap. 75, 3) to the proposed law seems to imply that the number ten has been already mentioned.

ὥστε τοῖς ὠνησαμένοις εἶναι[1] πρὸς τοὺς ἀντιποιη-
σομένους ὑπὲρ αὐτῆς[2] κρίσεις, τὴν δὲ[3] πενταετῆ
μισθοῦν χρόνον· τὸ δὲ προσιὸν ἐκ τῶν μισθώσεων
ἀργύριον εἰς τοὺς ὀψωνιασμοὺς τῶν στρατευομένων
ἀναλοῦσθαι καὶ εἰς τὰς μισθώσεις ὧν οἱ πόλεμοι
4 χορηγιῶν δέονται. "Νῦν μὲν γάρ," ἔφη,[4] " ὁ
φθόνος τῶν πενήτων ὁ πρὸς τοὺς πλουσίους, ὅσοι
σφετερισάμενοι τὰ κοινὰ διακατέχουσι, δίκαιός
ἐστι· καὶ οὐθὲν θαυμαστὸν εἰ τὰ κοινὰ πάντας
διανείμασθαι μᾶλλον ἀξιοῦσιν ἢ τοὺς ἀναιδεσ-
τάτους τε καὶ ὀλίγους κατέχειν· ἐὰν δ' ἀφιστα-
μένους αὐτῶν[5] ὁρῶσι τοὺς νῦν καρπουμένους καὶ τὰ
κοινὰ ὄντως κοινὰ γινόμενα, παύσονται φθονοῦντες
ἡμῖν, τήν τε ἐπιθυμίαν τῆς κατ' ἄνδρα διανομῆς
τῶν ἀγρῶν ἐπανήσουσι, μαθόντες ὅτι λυσιτελεσ-
τέρα τῆς μικρᾶς ἑκάστῳ μερίδος ἡ κοινὴ μετὰ
5 πάντων ἔσται κτῆσις. διδάσκωμεν[6] γὰρ αὐτούς,"
ἔλεγεν, " ὅσον τὸ διάφορον, καὶ ὡς εἷς μὲν ἕκαστος
τῶν πενήτων γῄδιον οὐ μέγα λαβὼν καὶ εἰ τύχοι
γείτονας ὀχληροὺς ἔχων οὔτ' αὐτὸς ἱκανὸς ἔσται
τοῦτο γεωργεῖν δι' ἀπορίαν, οὔτε τὸν μισθωσόμενον
ὅτι μὴ τὸν[7] γείτονα εὑρήσει· εἰ δὲ μεγάλοι κλῆροι
ποικίλας τε καὶ ἀξιολόγους ἔχοντες γεωργοῖς ἐργασίας ὑπὸ τοῦ κοινοῦ μισθοῖντο, πολλὰς οἴσουσι
προσόδους· καὶ ὅτι κρεῖττον αὐτοῖς ἐστιν, ὅταν
ἐξίωσιν ἐπὶ τοὺς πολέμους, ἐκ τοῦ δημοσίου
ταμείου τὸν ἐπισιτισμόν τε καὶ ὀψωνιασμὸν
λαμβάνειν ἢ ἐκ τῶν ἰδίων οἴκων εἰς τὸ ταμεῖον

---

[1] εἶναι O : οὐκ εἶναι Reiske, μὴ εἶναι Kayser, Jacoby.
[2] Reiske : αὐτῶν O, Jacoby.
[3] τὴν δὲ Kiessling, after Gelenius : καὶ A, om. B.
[4] ἔφη O : ἔφησεν Jacoby.   [5] Reudler : αὐτῆς O, Jacoby.

that the purchasers might be involved in litigation over it with any who should lay claim to it, and the other part should be let for five years; and that the money coming in from these rents should be used for the payment of the troops and the purchase of the supplies needed for the wars. " For, as things now stand," he said, " the envy of the poor against the rich who have appropriated and continue to occupy the public possessions is justified, and it is not at all to be wondered at if they demand that the public property should be divided among all the citizens rather than held by a few, and those the most shameless. Whereas, if they see the persons who are now enjoying them give them up and the public possessions become really public, they will cease to envy us and will give up their eagerness for the distribution of our fields to individuals, once they have learnt that joint ownership by all the citizens will be of greater advantage to them than the small portion that would be allotted to each. Let us show them, in fact," he said, " what a great difference it makes, and that if each one of the poor receives a small plot of ground and happens to have troublesome neighbours, he neither will be able to cultivate it himself, by reason of his poverty, nor will he find anyone to lease it of him but that neighbour, whereas if large allotments offering varied and worthwhile tasks for the husbandman are let by the state, they will bring in large revenues; and that it is better for them, when they set out for the wars, to receive both their provisions and their pay from the public treasury than to pay in their individual contributions

---

ἑκάστοτ᾽[1] εἰσφέρειν[2] τεθλιμμένων ἔστιν ὅτε τῶν βίων καὶ ἔτι μᾶλλον ἐν τῷ συμπορίζειν τὸ ἀργύριον ἐπιβαρησομένων."

LXXIV. Ταύτην εἰσηγησαμένου τὴν γνώμην Ἀππίου καὶ σφόδρα δόξαντος εὐδοκιμεῖν δεύτερος ἐρωτηθεὶς Αὖλος Σεμπρώνιος Ἀτρατῖνος ἔλεξεν·

"" Ἄππιον μὲν οὐ νῦν ἔχω πρῶτον ἐπαινεῖν, ὡς φρονῆσαί τε ἱκανώτατον πρὸ πολλοῦ τὰ μέλλοντα καὶ γνώμας τὰς καλλίστας τε καὶ ὠφελιμωτάτας ἀποδεικνύμενον βέβαιόν τε καὶ ἀμετακίνητον ἐν τοῖς κριθεῖσι καὶ οὔτε φόβῳ εἴκοντα οὔτε χάρισιν ὑποκατακλινόμενον. ἀεὶ γὰρ ἐπαινῶν αὐτὸν καὶ θαυμάζων διατελῶ τοῦ τε φρονίμου καὶ τῆς γενναιότητος ἣν παρὰ τὰ δεινὰ ἔχει. γνώμην τε οὐχ ἑτέραν, ἀλλὰ καὶ αὐτὸς τὴν αὐτὴν[3] ἀποδείκνυμαι, μικρὰ ἔτι προσθεὶς αὐτῇ, ἅ μοι παραλιπεῖν Ἄππιος 2 ἐδόκει. Ἕρνικας μὲν γὰρ καὶ Λατίνους, οἷς νεωστὶ δεδώκαμεν τὴν ἰσοπολιτείαν, οὐδ᾽ αὐτὸς οἶμαι δεῖν κληρουχεῖν τὰ ἡμέτερα. οὐ γὰρ ἐξ οὗ προσῆλθον εἰς τὴν φιλίαν ἡμῖν ταύτην τὴν γῆν κτησάμενοι ἔχομεν, ἀλλὰ παλαίτερον ἔτι τοῖς ἑαυτῶν κινδύνοις οὐθενὸς ἄλλου προσωφελήσαντος ἀφελόμενοι τοὺς ἐχθρούς. ἀποκρινώμεθά[4] τε αὐτοῖς ὅτι τὰς μὲν πρότερον ὑπαρχούσας ἡμῖν κτήσεις, ὅσας ἕκαστοι εἴχομεν ὅτε τὴν φιλίαν συνετιθέμεθα, ἰδίας τε καὶ ἀναφαιρέτους ἑκάστοις δεῖ μένειν, ὅσων δ᾽ ἂν ἀφ᾽ οὗ τὰς συνθήκας ἐποιησάμεθα κοινῇ στρατεύσαντες ἐκ πολέμου κύριοι γενώμεθα, τούτων ὑπάρξει τὸ 3 ἐπιβάλλον ἑκάστοις λάχος. ταῦτα γὰρ οὔτε τοῖς

---

[1] ἑκάστοτ᾽ Post, ἕκαστον Reiske, Jacoby : ἑκάστου O.
[2] εἰσφέρειν added by Sylburg.
[3] τὴν αὐτὴν Reiske : ταύτην O, Jacoby.

each time to the treasury out of their private estates, when, as sometimes happens, their means of livelihood are scanty and will be still further cramped by providing this money."

LXXIV. After Appius had introduced this motion and appeared to win great approval, Aulus Sempronius Atratinus, who was called upon next, said:

" This is not the first time that I have had occasion to praise Appius as a man highly capable of grasping eventualities long in advance, and as one always offering the most excellent and useful opinions, a man who is firm and unshaken in his judgements and neither yields to fear nor is swayed by favour. For I have never ceased to praise and admire him both for his prudence and the noble spirit he shows in the presence of danger. And it is not a different motion that I offer, but I too make the same one, merely adding a few details which Appius seemed to me to omit. As regards the Hernicans and the Latins, to whom we recently granted equal rights of citizenship, I too think they ought not to share in the allotment of our lands ; for it was not after they entered into friendship with us that we acquired this land which we now occupy, but still earlier, when by our own perilous efforts, without the assistance of anyone else, we took it from our enemies. Let us give them this answer : that the possessions which each of us already had when we entered into the treaty of friendship must remain the peculiar and inalienable property of each, but that in the case of all that we may come to possess through war when taking the field together, from the time we made the treaty, each shall have his share. For this arrangement will

---

4 ἀποκρινώμεθά Ba : ἀποκρινόμεθά R.

συμμάχοις ὡς ἀδικουμένοις ὀργῆς παρέξει δικαίας
προφάσεις, οὔτε τῷ δήμῳ δέος μὴ δόξῃ τὰ κερδαλεώ-
τερα πρὸ τῶν εὐπρεπεστέρων[1] αἱρεῖσθαι. τῇ τε
αἱρέσει τῶν ἀνδρῶν οὓς Ἄππιος ἠξίου ὁριστὰς
γενέσθαι τῆς δημοσίας γῆς πάνυ εὐδοκῶ. πολλὴν
γὰρ ἡμῖν τοῦτο οἴσει παρρησίαν πρὸς τοὺς δημοτικούς, ἐπεὶ νῦν γε ἄχθονται κατ' ἀμφότερα, καὶ ὅτι
αὐτοὶ τῶν δημοσίων οὐθὲν ἀπολαύουσι κτημάτων,
καὶ ὅτι ἐξ ἡμῶν τινες οὐ δικαίως αὐτὰ καρποῦνται.
ἐὰν δὲ δημοσιωθέντα ἴδωσι καὶ τὰς ἀπ' αὐτῶν
προσόδους εἰς τὰ κοινὰ καὶ ἀναγκαῖα δαπανωμένας,
οὐδὲν ὑπολήψονται σφίσι διαφέρειν τῆς γῆς ἢ τῶν
4 ἐξ αὐτῆς καρπῶν μετέχειν. ἐῶ γὰρ λέγειν ὅτι τῶν
ἀπόρων ἐνίους μᾶλλον εὐφραίνουσιν αἱ ἀλλότριαι
βλάβαι τῶν ἰδίων ὠφελειῶν. οὐ μὴν ἀποχρῆν γε
οἴομαι τούτων ἑκάτερον ἐν τῷ ψηφίσματι γραφέν,[2]
ἀλλὰ καὶ δι' ἄλλης τινὸς οἴομαι δεῖν θεραπείας
μετρίας τὸν δῆμον οἰκειώσασθαί τε καὶ ἀναλαβεῖν·
ἣν μετὰ μικρὸν ἐρῶ, τὴν αἰτίαν πρῶτον ὑμῖν ἀποδειξάμενος, μᾶλλον δὲ τὴν ἀνάγκην, δι' ἣν καὶ
τοῦτο πρακτέον ἡμῖν.

LXXV. '' Ἴστε δήπου τοὺς ἐν τῇ ἐκκλησίᾳ ῥη-
θέντας ὑπὸ τοῦ δημάρχου λόγους, ὅτε ἤρετο τῶν
ὑπάτων τὸν ἕτερον τοῦτον Οὐεργίνιον ἥντινα γνώμην ἔχει περὶ τῆς κληρουχίας, πότερα τοῖς μὲν
πολίταις συγχωρεῖ διανέμειν τὰ δημόσια, τοῖς δὲ
συμμάχοις οὐκ ἐᾷ, ἢ τῶν κοινῶν τῶν ἡμετέρων
οὐδ' ἡμῖν συγχωρεῖ μέρος λαγχάνειν. καὶ οὗτος
ὡμολόγησε τὸ καθ' ἡμᾶς μέρος οὐ κωλύειν τῆς

---

[1] Sylburg : εὐπρεπεστάτων O.
[2] γραφέν O : γράφειν Cobet, Jacoby. For this somewhat
rare use of the participle cf. i. 6, 3 ; ix. 32, 1 ; 43, 1.

neither afford our allies any just excuses for anger, as being wronged, nor cause the populace any fear of appearing to prefer their own interests to their good name. As to the appointment of the men proposed by Appius to delimit the public land, I quite agree with him. For this will afford us great frankness in dealing with the plebeians, since they are now displeased on both accounts—because they themselves reap no benefit from the public possessions and because some of us enjoy them contrary to justice. But if they see them restored to the public and the revenues therefrom applied to the necessary uses of the commonwealth, they will not suppose that it makes any difference to them whether it is the land or its produce that they share. I need not mention, of course, that some of the poor are more delighted with the losses of others than with their own advantages. However, I do not regard the entering of these two provisions in the decree as enough; but we ought in my opinion to gain the goodwill of the populace and relieve them by another moderate favour also, one which I shall presently name, after I have first shown you the reason, or rather the necessity, for our doing this also.

LXXV. " You are aware, no doubt, of the words spoken by the tribune in the assembly when he asked one of the consuls, Verginius here, what his opinion was concerning the allotment of the land, whether he consented to divide the public possessions among the citizens but not among the allies, or would not consent that even we should receive a share of what belongs to us all in common. And Verginius admitted that he was not attempting to hinder the allotting of the

κληρουχίας, ἐὰν ἅπασι[1] ταῦτα κράτιστα εἶναι δοκῇ·
καὶ ἡ συγχώρησις ἥδε τούς τε δημάρχους ἐποίησεν
ἡμῖν συναγωνιστὰς καὶ τὸν δῆμον ἐπιεικέστερον.
2 τί οὖν μαθόντες,[2] ἃ τότε συνεχωρήσαμεν, νῦν ἀνα-
θησόμεθα; ἢ τί πλέον ἡμῖν ἔσται τὰ γενναῖα καὶ
τὰ καλὰ πολιτευόμενοις, ἐὰν μὴ πείθωμεν τοὺς χρησομένους; οὐ
τευομένοις, ἐὰν μὴ πείθωμεν τοὺς χρησομένους; οὐ
πείσομεν δέ, καὶ τοῦτο οὐδεὶς ὑμῶν ἀγνοεῖ. χαλεπώτερα[3] γὰρ ἄν, τῶν μὴ τυγχανόντων, ἀποργισθεῖεν[4]
οἱ ψευσθέντες τῆς ἐλπίδος καὶ τὰ ὁμολογηθέντα μὴ
κομιζόμενοι. οἰχήσεται δὴ πάλιν φέρων αὐτοὺς ὁ
τὰ πρὸς ἡδονὴν πολιτευόμενος, καὶ οὐδὲ τῶν δημ-
3 άρχων τις ἔτι μεθ᾽ ἡμῶν στήσεται. τί οὖν ὑμῖν
πράττειν παραινῶ καὶ τί προστίθημι τῇ Ἀππίου
γνώμῃ, μάθετε, ἀλλὰ μὴ προεξαναστῆτε μηδὲ
θορυβήσητε πρὶν ἅπαντα ἀκούσητε ἃ λέγω. τοῖς
αἱρεθησομένοις ἐπὶ τὴν ἐξέτασιν τῆς χώρας καὶ
περιορισμόν, εἴτε δέκα ἀνδράσιν εἴθ᾽ ὁσοιδήποτε,
ἐπιτρέψατε διαγνῶναι τίνα τε αὐτῆς δεῖ καὶ ὁπόσην
κοινὴν εἶναι πάντων καὶ κατὰ πενταετίαν μισθου-
μένην αὔξειν τὰς τοῦ ταμιείου προσόδους· ὁπόσην
τ᾽ αὖ καὶ ἥντινα τοῖς δημόταις ἡμῶν διαιρεθῆναι·
ἣν δ᾽ ἂν ἐκεῖνοι κληροῦχον ἀποδείξωσι γῆν, ὑμᾶς
διαγνόντας εἴθ᾽ ἅπασιν εἴθ᾽ οἷς δὴ οὐκέτ᾽ ἔστι
κλῆρος εἴτε τοῖς ἐλάχιστον ἔχουσι τίμημα εἴθ᾽

---

[1] Jacoby : πᾶσι O. [2] μαθόντες R : παθόντες C.
[3] χαλεπώτερα Bb : χαλεπώτεροι R.
[4] Post : ἀποτίσειαν O, Jacoby.

---

[1] The verb given by the MSS. is almost certainly corrupt; for the meaning "take vengeance" the middle voice
of that verb is wanted. Post's emendation is very attractive

land so far as it related to us Romans, if this seemed best to everybody. This concession not only caused the tribunes to espouse our cause, but also rendered the populace more reasonable. What has come over us, then, that we are now to change our mind about what we then conceded? Or what advantage shall we gain by pursuing our noble and excellent principles of government, principles worthy of our supremacy, if we cannot persuade those who are to make use of them? But we shall not persuade them, and this not one of you fails to know. For, of all who fail to get what they want, those will feel the harshest resentment [1] who are cheated of their hopes and are not getting what has been agreed upon. Surely the politician whose principle it is to please will run off with them again, and after that not one even of the tribunes will stand by us. Hear, therefore, what I advise you to do, and the amendment I add to the motion of Appius; but do not rise up or create any disturbance before you have heard all I have to say. After you have appointed commissioners, whether ten or whatever number, to inspect the land and fix its boundaries, empower them to determine which and how great a part of it should be held in common and, by being let for five years, increase the revenues of the treasury, and again, how great a part and which should be divided among our plebeians. And whatever land they appoint to be allotted you should allot after determining whether it shall be distributed among all the citizens, or among those who have no land as yet, or among those who have the lowest property rating, or in whatever manner you shall

in the light of the somewhat similar passage in v. 67, 2; see also viii. 89, 3.

ὅπως ἂν βούλησθε κατανεῖμαι· τοὺς δ' ὁριστὰς
αὐτῆς ἄνδρας καὶ τὸ ὑμέτερον ψήφισμα, ὃ περὶ τῆς
κληρουχίας ἐξοίσετε, καὶ τἆλλα ὅσα δεῖ γενέσθαι,
ἐπειδὴ βραχὺς ὁ λειπόμενός ἐστι τῆς ἀρχῆς τοῖς
ὑπάτοις χρόνος, τοὺς εἰσιόντας ὑπάτους, ὡς ἂν
4 αὐτοῖς κράτιστα δοκῇ ἕξειν, ἐπιτελέσαι. οὔτε γὰρ
ὀλίγων τηλικαῦτα πράγματα δεῖται χρόνων, οὔτε
ἡ νῦν στασιάζουσα ἀρχὴ φρονιμώτερον ἂν κατα-
μάθοι τὰ συμφέροντα τῆς μετ' αὐτήν[1] ἀποδειχθη-
σομένης, ἐὰν ἐκείνη γε, ὥσπερ ἐλπίζομεν, ὁμονοῇ.
χρήσιμον δὲ πρᾶγμα ἐν πολλοῖς καὶ ἥκιστα σφαλερὸν ἀναβολή, καὶ πολλὰ ὁ χρόνος ἐν ἡμέρᾳ μιᾷ
μετατίθησι· καὶ τὸ μὴ στασιάζον ἐν τοῖς προεστη-
κόσι τῶν κοινῶν ἁπάντων ἀγαθῶν ἐν ταῖς πόλεσιν
αἴτιον. ἐγὼ μὲν δὴ ταύτην ἀποφαίνομαι γνώμην·
εἰ δέ τις ἄλλο κρεῖττον εἰσηγεῖται, λεγέτω."

LXXVI. Παυσαμένου δ' αὐτοῦ πολὺς ἔπαινος ἐκ
τῶν παρόντων ἐγένετο, καὶ οὐθεὶς τῶν μετ' ἐκεῖνον
ἐρωτηθέντων ἑτέραν γνώμην ἀποφαίνεται· γράφεται
δὴ μετὰ ταῦτα τὸ τῆς βουλῆς δόγμα τοιόνδε· ἄνδρας
ἐκ τῶν ὑπατικῶν αἱρεθῆναι[2] δέκα τοὺς πρεσβυτάτους, οἵτινες ὁρίσαντες τὴν δημοσίαν χώραν ἀπο-
δείξουσιν ὅσην τε δεῖ μισθοῦσθαι καὶ ὅσην τῷ
2 δήμῳ διαιρεθῆναι· τοῖς δ' ἰσοπολίταις τε καὶ συμμάχοις, ἐάν τινα ὕστερον ἐπικτήσωνται κοινῇ
στρατευσάμενοι, τὸ ἐπιβάλλον ἑκάστοις κατὰ τὰς
ὁμολογίας ὑπάρχειν μέρος· τὴν δ' αἵρεσιν τῶν ἀνδρῶν καὶ τὴν διανομὴν τῶν κλήρων καὶ τἆλλα ὅσα
δεῖ γενέσθαι τοὺς εἰσιόντας ἐπιτελέσαι ὑπάτους.

---

[1] μετ' αὐτὴν Kiessling : μεθ' ἑαυτὴν A, μετὰ ταύτην B.
[2] Jacoby : ἀποδειχθῆναι R (?), om. AB.

think proper. As regards the men who are to fix the
bounds of the land and the decree you will publish
concerning its division and everything else that is
necessary, I advise, since the present consuls have but
a short time to continue in office, that their successors
shall carry out these purposes in such manner as they
think will be for the best. For not only do matters
of such moment require no little time, but the present
consuls, who are at variance, can hardly be expected
to show greater insight in discovering what is advantageous than their successors, if, as we hope, the
latter shall be harmonious. For delay is in many
cases a useful thing and anything but dangerous, and
time brings about many changes in a single day ;
furthermore, the absence of dissension among those
who preside over the public business is the cause of
all the blessings enjoyed by states. As for me, this
is the opinion I have to express ; but if anyone has
anything better to propose, let him speak."

LXXVI. When Sempronius had ended, there was
much applause from those present, and not one of
the senators who were asked their opinion after him
expressed any different view. Thereupon the decree
of the senate was drawn up to this effect : that the
ten oldest ex-consuls should be appointed to determine the boundaries of the public land and to declare
how much of it ought to be let and how much divided
among the people ; that those enjoying the rights of
citizens and the allies, in case they later acquired
more land by a joint campaign, should each have
their allotted share, according to the treaties ; and
that the appointment of the decemvirs, the distribution of the allotments, and everything else that was
necessary should be carried out by the incoming

τοῦτο τὸ δόγμα εἰς τὸν δῆμον εἰσενεχθὲν τόν τε
Κάσσιον ἔπαυσε τῆς δημαγωγίας, καὶ τὴν ἀναρ-
ριπιζομένην ἐκ τῶν πενήτων στάσιν οὐκ εἴασε
περαιτέρω προελθεῖν.

LXXVII. Τῷ δ' ἐξῆς ἐνιαυτῷ τῆς ἑβδομηκοστῆς
καὶ τετάρτης ὀλυμπιάδος ἐνεστώσης, ἣν ἐνίκα στάδιον Ἄστυλος Συρακούσιος, Ἀθήνησι δ' ἄρχων ἦν
Λεώστρατος, Κοΐντου Φαβίου καὶ Σερουίου Κορ-
νηλίου τὴν ὑπατείαν παρειληφότων, ἄνδρες ἐκ τῶν
πατρικίων νέοι μὲν ἔτι τὴν ἡλικίαν, ἐπιφανέστατοι
δὲ τῶν ἄλλων κατὰ γ'[1] ἀξιώσεις προγόνων, καὶ διὰ
τὰς ἑταιρίας τε καὶ πλούτους μέγα δυνάμενοι, καὶ
ὡς νέοι τὰ πολιτικὰ πράττειν οὐδενὸς τῶν ἐν
ἀκμῇ χείρους, Καίσων Φάβιος, ἀδελφὸς τοῦ τότε
ὑπατεύοντος, καὶ Λεύκιος Οὐαλέριος Ποπλικόλας,
ἀδελφὸς[2] τοῦ καταλύσαντος τοὺς βασιλεῖς, τὴν
ταμιευτικὴν ἔχοντες ἐξουσίαν κατὰ τὸν αὐτὸν χρόνον καὶ διὰ τοῦτο ἐκκλησίαν συνάγειν ὄντες κύριοι,
τὸν ὑπατεύσαντα τῷ πρόσθεν ἐνιαυτῷ Σπόριον
Κάσσιον καὶ τολμήσαντα τοὺς περὶ τῆς διανομῆς
εἰσηγήσασθαι νόμους εἰσήγγειλαν εἰς τὸν δῆμον ἐπὶ
τυραννίδος αἰτίᾳ· καὶ προειπόντες ἡμέραν ῥητὴν
ἐκάλουν αὐτὸν ὡς ἐπὶ τοῦ δήμου τὴν δίκην ἀπο-
2 λογησόμενον. ὄχλου δὲ πλείστου συναχθέντος εἰς
τὴν ἀποδειχθεῖσαν ἡμέραν συγκαλέσαντες εἰς ἐκκλησίαν τὸ πλῆθος τά τε ἐμφανῆ τοῦ ἀνδρὸς ἔργα ὡς
ἐπ' οὐδενὶ χρηστῷ γενόμενα διεξῄεσαν· ὅτι Λατίνοις
μὲν πρῶτον, οἷς ἀπέχρη πολιτείας κοινῆς ἀξιω-
θῆναι, μέγα εὐτύχημα ἡγουμένοις εἰ καὶ ταύτης

---

[1] γε Steph.[2] : τε O.
[2] ἀδελφιδοῦς or ἀδελφόπαις Glareanus.

consuls. When this decree was laid before the populace, it not only put a stop to the demagoguery of Cassius, but also prevented the sedition that was being rekindled by the poor from going any farther.

LXXVII. The following year,[1] at the beginning of the seventy-fourth Olympiad (the one at which Astylus of Syracuse won the foot-race), when Leostratus was archon at Athens, and Quintus Fabius and Servius Cornelius had succeeded to the consulship, two patricians, young indeed in years, but the most distinguished of their body because of the prestige of their ancestors, men of great influence both on account of their bands of supporters and because of their wealth, and, for young men, inferior to none of mature age for their ability in civil affairs, namely, Caeso Fabius, brother of the then consul, and Lucius Valerius Publicola, brother[2] to the man who overthrew the kings, being quaestors at the same time and therefore having authority to assemble the populace, denounced before them Spurius Cassius, the consul of the preceding year, who had dared to propose the laws concerning the distribution of land, charging him with having aimed at tyranny ; and appointing a day, they summoned him to make his defence before the populace. When a very large crowd had assembled upon the day appointed, the two quaestors called the multitude together in assembly, and recounting all his overt actions, showed that they were calculated for no good purpose. First, in the case of the Latins, who would have been content with being accounted worthy of a common citizenship with the Romans, esteeming it a great piece of good luck to

---

[1] 483 B.C. For chaps. 77-79 cf. Livy ii. 41, 10-12.
[2] Or, more probably, nephew, as Glareanus preferred.

τύχοιεν, οὐ μόνον ἣν ᾔτουν πολιτείαν[1] ὕπατος ὢν ἐχαρίσατο, ἀλλ' ἔτι καὶ τῶν ἐκ τοῦ πολέμου λαφύρων, ἐὰν κοινὴ γένηται στρατεία, τὴν τρίτην ἐψηφίσατο δίδοσθαι· ἔπειτα Ἔρνικας, οὓς πολέμῳ χειρωθέντας ἀγαπᾶν ἐχρῆν εἰ μὴ καὶ τῆς αὐτῶν[2] χώρας ἀφαιρέσει τινὶ ζημιωθεῖεν, φίλους μὲν ἀνθ' ὑπηκόων ἐποίησε, πολίτας δ' ἀνθ' ὑποτελῶν, γῆς τε καὶ λείας ἣν ἂν ἐκ παντὸς κτήσωνται τὴν ἑτέραν 3 ἔταξε λαμβάνειν τρίτην μερίδι. ὥστε μεριζομένων εἰς τρεῖς κλήρους τῶν λαφύρων τοὺς μὲν ὑπηκόους τε καὶ ἐπήλυδας διμοιρίας λαμβάνειν, τοὺς δ' αὐθιγενεῖς καὶ ἡγεμόνας τρίτην μερίδα. ἐκ δὲ τούτου δυεῖν τῶν ἀτοπωτάτων θάτερον ἐπεδείκνυσαν αὐτοῖς συμβησόμενον, ἐάν τινας ἑτέρους διὰ πολλὰς καὶ μεγάλας εὐεργεσίας προέλωνται ταῖς αὐταῖς τιμῆσαι δωρεαῖς αἷς Λατίνους τε ἐτίμησαν καὶ τοὺς μηδ' ὁτιοῦν ἀγαθὸν ἀποδειξαμένους Ἔρνικας. μιᾶς γὰρ καταλειπομένης αὐτοῖς τρίτης μερίδος, ἢ οὐχ ἕξειν ὅ τι δώσουσιν ἐκείνοις μέρος, ἢ τὰ ὅμοια ψηφισαμένους μηδὲν ἑαυτοῖς καταλείψειν.

LXXVIII. Πρὸς δὲ τούτοις διεξῄεσαν ὅτι δημεῦσαι τὰ κοινὰ τῆς πόλεως ἐπιβαλόμενος,[3] οὔτε τῆς βουλῆς ψηφισαμένης οὔτε τῷ συνυπάτῳ δοκοῦν, βίᾳ κυροῦν ἐμέλλησε τὸν νόμον, ὃς οὐ καθ' ἓν τοῦτο μόνον ἦν ἀσύμφορός τε καὶ ἄδικος, ὅτι προβουλεύ-

---

[1] πολιτείαν BCmg : ὑπατείαν AC, ἰσοπολιτείαν Sylburg.
[2] αὐτῶν Post : αὐτῶν O, Jacoby.
[3] Sylburg : ἐπιβαλλόμενος O.

get even so much, he had as consul not only bestowed on them the citizenship they asked for, but had furthermore caused a vote to be passed that they should be given also the third part of the spoils of war on the occasion of any joint campaign. Again, in the case of the Hernicans, who, having been subdued in war, ought to have been content not to be punished by the loss of some part of their territory, he had made them friends instead of subjects, and citizens instead of tributaries, and had ordered that they should receive the second third of any land and booty that the Romans might acquire from any source. Thus the spoils were to be divided into three portions, the subjects of the Romans and aliens receiving two of them and the natives and dominant race the third part. They pointed out that as a result of this procedure one or the other of two most absurd situations would come about in case they should choose to honour any other nation, in return for many great services, by granting the same privileges with which they had honoured not only the Latins, but also the Hernicans, who had never done them the least service. For, as there would be but one third left for them, they would either have no part to bestow upon their benefactors or, if they granted them the like favour, they would leave nothing for themselves.

LXXVIII. Besides this they went on to relate that Cassius, in proposing to give to the people the common possessions of the state without a decree of the senate or the consent of his colleague, had intended to get the law passed by force—a law that was inexpedient and unjust, not for this reason alone, that, though the senate ought to have considered the measure first,

σαι δέον τὸ συνέδριον καί, εἰ δόξειεν ἐκείνῳ, κοινὴν
ἁπάντων εἶναι τῶν ἐν τέλει τὴν φιλανθρωπίαν,
2 ἑνὸς ἀνδρὸς ἐποίει τὴν χάριν, ἀλλὰ καὶ κατ᾽
ἐκεῖνο τὸ πάντων σχετλιώτατον, ὅτι λόγῳ μὲν
δόσις ἦν τοῖς πολίταις τῆς δημοσίας χώρας, ἔργῳ
δ᾽ ἀφαίρεσις, Ῥωμαίων μὲν τῶν κτησαμένων αὐτὴν μίαν μοῖραν ληψομένων, Ἑρνίκων δὲ καὶ
Λατίνων, οἷς οὐθὲν αὐτῆς¹ μετῆν, τὰς δύο· καὶ ὡς
οὐδὲ τοῖς δημάρχοις ἐναντιωθεῖσι καὶ παραλύειν ἐκ
τοῦ νόμου θάτερον ἀξιοῦσι μέρος τὸ κατὰ τὴν
ἰσομοιρίαν τῶν ἐπηλύδων ἐπείσθη, ἀλλὰ καὶ δημάρχοις καὶ συνυπάτῳ καὶ βουλῇ καὶ πᾶσι τοῖς
ὑπὲρ τοῦ κοινοῦ τὰ κράτιστα βουλευομένοις τἀναν-
3 τία πράττων διετέλεσε. διεξελθόντες δὲ ταῦτα καὶ
μάρτυρας αὐτῶν ἅπαντας τοὺς πολίτας ποιησάμενοι, μετὰ τοῦτο ἤδη καὶ τὰς ἀπορρήτους τῆς
τυραννίδος παρείχοντο πίστεις, ὡς χρήματά τε
συνενέγκαιεν αὐτῷ Λατῖνοι καὶ Ἕρνικες καὶ ὅπλα
παρασκευάσαιντο καὶ συμπορεύοιντο ὡς αὐτὸν οἱ
θρασύτατοι τῶν ἐν ταῖς πόλεσι νέων ἀπόρρητά τε
ποιούμενοι βουλευτήρια καὶ πολλὰ πρὸς τούτοις
ἕτερα ὑπηρετοῦντες· καὶ παρείχοντο τοὺς τούτων
μάρτυρας πολλοὺς μὲν ἀστούς, πολλοὺς δ᾽ ἐκ τῶν
ἄλλων συμμαχίδων πόλεων, οὔτε φαύλους οὔτε
4 ἀφανεῖς. οἷς ἐπίστευσεν ὁ δῆμος, καὶ οὔτε λόγοις
ἔτι ὑπαχθεὶς οὓς ὁ ἀνὴρ ἐκ πολλῆς παρασκευῆς
συγκειμένους διέθετο, οὔτε οἴκτῳ ἐνδοὺς τριῶν μὲν

---

¹ οἷς οὐθὲν αὐτῆς Kiessling : ἧς οὐθὲν αὐτοῖς O, Jacoby.

and, in case they approved of it, it ought to have been
a joint concession on the part of all the authorities, he
was making it the favour of one man, but also for
the further reason—the most outrageous of all—that,
though it was in name a grant of the public land to
the citizens, it was in reality a deprivation, since the
Romans, who had acquired it, were to receive but one
third, while the Hernicans and the Latins, who had
no claim to it at all, would get the other two thirds.
They further charged that even when the tribunes
opposed him and asked him to strike out the part of
the law granting equal shares to the aliens, he had
paid no heed to them, but continued to act in opposition to the tribunes, to his colleague, to the senate,
and to all who consulted the best interests of the
commonwealth. After they had enumerated these
charges and named as witnesses to their truth the
whole body of the citizens, they then at length proceeded to present the secret evidences [1] of his having
aimed at tyranny, showing that the Latins and the
Hernicans had contributed money to him and provided themselves with arms, and that the most daring
young men from their cities were resorting to him,
making secret plans, and serving him in many other
ways besides. And to prove the truth of these
charges they produced many witnesses, both residents
of Rome and others from the cities in alliance with
her, persons who were neither mean nor obscure.
In these the populace put confidence ; and without
either being moved now by the speech which the
man delivered—a speech which he had prepared
with much care,—or yielding to compassion when

---

[1] In place of " secret evidences " we should expect " secret
actions," as contrasted with his " overt actions " (chap. 77, 2).

αὐτῷ παίδων μεγάλην παρεχόντων εἰς ἔλεον ἐπικουρίαν, πολλῶν[1] δ' ἄλλων συγγενῶν τε καὶ ἑταίρων συνολοφυρομένων, οὔτε τῶν κατὰ πολέμους
ἔργων, δι' οὖς[2] ἐπὶ μήκιστον ἦλθε τιμῆς, φειδὼ
5 λαβών[3] τινα, καταψηφίζεται τὴν δίκην. οὕτως τε
ἄρα ἦν πικρὸς πρὸς τὸ τῆς τυραννίδος ὄνομα ὥστε
οὐδ' ἐν τῷ τιμήματι τῆς δίκης μετρίᾳ ὀργῇ ἐχρήσατο πρὸς αὐτόν, ἀλλὰ θανάτου ἐτίμησεν. εἰσῄει
γὰρ αὐτὸν δέος μὴ φυγὰς ἐλαθεὶς ἐκ τῆς πατρίδος
ἀνὴρ στρατηγῆσαι πολέμους τῶν τότε δεινότατος
ὅμοια δράσῃ Μαρκίῳ τά τε φίλια διαβάλλων[4] καὶ
τὰ ἐχθρὰ συνιστὰς καὶ πόλεμον ἄσπειστον ἐπαγάγῃ[5] τῇ πατρίδι. τοῦτο τὸ τέλος τῆς δίκης
λαβούσης ἀγαγόντες οἱ ταμίαι τὸν ἄνδρα ἐπὶ τὸν
ὑπερκείμενον τῆς ἀγορᾶς κρημνόν, ἁπάντων ὁρών-
των ἔρριψαν κατὰ τῆς πέτρας. αὕτη γὰρ ἦν τοῖς
τότε Ῥωμαίοις ἐπιχώριος τῶν ἐπὶ θανάτῳ ἁλόντων
ἡ κόλασις.

LXXIX. Ὁ μὲν οὖν πιθανώτερος τῶν παραδεδο-
μένων ὑπὲρ τοῦ ἀνδρὸς λόγων τοιόσδε ἐστίν· δεῖ δὲ
καὶ τὸν ἧσσον πιθανόν, ἐπειδὴ κἀκεῖνος πεπίστευται
ὑπὸ πολλῶν καὶ ἐν γραφαῖς ἀξιοχρέοις φέρεται, μὴ
παρελθεῖν. λέγεται δή τισιν ὡς, ἀδήλου πᾶσιν
οὔσης ἔτι τῆς ὑπ' αὐτοῦ συσκευαζομένης τυραννίδος, πρῶτος ὑποπτεύσας ὁ πατὴρ τοῦ Κασσίου
καὶ διὰ τῆς ἀκριβεστάτης βασάνου τὸ πρᾶγμα
ἐξετάσας ἧκεν ἐπὶ τὴν βουλήν· ἔπειτα κελεύσας
ἐλθεῖν τὸν υἱὸν μηνυτής τε καὶ κατήγορος αὐτοῦ
ἐγένετο· καταγνούσης δὲ καὶ τῆς βουλῆς ἀγαγὼν
2 αὐτὸν εἰς τὴν οἰκίαν ἀπέκτεινε. τὸ μὲν οὖν πικρὸν

---

[1] πολλῶν Cmg : πολλὴν ABC.
[2] δι' οὖς O : δι' ἃ Kiessling.   [3] λαβών ACmg : om. BC.

his three young sons contributed much to his appeal
for sympathy and many others, both relations and
friends, joined in bewailing his fate, or paying any
regard to his exploits in war, by which he had at-
tained to the greatest honour, they condemned him.
Indeed, they were so exasperated at the name of
tyranny that they did not moderate their resentment even in the degree of his punishment, but
sentenced him to death. For they were afraid that
if a man who was the ablest general of his time should
be driven from his country into exile, he might follow
the example of Marcius in dividing his own people and
uniting their enemies, and bring a relentless war upon
his country. This being the outcome of his trial, the
quaestors led him to the top of the precipice that
overlooks the Forum and in the presence of all the
citizens hurled him down from the rock. For this
was the traditional punishment at that time among
the Romans for those who were condemned to death.

LXXIX. Such is the more probable of the accounts
that have been handed down concerning this man ;
but I must not omit the less probable version, since
this also has been believed by many and is recorded
in histories of good authority. It is said, then, by
some that while the plan of Cassius to make himself
tyrant was as yet concealed from all the world, his
father was the first to suspect him, and that after
making the strictest inquiry into the matter he went
to the senate ; then, ordering his son to appear, he
became both informer and accuser, and when the
senate also had condemned him, he took him home
and put him to death. The harsh and inexorable

---

⁴ Sylburg : διαβαλὼν O.
⁵ ἐπαγάγῃ A : ἐπάγοι B.

καὶ ἀπαραίτητον τῆς τῶν πατέρων ὀργῆς εἰς
υἱοὺς[1] ἀδικοῦντας καὶ μάλιστα ἐν τοῖς τότε Ῥωμαίοις οὐδὲ ταύτην ἀπωθεῖται τὴν ἀπόφασιν[2]· ἐπεὶ
καὶ πρότερον Βροῦτος ὁ τοὺς βασιλεῖς ἐκβαλὼν
ἀμφοτέρους τοὺς υἱοὺς ἐδικαίωσε κατὰ τὸν τῶν
κακούργων νόμον ἀποθανεῖν, καὶ πελέκεσι τοὺς
αὐχένας ἀπεκόπησαν, ὅτι συμπράττειν τοῖς βασι-
λεῦσιν ἐδόκουν τὴν κάθοδον. καὶ μετὰ ταῦτα
Μάλλιος τὸν Γαλατικὸν πόλεμον[3] στρατηγῶν τὸν
υἱὸν ἀριστεύοντα κατὰ πόλεμον τῆς μὲν ἀνδρείας
ἕνεκα τοῖς ἀριστείοις στεφάνοις ἐκόσμησεν, ἀπεί-
θειαν δ᾽ ἐπικαλῶν, ὅτι οὐκ ἐν ᾧ ἐτάχθη φρουρίῳ
ἔμεινεν ἀλλὰ παρὰ τὴν ἐπιταγὴν τοῦ ἡγεμόνος
ἐξῆλθεν ἀγωνιούμενος, ὡς λιποτάκτην ἀπέκτεινε.
3 καὶ ἄλλοι πολλοὶ πατέρες, οἱ μὲν ἐπὶ μείζοσιν
αἰτίαις, οἱ δ᾽ ἐπ᾽ ἐλάττοσιν, οὔτε φειδὼ τῶν παίδων
οὔτε ἔλεον ἔσχον. κατὰ μὲν δὴ τοῦτ᾽ οὐκ ἀξιῶ,
ὥσπερ ἔφην, προβεβλῆσθαι τὸν λόγον ὡς ἀπίθανον·
ἐκεῖνα δέ με ἀνθέλκει τεκμηρίων ὄντα οὔτ᾽ ἐλά-
χιστα οὔτ᾽ ἀπίθανα[4] καὶ πρὸς τὴν ἑτέραν ἄγει
συγκατάθεσιν, ὅτι μετὰ τὸν θάνατον τοῦ Κασσίου
ἥ τε οἰκία κατεσκάφη καὶ μέχρι τοῦδε ἀνεῖται ὁ
τόπος αὐτῆς αἴθριος ἔξω τοῦ νεὼ τῆς Γῆς, ὃν
ὑστέροις ἡ πόλις κατεσκεύασε χρόνοις ἐν μέρει τινὶ
αὐτῆς κατὰ τὴν ἐπὶ Καρίνας φέρουσαν ὁδόν, καὶ τὰ
χρήματα αὐτοῦ τὸ κοινὸν ἀνέλαβεν· ἐξ ὧν ἀπαρχὰς
ἐν ἄλλοις τε ἱεροῖς ἀνέθηκε καὶ δὴ καὶ τῇ Δήμητρι

---

[1] υἱοὺς Sintenis, following Sylburg : τοὺς O.
[2] Sintenis : πρόφασιν O, Jacoby.
[3] Μάλλιος τὸν Γαλατικὸν πόλεμον Jacoby : μάλλιος ἐν τῷ
γαλατικῷ πολέμῳ O.   [4] οὔτ᾽ ἀπίθανα A : om. R.

---

[1] The noun is uncertain, as the MSS. give a corrupt form.

anger of fathers against their offending sons, particularly among the Romans of that time, does not
permit us to reject even this account.[1] For earlier Brutus, who expelled the kings, condemned both
his sons to die in accordance with the law concerning malefactors, and they were beheaded because
they were believed to have been helping to bring
about the restoration of the kings.[2] And at a later
time Manlius, when he was commander in the Gallic
war and his son distinguished himself in battle,
honoured him, indeed, for his bravery with the crowns
given for superior valour, but at the same time
accused him of disobedience in not staying in the
fort in which he was posted but leaving it, contrary
to the command of his general, in order to take part
in the struggle ; and he put him to death as a de-
serter. And many other fathers, some for greater
and others for lesser faults, have shown neither mercy
nor compassion to their sons. For this reason I do
not feel, as I said, that this account should be rejected
as improbable. But the following considerations,
which are arguments of no small weight and are not
lacking in probability, draw me in the other direction
and lead me to agree with the first tradition. In the
first place, after the death of Cassius his house was
razed to the ground and to this day its site remains
vacant, except for that part of it on which the state
afterwards built the temple of Tellus, which stands in
the street leading to the Carinae ; and again, his
goods were confiscated by the state, which dedicated
first-offerings from them in various temples, especially the bronze statues to Ceres, which by their

The word used by Dionysius here was clearly not λόγος, his
usual word for " account."   [2] See v. 8.

τοὺς χαλκέους ἀνδριάντας ἐπιγραφαῖς δηλοῦντας
4 ἀφ᾽ ὧν εἰσι χρημάτων ἀπαρχαί. εἰ δέ γε ὁ πατὴρ
μηνυτής τε καὶ κατήγορος καὶ κολαστὴς αὐτοῦ
ἐγένετο, οὔτ᾽ ἂν ἡ οἰκία αὐτοῦ κατεσκάφη οὔτε ἡ
οὐσία ἐδημεύθη. Ῥωμαίοις γὰρ οὐθὲν ἴδιόν ἐστι
κτῆμα ζώντων ἔτι τῶν πατέρων, ἀλλὰ καὶ τὰ
χρήματα καὶ τὰ σώματα τῶν παίδων ὅ τι βούλονται
διατιθέναι τοῖς πατράσιν ἀποδέδοται. ὥστε οὐκ
ἂν δήπου τὴν τοῦ πατρὸς οὐσίαν τοῦ μηνύσαντος
τὴν τυραννίδα ἐπὶ τοῖς τοῦ παιδὸς ἀδικήμασιν ἀφ-
αιρεῖσθαι καὶ δημεύειν ἡ πόλις ἠξίου. διὰ μὲν δὴ
ταῦτα τῷ προτέρῳ συγκατατίθεμαι τῶν λόγων
μᾶλλον· ἔθηκα δ᾽ ἀμφοτέρους, ἵνα ἐξῇ τοῖς ἀναγνω-
σομένοις ὁποτέρῳ βούλονται τῶν λόγων προσέχειν.

LXXX. Ἐπιβαλλομένων δέ τινων καὶ τοὺς παῖδας ἀποκτεῖναι τοῦ Κασσίου δεινὸν τὸ ἔθος ἔδοξεν
εἶναι τῇ βουλῇ καὶ ἀσύμφορον· καὶ συνελθοῦσα
ἐψηφίσατο ἀφεῖσθαι τὰ μειράκια τῆς τιμωρίας καὶ
ἐπὶ πάσῃ ἀδείᾳ ζῆν, μήτε φυγῇ μήτε ἀτιμίᾳ μήτε
ἄλλῃ συμφορᾷ ζημιωθέντα. καὶ ἐξ ἐκείνου τὸ ἔθος
τοῦτο Ῥωμαίοις ἐπιχώριον γέγονεν ἕως τῆς καθ᾽
ἡμᾶς διατηρούμενον ἡλικίας, ἀφεῖσθαι τιμωρίας
ἁπάσης τοὺς παῖδας ὧν ἂν οἱ πατέρες ἀδικήσωσιν,
ἐάν τε τυράννων ὄντες υἱοὶ τύχωσιν, ἐάν τε πατρο-
κτόνων, ἐάν τε προδοτῶν, ὃ μέγιστόν ἐστι παρ᾽
2 ἐκείνοις ἀδίκημα. οἵ τε καταλῦσαι τὸ ἔθος τοῦτο
ἐπιβαλόμενοι κατὰ τοὺς ἡμετέρους χρόνους μετὰ
τὴν συντέλειαν τοῦ Μαρσικοῦ τε καὶ ἐμφυλίου

---

[1] The inscription read, according to Livy (ii. 41, 10): EX
CASSIA FAMILIA DATUM.
[2] The Social War and the Sullan War. The former was

inscriptions [1] show of whose possessions they are the first-offerings. But if his father had been at once the informer, the accuser and the executioner of his son, neither his house would have been razed nor his estate confiscated. For the Romans have no property of their own while their fathers are still living, but fathers are permitted to dispose both of the goods and the persons of their sons as they wish. Consequently the state surely would never have seen fit, because of the crimes of the son, to take away and confiscate the estate of his father who had given information of his plan to set up a tyranny. For these reasons, therefore, I agree rather with the former of the two accounts ; but I have given both, to the end that my readers may adopt whichever one they please.

LXXX. When the attempt was made by some to put to death the sons of Cassius also, the senators looked upon the custom as cruel and harmful ; and having assembled, they voted that the penalty should be remitted in the case of the boys and that they should live in complete security, being punished by neither banishment, disfranchisement, nor any other misfortune. And from that time this custom has become established among the Romans and is observed down to our day, that the sons shall be exempt from all punishment for any crimes committed by their fathers, whether they happen to be the sons of tyrants, of parricides, or of traitors— treason being among the Romans the greatest crime. And those who attempted to abolish this custom in our times, after the end of the Marsic and civil wars, [2]

usually called *bellum Marsicum* (or *Italicum*) by Roman writers of the following two centuries.

πολέμου, καὶ τοὺς παῖδας τῶν ἐπικηρυχθέντων ἐπὶ
Σύλλα πατέρων ἀφελόμενοι τὸ μετιέναι τὰς πα-
τρίους ἀρχὰς καὶ βουλῆς μετέχειν καθ' ὃν ἐδυνά-
στευον αὐτοὶ χρόνον, ἐπίφθονόν τε ἀνθρώποις καὶ
νεμεσητὸν θεοῖς ἔργον ἔδοξαν ἀποδείξασθαι. τοι-
γάρτοι δίκη μὲν ἐκείνοις σὺν χρόνῳ τιμωρὸς οὐ
μεμπτὴ παρηκολούθησε, δι' ἣν ἐκ μεγίστου τέως[1]
αὐχήματος εἰς ταπεινότατον πτῶμα κατήχθησαν,[2]
καὶ οὐδὲ γένος τὸ ἐξ αὐτῶν ὅτι μὴ κατὰ γυναῖκας
3 ἔτι λείπεται· τὸ δ' ἔθος εἰς τὸν ἐξ ἀρχῆς κόσμον ὁ
τούτους καθελὼν ἀνὴρ ἀποκατέστησε. παρ' Ἕλ-
λησι δ' οὐχ οὕτως ἐνίοις ὁ νόμος ἔχει, ἀλλὰ τοὺς
ἐκ τυράννων γενομένους οἱ μὲν συναποκτιννύναι
τοῖς πατράσι δικαιοῦσιν, οἱ δ' ἀειφυγίᾳ κολάζου-
σιν, ὥσπερ οὐκ ἐνδεχομένης τῆς φύσεως χρηστοὺς
παῖδας ἐκ πονηρῶν πατέρων ἢ κακοὺς ἐξ ἀγαθῶν γενέσθαι. ἀλλ' ὑπὲρ μὲν τούτων εἴτε ὁ παρ'
Ἕλλησιν ἀμείνων νόμος εἴτε τὸ Ῥωμαίων ἔθος

---

[1] Reiske : τε O.   [2] Reiske : ἤχθησαν O.

---

[1] It was Julius Caesar (Dio Cassius xli. 18; Suetonius,
Iul. 41) who restored to the " children of the proscribed "
their civil rights of which they had been deprived by Sulla
(Plutarch, *Sulla* 31) ; in the intervening period of more than
three decades neither the aristocratic nor the popular party
had offered to relieve them of their disability. Dionysius in
describing the fate of those who had kept them from holding
office while they themselves were in power seems to have had
Pompey particularly in mind, though he probably wished his
words to be understood in general of the men prominently
identified with the Sullan régime. The description might
even apply to the family of Sulla, regarded as a dynasty ;

and took away from the sons of fathers who had been proscribed under Sulla the privilege of standing for the magistracies held by their fathers and of being members of the senate as long as their own domination lasted, were regarded as having done a thing deserving both the indignation of men and the vengeance of the gods. Accordingly, in the course of time a justifiable retribution dogged their steps as the avenger of their crimes, by which the perpetrators were reduced from the greatest height of glory they had once enjoyed to the lowest depths, and not even their posterity, except of the female line, now survives; but the custom was restored to its original status by the man who brought about their destruction.[1] Among some of the Greeks, however, this is not the practice, but certain of them think it proper to put to death the sons of tyrants together with their fathers; and others punish them with perpetual banishment, as if Nature would not permit virtuous sons to be the offspring of wicked fathers or evil sons of good fathers. But concerning these matters, I leave to the consideration of anyone who is so minded the question whether the practice prevalent among the Greeks is better or the custom of the Romans

Sulla himself did not experience a reversal of fortune, but his son Faustus was defeated and slain by Caesar's forces, and with him ended the male line of Sulla's descendants, even as Pompey's male line terminated with the death of his son Sextus. For some reason or other Dionysius forbore to mention by name any of the prominent Romans after Sulla, with the exception of a reference to the defeat of Crassus (ii. 6, 4) and mention of Augustus and his stepson Claudius Nero (the later emperor Tiberius) merely as a means of dating events (i. 7, 2; 3, 4). Another conspicuous example of this reluctance to name people prominent in his own times is found below in chap. 87, 7 f. See also i. 70, 4 and note.

κρεῖττον, ἀφίημι τῷ βουλομένῳ σκοπεῖν· ἐπάνειμι
δ' ἐπὶ τὰ ἑξῆς.

LXXXI. Μετὰ γὰρ τὸν τοῦ Κασσίου θάνατον οἱ
μὲν αὐξάνοντες τὴν ἀριστοκρατίαν θρασύτεροί τε
καὶ ὑπεροπτικώτεροι τῶν δημοτικῶν ἐγεγόνεσαν·
οἱ δ' ἐν ἀφανεῖ τῆς δόξης[1] φερόμενοι καὶ βίου[2] εἰς
ταπεινὰ συνεστάλησαν, καὶ ὡς ἄριστον ἀπολωλεκότες φύλακα τῆς δημοτικῆς μερίδος πολλὴν ἄνοιαν
ἑαυτῶν ἐπὶ τῇ καταδίκῃ κατηγόρουν.[3] τούτου δ'
αἴτιον ἦν ὅτι τὰ δόξαντα τῇ βουλῇ περὶ τῆς
κληρουχίας οὐκ ἔπραττον οἱ ὕπατοι, δέον αὐτοὺς
ἄνδρας τε ἀποδεῖξαι δέκα τοὺς ὁριοῦντας τὴν γῆν
καὶ γνώμην εἰσηγήσασθαι πόσην τε αὐτῆς καὶ τίσι
2 δεήσει νεμηθῆναι. συνῇσάν τε πολλοὶ κατὰ συστροφὰς περὶ τῆς ἀπάτης ἑκάστοτε διαλεγόμενοι,
καὶ ἐν αἰτίᾳ τοὺς προτέρους εἶχον δημάρχους ὡς
προδεδωκότας τὸ κοινόν· ἐκκλησίαι τε συνεχεῖς ὑπὸ
τῶν τότε δημάρχων ἐγίνοντο καὶ ἀπαιτήσεις τῆς
ὑποσχέσεως. ταῦτα συνιδόντες οἱ ὕπατοι γνώμην
ἐποιήσαντο πολέμων προφάσει τὸ παρακινοῦν ἐν
τῇ πόλει μέρος καὶ ταραττόμενον καταστεῖλαι[4].
ἔτυχε γὰρ ἐν τῷ αὐτῷ χρόνῳ λῃστηρίοις τε ὑπὸ
τῶν πλησιοχώρων πόλεων καὶ καταδρομαῖς τισιν ἡ
3 γῆ βλαπτομένη. τιμωρίας μὲν δὴ τῶν ἀδικούντων
ἕνεκα προύθεσαν τὰ τοῦ πολέμου σημεῖα καὶ τὰς
δυνάμεις τῆς πόλεως κατέγραφον· οὐ προσιόντων
δὲ τῇ καταγραφῇ τῶν ἀπόρων ἀδύνατοι ὄντες τὴν
ἐκ τῶν νόμων ἀνάγκην τοῖς ἀπειθοῦσι προσφέρειν
(προειστήκεσαν γὰρ τοῦ πλήθους οἱ δήμαρχοι καὶ

---

[1] τῆς δόξης Kiessling : τε δόξῃ AB, τῇ δόξῃ C.
[2] βίου C : βίῳ R.   [3] κατεγίγνωσκον Prou.
[4] καταστεῖλαι ACmg : om. R.

is superior; and I now return to the events that followed.

LXXXI. After the death of Cassius [1] those who sought to extend the power of the aristocracy had grown more daring and more contemptuous of the plebeians, while those of obscure reputation and fortune were humbled and abased, and feeling that they had lost the best guardian of the plebeian order, accused themselves of great folly in having condemned him. The reason for this was that the consuls were not carrying out the decree of the senate regarding the allotting of the land, though it was their duty to appoint the decemvirs to fix the boundaries of the land and to present a proposal as to how much of it ought to be distributed, and to whom. Many met in groups, always discussing this duplicity and accusing the former tribunes of having betrayed the commonwealth; and there were continual meetings of the assembly called by the tribunes then in office, and demands for the fulfilment of the promise. The consuls, perceiving this, determined to repress the turbulent and disorderly element in the city, taking the wars as a pretext. For it chanced that their territory was at that very time harassed by bands of robbers and forays from the neighbouring cities. To punish these aggressors, then, they brought out the war standards and began to enrol the forces of the commonwealth. And when the poor did not come forward to enlist, the consuls, being unable to make use of the compulsion of the laws against the disobedient—for the tribunes defended the plebeians

_____
[1] For chaps. 81-82, 4 _cf._ Livy ii. 42, 1.

κωλύσειν ἔμελλον, εἴ τις ἐπιχειρήσειεν ἢ τὰ σώματα
τῶν ἐκλειπόντων τὴν στρατείαν ἄγειν ἢ τὰ χρήματα φέρειν), ἀπειλαῖς χρησάμενοι πολλαῖς ὡς οὐκ
ἐπιτρέψοντες τοῖς ἀνασείουσι τὸ πλῆθος, λεληθυῖαν
ὑποψίαν κατέλιπον ὡς δικτάτορα ἀποδείξοντες, ὃς
ἔμελλε καταλύσας τὰς ἄλλας ἀρχὰς τὴν τυραννικὴν
4 καὶ ἀνυπεύθυνον μόνος ἕξειν ἐξουσίαν. ὡς δὲ ταύτην ἔλαβον τὴν ὑπόνοιαν οἱ δημοτικοί, δείσαντες
μὴ τὸν Ἄππιον ἀποδείξωσι πικρὸν ὄντα καὶ χα-
λεπόν, πάντα πρὸ τούτου πάσχειν ὑπέμενον.

LXXXII. Ἐπεὶ δὲ κατεγράφη τὰ στρατεύματα,
παραλαβόντες οἱ ὕπατοι τὰς δυνάμεις ἐξήγαγον ἐπὶ
τοὺς πολεμίους. Κορνήλιος μὲν οὖν εἰς τὴν Οὐιεντανῶν χώραν ἐμβαλὼν τὴν ἐγκαταληφθεῖσαν λείαν
ἐν αὐτῇ ἀπήλασε, καὶ μετὰ ταῦτα πρεσβευσαμένων
τῶν Οὐιεντανῶν τούς τε αἰχμαλώτους αὐτοῖς ἀπέλυσε χρημάτων καὶ ἀνοχὰς τοῦ πολέμου συνέθετο
ἐνιαυσίους. Φάβιος δὲ τὴν ἑτέραν δύναμιν ἔχων εἰς
τὴν Αἰκανῶν γῆν ἐνέβαλεν, ἔπειτ᾿ ἐκεῖθεν εἰς τὴν
2 Οὐολούσκων. χρόνον μὲν οὖν τινα οὐ πολὺν ἠνέσχοντο οἱ Οὐολοῦσκοι διαρπαζομένων αὐτοῖς καὶ
κειρομένων τῶν ἀγρῶν· ἔπειτα καταφρονήσαντες
τῶν Ῥωμαίων ὡς οὐ πολλῇ δυνάμει παρόντων ἐξ-
εβοήθουν ἐκ τῆς Ἀντιατῶν χώρας τὰ ὅπλα ἁρπάσαντες ἀθρόοι, ταχύτερα μᾶλλον ἢ ἀσφαλέστερα
βουλευσάμενοι. εἰ μὲν οὖν ἔφθασαν ἐσκεδασμένοις
τοῖς Ῥωμαίοις ἐπιφανέντες ἐκ τοῦ ἀπροσδοκήτου,
μεγάλην ἂν αὐτῶν εἰργάσαντο τροπήν· νῦν δὲ προ-
αισθόμενος τὴν ἔφοδον αὐτῶν ὁ ὕπατος διὰ τῶν
ἀποσταλέντων ἐπὶ τὰς κατασκοπάς, ἀνακλήσει
ταχείᾳ τοὺς ἐν ταῖς προνομαῖς ἐσκεδασμένους

and were prepared to prevent any attempt to seize
either the persons or the goods of those who failed to
serve—made many threats that they would not yield
to those who were stirring up the multitude, leaving
with them a lurking suspicion that they would appoint
a dictator, who would set aside the other magistracies and alone by himself possess a tyrannical
and irresponsible power. As soon as the plebeians
entertained this suspicion, fearing that Appius, a
harsh and stern man, would be the one appointed,
they were ready to submit to anything rather than
that.

LXXXII. When the armies had been enrolled, the
consuls took command and led them out against
their foes. Cornelius invaded the territory of the
Veientes and drove off all the booty that was found
there, and later, when the Veientes sent ambassadors,
he released their prisoners for a ransom and made a
truce with them for a year. Fabius, at the head of
the other army, marched into the country of the
Aequians, and from there into that of the Volscians.
For a short time the Volscians permitted their lands
to be plundered and laid waste; then, conceiving
contempt for the Romans, as they were not present
in any great force, they snatched up their arms and
set out from the territory of the Antiates in a body
to go to the rescue of their lands, having formed their
plans with greater precipitancy than regard for their
own safety. Now if they had surprised the Romans
by appearing unexpectedly to them while they were
dispersed, they might have inflicted a severe defeat
upon them; but as it was, the consul, being informed
of their approach by those he had sent out to reconnoitre, by a prompt recall drew in his men, then dis-

ἀναλαβών, τάξιν αὐτοῖς ἀπέδωκε τὴν εἰς πόλεμον
3 ἁρμόττουσαν. τοῖς δὲ Οὐολούσκοις σὺν καταφρονήσει καὶ θάρσει χωροῦσιν, ὡς παρὰ δόξαν ἐφάνη
συνεστῶσα ἐν κόσμῳ πᾶσα ἡ τῶν πολεμίων δύναμις, δέος ἐμπίπτει πρὸς τὴν ἀδόκητον ὄψιν, καὶ
τοῦ μὲν κοινοῦ τῆς ἀσφαλείας οὐδεμία φροντίς,[1] τῆς
δ᾽ ἰδίας ἑκάστῳ σωτηρίας πρόνοια. ὑποστρέψαντες
δὴ ὡς εἶχον ἕκαστοι τάχους ἔφευγον ἄλλοι κατ᾽
ἄλλας ὁδοὺς· καὶ οἱ μὲν πλείους ἀπεσώθησαν εἰς
τὴν πόλιν, ὀλίγον δέ τι[2] στῖφος, ὃ μάλιστα ἦν
συντεταγμένον, εἰς ὄρους τινὰ κορυφὴν ἀναδραμὸν
καὶ θέμενον ἐνταῦθα τὰ ὅπλα τὴν ἐπιοῦσαν νύκτα
διέμενε· ταῖς δ᾽ ἑξῆς ἡμέραις φρουρὰν περιστή-
σαντος τοῦ ὑπάτου τῷ λόφῳ καὶ πάσας διακλεί-
σαντος ὅπλοις τὰς ἐξόδους, λιμῷ βιασθὲν ὑποχείριον
4 γίνεται καὶ παραδίδωσι τὰ ὅπλα. ὁ δ᾽ ὕπατος
τήν τε λείαν ὅσῃ ἐπέτυχε καὶ τὰ λάφυρα καὶ τοὺς
αἰχμαλώτους ἀποδόσθαι κελεύσας τοῖς ταμίαις, εἰς
τὴν πόλιν ἀπήνεγκε τὸ ἀργύριον. καὶ μετ᾽ οὐ
πολὺν χρόνον ἀναστήσας τὴν δύναμιν ἐκ τῆς πολεμίας ἀπῆγεν ἐπ᾽ οἴκου τελευτῶντος ἤδη τοῦ ἔτους.

Ἐπιστάντων δὲ τῶν ἀρχαιρεσίων ἔδοξε τοῖς
πατρικίοις ἠρεθισμένον ὁρῶσι τὸν δῆμον καὶ μετα-
μελόμενον ἐπὶ τῇ Κασσίου καταδίκῃ, διὰ φυλακῆς
αὐτὸν ἔχειν, μή τι παρακινήσειε πάλιν εἰς δεκασμῶν
ἐλπίδα καὶ κλήρων διανομῆς[3] ὑπαχθεὶς ὑπ᾽ ἀνδρὸς
δημαγωγῆσαι δυνατοῦ τὸ τῆς ὑπατείας λαβόντος
ἀξίωμα. ἐφαίνετο δ᾽ αὐτοῖς ῥᾷστα κωλυθήσεσθαι

---

[1] οὐδεμία οὐδενὶ ἔτ᾽ ἦν φροντίς Reiske.
[2] τι B : om. R.
[3] Reiske : διανομὴν O.

persed in pillaging, and put them back into the proper order for battle. As for the Volscians, who were advancing contemptuously and confidently, when the entire army of the enemy unexpectedly appeared, drawn up in orderly array, they were struck with fear at the unlooked-for sight, and no longer was there any thought for their common safety, but every man consulted his own. Turning about, therefore, they fled, each with all the speed he could, some one way and some another, and the greater part got back safely to their city. A small body of them, however, which had been best kept in formation, ran up to the top of a hill, and standing to their arms, remained there during the following night ; but when in the course of the succeeding days the consul placed a guard round the hill and closed all the exits with armed troops, they were compelled by hunger to surrender and to deliver up their arms. The consul, after ordering the quaestors to sell the booty he had found, together with the spoils and the prisoners, brought the money back to the city. And not long afterwards, withdrawing his forces from the enemy's country, he returned home with them, as the year was now drawing to its close.

When the election of magistrates was at hand,[1] the patricians, perceiving that the people were exasperated and repented of having condemned Cassius, resolved to guard against them, lest they should create some fresh disturbance when encouraged to hope for bribes and a distribution of allotments by some man skilful in the arts of the demagogue who should have gained the prestige of the consulship. And it seemed to them that the people would be most

---

[1] For chaps. 82, 4-86, 9 cf. Livy ii. 42, 2-5.

τούτων τινὸς ὀρεγόμενος, εἰ γένοιτο ὕπατος ἀνὴρ
5 ἥκιστα δημοτικός. βουλευσάμενοι δὴ τοῦτο κελεύ-
ουσι μετιέναι τὴν ὑπατείαν τὸν ἕτερον τῶν κατ-
ηγορησάντων τοῦ Κασσίου, Καίσωνα Φάβιον
ἀδελφὸν ὄντα τοῦ τότε ὑπατεύοντος Κοΐντου, καὶ
ἐκ τῶν ἄλλων πατρικίων Λεύκιον Αἰμίλιον ἄνδρα
ἀριστοκρατικόν. τούτων δὲ μετιόντων τὴν ἀρχὴν
κωλύειν μὲν οὐχ οἷοί τ' ἦσαν οἱ δημοτικοί, καταλιπόντες δὲ τὰς ἀρχαιρεσίας ᾤχοντο ἐκ τοῦ πεδίου.
6 τὸ γὰρ τῆς λοχίτιδος ἐκκλησίας κῦρος ἐν ταῖς
ψηφοφορίαις περὶ τοὺς ἐπιφανεστάτους ἦν καὶ τὰ
πρῶτα τιμήματα ἔχοντας, καὶ σπάνιόν τι ἦν ὃ
ἐπεκύρουν οἱ διὰ μέσου· ὁ δὲ τελευταῖος λόχος, ἐν
ᾧ τὸ πλεῖστόν τε καὶ ἀπορώτατον τοῦ δημοτικοῦ
μέρος ἐψηφοφόρει, μιᾶς, ὡς καὶ πρότερον εἴρηται
μοι, τῆς ἐσχάτης ψήφου κύριος ἦν.

LXXXIII. Παραλαμβάνουσι δὴ τὴν ὑπατείαν
κατὰ τὸ ἑβδομηκοστόν τε καὶ διακοσιοστὸν ἔτος
ἀπὸ τοῦ συνοικισμοῦ τῆς Ῥώμης Λεύκιος Αἰμίλιος
Μαμέρκου υἱὸς καὶ Καίσων Φάβιος Καίσωνος υἱός,
ἄρχοντος Ἀθήνησι Νικοδήμου. οἷς κατ' εὐχὴν
συνέβη μηδὲν ὑπὸ τῆς πολιτικῆς ἐπιταραχθῆναι
διχοστασίας πολέμων τὴν πόλιν περιστάντων ἀλλο-
2 εθνῶν. ἐν ἅπασι μὲν οὖν ἔθνεσι καὶ τόποις Ἑλλήνων τε καὶ βαρβάρων φιλοῦσιν αἱ τῶν ἔξωθεν
κακῶν ἀνάπαυλαι ἐμφυλίους τε καὶ ἐνδήμους ἐγεί-
ρειν πολέμους, μάλιστα δὲ τοῦτο πάσχουσιν ὅσοι
πολεμιστὴν καὶ κακόπαθον αἱροῦνται βίον ἐλευ-
θερίας τε καὶ ἡγεμονίας πόθῳ. χαλεπαὶ γὰρ αἱ
μαθοῦσαι τοῦ πλείονος ἐφίεσθαι φύσεις ἐξειργό-

---

[1] The Campus Martius.

easily prevented from realizing any of these desires
if a man who was least democratic in his sympathies
should become consul.   Having come to this decision,
they ordered Caeso Fabius, one of the two persons
who had accused Cassius, and brother to Quintus,
who was consul at the time, and, from among
the other patricians, Lucius Aemilius, one of the
aristocratic party, to stand for the consulship.   When
these offered themselves for the office, the plebeians,
though they could do nothing to prevent it, did
leave the comitia and withdraw from the Field.[1]
For in the centuriate assembly the balance of power
in voting lay with the most important men and those
who had the highest property ratings, and it was
seldom that those of middling fortunes determined a
matter ; the last century, in which the most numerous and poorest part of the plebeians voted, had but
one vote, as I stated before,[2] which was always the
last to be called for.

LXXXIII. Accordingly, Lucius Aemilius, the son
of Mamercus, and Caeso Fabius, the son of Caeso,
succeeded to the consulship in the two hundred and
seventieth year [3] after the settlement of Rome, when
Nicodemus was archon at Athens.   It chanced fortunately that their consulship was not disturbed at
all by civil strife, since the state was beset by foreign
wars.   Now in all nations and places, both Greek and
barbarian, respites from evils from abroad are wont to
provoke civil and domestic wars ; and this happens
especially among those peoples who choose a life of
warfare and its hardships from a passion for liberty
and dominion.   For natures which have learned to
covet more than they have find it difficult, when

---

[2] See iv. 20, 5 ; vii. 59, 8.   [3] 482 B.C.

μεναι τῶν συνήθων ἔργων καρτερεῖν· καὶ διὰ τοῦτο
οἱ φρονιμώτατοι τῶν ἡγεμόνων ἀεί τινας ἐκ τῶν
ἀλλοεθνῶν ἀναζωπυροῦσιν ἔχθρας, κρείττονας ἡγούμενοι τῶν ἐντοπίων πολέμων τοὺς ἀλλοδαπούς.
3 τότε δ' οὖν, ὥσπερ ἔφην, κατὰ δαίμονα τοῖς ὑπάτοις συνέπεσον αἱ τῶν ὑπηκόων ἐπαναστάσεις.
Οὐολοῦσκοι γάρ, εἴτε τῇ πολιτικῇ Ῥωμαίων κινή-
σει πιστεύσαντες ὡς ἐκπεπολεμωμένου[1] τοῦ δημοτικοῦ πρὸς τοὺς ἐν τέλει, εἴτε τῆς προτέρας
ἥττης ἀμαχητὶ γενομένης αἰσχύνῃ παροξυνθέντες,
εἴτ' ἐπὶ[2] ταῖς ἑαυτῶν δυνάμεσι πολλαῖς οὔσαις
μέγα φρονήσαντες, εἴτε διὰ ταῦτα πάντα, πολεμεῖν
4 Ῥωμαίοις διέγνωσαν, καὶ συναγαγόντες ἐξ ἁπάσης
πόλεως τὴν νεότητα, μέρει μέν τινι τῆς δυνάμεως
ἐπὶ τὰς Ἑρνίκων τε καὶ Λατίνων πόλεις ἐστράτευ-
σαν, τῇ δὲ λοιπῇ, ἣ πλείστη τε ἦν καὶ κρατίστη,
τοὺς ἐπὶ τὰς πόλεις σφῶν ἥξοντας δέχεσθαι ἤμελ-
λον. ταῦτα μαθοῦσι Ῥωμαίοις ἔδοξε διχῇ νέμειν
τὰς δυνάμεις καὶ τῇ μὲν ἑτέρᾳ τὴν Ἑρνίκων τε
καὶ Λατίνων διὰ φυλακῆς ἔχειν, τῇ δ' ἑτέρᾳ τὴν
Οὐολούσκων λεηλατεῖν.

LXXXIV. Διακληρωσαμένων δὲ τῶν ὑπάτων
τὰς δυνάμεις, ὡς ἔστιν αὐτοῖς ἔθος, τὸ μὲν ἐπι-
κουρεῖν μέλλον τοῖς συμμάχοις στράτευμα Καίσων
Φάβιος παρέλαβε, θάτερον δὲ Λεύκιος ἔχων ἐπὶ τὴν
Ἀντιατῶν ἦγε πόλιν. γενόμενος δὲ πλησίον τῶν
ὁρίων καὶ κατιδὼν τὰς τῶν πολεμίων δυνάμεις, τότε
μὲν ἀντικατεστρατοπέδευσεν ἐπὶ λόφου, ταῖς δ'
ἑξῆς ἡμέραις ἐξιόντων εἰς τὸ πεδίον τῶν πολεμίων
θαμινὰ καὶ προκαλουμένων εἰς μάχην, ἡνίκα τὸν

---

[1] Kiessling : ἐκπολεμωμένου ABC.
[2] εἴτ' ἐπὶ added by Sylburg.

restrained from their usual employments, to remain patient, and for this reason the wisest leaders are always stirring up the embers of some foreign quarrels in the belief that wars waged abroad are better than those fought at home. Be that as it may, at the time in question, as I said, the uprisings of the subject nations occurred very fortunately for the consuls. For the Volscians, either relying on the domestic disquiet of the Romans, in the belief that the plebeians had been brought to a state of war with the authorities, or stung by the shame of their former defeat received without striking a blow, or priding themselves on their own forces, which were very numerous, or induced by all these motives, resolved to make war upon the Romans. And assembling the youth from every city, they marched with one part of their army against the cities of the Hernicans and Latins, while with the other, which was very numerous and powerful, they proposed to await the forces which should come against their own cities. The Romans, being informed of this, determined to divide their army into two bodies, with one of which they would keep guard over the territory of the Hernicans and Latins and with the other lay waste that of the Volscians.

LXXXIV. The consuls having drawn lots for the armies according to their custom, the army that was to aid their allies fell to Caeso Fabius, while Lucius at the head of the other marched upon Antium. When he drew near the border and caught sight of the enemy's army, he encamped for the time opposite to them upon a hill. In the days that followed the enemy frequently came out into the plain, challenging the consul to fight ; and when he

οἰκεῖον ἔχειν καιρὸν ὑπελάμβανεν, ἐξῆγε τὰς δυνά-
μεις· καὶ πρὶν εἰς χεῖρας ἐλθεῖν παρακλήσει τε
πολλῇ καὶ ἐπικελεύσει χρησάμενος, ἐκέλευσε
σημαίνειν τὸ πολεμικόν· καὶ οἱ στρατιῶται τὸ σύν-
ηθες ἀλαλάξαντες ἀθρόοι κατὰ σπείρας τε καὶ κατὰ
2 λόχους συνέβαλλον. ὡς δὲ τὰς λόγχας καὶ τὰ
σαυνία καὶ ὅσα εἶχον ἐκβόλα ἐξανάλωσαν, σπασά-
μενοι τὰ ξίφη συρράττουσιν ἀλλήλοις ἴσῃ τόλμῃ τε
καὶ ἐπιθυμίᾳ τοῦ ἀγῶνος ἑκάτεροι χρώμενοι· ἦν τε,
ὡς καὶ πρότερον ἔφην, παραπλήσιος αὐτοῖς ὁ τοῦ
ἀγῶνος τρόπος, καὶ οὔτε ἡ σοφία καὶ ἡ ἐμπειρία
Ῥωμαίων περὶ τὰς μάχας, ᾗ χρώμενοι τὰ πολλὰ
ἐπεκράτουν, οὔτε τὸ καρτερικὸν καὶ ταλαίπωρον ἐν
τοῖς πόνοις διὰ πολλῶν ἠσκημένον ἀγώνων ἐπ-
εκράτει· τὰ γὰρ αὐτὰ καὶ περὶ τοὺς πολεμίους ἦν,
ἐξ οὗ Μάρκιον ἡγεμόνα Ῥωμαίων οὐ τὸν ἀφανέ-
στατον στρατηλάτην ἔσχον· ἀλλ᾽ ἀντεῖχον ἑκάτεροι,
τῆς χώρας ἐν ᾗ τὸ πρῶτον ἔστησαν οὐχ ὑφιέμενοι.
3 ἔπειτα κατὰ μικρὸν οἱ Οὐολοῦσκοι ὑπεχώρουν ἐν
κόσμῳ τε καὶ τάξει δεχόμενοι τοὺς Ῥωμαίους.
στρατήγημα δὲ τοῦτ᾽ ἦν, ἵνα διασπάσωσί τε αὐτῶν
τὰς τάξεις καὶ ἐξ ὑπερδεξίου γένωνται[1] χωρίου.

LXXXV. Οἱ δ᾽ ὑπολαβόντες αὐτοὺς ἄρχειν φυγῆς ἠκολούθουν βάδην μὲν ἀπιοῦσι καὶ αὐτοὶ σὺν
κόσμῳ ἑπόμενοι, ἐπειδὴ δὲ δρόμῳ χωροῦντας ἐπὶ
τὸν χάρακα ἐθεάσαντο, ταχείᾳ καὶ αὐτοὶ διώξει
καὶ ἀσυντάκτῳ χρώμενοι. οἱ δὲ δὴ τελευταῖοί τε
καὶ ὀπισθοφυλακοῦντες λόχοι νεκρούς τε ἐσκύλευον,

---

[1] γένωνται O : ἐπιγένωνται or ἀγωνίσωνται Sylburg.

---

[1] In chap. 67, 3.
[2] The final verb of this sentence is uncertain ; the syntax

thought he had the suitable opportunity, he led out his army. Before they engaged, he exhorted and encouraged his troops at length, and then ordered the trumpets to sound the charge; and the soldiers, raising their usual battle-cry, attacked in close array both by cohorts and by centuries. After they had used up all their spears and javelins with the rest of their missile weapons, they drew their swords and rushed upon each other, both sides showing equal intrepidity and eagerness for the struggle. Their manner of fighting, as I said before,[1] was similar, and neither the skill and experience of the Romans in engagements, because of which they were generally victorious, nor their steadfastness and endurance of toil, acquired in many battles, now gave them any advantage, since the same qualities were possessed by the enemy also from the time that they had been commanded by Marcius, not the least distinguished general among the Romans; but both sides stood firm, without quitting the ground on which they had first taken their stand. Afterwards the Volscians began to retire, a little at a time, but in order and keeping their ranks, while receiving the Romans' onset. But this was a ruse designed to draw the enemy's ranks apart and to secure[2] a position above them.

LXXXV. The Romans, supposing that they were beginning flight, kept pace with them as they slowly withdrew, they too maintaining good order as they followed, but when they saw them running toward their camp, they also pursued swiftly and in disorder; and the centuries which were last and guarded the rear fell to stripping the dead, as if they had already

would be improved by either of Sylburg's conjectures, "attack" or "fight" "from a higher position."

ὡς κεκρατηκότες ἤδη τῶν πολεμίων, καὶ ἐφ'
2 ἁρπαγὴν τῆς χώρας ἐτράποντο. μαθόντες δ' οἱ
Οὐολοῦσκοι ταῦτα οἵ τε δόξαν παρασχόντες φυγῆς,
ἐπειδὴ τοῖς ἐρύμασι τοῦ χάρακος ἐπλησίασαν, ὑπο-
στραφέντες ἔστησαν, καὶ οἱ καταλειφθέντες ἐν τῷ
στρατοπέδῳ τὰς πύλας ἀναπετάσαντες ἐξέδραμον
ἀθρόοι κατὰ πολλὰ μέρη· γίνεταί τε αὐτῶν παλίντροπος ἡ μάχη· οἱ μὲν γὰρ διώκοντες ἔφευγον,
οἱ δὲ φεύγοντες ἐδίωκον. ἔνθα πολλοὶ καὶ ἀγαθοὶ
Ῥωμαίων θνήσκουσιν οἷα εἰκὸς ὠθούμενοι κατὰ
πρανοῦς χωρίου καὶ ὑπὸ πολλῶν ὀλίγοι κυκλω-
3 θέντες. ἀδελφὰ δὲ τούτοις ἔπασχον ὅσοι πρὸς[1]
σκῦλά τε καὶ ἁρπαγὰς τραπόμενοι τὸ ἐν κόσμῳ τε
καὶ τάξει ὑποχωρεῖν[2] ἀφῃρέθησαν· καὶ γὰρ καὶ[3] οὗτοι
καταληφθέντες ὑπὸ τῶν πολεμίων οἱ μὲν ἐσφάγη-
σαν, οἱ δ' αἰχμάλωτοι ἐλήφθησαν. ὅσοι δὲ τούτων
τε καὶ τῶν ἀπὸ τοῦ ὄρους ἀπαραχθέντων διεσώ-
θησαν, ὀψὲ τῆς ὥρας τῶν ἱππέων αὐτοῖς ἐπιβοηθη-
σάντων, ἀπῆλθον ἐπὶ τὸν χάρακα. ἐδόκει τε αὐτοῖς
συλλαβέσθαι τοῦ μὴ πασσυδὶ διαφθαρῆναι χειμὼν
πολὺς ἐξ οὐρανοῦ καταρραγεὶς καὶ σκότος, οἷον ἐν
ταῖς βαθείαις ὁμίχλαις γίνεται, ὃ τοῖς πολεμίοις
ὄκνον τῆς ἐπὶ πλέον διώξεως παρέσχεν οὐ δυνα-
4 μένοις τὰ πόρρω καθορᾶν. τῇ δ' ἐπιούσῃ νυκτὶ
ἀναστήσας τὴν στρατιὰν ὁ ὕπατος ἀπῆγε σιγῇ καὶ
ἐν κόσμῳ, λαθεῖν τοὺς πολεμίους προνοούμενος· καὶ
κατεστρατοπέδευσε παρὰ πόλει λεγομένῃ Λογγόλα
περὶ δείλην ὀψίαν, γήλοφον ἱκανὸν ἐρύκειν τοὺς
ἐπιόντας ἐκλεξάμενος. ἔνθα ὑπομένων τούς τε ὑπὸ

---

[1] Sylburg : περὶ O.
[2] ὑποχωρεῖν AC : ἀποχωρεῖν B.
[3] καὶ added by Sylburg.

conquered the enemy, and turned to plundering the
country. When the Volscians perceived this, not
only did those who had feigned flight face about and
stand their ground as soon as they drew near the
ramparts of their camp, but those also who had been
left behind in the camp opened the gates and ran out
in great numbers at several points. And now the
fortune of the battle was reversed ; for the pursuers
fled and the fugitives pursued. Here many brave
Romans lost their lives, as may well be imagined,
being driven down a declivity as they were and surrounded a few by many. And a like fate was suffered
by those who had turned to despoiling the dead and
to plundering and now found themselves deprived of
the opportunity of making an orderly and regular
retreat ; for these too were overtaken by the enemy,
and some of them were killed and others taken
prisoner. As many as came through safely, both of
these and of the others, who had been driven from
the hill, returned to their camp when the horse came
to their relief late in the day. It seemed, moreover,
that their escape from utter destruction had been due
in part to a violent rainstorm that burst from the sky
and to a darkness like that occurring in thick mists,
which made the enemy reluctant to pursue them any
farther, since they were unable to see things at a
distance. The following night the consul broke camp
and led his army away in silence and in good order,
taking care to escape the notice of the enemy ; and
late in the afternoon he encamped near a town called
Longula, having chosen a hill strong enough to keep
off any who might attack him. While he remained
there, he employed himself both in restoring with

τραυμάτων κάμνοντας ἀνεκτᾶτο θεραπείαις, καὶ
τοὺς ἀδημονοῦντας ἐπὶ τῇ παραδόξῳ τοῦ πάθους
αἰσχύνῃ παραμυθούμενος ἀνελάμβανε.

LXXXVI. Ῥωμαῖοι μὲν οὖν ἐν τούτοις ἦσαν·
Οὐολοῦσκοι δέ, ἐπειδὴ ἡμέρα τε ἐγένετο καὶ ἔγνωσαν τοὺς πολεμίους ἐκλελοιπότας τὸν χάρακα,
προσελθόντες[1] κατεστρατοπέδευσαν. σκυλεύσαντες
δὲ τοὺς τῶν πολεμίων νεκροὺς καὶ τοὺς ἡμιθνῆτας
οἷς σωθήσεσθαι ἐλπὶς ἦν ἀνελόμενοι ταφάς τε
ποιησάμενοι τῶν σφετέρων νεκρῶν, εἰς τὴν ἐγγυτάτω πόλιν Ἄντιον ἀνέζευξαν· ἔνθα παιανίζοντες
ἐπὶ τῇ νίκῃ καὶ θύοντες ἐν ἅπασιν ἱεροῖς εἰς εὐ-
παθείας καὶ ἡδονὰς ταῖς ἑξῆς ἡμέραις ἐτράποντο.
2 εἰ μὲν οὖν ἐπὶ τῆς τότε νίκης διέμειναν καὶ μηδὲν
ἐπεξειργάσαντο, καλὸν ἂν αὐτοῖς εἰλήφει τέλος ὁ
ἀγών. Ῥωμαῖοι γὰρ οὐκ ἂν ὑπέμειναν ἔτι προελθεῖν ἐκ τοῦ χάρακος ἐπὶ πολέμῳ, ἀγαπητῶς δ᾽ ἂν[2]
ἀπῆλθον ἐκ τῆς πολεμίας, κρείττονα τοῦ προδήλου
θανάτου τὴν ἄδοξον ἡγησάμενοι φυγήν. νῦν δὲ τοῦ
πλείονος ὀρεγόμενοι καὶ τὴν ἐκ τῆς προτέρας νίκης
3 δόξαν ἀπέβαλον. ἀκούοντες γὰρ παρά τε κατα-
σκόπων καὶ τῶν ἐκ τοῦ χάρακος ἀποδιδρασκόντων,[2]
ὅτι κομιδῇ τ᾽ εἰσὶν οἱ σωθέντες Ῥωμαίων ὀλίγοι
καὶ τούτων οἱ πλείους τραυματίαι, πολλὴν αὐτῶν
ἐποιήσαντο καταφρόνησιν, καὶ αὐτίκα τὰ ὅπλα
ἁρπάσαντες ἔθεον ἐπ᾽ αὐτούς. πολὺ δὲ καὶ τὸ
ἄνοπλον αὐτοῖς ἐκ τῆς πόλεως εἵπετο κατὰ θέαν
τοῦ ἀγῶνος καὶ ἅμα ἐφ᾽ ἁρπαγήν τε καὶ ὠφέλειαν.
4 ἐπεὶ δὲ προσβαλόντες τῷ λόφῳ τόν τε χάρακα

_____

[1] προσελθόντες Ba : προελθόντες R.
[2] ἀγαπητῶς δ᾽ ἂν Kiessling : ἀγαπητὸν δ᾽ ἂν εἰ (εἰ om. Ba)
O, ἀγαπητὸν δ᾽ ἂν ἦν εἰ Sylburg, Jacoby.

medical attention those who suffered from wounds and in raising the spirits of those who were disheartened at the unexpected disgrace of defeat by speaking words of encouragement to them.

LXXXVI. While the Romans were thus occupied, the Volscians, as soon as it was day and they learned that the enemy had left their entrenchments, came up and made camp. Then, having stripped the dead, taken up those whom, though half dead, there was hope of saving, and buried their own men, they retired to Antium, the nearest city; and there, singing songs of triumph for their victory and offering sacrifices in all their temples, they devoted themselves during the following days to merry-making and pleasures. Now if they had rested content with their present victory and had attempted nothing further, their struggle would have had a glorious end. For the Romans would not have dared to come out again from their camp to give battle, but would have been glad to withdraw from the enemy's country, considering inglorious flight better than certain death. But as it was, the Volscians, aiming at still more, threw away the glory of their former victory. For hearing both from scouts and from those who escaped from the enemy's camp that the Romans who had saved themselves were very few, and the greater part of these wounded, they conceived great contempt for them, and immediately seizing their arms, ran to attack them. Many unarmed people also followed them out of the city to witness the struggle and at the same time to secure plunder and booty. But when, after attacking the hill and surrounding the

---

³ ἀποδιδρασκόντων R : ἀποδεδρακόντων C, ἀποδεδρακότων Cobet.

περιέστησαν καὶ τὰ περισταυρώματα διασπᾶν ἐπ
εχείρουν, πρῶτοι μὲν οἱ τῶν Ῥωμαίων ἱππεῖς πεζοὶ
μαχόμενοι διὰ τὴν τοῦ χωρίου φύσιν ἐξέδραμον ἐπ'
αὐτούς, ἔπειτα τούτων κατόπιν οἱ καλούμενοι τριά
ριοι πυκνώσαντες τοὺς λόχους· οὗτοι δ' εἰσὶν οἱ
πρεσβύτατοι τῶν στρατευομένων, οἷς τὰ στρατό
πεδα ἐπιτρέπουσι φυλάττειν ὅταν ἐξίωσιν εἰς τὴν
μάχην, καὶ ἐφ' οὓς τελευταίους, ὅταν ἀθρόα γένηται
τῶν ἐν ἀκμῇ φθορά, σπανίζοντες ἑτέρας ἐπικουρίας
5 καταφεύγουσι διὰ τὴν ἀνάγκην. οἱ δὲ Οὐολοῦσκοι
κατ' ἀρχὰς μὲν ἐδέξαντο τὴν ἔφοδον αὐτῶν καὶ
μέχρι πολλοῦ διέμενον ἐκθύμως ἀγωνιζόμενοι,
ἔπειτα διὰ τὴν τοῦ χωρίου φύσιν μειονεκτοῦντες
ὑπεχώρουν, καὶ τέλος ὀλίγα μὲν τοὺς πολεμίους
καὶ οὐκ ἄξια λόγου ἐργασάμενοι, πλείω[1] δ' αὐτοὶ
παθόντες κακὰ ὑπεχώρησαν εἰς τὸ πεδίον. ἔνθα
καταστρατοπεδευσάμενοι ταῖς ἑξῆς ἡμέραις ἐξ
έταττον τὴν δύναμιν καὶ προυκαλοῦντο τοὺς Ῥω
μαίους εἰς μάχην, οἱ δ' οὐκ ἀντεξῆεσαν.

6 Ὡς δὲ τοῦτ' εἶδον, καταφρονήσαντες αὐτῶν οἱ
Οὐολοῦσκοι συνεκάλουν ἐκ τῶν πόλεων δυνάμεις
καὶ παρεσκευάζοντο ὡς ἐξελοῦντες πολυχειρίᾳ τὸ
φρούριον· ῥᾳδίως τε ἂν ἐξειργάσαντο μέγα ἔργον
ὑπάτου τε καὶ Ῥωμαϊκῆς δυνάμεως ἢ βίᾳ κρατή
σαντες ἢ καὶ ὁμολογίαις[2] (οὐδὲ γὰρ τῶν ἐπιτηδείων
ἔτι εὐπόρει τὸ χωρίον), ἔφθη δὲ πρότερον ἐπικουρία
Ῥωμαίοις ἐλθοῦσα, ὑφ' ἧς ἐκωλύθησαν οἱ Οὐολοῦ
7 σκοι τὸ κάλλιστον ἐπιθεῖναι τῷ πολέμῳ τέλος. ὁ
γὰρ ἕτερος τῶν ὑπάτων Καίσων Φάβιος μαθὼν ἐν
αἷς ἦν τύχαις ἡ παραταξαμένη Οὐολούσκοις δύναμις

─────
[1] Kiessling : πλέω O.
[2] καὶ ὁμολογίαις ABC : καθ' ὁμολογίας D (?).

camp, they endeavoured to pull down the palisades, first the Roman horse, obliged, from the nature of the ground, to fight on foot, sallied out against them, and, behind the horse, those they call the *triarii*, with their ranks closed. These are the oldest soldiers, to whom they commit the guarding of the camp when they go out to give battle, and they fall back of necessity upon these as their last hope when there has been a general slaughter of the younger men and they lack other reinforcements. The Volscians at first sustained their onset and continued to fight stubbornly for a long time ; then, being at a disadvantage because of the nature of the ground, they began to give way and at last, after inflicting slight and negligible injuries upon the enemy, while suffering more themselves, they retired to the plain. And encamping there, during the following days they repeatedly drew up in order of battle, challenging the Romans to fight ; but these did not come out against them.

When the Volscians saw this, they held them in contempt, and summoning forces from their cities, made preparations to capture the stronghold by their very numbers. And they might easily have performed a great exploit by taking both the consul and the Roman army either by force or even by capitulation, since the place was no longer well supplied with provisions either ; but reinforcements came in time to the Romans, thus preventing the Volscians from bringing the war to the most glorious conclusion. It seems that the other consul, Caeso Fabius, learning to what straits the army had been reduced which had been arrayed against the Volscians, proposed to

ἐβούλετο μὲν ὡς εἶχε τάχους ἅπασαν ἄγων τὴν
δύναμιν εὐθὺς ἐπιέναι τοῖς πολιορκοῦσι τὸ φρούριον.
ὡς δ' οὐκ ἐγίνετο αὐτῷ θυμομένῳ τε καὶ οἰωνοῖς
χρωμένῳ τὰ ἱερὰ καλά, ἀλλ' ἠναντιοῦτο πρὸς τὰς
ἐξόδους αὐτοῦ τὸ δαιμόνιον, αὐτὸς μὲν ὑπέμεινε,
τὰς δὲ κρατίστας ἐπιλεξάμενος σπείρας ἀπέστειλε
8 τῷ συνάρχοντι. αἱ δὲ διά τε ὀρῶν ἀφανῶς[1] καὶ
νύκτωρ τὰ πολλὰ ποιησάμεναι τὰς ὁδοὺς εἰσῆλθον
εἰς τὸν χάρακα τοὺς πολεμίους λαθοῦσαι. ὁ μὲν
οὖν Αἰμίλιος θρασύτερος ἐγεγόνει τῇ παρουσίᾳ τῶν
συμμάχων, οἱ δὲ πολέμιοι τῷ τε πλήθει τῷ σφε-
τέρῳ εἰκῇ[2] πίσυνοι καὶ διὰ τὸ μὴ ἐπεξιέναι τοὺς
Ῥωμαίους εἰς μάχην ἐπαρθέντες ἀνέβαινον ἐπὶ τὸ
ὄρος πυκνώσαντες τοὺς λόχους· καὶ οἱ Ῥωμαῖοι
παρέντες αὐτοὺς[3] ἀναβῆναι καθ' ἡσυχίαν καὶ πολλὰ
πονεῖν περὶ τῷ σταυρώματι ἐάσαντες, ἐπειδὴ τὰ
σημεῖα ἤρθη τῆς μάχης διασπάσαντες κατὰ πολλὰ
μέρη τὸν χάρακα ἐμπίπτουσιν αὐτοῖς· καὶ οἱ μὲν
εἰς χεῖρας καταστάντες τοῖς ξίφεσιν ἐμάχοντο, οἱ
δ' ἀπὸ τῶν ἐρυμάτων λίθοις τε καὶ σαυνίοις καὶ
λόγχαις τοὺς ἐπιόντας ἔβαλλον, βέλος τε[4] οὐδὲν
ἄσκοπον ἦν πεπιλημένων γε[5] ἐν βραχεῖ χωρίῳ πολ-
9 λῶν. ἀπαράττονται δὴ τοῦ λόφου πολλοὺς σφῶν
ἀποβαλόντες οἱ Οὐολοῦσκοι καὶ εἰς φυγὴν ὁρμή-
σαντες μόγις εἰς τὸν ἴδιον ἀποσῴζονται χάρακα.
Ῥωμαῖοι δ' ὡς ἐν ἀσφαλείᾳ τέλος[6] ὄντες ἤδη κατέβαινον ἐπὶ τοὺς ἀγροὺς αὐτῶν· ἐξ ὧν ἐπισιτισ-
μοὺς καὶ τἆλλα ὅσων σπάνις ἦν ἐν τῷ χάρακι
ἐλάμβανον.

LXXXVII. Ἐπειδὴ δὲ καθῆκεν ὁ τῶν ἀρχ-

---

[1] ὀρῶν ἀφανῶς Sintenis, ὀρῶν ἀφανεῖς Reudler : ὁδῶν ἀφα-
νῶν O.   [2] Sylburg : ἐκεῖ O.

march as quickly as possible with all his forces and
fall at once upon those who were besieging the
stronghold. Since, however, the victims and omens
were not favourable when he offered sacrifice and
consulted the auspices, but the gods opposed his
setting out, he himself remained behind, but chose
out and sent his best cohorts to his colleague. These,
making their way covertly through the mountains and
generally by night, entered the camp without being
perceived by the enemy. Aemilius, therefore, had
become emboldened by the arrival of these reinforcements, while the enemy, rashly trusting to their
numbers and elated because the Romans did not come
out to fight, proceeded to march up the hill in close
order. The Romans permitted them to come up
at their leisure and to spend their strength on
the palisade ; but when the signals for battle were
raised, they pulled down the ramparts in many places
and fell upon the enemy. Some of them, coming to
close quarters, fought with their swords, while others
from the ramparts hurled at their assailants stones,
javelins and spears ; and no missile failed of a mark
where many combatants were crowded together in a
limited space. Thus the Volscians were hurled back
from the hill after losing many of their number, and
turning to flight, barely got safely back to their own
camp. The Romans, feeling themselves secure at
last, now made descents into the enemy's fields, from
which they took provisions and everything else of
which there was a dearth in the camp.

LXXXVII. When the time for the election of

---

³ Sylburg : αὐτοῖς O.   ⁴ τε O : δ' Reiske, Jacoby.
⁵ γε Reiske : τε O.
⁶ τέλος Kiessling : τέως O, Jacoby.

αἱρεσιῶν καιρός, ὁ μὲν Αἰμίλιος ἔμεινεν ἐπὶ στρατοπέδου δι' αἰσχύνης ἔχων ἐπὶ συμφοραῖς οὐκ
εὐσχήμοσιν εἰς τὴν πόλιν εἰσελθεῖν τὸ κράτιστον
ἀπολωλεκὼς τῆς στρατιᾶς. ὁ δὲ συνύπατος αὐτοῦ
τοὺς ὑφ' ἑαυτὸν ἄρχοντας ἐπὶ στρατοπέδου καταλιπὼν εἰς τὴν Ῥώμην ᾤχετο· καὶ συγκαλέσας τὸν
ὄχλον ἐπὶ τὰς ἀρχαιρεσίας, οἷς μὲν ὁ δῆμος ἐβούλετο δοθῆναι τὴν ὑπατείαν ἀνδράσιν ἐκ τῶν ὑπα-
τευκότων οὐ προὔθηκε τὴν ψηφοφορίαν, ἐπειδὴ
οὐδ'[1] αὐτοὶ μετῄεσαν τὴν ἀρχὴν ἑκόντες, ὑπὲρ δὲ
τῶν μετιόντων τούς τε λόχους ἐκάλεσε καὶ τὰς
2 ψήφους ἀνέδωκεν. οὗτοι δ' ἦσαν οὓς ἡ βουλὴ προ-
είλετο καὶ οἷς παραγγέλλειν τὴν ἀρχὴν ἐκέλευσεν,
οὐ σφόδρα τῷ δήμῳ κεχαρισμένοι. καὶ ἀπεδείχθη-
σαν εἰς τὸν ἐπιόντα ἐνιαυτὸν ὕπατοι ὅ τε νεώτερος
ἀδελφὸς τοῦ προθέντος τὰς ἀρχαιρεσίας ὑπάτου,
Μάρκος Φάβιος Καίσωνος υἱός, καὶ Λεύκιος
Οὐαλέριος Μάρκου υἱός, ὁ τὸν τρὶς ὑπατεύσαντα
Κάσσιον κρίνας ἐπὶ τῇ τυραννίδι καὶ ἀποκτείνας.
3 Οὗτοι τὴν ἀρχὴν παραλαβόντες ὑπὲρ τῶν ἀπο-
θανόντων ἐν τῷ πρὸς Ἀντιάτας πολέμῳ στρατιωτῶν ἠξίουν ἑτέρους καταγράφειν, ἵνα τὸ ἐλλιπὲς
ἀναπληρωθῇ τῶν λόχων. καὶ δόγμα ποιησάμενοι
βουλῆς[2] προὔγραψαν ἡμέραν ἐν ᾗ παρεῖναι τοὺς
ἔχοντας ἡλικίαν στρατεύσιμον ἔδει.[3] μετὰ τοῦτο
θόρυβος ἦν πολὺς κατὰ τὴν πόλιν ὅλην[4] καὶ λόγοι
τῶν πενεστάτων στασιώδεις οὐκ ἀξιούντων οὔτε
βουλῆς δόγμασιν ὑπηρετεῖν οὔτε ὑπάτων ἐξουσίᾳ
πειθαρχεῖν, ὅτι τὰς περὶ τῆς κληρουχίας ὑποσχέσεις

<hr />

[1] Sylburg : οὐκ O.
[2] δόγμα ποιησαμένης τῆς βουλῆς Kiessling.

magistrates arrived,[1] Aemilius remained in camp,
being ashamed to enter the city after his ignominious
defeat, in which he had lost the best part of his army.
But his colleague, leaving his subordinate officers in
camp, went to Rome ; and assembling the people for
the election, he declined to propose for the voting
those among the ex-consuls on whom the populace
wished the consulship to be bestowed, since even
these men were not voluntary candidates, but he
called the centuries and took their votes in favour of
such as sought the office. These were men the senate
had selected and ordered to canvass for the office, men
not very acceptable to the populace. Those elected
consuls for the ensuing year were Marcus Fabius, son
of Caeso, the younger brother of the consul who
conducted the election, and Lucius Valerius, the son
of Marcus, the man who had accused Cassius, who
had been thrice consul, of aiming at tyranny and
caused him to be put to death.

These men, having taken office, asked for the levying of fresh troops to replace those who had perished
in the war against the Antiates, in order that the gaps
in the various centuries might be filled ; and having
obtained a decree of the senate, they appointed a day
on which all who were of military age must appear.
Thereupon there was a great tumult throughout the
city and seditious speeches were made by the poorest
citizens, who refused either to comply with the
decrees of the senate or to obey the authority of the
consuls, since they had violated the promises made

---

[1] For chaps. 87-89, 3 *cf.* Livy ii. 42, 6-9.

---

[2] ἐν ᾗ . . . ἔδει B : ἐν ᾗ τοὺς ἔχοντας ἡλικίαν στρατεύσιμον
ἥκειν ἔδει R.   [4] ὅλην B : om. R.

ἐψεύσαντο πρὸς αὐτούς· συνιόντες τε κατὰ πλῆθος
ἐπὶ τοὺς δημάρχους ὠνείδιζον αὐτοῖς προδοσίαν καὶ
κατεβόων ἐπικαλούμενοι τὴν ἐξ ἐκείνων συμμαχίαν.
4 τοῖς μὲν οὖν ἄλλοις οὐκ ἐδόκει καιρὸς ἁρμόττων
εἶναι πολέμου συνεστῶτος ὑπερορίου τὰς πολιτικὰς
ἔχθρας ἀναζωπυρεῖν, εἷς δέ τις ἐξ αὐτῶν Γάιος
Μαίνιος οὐκ ἔφη προδώσειν τοὺς δημοτικούς, οὐδ'
ἐπιτρέψειν τοῖς ὑπάτοις στρατιὰν καταγράφειν, ἐὰν
μὴ πρότερον ἀποδείξωσι τοὺς ὁριστὰς τῆς δημοσίας
γῆς καὶ τὸ περὶ τῆς κληρουχίας ψήφισμα γράψαντες
εἰς τὸν δῆμον ἐξενέγκωσιν. ἀντιλεγόντων δὲ πρὸς
ταῦτα τῶν ὑπάτων καὶ πρόφασιν ποιουμένων τοῦ
μηθὲν αὐτῷ συγχωρεῖν ὧν ἠξίου τὸν ἐν χερσὶν ὄντα
πόλεμον, οὐκ ἔφη προσέξειν αὐτοῖς τὸν νοῦν, ἀλλὰ
5 κωλύσειν ἁπάσῃ δυνάμει τὴν καταγραφήν. καὶ
ἐποίει ταῦτα· οὐ μὴν ἴσχυσέ γε μέχρι τέλους. οἱ
γὰρ ὕπατοι προελθόντες ἔξω τῆς πόλεως ἐν τῷ
παρακειμένῳ πεδίῳ τοὺς στρατηγικοὺς δίφρους
ἔθηκαν· ἐνταῦθα καὶ τὸν στρατιωτικὸν ἐποιοῦντο
κατάλογον, καὶ τοὺς οὐχ ὑπακούοντας τοῖς νόμοις,
ἐπειδὴ αὐτοὺς ἄγειν οὐχ οἷοί τ' ἦσαν, εἰς χρήματα
ἐζημίουν, ὅσοις μὲν χωρία ὑπῆρχεν, ἐκκόπτοντες
ταῦτα καὶ τὰς αὐλὰς καθαιροῦντες, ὅσων δὲ
γεωργικὸς ὁ βίος ἦν ἐν ἀλλοτρίοις κτήμασι, τούτων ἄγοντές τε καὶ φέροντες τὰ παρεσκευασμένα
πρὸς τὴν ἐργασίαν ζεύγη τε βοϊκὰ καὶ βοσκήματα
καὶ ὑποζύγια ἀχθοφόρα καὶ σκεύη παντοῖα οἷς γῆ
6 τ' ἐξεργάζεται καὶ καρποὶ συγκομίζονται. ὁ δὲ
κωλύων τὴν καταγραφὴν δήμαρχος οὐθὲν ἔτι ποιεῖν
ἦν δυνατός. οὐδενὸς γάρ εἰσι τῶν ἔξω τῆς πόλεως
οἱ τὴν δημαρχικὴν ἔχοντες ἐξουσίαν κύριοι· περι-

to them concerning the allotment of land. And going
in great numbers to the tribunes, they charged them
with treachery, and with loud outcries demanded
their assistance. Most of the tribunes did not regard it as a suitable time, when a foreign war had
arisen, to fan domestic hatreds into flame again; but
one of them, named Gaius Maenius, declared that he
would not betray the plebeians or permit the consuls
to levy an army unless they should first appoint
commissioners for fixing the boundaries of the public
land, draw up the decree of the senate for its allotment, and lay it before the people. When the consuls opposed this and made the war they had on their
hands an excuse for not granting anything he desired,
the tribune replied that he would pay no heed to
them, but would hinder the levy with all his power.
And this he attempted to do; nevertheless, he could
not prevail to the end. For the consuls, going outside the city, ordered their generals' chairs to be
placed in the near-by field [1]; and there they not only
enrolled the troops, but also fined those who refused
obedience to the laws, since it was not in their power
to seize their persons. If the disobedient owned
estates, they laid them waste and demolished their
country-houses; and if they were farmers who tilled
fields belonging to others, they stripped them of the
yokes of oxen, the cattle, and the beasts of burden
that were on hand for the work, and all kinds of implements with which the land is tilled and the crops
gathered. And the tribune who opposed the levy
was no longer able to do anything. For those who
are invested with the tribuneship possess no authority
over anything outside the city, since their jurisdic-

[1] The Campus Martius.

γέγραπται γὰρ αὐτῶν τὸ κράτος τοῖς τείχεσι, καὶ οὐδὲ ἀπαυλισθῆναι τῆς πόλεως αὐτοῖς θέμις, ὅτι μὴ πρὸς ἕνα καιρόν, ἐν ᾧ πᾶσαι θύουσιν αἱ τῆς πόλεως ἀρχαὶ κοινὴν ὑπὲρ τοῦ Λατίνων ἔθνους τῷ Διὶ θυσίαν ἐπὶ τὸ Ἀλβανῶν[1] ὄρος ἀναβαίνουσαι.

7 τοῦτο διαμένει μέχρι τῶν καθ' ἡμᾶς χρόνων τὸ ἔθος, τὸ μηδενὸς εἶναι τῶν ἔξω τῆς πόλεως τοὺς δημάρχους κυρίους· καὶ δὴ καὶ τὸν ἐμφύλιον Ῥωμαίων πόλεμον τὸν[2] ἐπὶ τῆς ἐμῆς ἡλικίας, ὃς μέγιστος τῶν πρὸ αὐτοῦ πολέμων ἐγένετο, ἡ κινήσασα πρόφασις ἐπὶ πολλαῖς ἄλλαις δόξασα μείζων[3] εἶναι καὶ ἀποχρῶσα[4] διαστῆσαι τὴν πόλιν ἥδε ἦν, ὅτι τῶν δημάρχων τινὲς ἐξεληλάσθαι τῆς πόλεως αἰτιώμενοι βίᾳ πρὸς τοῦ τότε κατέχοντος τὰ κατὰ τὴν Ἰταλίαν ἡγεμόνος, ἵνα μηδενὸς εἶεν ἔτι κύριοι, ἐπὶ τὸν ἐν τῇ Γαλατίᾳ τὰ στρατόπεδα κατέχοντα,

8 ὡς οὐκ ἔχοντες ὅποι τράπωνται, κατέφυγον. ὁ δὲ τῇ προφάσει ταύτῃ χρησάμενος, ὡς ἀρχῇ δήμου παναγεῖ τὸ κράτος ἀφαιρεθείσῃ παρὰ τοὺς ὅρκους τῶν προγόνων αὐτὸς ὁσίως καὶ σὺν δίκῃ βοηθῶν αὐτός τε σὺν τοῖς ὅπλοις ἦλθεν εἰς τὴν πόλιν καὶ τοὺς ἄνδρας ἐπὶ τὴν ἀρχὴν κατήγαγε.

LXXXVIII. Τότε δ' οὖν οἱ δημόται τῆς δημαρχικῆς ἐξουσίας οὐδὲν ἀπολαύοντες ὑφεῖντο τοῦ θράσους καὶ προσιόντες τοῖς ἐπὶ τῆς στρατολογίας τεταγμένοις τὸν ἱερὸν ὅρκον ὤμνυσαν, καὶ ὑπὸ τὰς

---

[1] Ἀλβανὸν Kiessling.
[2] τὸν added by Steph.
[3] μείζων ACmℝ : om. R.
[4] καὶ ἀποχρῶσα O : καὶ μόνη ἀποχρῶσα Reiske, Jacoby.

---

[1] Pompey.   [2] Caesar.

tion is limited by the city walls, and it is not lawful for them even to pass a night away from the
city, save on a single occasion, when all the magistrates of the commonwealth ascend the Alban Mount
and offer up a common sacrifice to Jupiter in behalf
of the Latin nation. This custom by which the
tribunes possess no authority over anything outside
the city continues to our times. And indeed the
motivating cause, among many others, of the civil
war among the Romans which occurred in my day and
was greater than any war before it, the cause which
seemed more important and sufficient to divide the
commonwealth, was this—that some of the tribunes,
complaining that they had been forcibly driven out of
the city by the general [1] who was then in control of
affairs in Italy, in order to deprive them henceforth
of any power, fled to the general [2] who commanded
the armies in Gaul, as having no place to turn to.
And the latter, availing himself of this excuse and
pretending to come with right and justice to the aid
of the sacrosanct magistracy of the people which
had been deprived of its authority contrary to the
oaths of the forefathers, entered the city himself in
arms and restored the men to their office.[3]

LXXXVIII. But on the occasion of which we are
now speaking the plebeians, receiving no assistance
from the tribunician power, moderated their boldness,
and coming to the persons appointed to raise the
levies, took the sacred oath and enlisted under their

[3] At the beginning of the year 49 B.C. Antony and
Q. Cassius, two of the new tribunes, and Curio, who had
just laid down that office, fled to Caesar, then encamped at
Ravenna. Attention has already been called (see chap. 80)
to Dionysius' avoidance of proper names when mentioning
persons of his own day.

σημείας[1] κατεγράφοντο. ἐπεὶ δὲ τὸ ἐλλιπὲς τῶν
λόχων ἐξεπληρώθη, διεκληρώσαντο τὰς ἡγεμονίας
τῶν στρατοπέδων οἱ ὕπατοι· καὶ ὁ μὲν Φάβιος
τὴν ἐπὶ τῇ βοηθείᾳ τῶν συμμάχων ἀποσταλεῖσαν
δύναμιν παρελάμβανεν, ὁ δὲ Οὐαλέριος τὴν ἐν
Οὐολούσκοις στρατοπεδεύουσαν ἄγων τοὺς νεωστὶ
2 καταγραφέντας. μαθοῦσι δὲ τὴν παρουσίαν αὐτοῦ
τοῖς πολεμίοις ἐδόκει στρατιάν τε ἑτέραν μετα-
πέμπεσθαι καὶ ἐν ἰσχυροτέρῳ τὸ στρατόπεδον
ποιήσασθαι χωρίῳ καὶ μηδὲν ἐκ τοῦ καταφρονεῖν
αὐτῶν ἔτι προπετὲς κινδύνευμα ὡς πρότερον ὑπομένειν. ἐγεγόνει ταῦτα διὰ ταχέων, ἀμφοτέροις τε
παρέστη τοῖς ἡγεμόσι τῶν δυνάμεων ὁμοία περὶ
τοῦ πολέμου γνώμη, τὰ ἑαυτῶν φυλάττειν ἐρύματα,
ἐάν τις ἐπίῃ, τοῖς δὲ τῶν πολεμίων ὡς βίᾳ κρατη-
3 θησομένοις μὴ ἐπιχειρεῖν. καὶ ὁ διὰ μέσου χρόνος
οὐκ ὀλίγος ἐγένετο φόβῳ τῶν ἐπιχειρήσεων τριβό-
μενος· οὐ μέντοι καὶ εἰς τέλος γε διαμένειν ἐν τοῖς
ἐγνωσμένοις ἐδυνήθησαν. ὁπότε γὰρ ἐπισιτισμοῦ
χάριν ἢ τῶν ἄλλων ἐπιτηδείων τινὸς ὧν ἀμφοτέροις
ἔδει[2] μοῖρά τις ἀποσταλείη τῆς στρατιᾶς, συμβολαί
τε αὐτῶν ἐγίνοντο καὶ πληγαί, καὶ τὸ νικᾶν οὐκ
ἀεὶ παρὰ τοῖς αὐτοῖς ἔμενε· πολλάκις δὲ συμπλεκο-
μένων ἀλλήλοις ἀπέθνησκόν τε οὐκ ὀλίγοι καὶ
4 τραυματίαι πλείους ἐγίνοντο. τοῖς μὲν οὖν Ῥωμαίοις τὸ ἀπαναλούμενον τῆς στρατιᾶς οὐδεμία
ποθὲν[3] ἐπικουρία[4] ἐξεπλήρου, τὸ δὲ τῶν Οὐολούσκων στρατόπεδον ἄλλων ἐπ' ἄλλοις ἡκόντων
πολλὴν αὔξησιν ἐλάμβανε· καὶ τούτῳ ἐπαρθέντες

---

[1] σημείας AB : σημαίας Portus, Jacoby.
[2] ἔδει Reiske : ἐδόκει O.
ποθὲν O : οἴκοθεν Kiessling.

standards. When the gaps in the several centuries
had been filled, the consuls drew lots for the command of the legions ; as a result, Fabius took over
the army which had been sent to the assistance of
the allies, while Valerius received the one which lay
encamped in the country of the Volscians, and took
with him the new levies. When the enemy were
informed of his arrival, they resolved to send for
another army and to encamp in a place of greater
strength, and no longer out of contempt for the
Romans to expose themselves to reckless danger, as
before. These resolutions were quickly carried out ;
and the commanders of the two armies both came to
the same decision regarding the war, namely, to defend their own entrenchments if they were attacked,
but to make no attempt upon those of the enemy in
the expectation of carrying them by assault. And
meanwhile not a little time was wasted, because
of their fear of making any attack upon each other.
Nevertheless, they were not able to abide by their
resolutions to the end. For whenever any detachments were sent out to bring in provisions or anything else that was necessary to the two armies,
there were encounters and blows were exchanged,
and the victory did not always rest with the same
side ; and since they frequently clashed, not a
few men were killed and more wounded. For the
Romans the wastage of their army was made good
by no replacements from any quarter[1] ; but the
army of the Volscians was greatly increased by the
arrival of one force after another, and their generals,

---

[1] Kiessling proposed " from home."

⁴ ἐπικουρία Ambrosch, Kiessling, ἐπιοῦσα ἐπικουρία Sintenis : ἐπιοῦσα O.

οἱ ἡγεμόνες ἐξῆγον ἐκ τοῦ χάρακος τὴν δύναμιν
ὡς εἰς μάχην.

LXXXIX. Ἐξελθόντων δὲ καὶ τῶν Ῥωμαίων
καὶ παραταξαμένων ἰσχυρὰ μάχη γίνεται καὶ ἱππέων καὶ πεζῶν καὶ ψιλῶν ἴσῃ πάντων χρωμένων
προθυμίᾳ τε καὶ ἐμπειρίᾳ, καὶ τὸ νικᾶν ἑκάστου
2 παρ' ἑαυτὸν μόνον τιθεμένου· ὡς δὲ νεκροί τε
αὐτῶν πολλοὶ ἑκατέρωθεν ἐν ᾧ ἐτάχθησαν χωρίῳ
πεσόντες ἔκειντο, καὶ ἡμιθνῆτες ἔτι πλείους τῶν
νεκρῶν,[1] οἱ δὲ παρὰ τὸν ἀγῶνα καὶ τὰ δεινὰ ἔτι
διαμένοντες ὀλίγοι ἦσαν, καὶ οὐδὲ οὗτοι δρᾶν τὰ
πολέμου ἔργα δυνάμενοι, βαρυνόντων μὲν αὐτοῖς
τῶν σκεπαστηρίων τὰς εὐωνύμους χεῖρας διὰ πλῆθος τῶν ἐμπεπηγότων βελῶν, καὶ οὐκ ἐώντων
ὑπομένειν τὰς προσβολάς, τετραμμένων δὲ τῶν
ἐγχειριδίων τὰς ἀκμάς, ἔστι δ' ὧν καὶ κατεαγότων
ὅλων, οἷς οὐθὲν ἔτι ἦν χρῆσθαι, τοῦ τε κόπου, ὃς δι'
ὅλης ἡμέρας ἀγωνιζομένοις αὐτοῖς πολὺς ἐγεγόνει,
παραλύοντος τὰ νεῦρα καὶ τὰς πληγὰς ἀσθενεῖς
ποιοῦντος, ἱδρῶτος δὲ καὶ δίψης καὶ ἄσθματος,
οἷα ἐν πνιγηρᾷ ὥρᾳ[2] ἔτους τοῖς πολὺν χρόνον
ἀγωνιζομένοις συμπίπτειν φιλεῖ, παρ' ἀμφοτέροις
γινομένων, τέλος οὐδὲν ἔλαβεν ἀξιόλογον ἡ μάχη,
ἀλλ' ἀγαπητῶς ἀμφότεροι τῶν στρατηγῶν ἀνα-
καλουμένων ἀπῆλθον ἐπὶ τοὺς ἑαυτῶν χάρακας· καὶ
οὐκέτι μετὰ τοῦτ' ἐξῄεσαν εἰς μάχην οὐδέτεροι,
ἀλλ' ἀντικαθήμενοι[3] παρεφύλαττον ἀλλήλων τὰς
3 ἕνεκα τῶν ἐπιτηδείων γινομένας ἐξόδους. ἔδοξε
μέντοι, ὡς[4] λόγος ἦν ἐν τῇ Ῥώμῃ πολύς, δυναμένη[5]

---

[1] τῶν νεκρῶν deleted by Reudler, Jacoby.
[2] ἐν πνιγηρᾷ ὥρᾳ Bb : ἐμπνίγει ὥρᾳ A.
[3] ἀλλ' ἀντικαθήμενοι A : ἀλλὰ καθήμενοι B.

elated at this, led out the army from the camp
ready for battle.

LXXXIX. When the Romans also came out and
drew up their forces, a sharp engagement ensued, not
only of the horse, but of the foot and the light-armed
troops as well, all showing equal ardour and experience and every man placing his hopes of victory in
himself alone. At last, however, the bodies of the
dead on both sides lay in great numbers where they
had fallen at the posts assigned to them, and the men
who were barely alive were even more numerous than
the dead, while those who still continued the fight
and faced its dangers were but few, and even these
were unable to perform the tasks of war ; for their
shields, because of the multitude of spears that had
stuck in them, weighed down their left arms and
would not permit them to sustain the enemy's onsets,
and their daggers had their edges blunted or in some
cases were entirely shattered and no longer of any use,
and the great weariness of the men, who had fought
the whole day, slackened their sinews and weakened
their blows, and sweat, thirst, and want of breath
afflicted both armies, as is wont to happen when
men fight long in the stifling heat of summer. Thus
the battle came to an end that was anything but
remarkable ; but both sides, as soon as their generals
ordered a retreat to be sounded, gladly returned to
their camps. After that neither army any longer
ventured out for battle, but lying over against one
another, they kept watch on each other's movements
when any detachments went out for supplies. It was
believed, however, according to the report common

---

⁴ ὡς Naber : καὶ O, Jacoby.
⁵ δυναμένη Naber : ὡς δυναμένη O, Jacoby.

τότε νικᾶν ἡ Ῥωμαίων δύναμις ἑκουσία μηδὲν
ἐργάσασθαι[1] λαμπρὸν διὰ μῖσός τε τοῦ ὑπάτου καὶ
ὀργὴν ἣν εἶχε πρὸς τοὺς πατρικίους ἐπὶ τῷ φενα-
κισμῷ τῆς κληρουχίας. αὐτοὶ δ' οἱ στρατιῶται τὸν
ὕπατον ὡς οὐχ ἱκανὸν στρατηγεῖν ᾐτιῶντο, γράμματα πέμποντες ὡς τοὺς ἐπιτηδείους ἑαυτῶν
ἕκαστοι.

Καὶ τὰ μὲν ἐπὶ στρατοπέδου γινόμενα τοιαῦτ'
ἦν· ἐν αὐτῇ δὲ τῇ Ῥώμῃ πολλὰ δαιμόνια σημεῖα
ἐφαίνετο δηλωτικὰ θείου χόλου κατά τε φωνὰς καὶ
4 ὄψεις ἀήθεις. πάντα δ' εἰς τοῦτο συνέτεινεν, ὡς οἵ
τε μάντεις καὶ οἱ τῶν ἱερῶν ἐξηγηταὶ συνενέγ-
καντες τὰς ἐμπειρίας ἀπέφαινον, τὸ[2] θεῶν χολοῦσθαι[3] τινας[4] ὅτι[5] οὐ κομίζονται τὰς νομίμους τιμάς,
οὐ καθαρῶς οὐδὲ ὁσίως ἐπιτελουμένων αὐτοῖς τῶν
ἱερῶν. ζήτησις δὴ μετὰ τοῦτο πολλὴ ἐκ πάντων
ἐγίνετο, καὶ σὺν χρόνῳ μήνυσις ἀποδίδοται τοῖς
ἱεροφάνταις ὅτι τῶν παρθένων μία τῶν φυλαττου-
σῶν τὸ ἱερὸν πῦρ, Ὀπιμία ὄνομα αὐτῇ, τὴν παρθε-
5 νίαν ἀφαιρεθεῖσα μιαίνει τὰ ἱερά. οἱ δ' ἔκ τε
βασάνων καὶ τῶν ἄλλων ἀποδείξεων μαθόντες ὅτι
τὸ μηνυόμενον ἦν ἀδίκημα[6] ἀληθές, αὐτὴν μὲν τῆς
κορυφῆς ἀφελόμενοι τὰ στέμματα καὶ πομπεύ-
σαντες δι' ἀγορᾶς ἐντὸς τείχους ζῶσαν κατώρυξαν·
δύο δὲ τοὺς ἐξελεγχθέντας διαπράξασθαι τὴν φθορὰν

[1] μηδὲν ἐργάσασθαι O : μηδὲν ἦν ἐργάσασθαι Jacoby.
[2] ἀπέφαινον, τὸ Post : ἀπεφαίνοντο O, Jacoby.
[3] χολοῦσθαι ACmg : om. BC, Jacoby.
[4] τινας Sylburg : τινες B, Jacoby, τινα A, and C (by correction).
[5] ὅτι Reiske : οἱ A (by correction), om. BC ; Jacoby
placed ὅτι before θεῶν and (with BC) omitted χολοῦσθαι.

in Rome, that the Roman army, though it was then in their power to conquer, deliberately refused to perform any brilliant action because of hatred for the consul and the resentment they felt against the patricians for having played a trick upon them in the matter of the allotment of land. Indeed, the soldiers themselves, in letters they sent to their friends, accused the consul of being unfit to command.

While these things were happening in the camp, in Rome itself many prodigies[1] in the way of unusual voices and sights occurred as indications of divine wrath. And they all pointed to this conclusion, as the augurs and the interpreters of religious matters declared, after pooling their experiences, that some of the gods were angered because they were not receiving their customary honours, as their rites were not being performed in a pure and holy manner. Thereupon strict inquiry was made by everyone, and at last information was given to the pontiffs that one of the virgins who guarded the sacred fire, Opimia[2] by name, had lost her virginity and was polluting the holy rites. The pontiffs, having by tortures and other proofs found that the information was true,[3] took from her head the fillets, and solemnly conducting her through the Forum, buried her alive inside the city walls. As for the two men who were convicted of violating her, they ordered them to be

---

[1] For chap. 89, 3-5 *cf.* Livy ii. 42, 10 f.

[2] Livy gives her name as Oppia.

[3] Literally, " a true crime "; but the word ἀδίκημα is suspicious, and was deleted by Kiessling ; Kayser proposed ἀσέβημα (" act of impiety ").

---

⁶ ἀδίκημα deleted by Kiessling ; Kayser proposed to read ἀσέβημα or ἁμάρτημα.

μαστιγώσαντες ἐν φανερῷ παραχρῆμα[1] ἀπέκτειναν.
καὶ μετὰ τοῦτο καλὰ τὰ ἱερὰ καὶ τὰ μαντεύματα ὡς
ἀφεικότων αὐτοῖς τῶν θεῶν τὸν χόλον, ἐγίνετο.

XC. Ὡς δὲ καθῆκεν ὁ τῶν ἀρχαιρεσιῶν χρόνος,
ἐλθόντων τῶν ὑπάτων πολλὴ σπουδὴ καὶ παράταξις
ἐγένετο τοῦ δήμου πρὸς τοὺς πατρικίους περὶ τῶν
παραληψομένων τὴν ἡγεμονίαν ἀνδρῶν. ἐκεῖνοι μὲν
γὰρ ἐκ τῶν νεωτέρων ἐβούλοντο τοὺς δραστηρίους
τε καὶ ἥκιστα δημοτικοὺς ἐπὶ τὴν ὑπατείαν προ-
αγαγεῖν· καὶ μετῄει τὴν ἀρχὴν κελευσθεὶς ὑπ' αὐτῶν
ὁ υἱὸς Ἀππίου Κλαυδίου τοῦ πολεμιωτάτου τῷ
δήμῳ δοκοῦντος εἶναι, μεστὸς αὐθαδείας ἀνὴρ καὶ
θράσους, ἑταίροις τε καὶ πελάταις ἁπάντων πλεῖστον τῶν καθ' ἡλικίαν δυνάμενος· ὁ δὲ δῆμος ἐκ
τῶν πρεσβυτέρων τε καὶ τῶν πεῖραν ἤδη δεδωκότων
τῆς ἐπιεικείας τοὺς προνοησομένους τοῦ κοινῇ συμφέροντος ὀνομάζων ἠξίου ποιεῖν ὑπάτους. αἵ τε
ἀρχαὶ διειστήκεσαν καὶ τὰς ἀλλήλων ἀνέλυον ἐξου-
2 σίας. ὁπότε μὲν γὰρ οἱ ὕπατοι καλοῖεν τὸ πλῆθος
ὡς ἀποδείξοντες τοὺς μετιόντας τὴν ἀρχὴν ὑπάτους,
οἱ δήμαρχοι τοῦ κωλύειν ὄντες κύριοι διέλυον τὰ
ἀρχαιρέσια, ὁπότε δ' αὖ πάλιν ἐκεῖνοι καλοῖεν ὡς
ἀρχαιρεσιάσοντα τὸν δῆμον, οὐκ ἐπέτρεπον οἱ
ὕπατοι τὴν ἐξουσίαν ἔχοντες τοῦ συγκαλεῖν τοὺς
λόχους καὶ τὰς ψήφους ἀναδιδόναι. κατηγορίαι τε
ἀλλήλων ἐγίνοντο καὶ συνεχεῖς ἁψιμαχίαι καθ'
ἑταιρίας συνισταμένων, ὥστε καὶ πληγὰς ἀλλήλοις
διδόναι τινὰς ὑπ' ὀργῆς, καὶ οὐ μακρὰν ἀποσχεῖν
3 τὴν στάσιν τῶν ὅπλων. ταῦτα μαθοῦσα ἡ βουλὴ

---

[1] παραχρῆμα placed before μετὰ τοῦτο by Reiske.

[1] For chaps. 90 f. cf. Livy ii. 43, 1 f.

scourged in public and then put to death at once. Thereupon the sacrifices and the auguries became favourable, as if the gods had given up their anger against them.

XC. When the time for the election of magistrates arrived [1] and the consuls had returned to Rome, there was great rivalry and marshalling of forces between the populace and the patricians concerning the persons who were to receive the chief magistracy. For the patricians desired to promote to the consulship those of the younger men who were energetic and least inclined to favour the plebeians ; and at their behest the son of the Appius Claudius who was regarded as the greatest enemy of the plebeians stood for the office, a man full of arrogance and daring and by reason of his friends and clients the most powerful man of his age. The populace, on their part, named from among the older men who had already given proof of their reasonableness those who were likely to consult the common good, and desired to make them consuls. The magistrates also were divided and sought to invalidate one another's authority. For whenever the consuls called an assembly of the multitude, to announce the candidates for the consulship, the tribunes, by virtue of their power to intervene, would dismiss the comitia ; and whenever the tribunes, in turn, called an assembly of the people to elect magistrates, the consuls, who had the power of calling the centuries together and of taking their votes, would not permit them to proceed. There were mutual accusations and continual skirmishes between them, each side uniting in factional groups, with the result that even angry blows were exchanged and the sedition stopped little short of armed violence.

πολὺν ἐσκόπει χρόνον ὅ τι χρήσεται τοῖς πράγμασιν, οὔτε βιάσασθαι δυναμένη τὸν δῆμον οὔτε
εἶξαι βουλομένη. ἦν δ᾿ ἡ μὲν αὐθαδεστέρα γνώμη
δικτάτορα ἑλέσθαι τῶν ἀρχαιρεσιῶν ἕνεκα, ὃν ἂν
ἡγῶνται κράτιστον εἶναι, τὸν δὲ λαβόντα τὴν ἐξουσίαν τούς τε νοσοποιοὺς ἐκ τῆς πόλεως ἐξελεῖν, καὶ
εἴ τι ἡμάρτηται ταῖς πρότερον ἀρχαῖς ἐπανορθώσασθαι, τόν τε κόσμον τοῦ πολιτεύματος ὃν βούλεται
καταστησάμενον ἀνδράσι τοῖς κρατίστοις ἀποδοῦναι
4 τὰς ἀρχάς· ἡ δ᾿ ἐπιεικεστέρα μεσοβασιλεῖς ἑλέσθαι
τοὺς πρεσβυτάτους τε καὶ τιμιωτάτους ἄνδρας,
οἷς ἐπιμελὲς ἔσται τὰ περὶ τὰς ἀρχάς, ὅπως κράτι-
σται γενήσονται, προνοηθῆναι, τὸν αὐτὸν τρόπον
ὅνπερ ἐπὶ τῶν βασιλέων τῶν ἐκλιπόντων ἐγίνοντο.
ταύτῃ προσθεμένων τῇ γνώμῃ τῶν πλειόνων ἀποδείκνυται πρὸς αὐτῶν μεσοβασιλεύς[1] Αὖλος Σεμπρώνιος Ἀτρατῖνος· αἱ δ᾿ ἄλλαι κατελύθησαν
5 ἀρχαί. οὗτος ἐπιτροπεύσας τὴν πόλιν ἀστασίαστον
ὅσας ἐξῆν ἡμέρας ἕτερον ἀποδείκνυσιν, ὥσπερ αὐτοῖς ἔθος ἦν, Σπόριον Λάρκιον. κἀκεῖνος συγκαλέσας τὴν λοχῖτιν ἐκκλησίαν καὶ τὰς ψήφους
κατὰ[2] τὰ τιμήματα ἀναδούς, ἐκ τῆς ἀμφοτέρων
εὐδοκήσεως ἀποδείκνυσιν ὑπάτους Γάιον Ἰούλιον,
τὸν ἐπικαλούμενον Ἴουλον, ἐκ τῶν φιλοδήμων,[3]
καὶ Κόιντον Φάβιον Καίσωνος υἱὸν τὸ δεύτερον ἐκ
8 τῶν ἀριστοκρατικῶν. καὶ ὁ μὲν[4] δῆμος οὐδὲν ἐκ
τῆς προτέρας ὑπατείας αὐτοῦ πεπονθὼς εἴασε

---

[1] ἀποδείκνυται . . . μεσοβασιλεὺς Cmg : ἀποδείκνυται . . .
μεσοβασιλεῖς ABC.   [2] κατὰ Sylburg : καὶ O.
[3] Jacoby : φιλοδημοτικῶν O, δημοτικῶν Cobet.
[4] μὲν added by Reiske.

The senate, being informed of all this, deliberated for a long time how it should deal with the situation, being neither able to force the populace to submit nor willing to yield. The bolder opinion in that body was for appointing a dictator, whomever they should consider to be the best, for the purpose of the election, and that the one receiving this power should banish the trouble-makers from the state, and if the former magistrates had been guilty of any error, that he should correct it, and then, after establishing the form of government he desired, should hand over the magistracies to the best men. The more moderate opinion was for choosing the oldest and most honoured senators as *interreges* to have charge of the election and see that it was carried out in the best manner, just as elections were formerly carried out upon the demise of their kings. The latter opinion having been approved by the majority, Aulus Sempronius Atratinus was appointed *interrex* by the senate and all the other magistracies were suspended. After he had administered the commonwealth without any sedition for as many days as it was lawful,[1] he appointed another *interrex*, according to their custom, naming Spurius Larcius. And Larcius, summoning the centuriate assembly and taking their votes according to the valuation of their property, named for consuls, with the approval of both sides, Gaius Julius, surnamed Iulus, one of the men friendly to the populace, and, to serve for the second time, Quintus Fabius, the son of Caeso, who belonged to the aristocratic party. The populace, who had suffered naught at his hands in his former consulship, permitted him to obtain this

---

[1] The period was five days ; see ii. 57, 2.

τυχεῖν ταύτης τῆς ἐξουσίας τὸ δεύτερον, μισῶν
τὸν Ἄππιον καὶ ὅτι ἐκεῖνος ἀτιμασθῆναι ἐδόκει
σφόδρα ἡδόμενος· τοῖς δ' ἐν τέλει διαπεπραγμένοις
δραστήριον ἄνδρα καὶ οὐθὲν ἐνδώσοντα τῷ δήμῳ
μαλακὸν ἐπὶ τὴν ὑπατείαν παρελθεῖν, κατὰ γνώμην
ἐδόκει κεχωρηκέναι τὰ τῆς διχοστασίας.

XCI. Ἐπὶ τῆς τούτων ἀρχῆς Αἰκανοὶ μὲν εἰς τὴν
Λατίνων χώραν ἐμβαλόντες ἀπήλασαν ἀνδράποδα
καὶ βοσκήματα πολλὰ ληστρικῇ ἐφόδῳ χρησάμενοι·
Τυρρηνῶν δ' οἱ καλούμενοι Οὐιεντανοὶ τῆς Ῥωμαίων γῆς πολλὴν ἠδίκησαν προνομαῖς. τῆς δὲ
βουλῆς τὸν μὲν πρὸς Αἰκανοὺς πόλεμον εἰς ἕτερον
ἀναβαλομένης χρόνον, παρὰ δὲ Οὐιεντανῶν δίκας
αἰτεῖν ψηφισαμένης,[1] Αἰκανοὶ μὲν ἐπειδὴ τὰ πρῶτα
αὐτοῖς κατὰ νοῦν ἐχώρησε, καὶ οὐθεὶς ὁ κωλύσων
τὰ λοιπὰ ἐφαίνετο, θράσει ἐπαρθέντες ἀλογίστῳ
ληστρικὴν μὲν οὐκέτι στρατείαν ἔγνωσαν ποιεῖσθαι,
δυνάμει δὲ βαρείᾳ ἐλάσαντες ἐπὶ πόλιν Ὀρτῶνα[2]
κατὰ κράτος αἱροῦσι· καὶ διαρπάσαντες τά τε ἐκ
τῆς χώρας καὶ τὰ τῆς πόλεως ἀπήεσαν εὐπορίαν
2 πολλὴν ἀγόμενοι. Οὐιεντανοὶ δὲ πρὸς τοὺς ἀπὸ
τῆς Ῥώμης ἥκοντας ἀποκρινάμενοι ὅτι οὐκ ἐξ
αὐτῶν εἴησαν οἱ προνομεύοντες τὴν χώραν, ἀλλ' ἐκ
τῶν ἄλλων Τυρρηνῶν, ἀπέλυσαν τοὺς ἄνδρας οὐθὲν
τῶν δικαίων ποιήσαντες· καὶ οἱ πρέσβεις ἐπι-
τυγχάνουσι τοῖς Οὐιεντανοῖς λείαν ἐκ τῆς αὐτῶν
χώρας ἄγουσι. ταῦτα παρ' αὐτῶν ἡ βουλὴ μαθοῦσα
πολεμεῖν τε ἐψηφίσατο Οὐιεντανοῖς καὶ τοὺς ὑπά-
3 τους ἀμφοτέρους ἐξάγειν τὴν στρατιάν. ἐγένετο

---

[1] δίκας αἰτεῖν ψηφισαμένης B : αἰτεῖν ψηφισαμένης ἀπολογίαν R.
[2] Sylburg : ὁρῶνα O.

power for the second time because they hated
Appius and were greatly pleased that he seemed
to have been deprived of an honour ; while those
in authority, having succeeded in advancing to the
consulship a man of action and one who would
show no weakness toward the populace, thought the
dissension had taken a course favourable to their
designs.

XCI. During the consulship of these men the
Aequians, making a raid into the territory of the
Latins after the manner of brigands, carried off a
great number of slaves and cattle ; and the people
of Tyrrhenia called the Veientes injured a large part
of the Roman territory by their forays. The senate
voted to put off the war against the Aequians to
another time, but to demand satisfaction of the
Veientes. The Aequians, accordingly, since their
first attempts had been successful and there appeared
to be no one to prevent their further operations, grew
elated with an unreasoning boldness, and resolving
no longer to send out a mere marauding expedition,
marched with a large force to Ortona and took it by
storm ; then, after plundering everything both in the
country and in the city, they returned home with
rich booty. As for the Veientes, they returned
answer to the ambassadors who came from Rome that
those who were ravaging their country were not from
their city, but from the other Tyrrhenian cities, and
then dismissed them without giving them any satisfaction ; and the ambassadors fell in with the Veientes
as these were driving off booty from the Roman territory. The senate, learning of these things from
the ambassadors, voted to declare war against the
Veientes and that both consuls should lead out

μὲν οὖν περὶ τοῦ δόγματος ἀμφιλογία, καὶ πολλοὶ
ἦσαν οἱ τὸν πόλεμον οὐκ ἐῶντες ἐκφέρειν τῆς τε
κληρουχίας ὑπομιμνήσκοντες τοὺς δημοτικούς, ἧς
γε πέμπτον ἔτος ἐψηφισμένης ὑπὸ τοῦ συνεδρίου
κενῇ πιστεύσαντες ἐλπίδι ἐξηπάτηντο, καὶ κοινὸν[1]
ἀποφαίνοντες πόλεμον, εἰ κοινῇ χρήσεται γνώμῃ
4 πᾶσα Τυρρηνία τοῖς ὁμοεθνέσι βοηθοῦσα. οὐ μὲν
ἴσχυσάν γε οἱ τῶν στασιαστῶν[2] λόγοι, ἀλλ' ἐκύρωσε
καὶ ὁ δῆμος τὸ τῆς βουλῆς δόγμα τῇ Σπορίου
Λαρκίου γνώμῃ τε καὶ παρακλήσει χρησάμενος.
καὶ μετὰ ταῦτ' ἐξῆγον τὰς δυνάμεις οἱ ὕπατοι·
στρατοπεδευσάμενοι δὲ χωρὶς ἀλλήλων οὐ μακρὰν
ἀπὸ[3] τῆς πόλεως καὶ μείναντες ἡμέρας συχνάς,
ἐπειδὴ οὐκ ἀντεξῆγον οἱ πολέμιοι τὰς δυνάμεις,
προνομεύσαντες αὐτῶν τῆς γῆς ὅσην ἐδύναντο
πλείστην ἀπῆγον ἐπ' οἴκου τὴν στρατιάν. ἄλλο
δ' ἐπὶ τῆς τούτων ὑπατείας λόγου ἄξιον οὐδὲν
ἐπράχθη.

---

[1] κοινὸν O : δεινὸν Post.
[2] Portus, Sylburg : στρατιωτῶν O.
[3] ἀπὸ B : om. R.

the army. There was a controversy,[1] to be sure, over the decree, and there were many who opposed engaging in the war and reminded the plebeians of the allotment of land, of which they had been defrauded after a vain hope, though the senate had passed the decree four years before; and they declared that there would be a general[2] war if all Tyrrhenia by common consent should assist their countrymen. However, the arguments of the seditious speakers did not prevail, but the populace also confirmed the decree of the senate, following the opinion and advice of Spurius Larcius. Thereupon the consuls marched out with their forces and encamped apart at no great distance from the city[3]; but after they had remained there a good many days and the enemy did not lead their forces out to meet them, they ravaged as large a part of their country as they could and then returned home with the army. Nothing else worthy of notice happened during their consulship.

[1] This was in the assembly; see just below.
[2] Post would emend "general" to "formidable."
[3] Veii is meant.

ΔΙΟΝΥΣΙΟΥ

ΑΛΙΚΑΡΝΑΣΕΩΣ

ΡΩΜΑΙΚΗΣ ΑΡΧΑΙΟΛΟΓΙΑΣ

ΛΟΓΟΣ ΕΝΑΤΟΣ

I. Τῷ δὲ μετὰ τούτους ἔτει διαφορᾶς γενομένης τῷ δήμῳ πρὸς τὴν βουλὴν περὶ τῶν ἀποδειχθησομένων ὑπάτων (οἱ μὲν γὰρ ἠξίουν ἀμφοτέρους ἐκ τῶν ἀριστοκρατικῶν ἐπὶ τὴν ἀρχὴν προαγαγεῖν, ὁ δὲ δῆμος ἐκ τῶν ἑαυτῷ κεχαρισμένων) γνωσιμαχήσαντες[1] τέλος[2] συνέπεισαν ἀλλήλους ἀφ' ἑκάστης μερίδος ὕπατον αἱρεθῆναι· καὶ ἀποδείκνυται Καίσων μὲν Φάβιος τὸ δεύτερον ὑπὸ τῆς βουλῆς, ὁ τὸν Κάσσιον ἐπὶ τῇ τυραννίδι κρίνας, Σπόριος δὲ Φούριος ὑπὸ τῶν δημοτικῶν, ἐπὶ τῆς ἑβδομηκοστῆς καὶ πέμπτης ὀλυμπιάδος ἄρχοντος Ἀθήνησι Καλλιάδου, καθ' ὃν χρόνον ἐστράτευσε[3] Ξέρξης ἐπὶ
2 τὴν Ἑλλάδα. ἄρτι δὲ παρειληφότων αὐτῶν τὴν

---

[1] πρὸς ἀλλήλους ἡ βουλὴ καὶ ὁ δῆμος after γνωσιμαχήσαντες deleted by Cobet.   [2] τέλος Portus : τέως ACmg, ἕως BC.
[3] Portus : ἐστρατοπέδευσε Ο.

---

[1] For chaps. 1-4 cf. Livy ii. 43.
[2] 479 B.C. Dionysius synchronized each Roman consul

THE ROMAN ANTIQUITIES

OF

DIONYSIUS OF HALICARNASSUS

BOOK IX

I. The following year,[1] a dispute having arisen between the populace and the senate concerning the men who were to be elected consuls, the senators demanding that both men promoted to that magistracy should be of the aristocratic party and the populace demanding that they be chosen from among such as were agreeable to them, after an obstinate struggle they finally convinced each other that a consul should be chosen from each party. Thus Caeso Fabius, who had accused Cassius of aiming at tyranny, was elected consul, for the second time, on the part of the senate, and Spurius Furius on the part of the populace, in the seventy-fifth Olympiad,[2] Calliades being archon at Athens, at the time when Xerxes made his expedition against Greece. They had no sooner taken office than ambassadors of the

ship with the Greek year in the course of which it began (see vol. i. pp. xxx f.). Calliades was archon in 480/79, and the arrival of Xerxes in Greece came at about the time he assumed office.

ἀρχὴν Λατίνων τε πρέσβεις ἧκον ἐπὶ τὴν βουλὴν
δεόμενοι πέμψαι σφίσι τὸν ἕτερον τῶν ὑπάτων μετὰ
δυνάμεως, ὃς οὐκ ἐάσει προσωτέρω χωρεῖν τὴν
Αἰκανῶν καταφρόνησιν, καὶ Τυρρηνία πᾶσα ἠγγέλ-
λετο κεκινημένη καὶ οὐ διὰ μακροῦ χωρήσουσα εἰς
πόλεμον. συνήχθη γὰρ εἰς κοινὴν ἐκκλησίαν τὸ
ἔθνος, καὶ πολλὰ Οὐιεντανῶν δεηθέντων συνάρασθαι σφίσι τοῦ κατὰ Ῥωμαίων πολέμου, τέλος
ἐξήνεγκεν ἐξεῖναι τοῖς βουλομένοις Τυρρηνῶν μετέχειν τῆς στρατείας· καὶ ἐγένετο χεὶρ ἀξιόμαχος ἡ
τοῖς Οὐιεντανοῖς ἑκουσίως τοῦ πολέμου συναραμένη.
ταῦτα μαθοῦσι τοῖς ἐν τέλει Ῥωμαίων ἔδοξε στρατιάς τε καταγράφειν καὶ τοὺς ὑπάτους ἀμφοτέρους ἐξιέναι, τὸν μὲν Αἰκανοῖς τε πολεμήσοντα καὶ
Λατίνοις τιμωρὸν ἐσόμενον, τὸν δ' ἐπὶ Τυρρηνίαν[1]
3 ἄξοντα τὰς δυνάμεις. ἀντέπραττε δὲ πρὸς ταῦτα
Σπόριος Ἰκίλιος[2] τῶν δημάρχων εἷς· καὶ συνάγων
εἰς ἐκκλησίαν τὸν δῆμον ὁσημέραι τὰς περὶ τῆς
κληρουχίας ὑποσχέσεις ἀπῄτει παρὰ τῆς βουλῆς
καὶ οὐδὲν ἔφη συγχωρήσειν οὔτε τῶν ἐπὶ πόλεμον[3] οὔτε τῶν κατὰ πόλιν ὑπ' αὐτῆς ψηφιζομένων
ἐπιτελεσθῆναι, ἐὰν μὴ τοὺς δέκα ἄνδρας ἀποδείξωσι πρῶτον[4] ὁριστὰς τῆς δημοσίας χώρας, καὶ
4 διέλωσι τὴν γῆν, ὡς ὑπέσχοντο, τῷ δήμῳ. ἀπορου-
μένῃ δὲ τῇ βουλῇ καὶ ἀμηχανούσῃ τί χρὴ ποιεῖν,
Ἄππιος Κλαύδιος ὑποτίθεται σκοπεῖν ὅπως δια-
στήσεται τὰ τῶν ἄλλων δημάρχων πρὸς αὐτόν,
διδάσκων ὅτι τὸν κωλύοντα καὶ ἐμποδὼν γινόμενον
τοῖς δόγμασι τῆς βουλῆς ἱερὸν ὄντα καὶ νόμῳ τὴν

---

[1] Naber : τυρρηνίας O, Jacoby.
[2] Sylburg : σικίλιος O (and so in later chapters).
[3] οὔτε τῶν ἐπὶ πόλεμον Sintenis : ἐπὶ τῶν πολεμίων O.

288

Latins came to the senate asking them to send to them one of the consuls with an army to put a check to the insolence of the Aequians, and at the same time word was brought that all Tyrrhenia was aroused and would soon go to war. For that nation had been convened in a general assembly and at the urgent solicitation of the Veientes for aid in their war against the Romans had passed a decree that any of the Tyrrhenians who so desired might take part in the campaign; and it was a sufficiently strong body of men that voluntarily aided the Veientes in the war. Upon learning of this the authorities in Rome resolved to raise armies and also that both consuls should take the field, one to make war on the Aequians and to aid the Latins, and the other to march with his forces against Tyrrhenia. All this was opposed by Spurius Icilius,[1] one of the tribunes, who, assembling the populace every day, demanded of the senate the performance of its promises relating to the allotment of land and said that he would allow none of their decrees, whether they concerned military or civil affairs, to take effect unless they should first appoint the decemvirs to fix the boundaries of the public land and divide it among the people as they had promised. When the senate was at a loss and did not know what to do, Appius Claudius suggested that they should consider how the other tribunes might be brought to dissent from Icilius, pointing out that there is no other method of putting an end to the power of a tribune who opposes and obstructs the decrees of the

---

[1] The MSS. give this name here and below as Sicilius. Livy calls him Licinius.

---

[4] πρῶτον O : πρότερον Kiessling, Jacoby.

ἐξουσίαν ἔχοντα ταύτην ἄλλως οὐκ ἔστι παῦσαι τῆς
δυναστείας, ἐὰν μή τις ἕτερος τῶν ἀπὸ τῆς ἴσης
τιμῆς καὶ τὴν αὐτὴν ἐξουσίαν ἐχόντων τἀναντία
πράττῃ[1] καί, οἷς ἂν ἐκεῖνος ἐμποδὼν γίνηται,[2]
5 ταῦτα κελεύῃ.[3] συνεβούλευέ τε τοῖς αὖθις παρα-
ληψομένοις τὴν ἀρχὴν ὑπάτοις τοῦτο πράττειν καὶ
σκοπεῖν ὅπως ἕξουσί τινας ἀεὶ τῶν δημάρχων
οἰκείους σφίσι καὶ φίλους, μίαν εἶναι λέγων τῆς
ἐξουσίας τοῦ ἀρχείου κατάλυσιν, ἐὰν στασιάζωσι
πρὸς ἀλλήλους οἱ ἄνδρες.

II. Ταύτην εἰσηγησαμένου τὴν γνώμην Ἀππίου
δόξαντες αὐτὸν ὀρθῶς παραινεῖν οἵ τε ὕπατοι καὶ
τῶν ἄλλων οἱ δυνατώτατοι πολλῇ θεραπείᾳ[4] δι-
επράξαντο τοὺς τέτταρας ἐκ τῶν δημάρχων οἰκεί-
2 ους τῇ βουλῇ γενέσθαι. οἱ δὲ τέως μὲν λόγῳ
μεταπείθειν τὸν Ἰκίλιον ἐπεχείρουν ἀποστῆναι τῶν
περὶ τῆς κληρουχίας πολιτευμάτων ἕως οἱ πόλεμοι
λάβωσι τέλος· ὡς δ' ἠναντιοῦτο καὶ διώμνυτο, λόγον
τέ τιν'[5] αὐθαδέστερον[6] εἰπεῖν ἐτόλμησε τοῦ δήμου
παρόντος, ὅτι μᾶλλον ἂν βούλοιτο Τυρρηνοὺς καὶ
τοὺς ἄλλους πολεμίους κρατήσαντας τῆς πόλεως
ἐπιδεῖν ἢ τοὺς κατέχοντας τὴν χώραν τὴν δημοσίαν
ἀφεῖναι, δόξαντες ἀφορμὴν εἰληφέναι καλὴν πρὸς
αὐθάδειαν τοσαύτην τοῦ τἀναντία λέγειν τε καὶ
πράττειν, οὐδὲ τοῦ δήμου τὸν λόγον ἡδέως δεξα-
μένου, κωλύειν αὐτὸν ἔφησαν, καὶ φανερῶς ἔπραττον ὅσα τῇ βουλῇ τε καὶ[7] τοῖς ὑπάτοις δοκοίη·

---

[1] πράττῃ B : πράττειν R.
[2] γίνηται AB : γένηται Jacoby.
[3] κελεύῃ Naber : κωλύῃ B, Jacoby, κωλύειν R, μὴ κωλύῃ
Reiske.

290

senate, since his person is sacred and this authority of his is legal, than for another of the men of equal rank and possessing the same power to oppose him and to order to be done what the other tries to obstruct. And he advised all succeeding consuls to do this and to consider how they might always have some of the tribunes well disposed and friendly to them, saying that the only method of destroying the power of their college was to sow dissension among its members.

II. When Appius had expressed this opinion, both the consuls and the more influential of the others, believing his advice to be sound, courted the other four tribunes so effectually as to make them well disposed toward the senate. These for a time endeavoured by argument to persuade Icilius to desist from his course with respect to the allotment of land till the wars should come to an end. But when he kept opposing them and swore that he would continue to do so, and had the assurance to make a rather insolent remark in the presence of the populace to the effect that he had rather see the Tyrrhenians and their other enemies masters of the city than leave unpunished those who were occupying the public land, they thought they had got an excellent opportunity for opposing so great insolence both by their words and by their acts, and since even the populace showed displeasure at his remark, they said they interposed their veto ; and they openly pursued such measures as were agreeable to both the senate and the consuls. Thus Icilius being de-

---

⁴ θεραπείᾳ B : δυναστείᾳ R.   ⁵ τιν' Post : τὸν O, Jacoby.
⁶ αὐθαδέστατον Sylburg.   ⁷ τε καὶ B : ἢ R.

3 μονωθεὶς δ' Ἰκίλιος οὐδενὸς ἔτι κύριος ἦν. μετὰ τοῦτο ἡ στρατιὰ κατεγράφετο, καὶ ὅσων ἔδει τῷ πολέμῳ πάντα ὑπηρετεῖτο, τὰ μὲν ἐκ τῶν δημοσίων, τὰ δ' ἐκ τῶν ἰδίων, ἁπάσῃ προθυμίᾳ· καὶ διὰ τάχους οἱ ὕπατοι διακληρωσάμενοι τὰ στρατεύματα ἐξῄεσαν, Σπόριος μὲν Φούριος ἐπὶ τὰς Αἰκανῶν πόλεις, Καίσων δὲ Φάβιος ἐπὶ Τυρρηνούς.

4 Σπορίῳ μὲν οὖν ἅπαντα κατὰ νοῦν ἐχώρησεν οὐχ ὑπομεινάντων εἰς χεῖρας ἐλθεῖν τῶν πολεμίων, καὶ πολλὰ ἐκ τῆς στρατείας ἐξεγένετο χρήματά τε καὶ σώματα λαβεῖν. ἐπῆλθε γὰρ ὀλίγου δεῖν πᾶσαν ὅσην οἱ πολέμιοι χώραν κατεῖχον, ἄγων καὶ φέρων, καὶ τὰ λάφυρα τοῖς στρατιώταις ἅπαντα ἐχαρίσατο.

5 δοκῶν δὲ καὶ τὸν πρὸ τοῦ χρόνον εἶναι φιλόδημος, ἔτι μᾶλλον ἐκ ταύτης τῆς στρατηγίας ἐθεράπευσε τὸ πλῆθος. καὶ ἐπειδὴ παρῆλθεν ὁ χρόνος τῆς στρατείας, ἄγων[1] τὴν δύναμιν ὁλόκληρόν τε καὶ ἀπαθῆ χρήμασιν εὔπορον κατέστησε τὴν πατρίδα.

III. Καίσων δὲ Φάβιος ὁ ἕτερος τῶν ὑπάτων, οὐδενὸς χεῖρον στρατηγήσας, ἀφῃρέθη τὸν ἐκ τῶν ἔργων ἔπαινον παρ' οὐδὲν ἁμάρτημα ἴδιον, ἀλλ' ὅτι τὸ δημοτικὸν οὐκ εἶχε κεχαρισμένον[2] αὐτῷ ἐξ οὗ τὸν ὕπατον Κάσσιον ἐπὶ τῇ τυραννίδι κρίνας[3] ἀπέ-
2 κτεινεν. οὔτε γὰρ ὅσα δέοι σὺν τάχει στρατηγῷ κελεύσαντι τοὺς ὑπηκόους πειθαρχεῖν, οὔθ' ὅσα τῷ προθύμῳ καὶ πρέποντι[4] χρησαμένους βίᾳ κατασχεῖν, οὔθ' ὅσα λάθρα τῶν ἀντιπολεμίων[5] χωρία εἰς

---

[1] ἄγων O : ἀπάγων Kiessling.
[2] κεχαρισμένον C : μένον R, εὔνουν Sintenis.
[3] κρίνας B : προσαγγείας A, Jacoby, εἰσαγγείας C.
[4] καὶ πρέποντι O : ἐν πρέποντι Reiske, ἐν πρέποντι καιρῷ Kayser, ἐπιτρέποντας καὶ Kiessling.
[5] Reiske : ἀντιπολέμων O.

serted by his colleagues, no longer had any authority.
After this the army was raised and everything that
was necessary for the war was supplied, partly from
public and partly from private sources, with all possible alacrity; and the consuls, having drawn lots
for the armies, set out in haste, Spurius Furius
marching against the cities of the Aequians and
Caeso Fabius against the Tyrrhenians. In the case
of Spurius everything succeeded according to his
wish, the enemy not daring to come to an engagement, so that in this expedition he had the opportunity of taking much booty in both money and
slaves. For he overran almost all the territory that
the enemy possessed, carrying and driving off everything, and he gave all the spoils to the soldiers.
Though he had been regarded even before this time
as a friend of the people, he gained the favour of
the multitude still more by his conduct in this command; and when the season for military operations
was over, he brought his army home intact and un-
scathed, and made the fatherland rich with the
money he had taken.

III. Caeso Fabius, the other consul, though as a
general his performance was second to none, was
nevertheless deprived of the praise that his achievements deserved, not through any fault of his own, but
because he did not enjoy the goodwill of the plebeians
from the time when he had denounced and put to
death the consul Cassius for aiming at a tyranny.
For they never showed any alacrity either in those
matters in which men under authority ought to yield
a prompt obedience to the orders of their general, or
when they should through eagerness and a sense of
duty seize positions by force, or when it was necessary

πλεονεξίαν εὔθετα σφετερίσασθαι, οὔτ' ἄλλο πράττειν οὐδὲν ἔτοιμοι ἦσαν ἐξ οὗ τιμήν τινα ὁ στρατηγὸς καὶ δόξαν ἀγαθὴν ἐξοίσεσθαι ἔμελλε. καὶ
τἆλλα μὲν¹ αὐτῶν, ὅσα ὑβρίζοντες τὸν ἡγεμόνα
διετέλουν, ἐκείνῳ τε² ἧττον λυπηρὰ ἦν καὶ τῇ
πόλει βλάβης οὐ μεγάλης αἴτια,³ ὃ δὲ τελευτῶντες
ἐξειργάσαντο κίνδυνον οὐ μικρὸν ἤνεγκε καὶ πολλὴν
3 αἰσχύνην ἀμφοῖν. γενομένης γὰρ παρατάξεως ἐν
τῷ μεταξὺ τῶν λόφων ἐφ' οἷς ἦσαν ἐστρατοπεδευ-
κότες ἀμφότεροι πάσῃ τῇ παρ' ἑκατέρων δυνάμει,
πολλὰ καὶ καλὰ ἔργα ἀποδειξάμενοι καὶ τοὺς πολεμίους ἀναγκάσαντες ἄρξαι φυγῆς, οὔτ' ἠκολούθησαν
ἀπιοῦσι τοῦ στρατηγοῦ πολλὰ ἐπικελεύοντος οὔτε
παραμείναντες ἐκπολιορκῆσαι τὸν χάρακα ἠθέλη-
σαν, ἀλλ' ἐάσαντες ἀτελὲς ἔργον καλὸν ἀπήεσαν
4 εἰς τὴν αὑτῶν στρατοπεδείαν. ἐπιχειρησάντων δ'
αὐτοκράτορα τὸν ὕπατον ἀναγορεῦσαί τινων μέγα
ἐμβοήσαντες⁴ ἀθρόοι κακιζούσῃ τῇ φωνῇ τὸν ἡγεμόνα ἐλοιδόρουν, ὡς πολλοὺς σφῶν καὶ ἀγαθοὺς
ἀπολωλεκότα δι' ἀπειρίαν τοῦ στρατηγεῖν· καὶ
ἄλλῃ πολλῇ βλασφημίᾳ καὶ ἀγανακτήσει χρησάμενοι λύειν τὸν χάρακα καὶ ἀπάγειν σφᾶς εἰς τὴν
πόλιν ἠξίουν, ὡς οὐχ ἱκανοὺς ἐσομένους, ἐὰν ἐπ-
5 ίωσιν οἱ πολέμιοι, δευτέραν ὑπομεῖναι μάχην. καὶ
οὔτε μεταδιδάσκοντος ἐπείθοντο τοῦ ἡγεμόνος,
οὔτε ὀλοφυρομένου καὶ ἱκετεύοντος ἔπασχόν τι
πρὸς τὰς δεήσεις, οὔτε ἀπειλὰς καὶ ἀνατάσεις,
ὁπότε καὶ ταύταις χρήσαιτο, δι' εὐλαβείας ἐλάμ-

---

¹ Steph. : om. ABC.
² Reiske : δὲ O.
³ αἴτια Sylburg : ἄξια O, Jacoby.
⁴ Sylburg : ἐμβοησάντων AB.

to occupy advantageous positions without the knowledge of the enemy, or in anything else from which the general would derive any honour and good repute. Most of their conduct, to be sure, by which they were continually insulting their general was neither very troublesome to him nor the occasion of any great harm to the commonwealth ; but their final action brought no small danger and great disgrace to both. For when the two armies had arrayed themselves in battle order in the space between the hills on which their camps were placed, using all the forces on either side, and the Romans had performed many gallant deeds and forced the enemy to begin flight, they neither pursued them as they retreated, notwithstanding the repeated exhortations of the general, nor were they willing to remain and take the enemy's camp by siege ; on the contrary, they left a glorious action unfinished and returned to their own camp. And when some of the soldiers attempted to salute the consul as *imperator*, all the rest joined in a loud outcry, reproaching and taunting their commander with the loss of many of their brave comrades through his want of ability to command ; and after many other insulting and indignant remarks they demanded that he break camp and lead them back to Rome, pretending that they would be unable, if the enemy attacked them, to sustain a second battle. And they neither gave heed when their commander endeavoured to show them the error of their course, nor were moved by his entreaties when he turned to lamentations and supplications, nor were they alarmed by the violence of his threats when he made

βανον, ἀλλὰ πρὸς ἅπαντα τραχυνόμενοι ταῦτα διέμενον. τοσαύτη δ' ἀναρχία καὶ καταφρόνησις τοῦ ἡγεμόνος τισὶν ἐξ αὐτῶν[1] παρέστη ὥστε περὶ μέσας νύκτας ἐξαναστάντες τάς τε σκηνὰς ἔλυον καὶ τὰ ὅπλα ἀνελάμβανον καὶ τοὺς τραυματίας ἐβάσταζον οὐδενὸς κελεύσαντος.

IV. Ταῦτα ὁ στρατηγὸς μαθὼν ἠναγκάσθη πᾶσι δοῦναι τὸ παράγγελμα τῆς ἐξόδου δείσας τὴν ἀναρχίαν αὐτῶν καὶ τὸ θράσος. οἱ δ' ὥσπερ ἐκ φυγῆς ἀνασωζόμενοι τάχει πολλῷ συνάπτουσι τῇ πόλει περὶ τὸν ὄρθρον. καὶ οἱ ἐπὶ τῶν τειχῶν ἀγνοήσαντες ὅτι φίλιον ἦν στράτευμα, ὅπλα τ' ἐνεδύοντο καὶ ἀλλήλους ἀνεκάλουν, ἥ τ' ἄλλη πόλις, ὡς ἐπὶ συμφορᾷ μεγάλῃ, ταραχῆς ἐγεγόνει μεστὴ καὶ θορύβου· καὶ οὐ πρότερον ἀνέῳξαν αὐτοῖς τὰς πύλας οἱ φύλακες ἢ[2] λαμπράν τε ἡμέραν γενέσθαι

2 καὶ γνωσθῆναι τὸ οἰκεῖον στράτευμα· ὥστε πρὸς τῇ αἰσχύνῃ ἦν ἐκ τοῦ καταλιπεῖν τὸν χάρακα ἠνέγκαντο καὶ κίνδυνον οὐ τὸν ἐλάχιστον αὐτοὺς ἀναρρῖψαι σκότους ἀπιόντας διὰ τῆς πολεμίας ἀτάκτως. εἰ γοῦν τοῦτο καταμαθόντες οἱ πολέμιοι ἐκ ποδὸς[3] ἀπιοῦσιν αὐτοῖς ἠκολούθησαν, οὐδὲν ἂν ἐκώλυσεν ἅπασαν ἀπολωλέναι τὴν στρατιάν. τῆς δ' ἀλόγου ταύτης ἀπάρσεως ἢ φυγῆς τὸ πρὸς τὸν ἡγεμόνα ἐκ τοῦ δήμου μῖσος, ὥσπερ ἔφην, αἴτιον ἦν, καὶ ὁ φθόνος τῆς ἐκείνου τιμῆς, ἵνα μὴ θριάμβου καταγωγῇ κοσμηθεὶς ἐπιφανέστατος γένη-

3 ται. τῇ δ' ἐξῆς ἡμέρᾳ μαθόντες οἱ Τυρρηνοὶ τὴν ἄπαρσιν τῶν Ῥωμαίων νεκρούς τ' αὐτῶν ἐσκύλευ-

---

[1] τισὶν ἐξ αὐτῶν Post (cf. chap. 9, 4) : πᾶσιν ἐξ αὐτῶν O, Jacoby.
[2] ἢ B : ἕως AC.

296

use of these too ; but they continued exasperated in the face of all these appeals. Indeed, some of them were possessed with such a spirit of disobedience and such contempt for their general that they rose up about midnight and without orders from anyone proceeded to strike their tents, take up their arms, and carry off their wounded.

IV. When the general was informed of this, he was forced to give the command for all to depart, so great was his fear of their disobedience and audacity. And the soldiers retired with as great precipitation as if they were saving themselves from a rout, and reached the city about daybreak. The guards upon the walls, not knowing that it was an army of friends, began to arm themselves and call out to one another, while all the rest of the city was full of confusion and turmoil, as if some great disaster had occurred ; and the guards did not open the gates to them till it was broad day and they could distinguish their own army. Thus, in addition to the ignominy they incurred in deserting their camp, they also exposed themselves to great danger in returning in the dark through the enemy's country, without observing any order. Certainly, if the Tyrrhenians had learned of it and had followed close on their heels as they departed, nothing could have prevented the army from being utterly destroyed. The motive of this unaccountable withdrawal or flight was, as I have said, the hatred of the populace against the general and the begrudging of any honour to him, lest he should be granted a triumph and so acquire the greatest glory. The next day the Tyrrhenians, having learned of the withdrawal of the Romans, stripped their dead, took

---

ᵃ ἐκ ποδὸς Sylburg : ἐκ παντὸς O.

σαν καὶ τραυματίας ἀράμενοι ἀπήνεγκαν τάς τε
καταλειφθείσας ἐν τῷ χάρακι παρασκευάς (πολλαὶ
δ᾽ ἦσαν ὡς εἰς χρόνιον παρεσκευασμέναι¹ πόλεμον)
διεφόρησαν, καὶ ὡς δὴ κρατοῦντες² τῆς χώρας
τῶν πολεμίων τὴν ἐγγυτάτω λεηλατήσαντες ἀπῆγον
τὴν στρατιάν.

V. Οἱ δὲ μετὰ τούτους ἀποδειχθέντες ὕπατοι,
Γνάιος Μάλλιος καὶ Μάρκος Φάβιος τὸ δεύτερον ἄρχειν αἱρεθείς, ψήφισμα τῆς βουλῆς ποιησαμένης στρατὸν ἐξάγειν ἐπὶ τὴν Οὐιεντανῶν πόλιν,
ὅσον ἂν πλεῖστον δυνηθῶσι, προὔθηκαν ἡμέραν ἐν
ᾗ τὸν κατάλογον ἔμελλον ποιήσεσθαι τῆς στρατιᾶς. γινομένου δ᾽ αὐτοῖς ἐμποδὼν ἐπὶ κωλύσει
τῆς καταγραφῆς ἑνὸς τῶν δημάρχων, Τιβερίου
Ποντοφικίου, καὶ τὸ περὶ τῆς κληρουχίας ψήφισμα ἀνακαλουμένου, θεραπεύσαντες τῶν συναρχόν-
των αὐτοῦ τινας, ὥσπερ ἐποίησαν οἱ πρὸ αὐτῶν
ὕπατοι, διέστησαν τὸ ἀρχεῖον· καὶ μετὰ τοῦτ᾽
ἔπραττον ἐπὶ πολλῆς ἐξουσίας τὰ δόξαντα τῇ
2 βουλῇ. γενομένης δὲ τῆς καταγραφῆς ἐν ὀλίγαις
ἡμέραις ἐξῇεσαν ἐπὶ τοὺς πολεμίους, δύο μὲν
ἑκάτερος ἄγων Ῥωμαίων τάγματα τῶν ἐξ αὐτῆς
καταγραφέντων τῆς πόλεως, οὐκ ἐλάττω δὲ ταύτης
χεῖρα τὴν ὑπὸ τῶν ἀποίκων τε καὶ ὑπηκόων ἀποσταλεῖσαν. ἀφίκετο δ᾽ αὐτοῖς παρὰ τοῦ Λατίνων
τε καὶ Ἑρνίκων ἔθνους διπλάσιον τοῦ κληθέντος
ἐπικουρικόν.³ οὐ μὴν ἐχρήσαντό γε παντί⁴·
πολλὴν δὲ χάριν αὐτοῖς εἰδέναι φήσαντες τῆς
προθυμίας ἀπέλυσαν τῆς ἀποσταλείσης δυνάμεως
3 τὴν ἡμίσειαν. ἔταξαν δὲ καὶ πρὸ τῆς πόλεως

___

¹ ἦσαν ὡς εἰς χ. παρεσκευασμέναι Steph. : ἦσαν ἐσκευασμέναι
ὡς εἰς χ. παρεσκευασμέναι ABC.

up and carried off their wounded, and plundered all
the stores they had left in their camp, which were
very abundant as having been prepared for a long
war ; then, like conquerors, they laid waste the
adjacent territory of the enemy, after which they
returned home with their army.

V. The succeeding consuls,[1] Gnaeus Manlius and
Marcus Fabius (the latter chosen for the second
time), in pursuance of a decree of the senate ordering
them to march against the Veientes with as large an
army as they could raise, appointed a day for levying
the troops. When Tiberius Pontificius, one of the
tribunes, opposed them by forbidding the levy and
called upon them to carry out the decree relating to
the allotment of land, they courted some of his colleagues, as their predecessors had done, and thus
divided the college of tribunes, after which they proceeded to carry out the will of the senate with full
liberty. The levy being completed in a few days, the
consuls took the field against the enemy, each of them
having with him two legions of Romans raised in the
city itself and a force no less numerous sent by their
colonies and subjects. Indeed, there came to them
from the Latin and the Hernican nations double the
number of auxiliaries they had called for ; they did
not, however, make use of this entire force, but stat-
ing that they were very grateful for their zeal, they
dismissed one half of the army that had been sent.
They also drew up before the city a third army,

---

[1] For chaps. 5-13 *cf.* Livy ii. 43, 11–47, 12.

[2] ὡς δὴ κρατοῦντες Cb : ὡς δημοκρατοῦντες ABCa, ὡς ἤδη
κρατοῦντες Sylburg, ὡς δῆλοι κρατοῦντες Kiessling.

[3] ἐπικουρικόν Reiske : ἐπικουρικοῦ O.

[1] παντί B : πάντη AC, τῷ παντὶ Hertlein.

τρίτον ἐκ δυεῖν ταγμάτων τῶν¹ ἐν ἀκμῇ στρατόν,
φύλακα τῆς χώρας ἐσόμενον, εἴ τις ἑτέρα δύναμις
πολεμίων ἐκ τοῦ ἀδοκήτου φανείη· τοὺς δ' ὑπὲρ
τὸν στρατιωτικὸν κατάλογον οἷς ἔτι δύναμις ἦν
ὅπλων χρήσεως ἐν τῇ πόλει κατέλιπον ἄκρας τε
καὶ τείχη φυλάξοντας.

4 Ἀγαγόντες δὲ πλησίον τῆς Οὐιεντανῶν πόλεως
τὰς δυνάμεις κατεστρατοπέδευσαν ἐπὶ λόφοις δυσὶν
οὐ μακρὰν ἀφεστηκόσιν ἀπ' ἀλλήλων. ἦν δὲ καὶ
ἡ τῶν πολεμίων δύναμις ἐξεστρατευμένη πρὸ τῆς
πόλεως πολλή τε καὶ ἀγαθή. συνεληλύθεσαν γὰρ
ἐξ ἁπάσης Τυρρηνίας οἱ δυνατώτατοι τοὺς ἑαυτῶν
πενέστας ἐπαγόμενοι, καὶ ἐγένετο τοῦ Ῥωμαϊκοῦ
5 στρατοῦ μεῖζον τὸ Τυρρηνικὸν οὐκ ὀλίγῳ. τοῖς
δ' ὑπάτοις τό τε πλῆθος ὁρῶσι τῶν πολεμίων καὶ
τὴν λαμπρότητα τῶν ὅπλων πολὺ δέος ἐνέπεσε μή
ποτ' οὐχ ἱκανοὶ γένωνται στασιαζούσῃ δυνάμει τῇ
σφετέρᾳ πρὸς ὁμονοοῦσαν τὴν τῶν πολεμίων ἀντι-
ταξάμενοι ὑπερβαλέσθαι· ἐδόκει τε αὐτοῖς ὀχυρω-
σαμένοις τὰ στρατόπεδα τρίβειν τὸν πόλεμον,
ἐκδεχομένοις εἴ τινα δώσει πλεονεξίας ἀφορμὴν
αὐτοῖς τὸ τῶν πολεμίων θράσος ἀλογίστῳ καταφρονήσει ἐπαρθέν. ἀκροβολισμοὶ δὴ μετὰ τοῦτο
συνεχεῖς ἐγίνοντο καὶ ψιλῶν συμπλοκαὶ βραχεῖαι,
μέγα δ' ἢ λαμπρὸν ἔργον οὐδέν.

VI. Οἱ δὲ Τυρρηνοὶ ἀχθόμενοι τῇ τριβῇ τοῦ
πολέμου δειλίαν τε ὠνείδιζον τοῖς Ῥωμαίοις,
ἐπειδὴ οὐκ ἐξῄεσαν εἰς μάχην, καὶ ὡς παρακεχωρη-
κότων αὐτῶν σφίσι τῆς ὑπαίθρου μέγα ἐφρόνουν.
καὶ ἔτι μᾶλλον ἐπήρθησαν εἰς ὑπεροψίαν τοῦ ἀντιπάλου στρατοῦ καὶ καταφρόνησιν τῶν ὑπάτων
2 δόξαντες καὶ τὸ θεῖον αὐτοῖς συμμαχεῖν. τοῦ γὰρ

consisting of two legions of the younger men, to serve as a garrison for the country in case any other hostile force should unexpectedly make its appearance ; the men who were above the military age but still had strength sufficient to bear arms they left in the city to guard the citadels and the walls.

When the consuls had led their forces close to the city of Veii, they encamped on two hills not far apart. The enemy's army, which was both large and valiant, had also taken the field and lay encamped before the city. For the most influential men from all Tyrrhenia had joined them with their dependents, with the result that the Tyrrhenians' army was not a little larger than that of the Romans. When the consuls saw the numbers of the enemy and the lustre of their arms, great fear came upon them lest, with their own forces rent by faction, they might not be able to prevail when arrayed against the harmonious forces of the enemy ; and they determined to fortify their camps and to prolong the war in the hope that the boldness of the enemy, encouraged by an ill-advised contempt for them, might afford them some opportunity of acting with advantage. After this there were continual skirmishes and brief clashes of the light-armed troops, but no important or signal action.

VI. The Tyrrhenians, being irked by the prolongation of the war, taunted the Romans with cowardice because they would not come out for battle, and believing that their foes had abandoned the field to them, they were greatly elated. They were still further inspired with scorn for the Roman army and contempt for the consuls when they thought that even the gods were fighting on their side. For

---

¹ Reiske : τὸν O.

ἑτέρου τῶν ὑπάτων Γναίου Μαλλίου κεραυνὸς εἰς
τὸ στρατήγιον ἐμπεσὼν τήν τε σκηνὴν διέσπασε
καὶ τὴν ἑστίαν ἀνέτρεψε[1] καὶ τῶν πολεμιστηρίων
ὅπλων τὰ μὲν ἐσπίλωσε, τὰ δὲ περιέκαυσε, τὰ δ'
εἰς τέλος ἠφάνισεν· ἀπέκτεινε δὲ καὶ τὸν λαμπρό-
τατον αὐτοῦ τῶν ἵππων, ᾧ παρὰ τοὺς ἀγῶνας
3 ἐχρῆτο, καὶ τῶν θεραπόντων τινάς. λεγόντων δὲ
τῶν μάντεων τοῦ τε χάρακος ἅλωσιν προσημαίνειν
τοὺς θεοὺς καὶ τῶν ἐπιφανεστάτων ἀνδρῶν ἀπώλειαν, ἀναστήσας τὴν δύναμιν ὁ Μάλλιος ἀπῆγε
περὶ μέσας νύκτας ἐπὶ τὸν ἕτερον χάρακα καὶ μετὰ
4 τοῦ συνάρχοντος κατεστρατοπέδευσε. μαθόντες
οὖν οἱ Τυρρηνοὶ τὴν ἀπανάστασιν[2] τοῦ στρατηγοῦ
καὶ δι' ἃς αἰτίας ἐγένετο παρά τινων αἰχμαλώτων
ἀκούσαντες ἐπήρθησάν τε ταῖς γνώμαις ἔτι μᾶλλον,
ὡς πολεμοῦντος τοῖς Ῥωμαίοις τοῦ δαιμονίου, καὶ
πολλὴν εἶχον ἐλπίδα κρατήσειν αὐτῶν· οἵ τε μάντεις
ἀκριβέστερον τῶν ἄλλοθί που δοκοῦντες ἐξητακέναι
τὰ μετάρσια, πόθεν τε αἱ τῶν κεραυνῶν γίνονται
βολαὶ καὶ τίνες αὐτοὺς ὑποδέχονται μετὰ τὰς πληγὰς ἀπιόντας τόποι, θεῶν τε οἷς ἕκαστοι ἀποδίδον-
ται καὶ τίνων ἀγαθῶν ἢ κακῶν μηνυταί, χωρεῖν
ὁμόσε τοῖς πολεμίοις παρῄνουν διαιρούμενοι τὸ
γενόμενον τοῖς Ῥωμαίοις σημεῖον κατὰ τάδε·
5 ἐπειδὴ τὸ βέλος εἰς ὑπάτου σκηνὴν κατέσκηψεν, ἐν
ᾗ τὸ στρατήγιον ἐνῆν, καὶ πᾶσαν αὐτὴν ἄχρι τῆς
ἑστίας ἠφάνισεν, ὅλῃ προσημαίνειν τὸ δαιμόνιον
τῇ στρατιᾷ τοῦ χάρακος ἔκλειψιν βίᾳ κρατηθέντος
6 καὶ τῶν ἐπιφανεστάτων ὄλεθρον. "Εἰ μὲν οὖν,"
ἔφασαν, "ἔμειναν ἐν ᾧ κατέσκηψε χωρίῳ τὸ βέλος
οἱ κατέχοντες αὐτὸ καὶ μὴ μετηνέγκαντο τὰ σημεῖα

---

[1] Sylburg : ἀνέστρεψε AB.

a thunderbolt, falling upon the headquarters of
Gnaeus Manlius, one of the consuls, tore the tent in
pieces, overturned the hearth, and tarnished some of
the weapons of war, while scorching or completely
destroying others. It killed also the finest of his
horses, the one he used in battle, and some of his
servants. And when the augurs declared that the
gods were foretelling the capture of the camp and
the death of the most important persons in it, Manlius
roused his forces about midnight and led them to the
other camp, where he took up quarters with his colleague. The Tyrrhenians, learning of the general's
departure and hearing from some of the prisoners the
reasons for his action, grew still more elated in mind,
since it seemed that the gods were making war upon
the Romans ; and they entertained great hopes of
conquering them. For their augurs, who are reputed
to have investigated with greater accuracy than those
anywhere else the signs that appear in the sky, determining where the thunderbolts come from, what
quarters receive them when they depart after striking, to which of the gods each kind of bolt is assigned,
and what good or evil it portends, advised them to
engage the enemy, interpreting the omen which had
appeared to the Romans on this wise : Since the bolt
had fallen upon the consul's tent, which was the
army's headquarters, and had utterly destroyed it
even to its hearth, the gods were foretelling to the
whole army the wiping out of their camp after it
should be taken by storm, and the death of the
principal persons in it. " If, now," they said, " the
occupants of the place where the bolt fell had
remained there instead of removing their standards

ὡς τοὺς ἑτέρους, μιᾶς τε παρεμβολῆς ἁλώσει καὶ
ἑνὸς ὀλέθρῳ στρατοῦ τὸ νεμεσῶν αὐτοῖς δαιμόνιον
ἀπεπλήρωσεν ἂν τὸν χόλον· ἐπειδὴ δὲ σοφώτεροι
τῶν θεῶν εἶναι ζητοῦντες εἰς τὸν ἕτερον χάρακα
μετεστρατοπεδεύσαντο,[1] καταλιπόντες ἔρημον τὸν
τόπον, ὡς οὐ τοῖς ἀνθρώποις τοῦ θεοῦ προδηλοῦντος
τὰς συμφοράς, ἀλλὰ τοῖς τόποις, κοινὸς ἅπασιν
αὐτοῖς ὁ παρὰ τοῦ δαίμονος ἥξει χόλος, τοῖς τε
7 ἀπαναστᾶσι καὶ τοῖς ὑποδεξαμένοις. καὶ ἐπειδὴ
ἁλῶναι σφῶν τὸν ἕτερον χάρακα βίᾳ θείας ἐπι-
θεσπιζούσης ἀνάγκης οὐ περιέμειναν τὸ χρεών,
ἀλλ' αὐτοὶ παρέδοσαν τοῖς ἐχθροῖς, ἐκεῖνος ὁ χάραξ
ὁ τὸν ἐκλειφθέντα ὑποδεξάμενος ἀντὶ τοῦ κατα-
λειφθέντος ἁλώσεται βίᾳ κρατηθείς."

VII. Ταῦτα παρὰ τῶν μάντεων οἱ Τυρρηνοὶ
ἀκούσαντες μέρει τινὶ τῆς ἑαυτῶν στρατιᾶς τὴν
ἐρημωθεῖσαν ὑπὸ τῶν Ῥωμαίων καταλαμβάνονται
στρατοπεδείαν ὡς ἐπιτείχισμα ποιησόμενοι τῆς
ἑτέρας· ἦν δὲ πάνυ ἐχυρὸν τὸ χωρίον καὶ τοῖς ἀπὸ
Ῥώμης ἐπὶ τὸ στρατόπεδον ἰοῦσι κωλύσεως ἐν
καλῷ κείμενον. πραγματευσάμενοι δὲ καὶ τἆλλα ἐξ
ὧν πλεονεκτήσειν τοὺς πολεμίους ἔμελλον, ἐξῆγον
2 εἰς τὸ πεδίον τὰς δυνάμεις. μενόντων δὲ τῶν
Ῥωμαίων ἐφ' ἡσυχίας προσιππεύοντες ἐξ[2] αὐτῶν
οἱ τολμηρότατοι καὶ πλησίον τοῦ χάρακος ἱστά-
μενοι, γυναῖκάς τε ἀπεκάλουν ἅπαντας καὶ τοὺς
ἡγεμόνας αὐτῶν τοῖς δειλοτάτοις τῶν ζῴων ἐοικέ-
ναι λέγοντες ἐκάκιζον, καὶ δυεῖν θάτερον ἠξίουν·
εἰ μὲν ἀντιποιοῦνται τῆς περὶ τὰ πολέμια ἀρετῆς,

---

[1] μετεστρατοπεδεύσαντο B : μετεστρατοπέδευσαν R.
[2] ἐξ B : πρὸς R.

to the other army, the divinity who was wroth with them would have satisfied his anger with the capture of a single camp and the destruction of a single army ; but since they endeavoured to be wiser than the gods and changed their quarters to the other camp, leaving the place deserted, as if the god had signified that the calamities should fall, not upon the men, but upon the places, the divine wrath will come upon all of them alike, both upon those who departed and upon those who received them. And since, when destiny had foretold that one camp should be taken by storm, they did not wait for their fate, but of their own accord handed their camp over to the enemy, the camp which received the deserted camp [1] shall be taken by storm instead of the one that was abandoned."

VII. The Tyrrhenians, hearing this from their augurs, sent a part of their army to take possession of the camp deserted by the Romans, with the intention of making it a fort to serve against the other camp. For the place was a very strong one and was conveniently situated for intercepting any who might come from Rome to the enemy's camp. After they had also made the other dispositions calculated to give them an advantage over the enemy, they led out their forces into the plain. Then, when the Romans remained quiet, the boldest of the Tyrrhenians rode up and, halting near the camp, called them all women and taunted their leaders, likening them to the most cowardly of animals ; and they challenged them to do one of two things—either to descend into the plain, if they laid claim to any war-

---

[1] *i.e.*, the men from the deserted camp. The word "camp" in this passage refers now to the site, now to the occupants.

καταβάντας εἰς τὸ πεδίον μιᾷ τὸν ἀγῶνα κρῖναι
μάχῃ, εἰ δ' ὁμολογοῦσιν εἶναι κακοί, παραδόντας
τὰ ὅπλα τοῖς κρείττοσι καὶ δίκας ὑποσχόντας ὧν
ἔδρασαν μηδενὸς ἔτι τῶν μεγάλων ἑαυτοὺς ἀξιοῦν.
3 τοῦτ' ἐποίουν ὁσημέραι καὶ ἐπεὶ οὐδὲν ἐπέραινον,
ἀποτειχίζειν αὐτοὺς ἔγνωσαν ὡς λιμῷ προσαναγκάσοντες παραστῆναι. οἱ δ' ὕπατοι περιεώρων τὰ
γινόμενα μέχρι πολλοῦ, δι' ἀνανδρίαν μὲν ἢ μαλα-
κίαν οὐδεμίαν (ἀμφότεροι γὰρ εὔψυχοί τε καὶ
φιλοπόλεμοι ἦσαν), τὸ δὲ τῶν στρατιωτῶν ἐθελό-
κακόν τε καὶ ἀπρόθυμον, διαμένον ἐν τοῖς δημοτικοῖς ἐξ οὗ περὶ τῆς κληρουχίας διεστασίασαν,
ὑφορώμενοι· ἔτι γὰρ αὐτοῖς ἔναυλα καὶ πρὸ ὀμμά-
των ἦν ἃ τῷ παρελθόντι ἐνιαυτῷ κατὰ τὸ ἔγκοτον
τῆς πρὸς[1] τὸν ὕπατον τιμῆς αἰσχρὰ καὶ ἀνάξια
τῆς πόλεως εἰργάσαντο, παραχωρήσαντες τῆς νίκης
τοῖς ἡττηθεῖσι καὶ φυγῆς ὄνειδος οὐκ ἀληθὲς ὑπο-
μείναντες, ἵνα μὴ καταγάγῃ τὸν ἐπινίκιον θρίαμβον
ὁ ἀνήρ.

VIII. Βουλόμενοι δὴ τὸ στασιάζον ἐκ τῆς στρατιᾶς ἐξελεῖν εἰς τέλος καὶ καταστῆσαι πάλιν εἰς
τὴν ἐξ ἀρχῆς ὁμόνοιαν ἅπαν τὸ πλῆθος, καὶ εἰς ἓν
τοῦτο πᾶσαν εἰσφερόμενοι βουλήν τε καὶ πρόνοιαν,
ἐπειδὴ οὔτε κολάσει μέρους τινὸς σωφρονέστερον
ἀποδοῦναι τὸ λοιπὸν ἦν, πολὺ καὶ αὔθαδες ὑπάρχον
καὶ τὰ ὅπλα ἐν ταῖς χερσὶν ἔχον, οὔτε πειθοῖ
προσαγαγέσθαι λόγων τοὺς οὐδὲ[2] πεισθῆναι βουλομένους, δύο ταύτας ὑπέλαβον ἔσεσθαι[3] τῶν
στασιαζόντων αἰτίας τῆς διαλλαγῆς, τοῖς μὲν ἐπι-

---

[1] πρὸς O : περὶ Reiske.
[2] Reiske : οὔτε O.
[3] ἔσεσθαι B : om. R.

like valour, and decide the contest by a single battle,
or, if they owned themselves to be cowards, to deliver
up their arms to those who were their betters, and
after paying the penalty for their deeds, never again
to hold themselves worthy of greatness. This they
did every day, and when it had no effect, they resolved to block them off by a wall with the purpose
of starving them into surrender. The consuls permitted this to go on for a considerable time, not
through any cowardice or weakness—for they were
both men of spirit and fond of war—but because they
feared the soldiers' wilful shirking of duty and their
apathy, which had persisted among the plebeians
ever since the sedition over the allotment of land.
For they still had ringing in their ears and fresh
before their eyes the shameful behaviour, unworthy
of the commonwealth, which the soldiers, because of
their begrudging the honour that would come to the
consul, had been guilty of the year before, when they
had yielded up the victory to the vanquished and endured the false reproach of flight in order that their
general might not celebrate the triumph awarded
for victory.

VIII. Desiring, therefore, to banish sedition from
the army once and for all and to restore the whole
rank and file to their original harmony, and devot-
ing to this single end all their counsel and all their
thought, since it was not in their power by punishing
some of them to reform the rest, who were numerous,
bold, and had arms in their hands, or to attempt by
the persuasion of words to win over those who did
not even wish to be persuaded, they assumed that
the following two motives would bring about the reconciliation of the seditious : first, for those of a more

εικεστέρας μετειληφόσι φύσεως (ἐνῆν γάρ τι καὶ
τοιοῦτον ἐν τῷ πολλῷ[1]) τὴν ἐπὶ τοῖς ὀνειδισμοῖς
τῶν πολεμίων αἰσχύνην, τοῖς δὲ δυσαγώγοις ἐπὶ τὸ
καλόν, ἣν ἅπασα δέδοικεν ἀνθρώπου φύσις ἀνάγκην.
2 ἵνα δὴ ταῦτα γένοιτο ἀμφότερα, ἐφῆκαν τοῖς πολεμίοις λόγῳ τε αἰσχύνειν κακίζοντας σφῶν ὡς
ἄνανδρον τὴν ἡσυχίαν, καὶ ἔργοις ὑπεροψίας τε καὶ
καταφρονήσεως πολλοῖς[2] γινομένοις[3] ἀναγκάζειν
ἀγαθοὺς γενέσθαι τοὺς ἑκουσίως εἶναι μὴ βουλομένους. γινομένων γὰρ τούτων πολλὰς ἐλπίδας
εἶχον ἥξειν ἐπὶ τὸ στρατήγιον ἅπαντας ἀγανακτοῦντας καὶ καταβοῶντας καὶ κελεύοντας ἡγεῖσθαι
3 σφῶν ἐπὶ τοὺς πολεμίους· ὅπερ καὶ συνέβη. ὡς
γὰρ ἤρξαντο τὰς ἐξόδους τοῦ χάρακος ἀποταφρεύ-
ειν τε καὶ ἀποσταυροῦν οἱ πολέμιοι, δυσανασχετή-
σαντες οἱ Ῥωμαῖοι ἐπὶ τῷ ἔργῳ, τέως μὲν κατ᾽
ὀλίγους, ἔπειτ᾽ ἀθρόοι συντρέχοντες ἐπὶ τὰς σκηνὰς
τῶν ὑπάτων ἐκεκράγεσάν τε καὶ προδοσίαν αὐτοῖς
ἐνεκάλουν, καὶ εἰ μή τις ἡγήσεται σφίσι τῆς ἐξόδου,
δίχα ἐκείνων αὐτοὶ τὰ ὅπλα ἔχοντες ἐπὶ τοὺς
4 πολεμίους ἔλεγον ἐξελεύσεσθαι. ὡς δ᾽ ἐξ ἁπάντων
ἐγίνετο τοῦτο, παρεῖναι τὸν χρόνον ὃν περιέμενον
οἱ στρατηγοὶ νομίσαντες ἐκέλευον τοῖς ὑπηρέταις
συγκαλεῖν τὸ πλῆθος εἰς ἐκκλησίαν· καὶ προελθὼν
Φάβιος τοιάδε εἶπε·

IX. "Βραδεῖα μὲν ἡ ἀγανάκτησις ὑμῶν γίνεται
περὶ ὧν ὑβρίζεσθε ὑπὸ τῶν πολεμίων, ἄνδρες στρα-

[1] ἐν τῷ πολλῷ πλήθει Reiske.
[2] Cary : πολλῆς O, Jacoby.
[3] γινομένοις Kiessling, γενομένοις Sintenis : γινομένης B,
γενομένης AC, γέμουσιν Reiske, om. Kayser.

reasonable disposition (for there was an admixture of these also among the mass of the troops), the shame of being taunted by the enemy, and second, for those who were not easily led to adopt the honourable course, the thing of which all human nature stands in dread—necessity. In order, then, to accomplish both these results, they allowed the enemy not only to shame them by words, as when they branded their inaction as cowardice, but also by repeated deeds of scorn and contempt [1] to compel those to show themselves brave men who were not disposed to be so of their own accord. For if these insults should be continued, they had great hopes that all the soldiers would come to headquarters, giving vent to their indignation, reproaching the consuls, and demanding that they lead them against the enemy ; and that is just what happened. For when the enemy began to block the outlets of the camp with ditches and palisades, the Romans, growing indignant at their action, ran to the tents of the consuls, first in small numbers and then in a body, and crying out, accused them of treachery, and declared that if no one would lead them in a sortie, they themselves would take their arms and without their generals sally out against the enemy. This being the general cry, the consuls thought the opportunity for which they had been waiting had now come, and they ordered the lictors to call the troops to an assembly. Then Fabius, coming forward, spoke as follows :

IX. " Long delayed is your indignation at the insults you are receiving from the enemy, soldiers and

---

[1] The text is uncertain here. Reiske wished to read " by deeds full of great scorn and contempt " ; Kayser proposed " by deeds of great scorn and contempt."

τιῶταί τε καὶ ἡγεμόνες· καὶ τὸ βουλόμενον ἑκάστου
χωρεῖν ὁμόσε τοῖς ἐναντίοις πολὺ τοῦ δέοντος
ὕστερον φαινόμενον ἄωρόν ἐστι. παλαίτερον γὰρ
ἔτι τοῦθ' ὑμᾶς ἔδει πράττειν, ὅτε πρῶτον αὐτοὺς
εἴδετε καταβαίνοντας ἐκ τῶν ἐρυμάτων καὶ μάχης
ἄρχειν βουλομένους. τότε γὰρ δήπου καλὸς ὁ περὶ
τῆς ἡγεμονίας ἦν ἀγὼν καὶ τοῦ Ῥωμαίων φρονήματος ἄξιος· νῦν δ' ἀναγκαῖος ἤδη γίνεται, καὶ
οὐδ' ἂν τὸ κράτιστον λάβῃ τέλος, ὁμοίως καλός.
2 εὖ δὲ καὶ νῦν ποιεῖτε ὅμως ἐπανορθώσασθαι τὴν
βραδυτῆτα βουλόμενοι καὶ τὰ παραλειφθέντα ἀναλαβεῖν, καὶ πολλὴ χάρις ὑμῖν τῆς ἐπὶ τὰ κράτιστα
ὁρμῆς, εἴτ'[1] ὑπ' ἀρετῆς γίνεται (κρεῖττον γάρ ἐστιν
ὀψὲ ἄρξασθαι τὰ δέοντα πράττειν ἢ μηδέποτε), εἴτ'
οὖν ἅπαντες ὁμοίους ἔχετε περὶ τῶν συμφερόντων
λογισμούς, καὶ ἡ προθυμία τῆς ἐπὶ τὸν ἀγῶνα
3 ὁρμῆς ἅπαντας ἡ αὐτὴ κατείληφε. νῦν δὲ[2] φοβού-
μεθα μὴ τὰ περὶ τῆς κληρουχίας προσκρούσματα
τῶν δημοτικῶν πρὸς τοὺς ἐν τέλει μεγάλης αἴτια
τῷ κοινῷ γένηται βλάβης· ὑποψία τε ἡμᾶς κατ-
είληφεν ὡς ἡ περὶ τῆς ἐξόδου καταβοὴ καὶ ἀγανάκτησις οὐκ ἀπὸ τῆς αὐτῆς προαιρέσεως παρὰ
πάντων γίνεται, ἀλλ' οἱ μὲν ὡς τιμωρησόμενοι τοὺς
πολεμίους προθυμεῖσθε τοῦ χάρακος ἐξελθεῖν, οἱ
4 δ' ὡς ἀποδρασόμενοι. ἐξ ὧν δὲ παρέστηκεν ἡμῖν
ταῦτα ὑποπτεύειν οὐ μαντεῖαί[3] εἰσιν οὐδὲ στοχασμοί,
ἀλλ' ἔργα ἐμφανῆ καὶ οὐδὲ ταῦτα παλαιά, ἀλλ' ἐν
τῷ παρελθόντι ἐνιαυτῷ γενόμενα, ὡς ἅπαντες ἴστε,
ὅτε ἐπὶ τοὺς αὐτοὺς πολεμίους τούτους πολλῆς καὶ
ἀγαθῆς ἐξελθούσης στρατιᾶς καὶ τῆς πρώτης μάχης

---

[1] Reiske : εἴ γε O, Jacoby.
[2] Sylburg : δὴ ABC.

officers, and the eagerness which you one and all have to come to grips with your opponents, by showing itself much too late, is untimely. For you should have done this still earlier, when you first saw them come down from their entrenchments and eager to begin battle. Then, no doubt, the contest for the supremacy would have been glorious and worthy of the Roman spirit; as things are, it is already becoming a matter of necessity, and however successful its outcome may be, it will not be equally glorious. Yet even now you do well in desiring to atone for your slowness and to retrieve what you have lost by neglect, and great thanks are due to you for your eagerness to follow the best course, whether this springs from valour—for it is better to begin late to do one's duty than never—or whether indeed you have all come to the same logical conclusions as to what is expedient, and the same eagerness for rushing into battle has seized all of you. But as it is, we are afraid that the grievances of the plebeians against the authorities over the allotment of land may be the cause of great mischief to the commonwealth. And the suspicion has come to us that this clamour and indignation about a sortie do not spring from the same motive with all of you, but that while some desire to go out of the camp in order to take revenge on the enemy, others do so in order to run away. As for the reasons which have induced us to entertain these suspicions, they are neither divinations nor conjectures, but overt deeds, and deeds, too, that happened, not long ago, but only last year, as you all know. For when a large and excellent army had taken the field against this very

---

³ Sylburg : μάντεις O.

τὸ κράτιστον ἡμῖν λαβούσης τέλος, δυνηθέντος ἂν
τοῦ τότε ἄγοντος ὑμᾶς ὑπάτου Καίσωνος, ἀδελφοῦ
δ' ἐμοῦ τουδί, καὶ τὸν χάρακα τῶν πολεμίων
ἐξελεῖν καὶ νίκην τῇ πατρίδι καταγαγεῖν λαμπρο-
τάτην, φθονήσαντες αὐτῷ δόξης τινές, ὅτι δημοτικὸς οὐκ ἦν οὐδὲ τὰ κεχαρισμένα τοῖς πένησι
διετέλει πολιτευόμενος, τῇ πρώτῃ νυκτὶ μετὰ τὴν
μάχην ἀνασπάσαντες τὰς σκηνὰς ἄνευ παραγγέλματος ἀπέδρασαν ἐκ τοῦ χάρακος, οὔτε τὸν κίνδυνον
ἐνθυμηθέντες τὸν καταληψόμενον αὐτοὺς ἀτάκτως
καὶ χωρὶς ἡγεμόνος ἀπιόντας ἐκ πολεμίας γῆς καὶ
ταῦτα ἐν νυκτί, οὔτε τὴν αἰσχύνην ὅση καθέξει
αὐτοὺς ἔμελλεν ὑπολογισάμενοι, ὅτι παρεχώρουν
τοῖς πολεμίοις τῆς ἡγεμονίας, τὸ γοῦν ἐφ' ἑαυτοῖς[1]
μέρος, καὶ ταῦτα οἱ νικήσαντες τοῖς κεκρατημένοις.
5 τούτους δὴ τοὺς ἄνδρας ὀρρωδοῦντες, ὦ ταξίαρχοί
τε καὶ λοχαγοὶ καὶ στρατιῶται, τοὺς οὔτ' ἄρχειν
δυναμένους οὔτ' ἄρχεσθαι βουλομένους πολλοὺς καὶ
αὐθάδεις ὄντας καὶ τὰ ὅπλα ἔχοντας ἐν χερσίν,
οὔτε πρότερον ἐβουλόμεθα μάχην συνάπτειν οὔτε
νῦν ἔτι θαρσοῦμεν ἐπὶ τοιούτοις συμμάχοις τὸν
ὑπὲρ τῶν μεγίστων ἀγῶνα ἄρασθαι, μὴ κωλύματα
καὶ βλάβαι γένωνται τοῖς ἅπαντα τὰ καθ' ἑαυτοὺς
6 πρόθυμα παρεχομένοις. εἰ μέντοι κἀκείνων ὁ θεὸς
ἐπὶ τὰ κρείττω τὸν νοῦν ἄγει νυνὶ καὶ[2] κατα-
βαλόντες τὸ στασιάζον, ὑφ' οὗ[3] πολλὰ καὶ μεγάλα
βλάπτεται τὸ κοινόν, ἤ γε δὴ[4] εἰς τοὺς τῆς εἰρήνης
ἀναβαλόμενοι καιρούς, ἐπανορθώσασθαι βούλονται
τὰ παρελθόντα ὀνείδη τῇ νῦν ἀρετῇ, μηδὲν ἔτι τὸ

---

[1] ἑαυτοῖς B : ἑαυτοὺς A.
[2] καὶ added by Sintenis.
[3] νῦν after οὗ deleted by Reiske.

enemy and the first battle had had the most successful outcome for us, so that your commander at the time, the consul Caeso, my brother here, could not only have taken the enemy's camp, but also have brought back a most glorious victory for the fatherland, some of the soldiers, begrudging him the glory because he was not a friend of the people and did not constantly pursue such a course as was pleasing to the poor, struck their tents the first night after the battle and without orders ran away from the camp, neither taking thought for the danger they would incur in retreating from a hostile country in disorderly fashion and without a general, and that too in the night, nor taking into account all the disgrace that was sure to come upon them for yielding the supremacy to the enemy, as far at least as in them lay, and yielding it, moreover, as victors to the vanquished.   Being afraid, therefore, tribunes, centurions, and soldiers, of these men who are neither able to command nor willing to obey, who are numerous and bold and have their weapons in their hands, we have been unwilling hitherto to join battle and dare not even now, with such men to support us, engage in a life-and-death struggle, lest they prove hindrances and detriments to those who are displaying all the alacrity in their power.   If, however, Heaven is turning the minds of even these men to better ways at the present time, and if, laying aside their seditious spirit, from which the commonwealth is suffering very great harm, or at least postponing it till times of peace, they wish to redeem their past disgraces by their present valour, let there be no further hindrance to your advancing

---

⁴ ἤ γε δὴ Sintenis : εἰ γε δὴ B, om. R.

κωλῦσον ἔστω χωρεῖν ὑμᾶς ἐπὶ τοὺς πολεμίους, τὰς
ἀγαθὰς προβαλλομένους ἐλπίδας.

7 "'Ἔχομεν δὲ πολλὰς μὲν καὶ ἄλλας ἀφορμὰς εἰς
τὸ νικᾶν, μεγίστας δὲ καὶ κυριωτάτας ἃς τὸ τῶν
πολεμίων ἀνόητον ἡμῖν παρέχει, οἵ γε πλήθει
στρατιᾶς μακρῷ προὔχοντες ἡμῶν, καὶ τούτῳ μόνῳ
δυνηθέντες ἂν πρὸς τὰς ἡμετέρας τόλμας τε καὶ
ἐμπειρίας ἀντέχειν, ἀπεστερήκασι τῆς μόνης ὠφελείας ἑαυτοὺς ἀπαναλώσαντες τὸ πλεῖον τῆς δυνά-
8 μεως μέρος εἰς τὰς τῶν φρουρίων φυλακάς. ἔπειτα
δέον αὐτοὺς σὺν εὐλαβείᾳ καὶ λογισμῷ σώφρονι
πράττειν ἕκαστα, ἐνθυμουμένους πρὸς οἵους ἄνδρας
καὶ πολὺ[1] ἀλκιμωτέρους αὐτῶν ὁ κίνδυνος ἔσται,
θρασέως καὶ ἀπερισκέπτως ἐπὶ τὸν ἀγῶνα χωροῦσιν, ὡς ἄμαχοι δή τινες[2] καὶ ὡς ἡμῶν κατα-
πεπληγότων αὐτούς. αἱ γοῦν ἀποταφρεύσεις καὶ
αἱ μέχρι τοῦ χάρακος ἡμῶν καθιππεύσεις καὶ
τὰ πολλὰ ἐν λόγοις τε καὶ ἔργοις ὑβρίσματα τοῦτο
9 δύναται. ταῦτά τε δὴ ἐνθυμούμενοι καὶ τῶν προτέρων ἀγώνων μεμνημένοι, πολλῶν ὄντων καὶ καλῶν,
ἐν οἷς αὐτοὺς ἐνικᾶτε, χωρεῖτε μετὰ προθυμίας καὶ
ἐπὶ τόνδε τὸν ἀγῶνα· καὶ ἐν ᾧ ἂν ὑμῶν ἕκαστος
χωρίῳ ταχθῇ, τοῦτο ὑπολαβέτω καὶ οἶκον εἶναι καὶ
κλῆρον καὶ πατρίδα· καὶ ὅ τε σώζων τὸν παρα-
στάτην ἑαυτῷ πράττειν τὴν σωτηρίαν ὑπολαβέτω,
καὶ ὁ ἐγκαταλιπὼν τὸν πέλας ἑαυτὸν ἡγείσθω τοῖς
πολεμίοις προδιδόναι. μάλιστα δ' ἐκεῖνο μεμνῆσθαι
προσῆκεν,[3] ὅτι μενόντων μὲν ἀνδρῶν καὶ μαχο-
μένων ὀλίγον τὸ ἀπολλύμενόν ἐστιν, ἐγκλινάντων
δὲ καὶ φευγόντων κομιδῇ βραχὺ τὸ σωζόμενον.'"

---

[1] καὶ πολύ B : om. C, καὶ R. Garrer and Jacoby reject
καὶ πολύ ἀλκιμωτέρους αὐτῶν as a gloss.

against the foe, setting before your eyes the fair hopes of victory.

" We have many resources for winning, but greatest and most decisive are those afforded us by the folly of the enemy. For though they far exceed us in the size of their army, and for that reason alone might have withstood our courage and experience, they have deprived themselves of their only advantage by using up the greater part of their forces in garrisoning the forts. In the next place, when they ought to act with caution and sober reason in everything they do, bearing in mind against what kind of men, actually far superior to them in valour,[1] the hazard will be, they enter the struggle recklessly and incautiously, as if forsooth they were some invincible warriors and as if we stood in terror of them. At any rate, their digging of ditches round our camp, their riding up to our entrenchments, and their many insults both in words and actions indicate this. Bearing these thoughts in mind, then, and remembering the many glorious battles of the past in which you have overcome them, enter with alacrity into this contest also. And let every one of you look upon the spot in which he shall be posted as his house, his lot of land, and his country. Let him who saves the man beside him feel that he is effecting his own safety, and let him who forsakes his comrade feel that he is delivering himself up to the enemy. But, above all, you should remember this, that when men stand their ground and fight their losses are small, but when they give way and flee very few are saved."

[1] The clause " actually far superior to them in valour " looks suspiciously like a gloss ; see the critical note.

ᵃ δή τινες R : τινες B, Jacoby.   ᵇ προσῆκεν A : προσῆκει R.

X. Ἔτι δ᾽ αὐτοῦ λέγοντος τὰ εἰς τὸ γενναῖον
ἐπαγωγὰ καὶ πολλὰ μεταξὺ τῶν λόγων ἐκχέοντος
δάκρυα, λοχαγῶν τε καὶ ταξιάρχων καὶ τῶν ἄλλων
στρατιωτῶν ἕκαστον ᾧ συνῄδει τι λαμπρὸν ἔργον
ἐν μάχαις ἀποδειξαμένῳ κατ᾽ ὄνομα ἀνακαλοῦντος,
καὶ πολλὰ καὶ μεγάλα τοῖς ἀριστεύσασι κατὰ τὴν
μάχην φιλάνθρωπα δώσειν ὑπισχνουμένου πρὸς
τὸ τῶν πράξεων μέγεθος, τιμάς τε καὶ πλούτους
καὶ τὰς ἄλλας βοηθείας, ἀναβοήσεις ἐξ ἁπάντων
ἐγίνοντο θαρρεῖν τε παρακελευομένων καὶ ἄγειν ἐπὶ
2 τὸν ἀγῶνα ἀξιούντων. ἐπειδὴ δ᾽ ἐπαύσατο, προ-
έρχεταί τις ἐκ τοῦ πλήθους, Μάρκος Φλαβόληιος
ὄνομα, ἀνὴρ δημοτικὸς μὲν καὶ αὐτουργός, οὐ μὴν
τῶν ἀπερριμμένων τις, ἀλλὰ τῶν ἐπαινουμένων δι᾽
ἀρετὴν καὶ τὰ πολέμια ἄλκιμος, καὶ δι᾽ ἄμφω
ταῦτα ἑνὸς τῶν ταγμάτων τῇ λαμπροτάτῃ ἀρχῇ
κεκοσμημένος, ᾗ τὰς ἑξήκοντα ἑκατονταρχίας ἕπε-
σθαί τε καὶ τὸ κελευόμενον ὑπηρετεῖν κελεύει ὁ[1] νόμος. τούτους Ῥωμαῖοι τοὺς ἡγεμόνας τῇ πατρίῳ
3 γλώττῃ πριμοπίλους καλοῦσιν. οὗτος ὁ ἀνὴρ (ἦν
δὲ πρὸς τοῖς ἄλλοις μέγας τε καὶ καλὸς ἰδεῖν) στὰς
ὅθεν ἅπασιν ἔμελλεν ἔσεσθαι φανερός, "Ἐπεὶ
τοῦτο,[2]" ἔφησεν, "ὦ ὕπατοι, δεδοίκατε, μὴ τὰ
ἔργα ἡμῶν οὐχ ὅμοια γένηται τοῖς λόγοις, ἐγὼ
πρῶτος ὑμῖν ὑπὲρ ἐμαυτοῦ τὸ βέβαιον τῆς ὑποσχέσεως ἐκ τῆς μεγίστης πίστεως παρέξομαι· καὶ
ὑμεῖς δ᾽, ὦ πολῖταί τε καὶ τῆς αὐτῆς κοινωνοὶ
τύχης, ὅσοι διεγνώκατε[3] εἰς ἴσον καταστῆσαι τὰ
ἔργα τοῖς λόγοις, οὐκ ἂν ἁμαρτάνοιτε τὸ αὐτὸ ποι-
4 οῦντες ἐμοί." ταῦτ᾽ εἰπὼν καὶ τὸ ξίφος ἀνατείνας

_____

[1] ὁ added by Kiessling.
[2] ἐπεὶ τοῦτο Sintenis : ἐπὶ τοῦτο A, ἐπὶ τούτῳ B.

X. While he was yet uttering these encourage-
ments to bravery and accompanying his words with
many tears, calling by name each one of the centurions, tribunes, and common soldiers whom he knew
to have performed some gallant action in battle, and
promising to those who should distinguish themselves
in this engagement many great rewards in propor-
tion to the magnitude of their deeds, such as honours,
riches, and all the other advantages, shouts arose
from all of them as they bade him be of good cheer
and demanded that he lead them to battle. As
soon as he had done speaking, there came forward
from the throng a man named Marcus Flavoleius,[1] a
plebeian and small farmer, though not one of the
rabble but one celebrated for his merits and valiant
in war and on both these accounts honoured with the
most conspicuous command in one of the legions—
a command which the sixty centuries are enjoined
by the law to follow and obey. These officers the
Romans call in their own tongue *primipili*. This man,
who, besides his other recommendations, was tall and
fair to look upon, taking his stand where he would
be in full view of all, said : " Since this is what you
fear, consuls, that our actions will not agree with our
words, I will be the first to give you in my own name
the assurance for the performance of my promise by
the greatest pledge I can give. And you too, fellow
citizens and sharers of the same fortune, as many of
you as are resolved to make your actions match your
words, will make no mistake in following my example." Having said this, he held up his sword and

---

[1] For chap. 10, 2-4 *cf.* Livy ii. 45, 13 f.

---

³ διεγνώκατε O : δὴ ἐγνώκατε Reiske.

ὤμοσε τὸν ἐπιχώριόν τε Ῥωμαίοις καὶ κράτιστον
ὅρκον, τὴν ἀγαθὴν ἑαυτοῦ πίστιν, νικήσας τοὺς
πολεμίους ἥξειν εἰς τὴν πόλιν, ἄλλως δ' οὔ. τοῦτον
ὀμόσαντος τοῦ Φλαβοληίου τὸν ὅρκον πολὺς ἐξ
ἁπάντων ἔπαινος ἐγένετο· καὶ αὐτίκα οἵ τε ὕπατοι
ἀμφότεροι τὸ αὐτὸ ἔδρων καὶ οἱ τὰς ἐλάττους
ἔχοντες στρατηγίας χιλίαρχοί τε καὶ λοχαγοί,
5 τελευτῶσα δ' ἡ πληθύς. ἐπεὶ δὲ τοῦτ' ἐγένετο,
πολλὴ μὲν εὐθυμία πᾶσιν ἐνέπεσε, πολλὴ δὲ φιλότης
ἀλλήλων, θάρσος τε αὖ καὶ μένος· καὶ ἀπελθόντες
ἐκ τῆς ἐκκλησίας, οἱ μὲν ἵπποις[1] χαλινοὺς ἐνέβαλλον,[2] οἱ δὲ ξίφη καὶ λόγχας ἔθηγον, οἱ δὲ τὰ σκεπα-
στήρια τῶν ὅπλων ἐξέματτον· καὶ δι' ὀλίγου[3] πᾶσα
6 ἦν ἕτοιμος εἰς τὸν ἀγῶνα ἡ στρατιά. οἱ δ' ὕπατοι
τοὺς θεοὺς εὐχαῖς τε καὶ θυσίαις καὶ λιταῖς ἐπι-
καλεσάμενοι τῆς ἐξόδου σφίσι γενέσθαι ἡγεμόνας,
ἐξῆγον ἐκ τοῦ χάρακος ἐν τάξει καὶ κόσμῳ τὸν
στρατόν. καὶ οἱ Τυρρηνοὶ κατιόντας αὐτοὺς ἐκ
τῶν ἐρυμάτων ἰδόντες ἐθαύμασάν τε καὶ ἀντεπεξ-
ῄεσαν ἁπάσῃ τῇ δυνάμει.

XI. Ὡς δ' εἰς τὸ πεδίον ἀμφότεροι κατέστησαν
καὶ τὸ πολεμικὸν ἐσήμηναν αἱ σάλπιγγες, ἔθεον
ἀλαλάξαντες ὁμόσε· καὶ συμπεσόντες ἀλλήλοις
ἱππεῖς τε[4] ἱππεῦσι καὶ πεζοὶ πεζοῖς ἐμάχοντο, καὶ
πολὺς ἐξ ἀμφοτέρων ἐγίνετο φόνος. οἱ μὲν οὖν
τὸ δεξιὸν ἔχοντες τῶν Ῥωμαίων κέρας, οὗ τὴν
ἡγεμονίαν εἶχεν ὁ ἕτερος τῶν ὑπάτων Μάλλιος, ἐξ-
έωσαν τὸ καθ' ἑαυτοὺς μέρος, καὶ καταβάντες ἀπὸ
τῶν ἵππων ἐμάχοντο πεζοί. οἱ δ' ἐν τῷ εὐωνύμῳ
κέρατι ταχθέντες ὑπὸ τοῦ δεξιοῦ τῶν πολεμίων

___

[1] ἵπποις B : ἱππεῖς AC.
[2] ἐνέβαλλον Bb : ἐνέβαλον R.

took the oath traditional among the Romans and regarded by them as the mightiest of all, swearing by his own good faith that he would return to Rome victorious over the enemy, or not at all. After Flavoleius had taken this oath there was great applause from all; and immediately both the consuls did the same, as did also the subordinate officers, both tribunes and centurions, and last of all the rank and file. When this had been done, great cheerfulness came upon them all and great affection for one another and also confidence and ardour. And going from the assembly, some bridled their horses, others sharpened their swords and spears, and still others cleaned their defensive arms; and in a short time the whole army was ready for the combat. The consuls, after invoking the gods by vows, sacrifices, and prayers to be their guides as they marched out, led the army out of the camp in regular order and formation. The Tyrrhenians, seeing them come down from their entrenchments, were surprised and marched out with their whole force to meet them.

XI. When both armies had come into the plain and the trumpets had sounded the charge, they raised their war-cries and ran to close quarters; and engaging, horse with horse and foot with foot, they fought there, and great was the slaughter on both sides. The troops on the right wing of the Romans, commanded by Manlius, one of the consuls, repulsed the part of the enemy that stood opposite to them, and quitting their horses, fought on foot. But those on the left wing were being surrounded by the enemy's

----

³ δι' ὀλίγου A : ὀλίγου B, Jacoby.
⁴ τε B : om. R.

2 ἐκυκλοῦντο. ἦν γὰρ ἡ Τυρρηνῶν φάλαγξ κατὰ τοῦτο τὸ χωρίον ὑπερπετής τε καὶ οὐκ ὀλίγῳ μείζων τῆς ἑτέρας. παρερρήγνυτο δὴ ταύτῃ τὸ Ῥωμαϊκὸν στράτευμα καὶ πολλὰς πληγὰς ἐλάμβανεν. ἡγεῖτο δὲ τούτου τοῦ κέρως Κόιντος Φάβιος, πρεσβευτὴς καὶ ἀντιστράτηγος ὤν, ὁ δὶς ὑπατεύσας· καὶ μέχρι πολλοῦ ἀντεῖχε τραύματα λαμβάνων παντοδαπά, ἔπειτα λόγχῃ βληθεὶς εἰς τὰ στέρνα μέχρι τῶν σπλάγχνων ἐλθούσης τῆς αἰχμῆς ἔξαιμος 3 γενόμενος πίπτει. ὡς δὲ τοῦτ᾽ ἤκουσεν ὁ ἕτερος τῶν ὑπάτων, Μάρκος Φάβιος (ἦν δὲ κατὰ μέσην τὴν φάλαγγα τεταγμένος) τοὺς κρατίστους τῶν λόχων ἀναλαβὼν καὶ τὸν ἕτερον τῶν ἀδελφῶν Καίσωνα Φάβιον ἀνακαλεσάμενος, παρήλαυνεν τὴν[1] ἑαυτοῦ φάλαγγα καὶ μέχρι πολλοῦ προελθών, ἐπειδὴ παρήλλαξεν[2] τὸ δεξιὸν τῶν πολεμίων κέρας, ἤλαυνεν ἐπὶ τοὺς κυκλουμένους. ἐμπεσὼν δ᾽ αὐτοῖς φόνον τε τοῖς ἐν χερσὶ ποιεῖ πολὺν καὶ φυγὴν τῶν πρόσω, τόν τε ἀδελφὸν ἔτι ἐμπνέοντα κατα- 4 λαβὼν αἴρεται. ἐκεῖνος μὲν οὖν οὐ πολὺν ἔτι χρόνον ἐπιβιοὺς ἀποθνήσκει· τοῖς δὲ τιμωροῦσιν αὐτῷ θυμὸς ἔτι πλείων παρέστη καὶ μείζων[3] πρὸς τὸ ἀντίπαλον· καὶ οὐδὲν ἔτι τῆς ἰδίας ψυχῆς προνοούμενοι σὺν ὀλίγοις εἰς μέσους ἐμπεσόντες τοὺς μάλιστα συνεστηκότας τῶν πολεμίων, σωροὺς ἐξ- 5 επλήρουν νεκρῶν. κατὰ μὲν δὴ τοῦτο τὸ μέρος

---

[1] ἐπὶ before τὴν deleted by Gelenius.
[2] Portus : παρήλλαξαν O.
[3] πλείων παρέστη καὶ μείζων A : μείζων παρέστη B.

---

[1] Dionysius employs ἀνθύπατος, the usual Greek word for "proconsul" or the adjective "proconsular," only in con-

right wing, since the Tyrrhenians' line at this point
outflanked that of the Romans and was considerably
deeper. Thus the Roman army was being broken
in this sector and was receiving many blows. This
wing was commanded by Quintus Fabius, who was
a legate and proconsul [1] and had been twice consul.
He maintained the fight for a long time, receiving
wounds of all kinds till, being struck in the breast
by a spear, the point of which pierced his bowels, he
fell through loss of blood. When Marcus Fabius, the
other consul, who commanded in the centre, was
informed of this, he took with him the best of the
centuries, and summoning Caeso Fabius, his other
brother, he passed beyond his own line, and advancing a long way, till he had got beyond the enemy's
right wing, he turned upon those who were en-
circling his men, and charging them, caused great
slaughter among all whom he encountered, and also
put to flight those who were at a distance; and finding his brother still breathing, he took him up. The
man lived only a short time after that; but his death
filled his avengers with still more and greater anger
against the foe and, heedless now of their own lives,
they rushed with a few followers into the densest
ranks of the enemy and made large heaps of their
dead bodies. In this part of their line, therefore, the

---

nexion with a person possessing the *imperium* (see chaps.
16, 3-4; 17, 5; 63, 2; *cf.* xi. 62, 1), but when, as in the
present passage and one other (chap. 12, 5), he is speaking
of a proconsul in a subordinate position, he uses the term
ἀντιστράτηγος. The latter term was used by most writers for
" propraetor," and the phrase πρεσβευτὴς καὶ ἀντιστράτηγος
was the Greek equivalent for *legatus pro praetore*; but at
the period with which we are here concerned the praetorship
had not been set off as yet from the consulship.

ἔκαμεν ἡ Τυρρηνῶν φάλαγξ, καὶ οἱ πρότερον
ὠσάμενοι τοὺς πολεμίους ὑπὸ τῶν κεκρατημένων
ἀνεκόπησαν· οἱ δὲ τὸ εὐώνυμον ἔχοντες κέρας,
ἔνθα ὁ Μάλλιος ἦν,[1] κάμνοντες ἤδη καὶ φυγῆς
ἄρχοντες ἐτρέψαντο τοὺς καθ' ἑαυτούς. παλτῷ
γάρ τις βαλὼν τὸν Μάλλιον διὰ τοῦ γόνατος ἄχρι
τῆς ἰγνύας διήρεισε τὴν λόγχην· καὶ τὸν μὲν οἱ
πέριξ ἄραντες ἐπὶ τὴν παρεμβολὴν ἀπεκόμιζον,
οἱ δὲ πολέμιοι τὸν ἡγεμόνα τῶν Ῥωμαίων τεθνη-
κέναι δόξαντες ἐπερρώσθησαν, καὶ παραβοηθη-
σάντων αὐτοῖς τῶν ἑτέρων ἐνέκειντο τοῖς Ῥωμαίοις
6 οὐκ ἔχουσιν ἡγεμόνα. ἠναγκάσθησαν δὲ πάλιν οἱ
Φάβιοι καταλιπόντες τὸ εὐώνυμον κέρας[2] τῷ δεξιῷ
βοηθεῖν· καὶ οἱ Τυρρηνοὶ προσιόντας αὐτοὺς στίφει
καρτερῷ μαθόντες τῆς μὲν ἐπὶ πλέον διώξεως
ἀποτρέπονται, πυκνώσαντες δὲ τοὺς λόχους ἐμάχοντο ἐν τάξει, καὶ πολλοὺς μὲν τῶν σφετέρων
ἀπέβαλον, πολλοὺς δὲ καὶ τῶν Ῥωμαίων ἀπέκτειναν.

XII. Ἐν ᾧ δὲ ταῦτ' ἐγίνετο, οἱ τὸν χάρακα τὸν
ἐκλειφθέντα ὑπὸ τοῦ Μαλλίου καταλαβόμενοι Τυρρηνοὶ συνθήματος ἀρθέντος ἀπὸ[3] τοῦ στρατηγίου[4]
σὺν τάχει πολλῷ καὶ προθυμίᾳ μεγάλῃ χωροῦντες
ἐπὶ τὸν ἕτερον ἠπείγοντο τῶν Ῥωμαίων χάρακα,
ὡς οὐκ ἀξιοχρέῳ δυνάμει φυλαττόμενον. καὶ ἦν ἡ
δόξα αὐτῶν ἀληθής. ἔξω γὰρ τῶν τριαρίων καὶ
ὀλίγων ἄλλων τῶν ἐν ἀκμῇ τὸ λοιπὸν πλῆθος
ἐμπόρων τε καὶ θεραπόντων καὶ χειροτεχνῶν ἦν ἐν
αὐτῷ· γίνεταί τε πολλῶν εἰς ὀλίγον συνελαθέντων
χωρίον (περὶ γὰρ ταῖς πύλαις ὁ ἀγὼν ἦν) ὀξεῖα καὶ

---

[1] ἔνθα ὁ Μάλλιος ἦν placed here by Kiessling, after ἄρχοντες by O; deleted by Jacoby.

Tyrrhenians were hard pressed, and those who earlier
had forced their enemies to give ground were now
repulsed by those they had conquered; but those on
the left wing, where Manlius was,[1] though they were
already in distress and beginning to flee, put their
opponents to flight. For when Manlius had been
struck in the knee with a javelin by an opponent who
thrust the point through to the hamstrings, and those
about him took him up and were carrying him back
to the camp, the enemy, believing the Roman commander to be dead, took heart and, the rest coming
to their assistance, pressed hard upon the Romans
who now had no commander. This obliged the Fabii
to quit their left wing once more and rush to the
relief of the right; and the Tyrrhenians, learning
that they were approaching in a strong body, gave
over further pursuit, and closing their ranks, fought
in good order, losing a large number of their own
men, but also killing many of the Romans.

XII. In the meantime the Tyrrhenians who had
possessed themselves of the camp abandoned by
Manlius, as soon as the signal for battle was given at
headquarters, ran with great haste and alacrity to the
other camp of the Romans, suspecting that it was not
guarded by a sufficient force. And their belief was
correct. For, apart from the *triarii* and a few younger
troops, the rest of the crowd then in the camp consisted of merchants, servants and artificers; and
with many crowded into a small space—for the
struggle was for the gates of the camp—a sharp and

---

[1] This awkward explanation may be an interpolation.

---

² κέρας A : μέρος B.   ³ ἀπὸ B : ὑπὸ R.
     ⁴ Reiske : στρατηγοῦ O.

χαλεπὴ μάχη, καὶ νεκροὶ παρ' ἀμφοτέρων πολλοί.
2 ἐν τούτῳ τῷ ἔργῳ ὅ τε ὕπατος Μάλλιος[1] ἐκβοηθῶν
ἅμα τοῖς ἱππεῦσιν, ἐπειδὴ ὁ ἵππος ἔπεσε, συγκατ-
ενεχθεὶς καὶ ἀδύνατος ὢν ἀναστῆναι ὑπὸ πλήθους
τραυμάτων, ἀποθνῄσκει καὶ πολλοὶ καὶ ἀγαθοὶ περὶ
αὐτὸν ἄλλοι νέοι. μετὰ δὲ τὸ πάθος τοῦτο εὐθὺς
ὁ χάραξ ἡλίσκετο, καὶ τέλος εἶχε τοῖς Τυρρηνοῖς
3 τὰ μαντεύματα. εἰ μὲν οὖν ἐταμιεύσαντο τὴν
παροῦσαν εὐτυχίαν καὶ διὰ φυλακῆς εἶχον[2] τὸν
χάρακα, τάς τε ἀποσκευὰς τῶν Ῥωμαίων κατέσχον
ἂν[3] καὶ αὐτοὺς αἰσχρῶς ἀπελθεῖν ἠνάγκασαν[4]· νῦν
δὲ πρὸς ἁρπαγὴν τῶν ἀπολειφθέντων τραπόμενοι
καὶ ἀναψύχοντες τὸ λοιπὸν[5] οἱ πλείους καλὴν ἄγραν
ἐκ τῶν χειρῶν ἀφῃρέθησαν. ὡς γὰρ ἀπηγγέλθη
θατέρῳ τῶν ὑπάτων ἡ τοῦ χάρακος ἅλωσις,
ἠπείγετο σὺν τοῖς ἀρίστοις ἱππέων τε καὶ πεζῶν.
4 καὶ οἱ Τυρρηνοὶ μαθόντες αὐτὸν ἐπιόντα περι-
εστεφάνωσαν τὸν χάρακα, μάχη τ' αὐτῶν γίνεται
καρτερὰ τῶν μὲν ἀνασώσασθαι βουλομένων τὰ
σφέτερα, τῶν δὲ μὴ πασσυδὶ διαφθαρῶσιν ἁλόντος
τοῦ χάρακος δεδοικότων. χρόνου δὲ γινομένου
πλείονος καὶ τῶν Τυρρηνῶν πολλὰ πλεονεκτούντων
(ἦν γὰρ αὐτοῖς ἐξ ὑπερδεξίων τε χωρίων[6] καὶ πρὸς
ἀνθρώπους δι' ἡμέρας ὅλης κεκμηκότας ἡ μάχη[7]),
5 Τίτος Σίκκιος ὁ πρεσβευτὴς καὶ ἀντιστράτηγος,
κοινωσάμενος τῷ ὑπάτῳ τὴν αὐτοῦ διάνοιαν τὸ
ἀνακλητικὸν ἐκέλευε σημαίνειν, καὶ καθ' ἓν ἅπαντας

---

[1] ὅ τε ὕπατος μάλλιος B : ὅ τε μάλλιος ὕπατος R. Kiessling
and Jacoby rejected Μάλλιος.
[2] εἶχον O : ἔσχον Steph.[3], Jacoby.
[3] ἄν added by Cobet. [4] Sylburg : ἠνάγκαζον O.
[5] τὸ λοιπὸν B : om. R.
[6] τε χωρίων Reiske : τὸ χωρίον O.

severe engagement followed, and there were many dead on both sides. During this action the consul Manlius was coming out with the cavalry to the relief of his men, when his horse fell; and he, falling with him and being unable to rise because of his many wounds, died there, and likewise many brave young men at his side. After this disaster the camp was soon taken, and the Tyrrhenians' prophecies had their fulfilment. Now if they had husbanded the good fortune that was then theirs and had kept the camp under guard, they would have got possession of the Romans' baggage and forced them to a shameful retreat; but as it was, by turning to plundering what had been left behind and from then on refreshing themselves, as most of them did, they allowed a fine booty to escape out of their hands. For as soon as word of the taking of the camp reached the other consul, he hastened thither with the flower of both horse and foot. The Tyrrhenians, informed of his approach, formed a circle round the camp and a sharp battle occurred between them, as the Romans endeavoured to recover what was theirs and the enemy feared being annihilated if their camp should be taken. When considerable time passed and the Tyrrhenians had many advantages, since they fought from higher ground and against men spent with fighting the whole day, Titus Siccius, the legate and proconsul,[1] after communicating his plan to the consul, ordered that a retreat should be sounded and

[1] See note on chap. 11, 2.

---

[7] ἡ μάχη Sylburg : τῇ μάχη O.

γενομένους μιᾷ προσβάλλειν πλευρᾷ τοῦ χάρακος,
καθ' ὃ μάλιστα τὸ χωρίον ἦν ἐπιμαχώτατον[1]· τὰ
δὲ κατὰ τὰς πύλας εἴασε μέρη κατά τινα εἰκότα
λογισμόν, ὃς οὐκ ἐψεύσατο αὐτόν, ὅτι σωθήσεσθαι
μὲν ἐλπίσαντες οἱ Τυρρηνοὶ[2] μεθήσονται τοῦ χάρακος, ἐν ἀπογνώσει δὲ τούτου γενόμενοι κυκλώ-
σεώς τε πάντοθεν ὑπὸ τῶν πολεμίων γενομένης καὶ
οὐδεμιᾶς ὑπαρχούσης ἐξόδου ἀναγκαῖον ἕξουσι τὸ
6 εὔτολμον. γενομένης δὲ καθ' ἓν χωρίον τῆς προσ-
βολῆς οὐκέτι πρὸς ἀλκὴν οἱ Τυρρηνοὶ ἐτράποντο,
ἀλλ' ἀνοίξαντες τὰς πύλας ἐπὶ τὸν ἑαυτῶν ἀν-
εσώζοντο χάρακα.

XIII. Ὁ δ' ὕπατος ἐπειδὴ τὸ δεινὸν ἀπεώσατο,
παρεβοήθει πάλιν τοῖς ἐν τῷ πεδίῳ. αὕτη μεγίστη
λέγεται τῶν πρὸ αὐτῆς γενέσθαι Ῥωμαίοις[3] μάχη,
πλήθει τε ἀνθρώπων καὶ μήκει χρόνου καὶ τῷ
ἀγχιστρόφῳ τῆς τύχης. αὐτῶν μὲν γὰρ τῶν ἐκ
τῆς πόλεως Ῥωμαίων ἡ κρατίστη τε καὶ ἐπίλεκτος
ἀκμὴ δισμυρίων μάλιστα πεζῶν ἐγένετο καὶ τῶν
συντεταγμένων τοῖς τέτταρσι τάγμασιν ἱππέων
ὁμοῦ τι χιλίων καὶ διακοσίων, ἀποίκων δὲ[4] καὶ
2 συμμάχων ἕτερα τοσαύτη. χρόνος δ' ἐμηκύνθη τοῦ
ἀγῶνος ὀλίγῳ πρότερον τῆς μεσημβρίας ἀρξάμενος
μέχρι δύσεως ἡλίου. τὰ δὲ τῆς τύχης μέχρι πολλοῦ τῇδε καὶ τῇδε νίκαις τε καὶ ἥτταις[5] ταλαντευό-
μενα διέμεινεν· ὑπάτου δὲ θάνατος ἐγένετο καὶ
πρεσβευτοῦ δὶς ὑπατεύσαντος καὶ ἄλλων πολλῶν
ἡγεμόνων καὶ ταξιάρχων καὶ λοχαγῶν, ὅσων
οὐδέπω πρότερον. τὸ μέντοι κράτος τοῦ ἀγῶνος

---

[1] Possibly an error for ἐπίμαχον.
[2] οἱ τυρρηνοί B : om. R.
[3] ῥωμαίοις B : ῥωμαίων R.
[4] δὲ B : τε R.

that all the men should assemble in a single body and assault one side of the camp where it was most easy of attack. He left free from attack the parts next the gates, reasoning plausibly—and in this he was not deceived—that if the Tyrrhenians saw any hope of saving themselves, they would abandon the camp, whereas, if they despaired of this, finding themselves surrounded on all sides and no way of escape left, necessity would make them brave. And when the attack was directed against one point only, the Tyrrhenians no longer resisted, but opening the gates, made their way back in safety to their own camp.

XIII. The consul, after he had averted the danger, returned once more to the assistance of those who were in the plain. This battle is said to have been greater than any the Romans had previously fought as regards not only the numbers of the combatants, but also the time it lasted and its sudden turns of fortune. For of the Romans themselves from the city the flower and choice of their youth consisted of about 20,000 foot and some 1200 horse attached to the four legions, while from their colonies and allies there was another force equally large. As for the duration of the battle, it began a little before noon and lasted till sunset. Its fortunes continued for a long time shifting to and fro with alternating victories and defeats. A consul was slain, as well as a legate who had himself been twice consul, and many other commanders, tribunes and centurions—more indeed than in any previous battle. But the victory in

---

¹ νίκαις τε καὶ ἥτταις Bb : νίκας τε καὶ ἥττας ABaC.

ἐδόκει περὶ τοὺς Ῥωμαίους γεγονέναι κατ' ἄλλο
μὲν οὐδέν, ὅτι δὲ τῇ ἐπιούσῃ νυκτὶ καταλιπόντες
3 τὸν χάρακα οἱ Τυρρηνοὶ ἀνέζευξαν. τῇ δ' ἐξῆς
ἡμέρᾳ πρὸς ἁρπαγὰς τῆς ἐκλειφθείσης ὑπὸ τῶν
Τυρρηνῶν παρεμβολῆς οἱ Ῥωμαῖοι τραπόμενοι καὶ
ταφὰς ποιησάμενοι τῶν σφετέρων νεκρῶν ἀπῆλθον
εἰς τὸν ἑαυτῶν χάρακα. ἐκεῖ δ' ἐκκλησίαν ποιησάμενοι τοῖς ἀγωνισαμένοις λαμπρῶς τὰς ἀριστείους
ἀπέδοσαν τιμάς, πρώτῳ μὲν Καίσωνι Φαβίῳ τῷ
τοῦ ὑπάτου ἀδελφῷ μεγάλα καὶ θαυμαστὰ ἔργα
ἀποδειξαμένῳ, δευτέρῳ δὲ τῷ Σικκίῳ, τῷ διαπραξαμένῳ[1] τὸν χάρακα ἀνασώσασθαι, τρίτῳ δὲ
Μάρκῳ Φλαβολήῳ τῷ ἡγεμόνι τοῦ τάγματος, τοῦ
θ' ὅρκου χάριν καὶ τῆς παρὰ τὰ δεινὰ ῥώμης.[2]
4 διαπραξάμενοι δὲ ταῦτα καὶ μείναντες ἡμέρας
ὀλίγας ἐπὶ τοῦ χάρακος, ὡς οὐδεὶς ἀντεπεξῄει
τῶν πολεμίων μαχησόμενος, ἀπῄεσαν ἐπ' οἴκου.
πάντων δὲ τῶν κατὰ τὴν πόλιν, ὡς ἐπὶ μεγίστῳ
ἀγῶνι κάλλιστον τέλος εἰληφότι, τὴν ἐπινίκιον τιμὴν τοῦ θριάμβου τῷ περιόντι ὑπάτῳ προσθεῖναι
βουλομένων, ἠρνήσατο τὴν χάριν αὐτῶν ὁ ὕπατος,
οὔτε ὅσιον εἶναι λέγων οὔτε θεμιτὸν ἐπ' ἀδελφοῦ
θανάτῳ καὶ συνάρχοντος ἀποβολῇ πομπεύειν καὶ
στεφανηφορεῖν· ἀποθεὶς δὲ τὰς σημείας[3] καὶ τοὺς
στρατιώτας ἀπολύσας ἐπὶ τὰ οἰκεῖα τὴν ὑπατείαν
ἀπωμόσατο, δυεῖν ἔτι μηνῶν εἰς τὸν ἐνιαύσιον
χρόνον λειπομένων, ἀδύνατος ὢν τὰ τῆς ἀρχῆς ἔτι

---

[1] διαπραξαμένῳ B : διαταξαμένῳ C, διαφρασαμένῳ ACmg.
[2] ῥώμης O : τόλμης Kiessling, ὁρμῆς Grasberger.
[3] σημείας O : σημαίας Sylburg, Jacoby. The form σημεία
is given by the MSS. in several passages in the chapters that
follow, but has been regularly emended by the editors.

the struggle seemed to rest with the Romans, for this
one reason alone, that the Tyrrhenians left their camp
the following night and withdrew. The next day the
Romans turned to plundering the camp which had
been abandoned by the Tyrrhenians, and having
buried their dead, returned to their own camp.
There, having called an assembly of the soldiers, they
distributed the rewards of valour to those who had
distinguished themselves in the battle, as follows :
first, to Caeso Fabius, the consul's brother, who had
performed great and remarkable exploits ; next, to
Siccius, who had brought about the recovery of their
camp ; and third, to Marcus Flavoleius, the commander [1] of the legion, on account of both the oath
he had taken and the prowess [2] he had shown in the
midst of danger. After attending to these things
they remained a few days in the camp ; then, when
none of the enemy came out to fight against them,
they returned home. Though all in the city wished
to honour the surviving consul with the victor's reward of a triumph because of a most glorious outcome
to a very great battle, the consul declined the favour
they offered, saying that it was neither right nor lawful for him to ride in procession and wear a crown
of laurel after the death of his brother and the loss of
his colleague. But after putting away the standards
and dismissing the soldiers to their homes he resigned
the consulship when two months still remained to
complete his year's term, since he was no longer
capable of performing the duties of the office. For

---

[1] The *primipilus* ; see chap. 10, 2.

[2] The word here rendered " prowess " is perhaps corrupt ;
we should expect a word like " intrepidity." See the critical
note.

πράττειν. ἐταλαιπώρει γὰρ ὑπὸ τραύματος ἐξαισίου καὶ ἦν κλινοπετής.

XIV. Ἑλομένης δὲ τῆς βουλῆς μεσοβασιλεῖς τῶν ἀρχαιρεσίων ἕνεκα, καὶ τοῦ δευτέρου μεσοβασιλέως συγκαλέσαντος εἰς τὸ πεδίον τοὺς λόχους,[1] ἀποδείκνυται Καίσων Φάβιος ὁ τὰ ἀριστεῖα λαβὼν ἐκ τῆς μάχης, ἀδελφὸς δὲ τοῦ τὴν ἀρχὴν ἀποθεμένου, τὸ τρίτον ὕπατος καὶ σὺν αὐτῷ Τίτος Οὐεργίνιος. οὗτοι διαλαχόντες τὰς δυνάμεις ἐξῄεσαν εἰς τὴν ὕπαιθρον, Φάβιος μὲν Αἰκανοῖς πολεμήσων προνομεύουσι τοὺς Λατίνων ἀγροὺς 2 Οὐεργίνιος δὲ Οὐιεντανοῖς. Αἰκανοὶ μὲν οὖν ἐπειδὴ στρατὸν ἐλευσόμενον ἐπ' αὐτοὺς ἔγνωσαν, ἀναστάντες ἐκ τῆς πολεμίας διὰ τάχους ἀπῆλθον εἰς τὰς ἑαυτῶν πόλεις· καὶ μετὰ ταῦτα λεηλατουμένης τῆς σφετέρας γῆς ἠνείχοντο, ὥστε πολλῶν κρατῆσαι χρημάτων τὸν ὕπατον καὶ σωμάτων καὶ τῆς ἄλλης λείας[2] ἐξ ἐφόδου. Οὐιεντανοὶ δὲ κατ' ἀρχὰς ἐντὸς τείχους μένοντες, ἐπειδὴ καιρὸν ἔχειν ἔδοξαν ἐπιτήδειον, ἐπέθεντο τοῖς πολεμίοις ἐσκεδασμένοις ἀνὰ τὰ πεδία καὶ πρὸς ἁρπαγὴν τετραμμένοις 3 τῆς λείας. ἔχοντες δὲ πολλὴν καὶ συντεταγμένην δύναμιν ἐμβάλλουσιν εἰς αὐτούς, καὶ τήν τε λείαν ἀφαιροῦνται καὶ τοὺς ὁμόσε χωροῦντας οὓς μὲν ἀποκτείνουσιν, οὓς δ' εἰς φυγὴν τρέπουσι· καὶ εἰ μὴ Τίτος Σίκκιος πρεσβευτὴς τότ' ὢν στίφει συντεταγμένῳ πεζῶν τε καὶ ἱππέων παραβοηθήσας ἐπέσχεν αὐτούς, οὐδὲν ἂν τὸ κωλῦσον ἦν ἅπασαν ἀπολέσθαι τὴν στρατιάν. ἐκείνου δ' ἐμποδὼν

---

[1] λόχους Schwegler : ὄχλους O.
[2] τῆς ἄλλης λείας Reiske, ἄλλης λείας Sintenis : τῆς λείας O, πολλῆς λείας Cmg.

330

he was still suffering from a horrible wound and
obliged to keep his bed.

XIV. The senate[1] chose *interreges* to preside at the
election of magistrates, and the second *interrex* having
assembled the centuries in the Field,[2] Caeso Fabius,
the one who had been awarded the prize for valour
in the battle, and brother to the man who had abdi-
cated his magistracy, was chosen consul for the third
time, and with him Titus Verginius. These, having
drawn lots for the armies, took the field, Fabius
to war against the Aequians, who were plundering
the fields of the Latins, and Verginius against the
Veientes. The Aequians, when they learned that an
army was going to come against them, hastily evacu-
ated the enemy's country and returned to their own
cities ; and after that they permitted their own
territory to be ravaged, so that the consul possessed
himself at the first blow of large amounts of money,
many slaves, and much booty of other sorts. As for
the Veientes, they at first remained within their
walls ; but as soon as they thought they had a favourable opportunity, they fell upon the enemy as they
were dispersed over the plains and occupied in seizing
booty. And attacking them with a large army in
good order, they not only took away their booty, but
also killed or put to flight all who engaged them.
Indeed, if Titus Siccius, who was legate at the time,
had not come to their relief with a body of foot and
horse in good order and held the foe in check, nothing
could have prevented the army from being utterly
destroyed. But when he got in the enemy's way,

---

[1] *Cf.* Livy ii. 48, 1-7.
[2] The Campus Martius.

γενομένου συνελθεῖν ἔφθασαν οἱ λοιποὶ οἱ καθ' ἕνα
διεσκεδασμένοι· πάντες δ' ἐν ταὐτῷ γενόμενοι
λόφον τινὰ καταλαμβάνονται περὶ δείλην ὀψίαν,
4 καὶ τὴν ἐπιοῦσαν νύκτα ἐν τούτῳ ἔμειναν. ἐπαρθέντες δὲ Οὐιεντανοὶ τῷ κατορθώματι πλησίον τοῦ
λόφου τίθενται τὰ ὅπλα, καὶ τοὺς ἐκ τῆς πόλεως
ἐκάλουν ὡς κατακεκλεικότες τοὺς Ῥωμαίους εἰς
χωρίον ἔνθα οὐδὲν τῶν ἐπιτηδείων ἔμελλον ἕξειν,
καὶ προσαναγκάσοντες οὐκ εἰς μακρὰν παραδοῦναι
σφίσι τὰ ὅπλα. γίνεταί τε αὐτῶν συχνοῦ ἐλθόντος
ὄχλου δύο στρατεύματα περὶ τὰς ἐπιμάχους λαγό-
νας τοῦ λόφου, πολλά τ'[1] ἄλλα φρούρια βραχύτερα
κατὰ τοὺς ἧττον ἐπικαίρους τόπους· καὶ πάντα ἦν
μεστὰ ὅπλων.

5 Ὁ δ' ἕτερος τῶν ὑπάτων Φάβιος γραμμάτων
παρὰ τοῦ συνάρχοντος ἀφικομένων ἐπιγνοὺς ὡς[2] ἐν
ἐσχάτοις εἰσὶν οἱ κατακλεισθέντες ἐν τῷ λόφῳ, καὶ
κινδυνεύσουσιν, εἰ μή τις αὐτοῖς βοηθήσει, λιμῷ
ἁλῶναι, ἀναστήσας τὸν στρατὸν ἦγεν ἐπὶ τοὺς
Οὐιεντανοὺς σὺν τάχει· καὶ εἰ μιᾷ βραδύτερον
ἡμέρᾳ διήνυσε τὴν ὁδόν, οὐδὲν ἂν ὤνησεν, ἀλλὰ
διεφθαρμένην τὴν ἐκεῖ στρατιὰν κατέλαβε. πιεζόμενοι γὰρ τῇ σπάνει τῶν ἀναγκαίων οἱ κατέχοντες
τὸν λόφον ἐξῆλθον ὡς τὸν εὐπρεπέστατον αἱρησό-
μενοι τῶν θανάτων, καὶ συμβαλόντες τοῖς πολεμίοις ἐμάχοντο κεκμηκότες οἱ πλείους τὰ σώματα
λιμῷ τε καὶ δίψῃ καὶ ἀγρυπνίᾳ καὶ τῇ ἄλλῃ κακώ-
6 σει. μετ' οὐ πολὺ δ' ὡς τὸ τοῦ Φαβίου στράτευμα
προσιὸν ὤφθη πολύ τε καὶ συντεταγμένον, θάρσος
μὲν ἔφερε τοῖς σφετέροις, δέος δὲ τοῖς πολεμίοις·

[1] τε Reiske : δὲ O.
[2] ὡς Post : ὡς ὅτι R, ὅτι B, Jacoby.

the rest of the troops, who had been scattered one
here and one there, succeeded in getting together
before it was too late; and being now all united, they
occupied a hill late in the afternoon and remained
there the following night. The Veientes, elated by
their success, encamped near the hill and sent for
their forces in the city, imagining that they had
shut up the Romans in a place where they could
not get any provisions, and that they would soon
force them to deliver up their arms to them. And
when a great multitude of their men had arrived,
there were now two armies posted on the two
sides of the hill that could be assailed, as well as
many smaller detachments to guard the less vulner-
able positions; and every place was full of armed
men.

The other consul, Fabius, learning from a letter
that came from his colleague that the troops shut up
on the hill were in the direst straits and would be in
danger of being reduced by famine unless someone
came to their relief, broke camp and marched in haste
against the Veientes. Indeed, if he had been one
day later in completing his march, he would have
been of no help, but would have found the army there
destroyed. For the men holding the hill, distressed
by the lack of provisions, had sallied out, ready to
choose the most honourable death; and having engaged the enemy, they were then fighting, though
the bodies of most of them were weakened by hunger,
thirst, want of sleep, and every other hardship. But
after a short time, when the army of Fabius, which
was very large and drawn up in order of battle, was
seen approaching, it brought confidence to their own
men and fear to the enemy; and the Tyrrhenians,

καὶ οἱ Τυρρηνοὶ οὐκέτι ἀξιόμαχοι εἶναι νομίσαντες πρὸς ἀγαθήν τε καὶ ἀκμῆτα δύναμιν εἰς ἀγῶνα χωρεῖν, ᾤχοντο ἐκλιπόντες τοὺς χάρακας. ὡς δ' εἰς ταὐτὸ συνῆλθον αἱ τῶν Ῥωμαίων δυνάμεις ἀμφότεραι, στρατόπεδόν τε ποιοῦνται μέγα πλησίον τῆς πόλεως ἐν ἐχυρῷ, καὶ πολλὰς ἡμέρας αὐτόθι διατρίψαντες καὶ τὴν ἀρίστην τῶν Οὐιεντανῶν χώραν λεηλατήσαντες ἀπῆγον ἐπ' οἴκου τὴν στρα-
7 τιάν. ὡς δ' ἔγνωσαν οἱ Οὐιεντανοὶ τὰς δυνάμεις τῶν Ῥωμαίων ἀφειμένας ἀπὸ τῶν σημείων, τὴν εὔζωνον ἀναλαβόντες νεότητα, ἥν τε αὐτοὶ συντεταγμένην εἶχον καὶ τὴν παρὰ τῶν πλησιοχώρων παροῦσαν, ἐμβάλλουσιν εἰς τὰ προσκείμενα τῇ σφετέρᾳ χώρᾳ πεδία, καὶ διαρπάζουσι καρπῶν τε καὶ βοσκημάτων καὶ ἀνθρώπων ὄντα μεστά. κατέβησαν γὰρ ἐκ τῶν ἐρυμάτων οἱ γεωργοὶ χιλοῦ τε τῶν βοσκημάτων ἕνεκα καὶ ἐργασίας τῶν ἀγρῶν πιστεύοντες τῇ σφετέρᾳ στρατιᾷ προκαθημένῃ καὶ οὐ φθάσαντες ἀπελθούσης ἀνασκευάσασθαι[1] πάλιν, οὐκ ἂν[2] ἐλπίσαντες τοσαῦτα κεκακωμένους τοὺς Οὐιεντανοὺς ταχεῖαν οὕτως ἀντεπιχείρησιν κατὰ
8 τοῦ ἀντιπάλου ποιήσασθαι.[3] αὕτη χρόνου μὲν μήκει βραχεῖα ἐγένετο ἡ τῶν Οὐιεντανῶν εἰς τὴν Ῥωμαίων γῆν ἐμβολή, πλήθει δὲ χώρας ἣν ἐπῆλθον ἐν τοῖς[4] πάνυ μεγάλη, καὶ ἀχθηδόνα σὺν αἰσχύνῃ Ῥωμαίοις ἀήθη παρέσχεν ἄχρι Τεβέριός τε ποταμοῦ καὶ ὅρους Ἰανίκλου στάδια τῆς Ῥώμης οὐδ' εἴκοσιν ἀφεστῶτος ἀφικομένη. ἡ[5] κωλύσουσα

---

[1] ἀνασκευάσασθαι BCmg : ἀνασκευάσαντες AC.
[2] οὐκ ἂν ἐλπίσαντες B : οὐκ ἐλπίσαντες A, Jacoby, οὐδ' ἐλπίσαντες Kiessling.
[3] ποιήσασθαι ABC : ποιήσεσθαι Steph., Jacoby.

believing themselves no longer to be strong enough
to engage in battle with a valiant and fresh army,
abandoned their camps and withdrew. When the
two armies of the Romans had come together, they
made a large camp in a strong position near the city ;
then, after remaining there many days and plundering the best part of the territory of the Veientes, the
generals led the army home. When the Veientes
heard that the forces of the Romans had been discharged from the standards, taking the light-armed
youth, not only their own which they had already
assembled, but also that of their neighbours which
was then present, they made an incursion into the
plains bordering upon their own territory, which were
full of corn, cattle and men, and plundered them.
For the husbandmen had come down from the strongholds to get feed for their cattle and to till their lands,
relying upon the protection of their army, which then
lay encamped between them and the enemy ; and
after this army had retired, they had made no haste
to move back, as they did not expect the Veientes,
after having suffered so many defeats, to make a
return attack so promptly against the foe. This
irruption of the Veientes into the Romans' country,
though brief in point of the time it lasted, was very
serious with respect to the amount of territory they
overran ; and it caused the Romans unusual vexation,
mingled with shame, since it extended as far as the
river Tiber and Mount Janiculum, which is not
twenty stades from Rome.[1] For there was no force

---

[1] In chap. 24, 3 the distance is given as 16 stades (2 miles).

---

[4] Kiessling : ταῖς O.
[5] ἡ A : om. B, but three letters deleted before κωλύσουσα.

335

γὰρ δύναμις ἐπὶ πλεῖον χωρεῖν τὰ πολέμια οὐκ ἦν
ὑπὸ[1] σημείαις. ἔφθασε γοῦν τὸ τῶν Οὐιεντανῶν
στράτευμα πρὶν[2] συνελθεῖν τε καὶ λοχισθῆναι τοὺς
Ῥωμαίους ἀπελθόν.

XV. Συναχθείσης δὲ μετὰ τοῦτο τῆς[3] βουλῆς
ὑπὸ τῶν ὑπάτων καὶ σκέψεως γενομένης τίνα χρὴ
πολεμεῖν τοῖς Οὐιεντανοῖς τρόπον, ἡ νικῶσα ἦν
γνώμη στράτευμα συνεστηκὸς ἔχειν ἐπὶ τοῖς ὁρίοις,
ὃ διὰ φυλακῆς ἕξει τὴν χώραν θυραυλοῦν καὶ αἰεὶ
μένον ἐν τοῖς ὅπλοις. ἐλύπει δ' αὐτοὺς ἥ τε εἰς
τοὺς φρουροὺς δαπάνη πολλὴ σφόδρα ἐσομένη, τοῦ
τε κοινοῦ ταμείου διὰ τὰς συνεχεῖς στρατείας
ἐξαναλωμένου[4] καὶ τῶν ἰδίων βίων ἀπειρηκότων
ταῖς εἰσφοραῖς· καὶ ἔτι μᾶλλον ἡ τῶν ἀποσταλησο-
μένων φρουρῶν καταγραφὴ τίνα τρόπον ἂν γένοιτο,
ὡς οὐκ ἂν ἑκουσίων γέ τινων[5] προκαθημένων[6]
ἁπάντων καὶ μὴ ἐκ διαδοχῆς ἀλλὰ συνεχῶς ταλαι-
2 πωρεῖν ὑποστησομένων. ἀδημονούσης δ' αὐτῆς
ἐπ' ἀμφοτέροις τούτοις συγκαλέσαντες οἱ δύο[7]
Φάβιοι τοὺς μετέχοντας τοῦ σφετέρου γένους καὶ
βουλευσάμενοι μετ' αὐτῶν ὑπέσχοντο τῇ βουλῇ
τοῦτο τὸ κινδύνευμα αὐτοὶ περὶ πάντων ἑκόντες
ὑπομενεῖν, πελάτας τε τοὺς ἑαυτῶν ἐπαγόμενοι καὶ
φίλους καὶ τέλεσι τοῖς ἰδίοις, ὅσον ἂν χρόνον ὁ
3 πόλεμος διαμένῃ, στρατευόμενοι. ἀγασθέντων δ'
αὐτοὺς ἁπάντων τοῦ γενναίου τῆς προθυμίας καὶ
τὸ νικᾶν παρ' ἓν τοῦτο τὸ ἔργον τιθεμένων, κλεινοὶ

---

[1] Portus : ἐπὶ O.   [2] πρὶν O : πρὶν ἢ Jacoby.
[3] τῆς added by Sylburg.
[4] ἐξαναλωμένου Ba : ἐξαναλουμένου R.
[5] After τινων Kayser proposed to add ὀλίγων.
[6] Kiessling : προκειμένων A, Jacoby, προκείμενον B, προ-
κινδυνεύειν Köstlin.   [7] δύο B : om. R.

then under the standards to stop the enemy's further progress ; at any rate, the army of the Veientes had gone before the Romans could assemble and be assigned to centuries.

XV. When the senate [1] was later called together by the consuls and had deliberated in what manner the war should be carried on against the Veientes, the opinion which prevailed was to maintain a standing army upon the frontiers, which should keep guard over the Roman territory, camping in the open and always remaining under arms. But the expense of maintaining the garrisons, which would be very great, grieved them, since the public treasury was exhausted as a result of the continual campaigns, and their private fortunes had proved unequal to the burden of the war-taxes. And they were grieved still more by the problem of enlisting the garrisons which were to be sent out, how that could be accomplished, there being little probability that a few men would, willingly at least, serve as a bulwark in defence of all and submit to hardships, not in successive shifts, but continuously. While the senate was troubled on both these accounts, the two Fabii assembled all the members of their clan, and having consulted with them, promised the senate that they themselves would voluntarily undertake this risk in defence of all the citizens, taking along with them their clients and friends, and would at their own expense continue in arms as long as the war should last. All admired them for their noble devotion and placed their hopes of victory in this single undertaking ; and while they

[1] *Cf.* Livy ii. 48, 8—49, 8.

καὶ περιβόητοι καθ' ὅλην τὴν πόλιν ὄντες ἐξῄεσαν
ἀναλαβόντες τὰ ὅπλα σὺν εὐχαῖς καὶ θυσίαις.
ἡγεῖτο δ' αὐτῶν Μάρκος Φάβιος ὁ τῷ παρελθόντι
ὑπατεύσας ἔτει καὶ νικήσας[1] τοὺς Τυρρηνοὺς τῇ
μάχῃ, τετρακισχιλίους μάλιστα ἐπαγόμενος, ὧν
τὸ μὲν πλεῖον πελατῶν τε καὶ ἑταίρων ἦν, ἐκ
δὲ τοῦ Φαβίων γένους ἓξ καὶ τριακόσιοι ἄνδρες.
εἵπετο δ' αὐτοῖς· μετ' οὐ πολὺ καὶ ἡ Ῥωμαίων
δύναμις, ἧς ἡγεῖτο Καίσων Φάβιος ὁ ἕτερος τῶν
ὑπάτων.

4 Γενόμενοι δὲ ποταμοῦ Κρεμέρας[2] πλησίον, ὃς
οὐ μακρὰν ἀπέχει τῆς Οὐιεντανῶν πόλεως, ὑπὲρ
ὄχθου τινὸς ἀποτόμου καὶ περιρρῶγος ἐπετείχιζον
αὐτοῖς φρούριον ἱκανὸν φυλάττεσθαι τοσαύτῃ στρατιᾷ τάφρους τε ὀρυξάμενοι περὶ αὐτὸ διπλᾶς καὶ
πύργους ἐγείραντες πυκνούς· καὶ ὠνομάσθη τὸ
φρούριον ἐπὶ τοῦ ποταμοῦ Κρεμέρα. οἷα δὲ
πολυχειρίας τε ἐργαζομένης καὶ ὑπάτου συλλαμβά-
νοντος θᾶττον ἢ κατὰ δόξαν ἐτελέσθη τὸ ἔργον.
5 καὶ μετὰ τοῦτ' ἐξαγαγὼν τὴν δύναμιν παρήλασεν
ἐπὶ θάτερα[3] μέρη τῆς Οὐιεντανῶν χώρας τὰ πρὸς
τὴν ἄλλην ἐστραμμένα Τυρρηνίαν, ἔνθα ἦν τοῖς
Οὐιεντανοῖς τὰ βοσκήματα, οὐδέποτε στρατὸν
ἥξειν Ῥωμαίων ἐκεῖ προσδεχομένοις. περιβαλό-
μενος δὲ πολλὴν λείαν ἀπῆγεν ἐπὶ τὸ νεόκτιστον
φρούριον, χαίρων ἐπὶ τῇ ἄγρᾳ κατ' ἀμφότερα, τῆς
τε οὐ διὰ μακροῦ τῶν πολεμίων τιμωρίας ἕνεκα,
καὶ ὅτι τοῖς φρουροῖς τοῦ χωρίου πολλὴν ἔμελλε
παρέξειν εὐπορίαν. οὐδὲν γὰρ οὔτ' εἰς τὸ δημόσιον

---

[1] Sylburg : ἐνίκησε O.
[2] Portus : κρεμέρα O.
[3] τὰ after θάτερα deleted by Reiske.

were being acclaimed and their names were on the lips of all, they took their arms and marched forth, accompanied by vows and sacrifices. Their leader was Marcus Fabius, the man who had been consul the preceding year and had conquered the Tyrrhenians in the late battle; those he took with him were about four thousand in number, the greater part of them being clients and friends, while of the Fabian clan there were three hundred and six men. They were followed a little later by the Roman army under the command of Caeso Fabius, one of the consuls.

When they came near the river Cremera, which is not far from the city of the Veientes, they built upon a steep and craggy hill a fortress to command their territory, as large as could be garrisoned by an army of such size, surrounding it with a double ditch and erecting frequent towers; and the fortress was named Cremera, after the river. Since many hands were employed at this work and the consul himself assisted them, it was completed sooner than might have been expected. After that the consul marched out with the army and went past the city to the other side of the territory of the Veientes, the side facing toward the rest of Tyrrhenia, where the Veientes kept their herds, not expecting that a Roman army would ever come there; and having possessed himself of much booty, he returned to the newly erected fortress. This quarry afforded him great satisfaction for two reasons—first, because he had so promptly retaliated upon the enemy, and again, because it would furnish abundant supplies to the garrison of the stronghold. For he neither turned over any part of

ἀνήνεγκεν,[1] οὔτε τοῖς στρατιώταις[2] ἀπένειμεν, ἀλλὰ
καὶ πρόβατα καὶ ὑποζύγια καὶ ζεύγη βοεικὰ καὶ
σίδηρον καὶ τἆλλα ὅσα εἰς γεωργίαν ἐπιτήδεια
6 ἦν τοῖς περιπόλοις τῆς χώρας ἐχαρίσατο. ταῦτα
διαπραξάμενος ἀπῆγεν ἐπ᾽ οἴκου τὴν στρατιάν.
τοῖς δὲ Οὐιεντανοῖς μετὰ τὸν ἐπιτειχισμὸν τοῦ
χωρίου κακῶς πάνυ τὰ πράγματ᾽ εἶχεν, οὔτε τὴν
γῆν ἔτι δυναμένοις ἀσφαλῶς γεωργεῖν οὔτε τὰς
7 ἔξωθεν εἰσαγομένας ἀγορὰς δέχεσθαι.[3] νείμαντες
γὰρ εἰς τέτταρα μέρη τὴν στρατιὰν οἱ Φάβιοι, τῷ
μὲν ἑνὶ διεφύλαττον τὸ χωρίον, τοῖς δὲ τρισὶ τὴν
χώραν τῶν πολεμίων ἄγοντές τε καὶ φέροντες ἀεὶ
διετέλουν· καὶ πολλάκις τῶν Οὐιεντανῶν ἐκ τοῦ
φανεροῦ τε αὐτοῖς ἐπιτιθεμένων[4] χειρὶ οὐκ ὀλίγῃ
καὶ εἰς χωρία ἐνέδραις κατεχόμενα ὑπαγομένων,
περιῆσαν ἀμφοτέρως καὶ πολλοὺς νεκροὺς ποιήσαντες ἀσφαλῶς ἀπῄεσαν εἰς τὸ χωρίον· ὥστε
οὐδ᾽ ὁμόσε χωρεῖν αὐτοῖς ἔτι οἱ πολέμιοι ἐτόλμων,
ἀλλὰ τειχήρεις μένοντες τὰ πολλὰ καὶ κλέπτοντες
τὰς ἐξόδους διετέλουν· καὶ ὁ μὲν χειμὼν ἐκεῖνος
ἐτελεύτα.[5]

XVI. Τῷ δὲ κατόπιν ἔτει Λευκίου τε Αἰμιλίου
καὶ Γαΐου Σερουϊλίου[6] τὴν ὑπατείαν παρειληφότων
ἀπηγγέλη Ῥωμαίοις ὅτι Οὐολοῦσκοι καὶ Αἰκανοὶ[7]
συνθήκας πεποίηνται στρατιὰς κατ᾽ αὐτῶν ἅμα
ἐξάγειν καὶ οὐ διὰ μακροῦ εἰς τὴν χώραν ἐμβαλοῦσι·
καὶ ἦν ἀληθῆ τὰ λεγόμενα. θᾶττον γοῦν ἢ προσ-

---

[1] Tegge : ἀπήνεγκεν O.
[2] στρατιώταις Kiessling, στρατευομένοις Kayser : στρατευομένοις ἰδιώταις O.   [3] δέχεσθαι BbCmg : om. R.
[4] Cary : ἐπιθεμένων O, Jacoby.

the spoils to the treasury nor distributed any to the soldiers, but presented all the cattle, the beasts of burden, the yokes of oxen, the iron, and the other implements of husbandry to the patrols of the country. After accomplishing this he led the army home. The Veientes found themselves in very dire straits after the erection of the frontier stronghold, since they could no longer either till their land in safety or receive the provisions that were imported from abroad. For the Fabii had divided their army into four bodies, with one of which they guarded the stronghold, while with the other three they continually pillaged the enemy's country; and often, when the Veientes openly attacked them with a considerable force or endeavoured to entice them into places beset with ambuscades, the Fabii had the advantage in both situations, and after killing many of them, would retire safely to their stronghold. Consequently the enemy no longer dared to engage them, but remained shut up within their walls for the most part, and only ventured out by stealth. Thus ended that winter.

XVI. The next year,[1] when Lucius Aemilius and Gaius Servilius had assumed the consulship, the Romans were informed that the Volscians and the Aequians had entered into an agreement to lead out armies against them at the same time, and that they would soon make an irruption into their territory. And this information was true. At all events, sooner

[1] For chaps. 16-17, 3 cf. Livy ii. 49, 9-12.

---

⁵ ἐτελεύτα O : οὕτως ἐτελεύτα Reiske, Jacoby.
⁶ Σερουΐλίου Sigonius : σεργίου O (and similarly below).
⁷ αἰκανοὶ Bb : λευκανοὶ ABa.

ἐδόκα τις ἀμφότεροι τὰς δυνάμεις ἔχοντες ἐδῄουν
τὴν κατὰ σφᾶς ἕκαστοι χώραν, ὡς οὐχ ἱκανῶν
ἐσομένων Ῥωμαίων τῷ τε Τυρρηνικῷ πολέμῳ
2 ἀντέχειν καὶ σφᾶς ἐπιόντας δέχεσθαι. καὶ ἕτεροι
αὖθις ἥκοντες ἐκπεπολεμῶσθαι πρὸς αὐτοὺς Τυρρηνίαν ἀπήγγελλον ὅλην καὶ παρεσκευάσθαι Οὐιεντανοῖς κοινὴν ἀποστέλλειν συμμαχίαν. κατέφυγον
γὰρ ὡς αὐτοὺς ἀδύνατοι ὄντες ἐξελεῖν δι' ἑαυτῶν
τὸ φρούριον Οὐιεντανοί, συγγενείας τε ὑπομιμνήσκοντες καὶ φιλίας καὶ ὅσους μετ' αὐτῶν ἤραντο
πολέμους διεξιόντες· ἀντὶ πάντων δὲ τούτων
ἀξιοῦντες συνάρασθαι σφίσι τοῦ κατὰ Ῥωμαίων
πολέμου, ὡς σφῶν τε προκαθημένων Τυρρηνίας
ὅλης καὶ τὸν πόλεμον ἀνακωχευόντων τὸν ἀπὸ
Ῥώμης ῥέοντα κατὰ πάντων τῶν ὁμοεθνῶν. καὶ
οἱ Τυρρηνοὶ πεισθέντες ὑπέσχοντο πέμψειν αὐτοῖς
ὅσην ἠξίουν συμμαχίαν.
3 Ταῦτα ἡ βουλὴ μαθοῦσα ἐψηφίσατο τρισσὰς
ἐκπέμψαι[1] στρατιάς, καὶ γενομένων ἐν τάχει τῶν
καταλόγων Λεύκιος μὲν Αἰμίλιος ἐπὶ Τυρρηνοὺς
ἐπέμφθη· συνῆρατο δ' αὐτῷ τῆς ἐξόδου Καίσων
Φάβιος, ὁ νεωστὶ τὴν ἀρχὴν ἀποθέμενος, δεηθεὶς
τῆς βουλῆς ἐπιτρέψαι αὐτῷ τοῖς ἐν Κρεμέρᾳ συγ-
γενέσιν, οὓς ὁ ἀδελφὸς αὐτοῦ φρουρήσοντας τὸ
χωρίον ἐξήγαγε, συνεῖναί τε καὶ τῶν αὐτῶν ἀγώνων μετέχειν· καὶ ἐξῆλθε σὺν τοῖς ἀμφ' αὐτὸν
4 ἐξουσίᾳ κοσμηθεὶς ἀνθυπάτῳ. Γάιος δὲ Σερουΐλιος
ὁ ἕτερος τῶν ὑπάτων ἐπὶ Οὐολούσκους ἐστράτευσε,
Σερούιος δὲ Φούριος ἀνθύπατος ἐπὶ τὸ Αἰκανῶν
ἔθνος. ἑκάστῳ δ' αὐτῶν δύο μὲν τάγματα Ῥωμαίων εἵπετο, Λατίνων δὲ καὶ Ἑρνίκων καὶ τῶν

---

[1] Cobet : ἐκπέμψειν O, Jacoby.

than anyone was expecting, both nations with their armies were ravaging the parts of the Roman territory that adjoined their own, in the belief that the Romans would not be able to cope with the Tyrrhenian war and at the same time to withstand their own attack. And again other messengers came reporting that all Tyrrhenia had become hostile to them and was prepared to send joint reinforcements to the Veientes. For the latter, finding themselves unable to destroy the fortress by themselves alone, had turned to them for help, reminding them of their kinship and friendship, and enumerating the many wars they had waged in common. In view of all this, they asked them to assist them in their war against the Romans, since they were now serving as a bulwark for all Tyrrhenia and stemming the torrent of war which was rushing from Rome upon all the peoples of their race. The Tyrrhenians were persuaded, and promised to send them as large a force of auxiliaries as they asked for.

The senate, being informed of this, resolved to send three armies into the field ; and the levies were speedily raised. Lucius Aemilius was sent against the Tyrrhenians ; and taking part in the expedition with him was Caeso Fabius, the man who had recently resigned the consulship, having now asked leave of the senate to join his kinsmen on the Cremera whom his brother had led out to garrison that place, and to take part in the same contests as they ; and invested with the proconsular power, he set out with his followers. Gaius Servilius, the other consul, marched against the Volscians, and Servius Furius, the proconsul, against the Aequians. Each of them was at the head of two legions of Romans and an equally

ἄλλων συμμάχων οὐκ ἐλάττω τῆς Ῥωμαϊκῆς δυνάμεως. τῷ μὲν οὖν ἀνθυπάτῳ Σερουΐῳ κατὰ
νοῦν ὁ πόλεμος ἐχώρησε καὶ σὺν τάχει. μιᾷ γὰρ
ἐτρέψατο τοὺς Αἰκανοὺς μάχῃ καὶ ταύτῃ δίχα
πόνου, τῇ πρώτῃ τοὺς πολεμίους ἐκπλήξας ἐφόδῳ,
καὶ τὸ λοιπὸν ἐδῄου τὴν γῆν αὐτῶν καταπεφευγό-
5 των εἰς τὰ ἐρύματα. Σερουϊλίῳ δὲ θατέρῳ τῶν
ὑπάτων ὑπὸ σπουδῆς τε καὶ αὐθαδείας ἐπὶ τὸν
ἀγῶνα χωρήσαντι πολὺ τὸ παρὰ γνώμην ἀπήντησε,
καρτερῶς πάνυ τῶν Οὐολούσκων ἀντιταξαμένων,
ὥστε ἠναγκάσθη πολλοὺς καὶ ἀγαθοὺς ἄνδρας
ἀπολέσας μηκέτι χωρεῖν ὁμόσε τοῖς πολεμίοις, ἀλλ'
ἐν τῷ χάρακι ὑπομένων ἀκροβολισμοῖς καὶ ψιλῶν
συμπλοκαῖς διαφέρειν[1] τὸν πόλεμον.

6   Λεύκιος δ' Αἰμίλιος, ὁ πεμφθεὶς ἐπὶ Τυρρηνούς,
εὑρὼν ἐξεστρατευμένους πρὸ τῆς πόλεως τοὺς
Οὐιεντανοὺς καὶ σὺν αὐτοῖς πολὺ τὸ παρὰ τῶν
ὁμοεθνῶν ἐπικουρικόν, οὐδὲν ἔτι μελλήσας ἔργου
εἴχετο· ἡμέραν δὲ μίαν[2] ἀφ' ἧς τὸν χάρακα ἔθετο
διαλιπὼν ἐξῆγε τὰς δυνάμεις εἰς μάχην, θρασέως
πάνυ τῶν Οὐιεντανῶν ὁμόσε χωρούντων. ἰσορ-
ρόπου δὲ τοῦ ἀγῶνος γινομένου τοὺς ἱππεῖς ἀναλαβὼν ἐνσείει τοῖς πολεμίοις κατὰ τὸ δεξιὸν κέρας,
καί, ἐπειδὴ τοῦτο διεσάλευσεν, ἐπὶ θάτερον ἐχώρει,
ὅπου μὲν ἱππάσιμον εἴη χωρίον ἀπὸ τῶν ἵππων
μαχόμενος, ὅπου δ' ἄνιππον ἀποκαταβαίνων τε καὶ
πεζὸς ἀγωνιζόμενος. πονούντων δὲ τῶν κεράτων
ἀμφοτέρων οὐδ' οἱ κατὰ μέσον ἔτι ἀντεῖχον, ἀλλ'
ἐξεώσθησαν ὑπὸ τῶν πεζῶν, καὶ μετὰ τοῦτο πάντες
7 ἔφυγον ἐπὶ τὸν χάρακα. ὁ δ' Αἰμίλιος ἠκολούθει

---

[1] ἔγνω after διαφέρειν deleted by Cobet.
[2] μίαν added here by Capps, after ἔθετο by Kiessling.

strong force of Latins, Hernicans and the other allies. In the case of the proconsul Servius the war went according to his wish and was soon over. For in a single battle he routed the Aequians, and that without any trouble, having terrified the enemy at the first onset; and thereafter he laid waste their country, as the people had taken refuge in their forts. But Servilius, one of the consuls, having rushed into battle in a precipitate and headstrong fashion, found himself greatly disappointed in his expectations, as the Volscians offered a very stout resistance, with the result that after losing many brave men he was forced to give up engaging in pitched battles with them any longer, but remaining in his camp, to carry through the war by means of skirmishes and engagements of the light-armed troops.

Lucius Aemilius, who had been sent against the Tyrrhenians, finding that the Veientes had taken the field before their city together with a large number of auxiliaries of the same race, set to work without further delay; and letting only a single day pass after making camp, he led out his forces to battle, in which the Veientes joined with great confidence. When the contest continued doubtful, he took the horse and charged the right wing of the enemy; then, after throwing that into confusion, he proceeded to the other wing, fighting on horseback where the ground would permit, and where it would not, dismounting and fighting on foot. When both of the enemy's wings were in distress, those in the centre could no longer hold out either, but were thrust back by the Roman foot; and after that they all fled to their camp. Aemilius followed them in their flight

τοῖς φεύγουσι συντεταγμένην τὴν δύναμιν ἔχων καὶ πολλοὺς διέφθειρε. γενόμενος δὲ πλησίον τοῦ χάρακος καὶ προσβαλὼν ἐκ διαδοχῆς ἐκείνῃ τε παρέμεινε τὴν ἡμέραν καὶ τὴν ἐπιοῦσαν νύκτα, τῇ δ' ἑξῆς ἡμέρᾳ κόπῳ τε καὶ τραύμασι τῶν πολεμίων καὶ ἀγρυπνίᾳ ἀπειρηκότων ἐγκρατὴς γίνεται τοῦ χάρακος. οἱ δὲ Τυρρηνοί, ὡς εἶδον ἐπιβαίνοντας ἤδη τοὺς Ῥωμαίους τοῖς περισταυρώμασιν, ἐκλιπόντες τὸ στρατόπεδον ἔφευγον, οἱ μὲν εἰς τὴν 8 πόλιν, οἱ δ' εἰς τὰ πλησίον ὄρη. ταύτην μὲν οὖν τὴν ἡμέραν ἐν τῷ χάρακι τῶν πολεμίων ἔμεινεν ὁ ὕπατος, τῇ δ' ἑξῆς ἡμέρᾳ στεφανώσας τοὺς ἀριστεύσαντας ἐν τῇ μάχῃ ταῖς ἐκπρεπεστάταις[1] δωρεαῖς, πάντα τὰ ἐγκαταλειφθέντα[2] ἐν τῷ χάρακι ὑποζύγιά τε καὶ ἀνδράποδα καὶ σκηνὰς πολλῶν ἀγαθῶν γεμούσας τοῖς στρατιώταις ἐχαρίσατο. καὶ ἐγένετο ἐν πολλῇ εὐπορίᾳ τὸ τῶν Ῥωμαίων στράτευμα ὡς ἐξ οὐδεμιᾶς ἑτέρας πώποτε μάχης. ἁβροδίαιτον γὰρ δὴ καὶ πολυτελὲς τὸ τῶν Τυρρηνῶν ἔθνος ἦν, οἴκοι τε καὶ ἐπὶ στρατοπέδου περιαγόμενον[3] ἔξω τῶν ἀναγκαίων πλούτου τε καὶ τέχνης ἔργα παντοῖα πρὸς ἡδονὰς μεμηχανημένα καὶ τρυφάς.

XVII. Ταῖς δ' ἑξῆς ἡμέραις ἀπειρηκότες ἤδη τοῖς κακοῖς οἱ Οὐιεντανοὶ τοὺς πρεσβυτάτους τῶν πολιτῶν ἱκετηρίας φέροντας ἀπέστειλαν ὡς τὸν ὕπατον ὑπὲρ τῆς εἰρήνης διαλεξομένους. καὶ οἱ ἄνδρες ὀλοφυρόμενοί τε καὶ ἀντιβολοῦντες καὶ τἆλλ' ὅσα ἐπαγωγὰ ἦν εἰς ἔλεον μετὰ πολλῶν δακρύων διεξιόντες πείθουσι τὸν ὕπατον ἐπιτρέψαι

---

[1] ἐν τῇ μάχῃ ταῖς ἐκπρεπεστάταις Reiske : ἐν ταῖς μάχαις ἐκπρεπεστάταις O, ἐν ταῖς μάχαις ταῖς ἐκπρεπεστάταις Jacoby.

with his army in good order and killed many of them.
When he came near their camp, he attacked it with
relays of fresh troops, remaining there all that day
and the following night ; and the next day, when the
enemy were spent with weariness, wounds and want
of sleep, he made himself master of the camp. The
Tyrrhenians, when they saw the Romans already
mounting the palisades, left their camp and fled,
some to the city and some to the neighbouring hills.
That day the consul remained in the enemy's camp ;
and on the next day he rewarded with the most
magnificent presents those who had distinguished
themselves in the battle, and gave to the soldiers all
the beasts of burden and slaves that had been left
behind in the camp, together with the tents, which
were full of many valuables. And the Roman army
found itself in greater opulence than after any
former battle. For the Tyrrhenians were a people
of dainty and expensive tastes, both at home and
in the field carrying about with them, besides the
necessities, costly and artistic articles of all kinds
designed for pleasure and luxury.

XVII. In the course of the following days the
Veientes, yielding at last to their misfortunes, sent
their oldest citizens to the consul with the tokens of
suppliants to treat for peace. These men, resorting
to lamentations and entreaties and with many tears
rehearsing every argument calculated to rouse compassion, endeavoured to persuade the consul to let

---

² ἐγκαταλειφθέντα O : ἐγκαταληφθέντα Reiske, Jacoby.
³ Gelenius : ὑπεραγόμενον O, ὑπεραγάμενον Reiske.

σφίσι πρεσβευτὰς[1] εἰς ῾Ρώμην ἀποστεῖλαι[2] τοὺς
ὑπὲρ τῆς καταλύσεως τοῦ πολέμου πρὸς τὴν βουλὴν
διαλεξομένους, ἕως δ' ἂν οἱ πρέσβεις ἀφίκωνται
φέροντες τὰς ἀποκρίσεις, μηδὲν αὐτῶν κακουργεῖν
τὴν χώραν. ἵνα δ' αὐτοῖς ἐγγένηται ταῦτα πράττειν, σῖτόν τε ὡμολόγησαν τῇ ῾Ρωμαίων στρατιᾷ
διμήνου παρέξειν καὶ χρήματα εἰς ὀψωνιασμὸν ἐξ
2 μηνῶν, ὡς ὁ κρατῶν ἔταξε. καὶ ὁ μὲν ὕπατος
λαβὼν τὰ κομισθέντα καὶ διαδοὺς τῇ στρατιᾷ
ποιεῖται τὰς πρὸς αὐτοὺς ἀνοχάς. ἡ δὲ βουλὴ τῆς
πρεσβείας ἀκούσασα καὶ τὰ τοῦ ὑπάτου γράμματα
δεξαμένη[3] πολλὴν ποιουμένου παράκλησιν καὶ παρ-
αινοῦντος[3] ὡς τάχιστα καταθέσθαι τὸν πρὸς τοὺς
Τυρρηνοὺς πόλεμον, δόγμα ἐξήνεγκε διδόναι τὴν
εἰρήνην, ὡς ᾐτοῦντο οἱ πολέμιοι· ἐφ' οἷς δὲ δικαίοις
αὕτη γενήσεται,[4] τὸν ὕπατον καταστήσασθαι Λεύκιον Αἰμίλιον, ὡς ἂν αὐτῷ φανῇ κράτιστα ἕξειν.
3 ταύτας λαβὼν τὰς ἀποκρίσεις ὁ ὕπατος σπένδεται
πρὸς τοὺς Οὐιεντανούς, ἐπιεικεστέραν μᾶλλον ἢ
συμφορωτέραν τοῖς κεκρατηκόσι ποιησάμενος εἰρήνην, οὔτε χώραν αὐτῶν ἀποτεμόμενος οὔτε χρημάτων ἄλλων ἐπιθεὶς ζημίαν, οὔτε ὁμήρων δόσει τὸ
4 πιστὸν ἐν[5] τοῖς συγκειμένοις βεβαιωσάμενος. τοῦτ'
αὐτῷ μέγαν ἤνεγκε φθόνον, καὶ τοῦ μὴ λαβεῖν
παρὰ τῆς βουλῆς τὰς ἐπὶ τοῖς κατωρθωμένοις
χάριτας αἴτιον ἐγένετο. ἐνέστησαν γὰρ αὐτῷ τὸν
θρίαμβον αἰτουμένῳ τὴν αὐθάδειαν αἰτιώμενοι
τῶν συνθηκῶν, ὅτι οὐ μετὰ κοινῆς γνώμης αὐτὰς
ἔπραξεν. ἵνα δὲ μὴ πρὸς ὕβριν ἢ πρὸς ὀργὴν λάβῃ

---

[1] πρεσβευτὰς Reiske : τοὺς πρεσβευτὰς AB, Jacoby.
[2] ἀποστεῖλαι placed here by Sylburg, Jacoby, after πολέμου
by O.

them send ambassadors to Rome to treat with the
senate for a termination of the war, and until the
ambassadors should return with the senate's answer,
to do no injury to their country. In order to obtain
these concessions, they promised to supply the Roman
army with corn for two months and with money for
their pay for six months, as the victor commanded.
And the consul, after receiving what they brought
and distributing it among his men, made the truce
with them. The senate, having heard the ambassadors and received the letter of the consul, in which
he earnestly recommended and urged putting an end
to the war with the Tyrrhenians as soon as possible,
passed a decree to grant peace as the enemy desired ;
as to the terms on which the peace should be made,
they left them for the consul Lucius Aemilius to
determine in such manner as he should think best.
The consul, having received this answer, concluded a
peace with the Veientes that was more equitable than
advantageous to the conquerors ; for he neither took
from them any part of their territory, nor imposed
on them any further fine of money, nor compelled
them to give hostages as security for the performance
of their agreement. This action brought upon him
great odium and was the reason for his not receiving
from the senate the rewards due for his success ; for
when he requested the customary triumph, they
opposed it, censuring his arbitrary behaviour in the
matter of the treaty, in that he had concluded it
without their concurrence. But lest he should take
this action as an insult and evidence of their anger,

---

³ δεξαμένη O : ἀναλεξαμένη Cobet, Jacoby.
⁴ Baumann : γένηται O.
⁵ ἐν O : om. Reiske.

τὸ πρᾶγμα, ἐπὶ Ουολούσκους αὐτὸν ἐψηφίσαντο
τὴν δύναμιν ἀπάγειν ἐπικουρίας τοῦ συνάρχοντος
ἕνεκα, εἰ δύναιτο κατορθώσας τὸν ἐκεῖ πόλεμον
(ἦν γὰρ ἐν αὐτῷ πολὺ τὸ ἀνδρεῖον) ἀφανίσαι τὰς
ἐπὶ τοῖς προτέροις ἁμαρτήμασιν ὀργάς. ὁ δ' ἀνὴρ
ἀγανακτῶν ἐπὶ τῇ ἀτιμίᾳ πολλὴν ἐποιήσατο τῆς
βουλῆς ἐν τῷ δήμῳ κατηγορίαν, ὡς[1] ἀχθομένης ἐπὶ
τῷ λελύσθαι τὸν πρὸς τοὺς Τυρρηνοὺς πόλεμον.
ἔφη δὲ τοῦτ' αὐτοὺς ἐξ ἐπιβουλῆς καὶ ὑπεροψίας τῶν πενήτων ποιεῖν, ἵνα μὴ τῶν ὑπερορίων
ἀπαλλαγέντες πολέμων ἀπαιτῶσι τὰς περὶ τῆς
κληρουχίας ὑποσχέσεις, πολλοστὸν ἔτος ἤδη
5 φενακιζόμενοι πρὸς αὐτῶν. ταῦτα καὶ πολλὰ
τούτοις ὅμοια δι'[2] ὀργῆς ἀκράτου τῶν πατρικίων
ὀνείδη κατασκεδάσας, τήν τε συστρατευσαμένην
αὐτῷ δύναμιν ἀπέλυσε τῶν σημείων καὶ τὴν μετὰ
Φουρίου τοῦ ἀνθυπάτου διατρίβουσαν ἐν Αἰκανοῖς
μεταπεμψάμενος ἀφῆκεν ἐπὶ τὰ σφέτερα· ἐξ ὧν
πολλὴν πάλιν ἐποίησεν ἐξουσίαν τοῖς δημάρχοις
κατηγορεῖν τῶν βουλευτῶν ἐν ταῖς ἐκκλησίαις καὶ
διιστάναι τοὺς πένητας ἀπὸ τῶν εὐπόρων.

XVIII. Μετὰ δὲ τούτους παραλαμβάνουσι τὴν
ὑπατείαν Γάιος Ὁράτιος καὶ Τίτος Μενήνιος ἐπὶ
τῆς ἑβδομηκοστῆς καὶ ἕκτης ὀλυμπιάδος, ἣν ἐνίκα
στάδιον Σκάμανδρος Μιτυληναῖος, ἄρχοντος Ἀθήνησι Φαίδωνος. τούτοις κατ' ἀρχὰς μὲν ὁ πολιτικὸς θόρυβος ἐμποδὼν ἐγένετο πράττειν τὰ κοινά,
ἠρεθισμένου τοῦ δήμου καὶ οὐδὲν ἐῶντος ἕτερον

----

[1] ὡς B : om. R.
[2] δι' Kiessling : καὶ δι' O. Retaining καί, Reiske supplied συνείρας, Jacoby εἰπών, after ὅμοια.

they ordered him to march with his army against the
Volscians in order to bear aid to his colleague, on the
chance that if he succeeded in the war there—for
he was a man of great bravery—he might blot out
the resentment for his former errors. But Aemilius,
angry at this slight upon his honour, inveighed violently against the senate in the popular assembly,
accusing them of being displeased that the war against
the Tyrrhenians was ended. He declared that they
were doing this with treacherous intent and through
contempt of the poor, lest these, when freed from
foreign wars, should demand the per ormance of the
promises concerning the allotment of land with which
they had been cajoled by them for so many years
already. After he had in his ungovernable resentment poured forth these and many similar reproaches
against the patricians, he not only dismissed from
the standards the army that had served under him,
but also sent for the forces that were tarrying in the
country of the Aequians under Furius the proconsul
and dismissed them to their homes. Thereby he
once more gave the tribunes a considerable warrant
for accusing the senators in the meetings of the
assembly and sowing dissension between the poor
and the rich.

XVIII. These consuls were succeeded by Gaius
Horatius and Titus Menenius [1] in the seventy-sixth
Olympiad [2] (the one at which Scamander of Mitylene
won the foot-race), when Phaedo was archon at
Athens. The new consuls were at first hindered from
transacting the public business by the domestic disturbance, the populace being exasperated and not
permitting any other public business to be carried on

---

[1] Cf. Livy ii. 51, 1.   [2] 475 B.C.

ἐπιτελεῖσθαι τῶν κοινῶν ἕως ἂν μερίσηται τὴν δημοσίαν γῆν, χρόνῳ δ' ὕστερον εἶξε τὰ παρακινοῦν-
τα καὶ ταραττόμενα τῇ ἀνάγκῃ συγχωρήσαντα
2 καὶ ἐπὶ τὰς στρατείας ἑκούσια ἦλθε. Τυρρηνῶν
γὰρ αἱ μὴ μετασχοῦσαι τῆς εἰρήνης ἕνδεκα πόλεις
ἀγορὰν ποιησάμεναι κοινὴν κατηγόρουν τοῦ Οὐιεντανῶν ἔθνους ὅτι τὸν πρὸς Ῥωμαίους πόλεμον οὐ
μετὰ κοινῆς γνώμης κατελύσαντο, καὶ δυεῖν θάτερον
αὐτοὺς ἠξίουν πράττειν, ἢ λύειν τὰ πρὸς Ῥωμαίους
3 ὁμολογηθέντα ἢ πολεμεῖν σφίσι μετ' ἐκείνων. οἱ δὲ
Οὐιεντανοὶ τῆς μὲν εἰρήνης τὴν ἀνάγκην ᾐτιῶντο,
ὅπως δ' ἂν αὐτὴν καταλύσαιντο εὐπρεπῶς εἰς
κοινὸν ἐτίθεσαν σκοπεῖν. ἔπειτα ὑποτίθεταί τις
αὐτοῖς ἔγκλημα ποιησαμένοις τὸν ἐπιτειχισμὸν τῆς
Κρεμέρας καὶ τὸ μὴ ἀπανίστασθαι τοὺς φρουροὺς
ἀπ' αὐτῆς, λόγῳ μὲν πρῶτον[1] ἀξιοῦν τοὺς ἐκλιπεῖν
τὸ χωρίον, ἐὰν δὲ μὴ πείθωσι, πολιορκεῖν τὸ φρούριον, καὶ ταύτην ἀρχὴν ποιήσασθαι τοῦ πολέμου.
4 ταῦτα συνθέμενοι ἀπηλλάττοντο ἐκ τοῦ συλλόγου·
καὶ μετ' οὐ πολὺ Οὐιεντανοὶ μὲν ἀποστείλαντες
πρεσβείαν ὡς τοὺς Φαβίους ἀπῄτουν παρ' αὐτῶν
τὸ φρούριον, Τυρρηνία δὲ πᾶσα ἦν ἐν τοῖς ὅπλοις.
ταῦτα Ῥωμαῖοι αἰσθόμενοι Φαβίων αὐτοῖς ἐπιστειλάντων[2] ἔγνωσαν ἀμφοτέρους ἐκπορεύεσθαι
τοὺς ὑπάτους ἐπὶ τὸν πόλεμον, τόν τε ἀπὸ Τυρρηνίας ἐπαγόμενον σφίσι καὶ τὸν ἔτι πρὸς Οὐο-
5 λούσκους συνεστῶτα. Ὁράτιος μὲν οὖν ἄγων δύο
τάγματα καὶ ἀπὸ τῶν ἄλλων συμμάχων τοὺς
ἱκανοὺς ἐξήγαγε τὴν δύναμιν ἐπὶ Οὐολούσκους,

[1] πρῶτον B : om. R.
[2] ἐπιστειλάντων C, by correction, Reiske : ἀποστειλάντων
ABC.

until they should divide up among themselves the public land; but after a time the seditious and turbulent elements yielded to necessity and came in voluntarily to be enlisted. For the eleven cities of the Tyrrhenians which had had no part in the peace, holding a general assembly, inveighed against the Veientes for having put an end to the war with the Romans without the general consent of the nation, and demanded that they do one of two things —either break the compact they had made with the Romans, or join with the Romans in making war upon the rest of the Tyrrhenians. But the Veientes laid the blame for the peace upon necessity, and proposed that the assembly consider how they might break it with decency. Upon this someone suggested to them that they should make formal complaint of the erection of the frontier stronghold on the Cremera and of the failure of its garrison to withdraw from there, and then should first make an oral demand that they evacuate the place, and, if they refused, should lay siege to the fortress and make this action the beginning of the war. Having agreed on this course, they left the assembly; and not long afterwards the Veientes sent ambassadors to the Fabii to demand from them the fortress, and all Tyrrhenia was in arms. The Romans, learning of these things through letters from the Fabii, resolved that both the consuls should take the field, one to command in the war that was coming upon them from Tyrrhenia and the other to prosecute the war which was still going on with the Volscians. Horatius, accordingly, marched against the Volscians with two legions and an adequate force of the allies, and Menenius was

Μενήνιος δὲ τοσαύτην στρατιὰν ἑτέραν ἄγων ἐπὶ
Τυρρηνοὺς ἔμελλε ποιεῖσθαι τὴν ἔξοδον. παρα-
σκευαζομένου δ' αὐτοῦ καὶ τρίβοντος τὸν χρόνον
ἔφθη τὸ ἐν Κρεμέρᾳ φρούριον ἐξαιρεθὲν ὑπὸ τῶν
πολεμίων καὶ τὸ Φαβίων γένος ἅπαν ἀπολόμενον.
περὶ δὲ τῆς κατασχούσης τοὺς ἄνδρας συμφορᾶς
διττὸς φέρεται λόγος, ὁ μὲν ἧττον πιθανός, ὁ δὲ
μᾶλλον τῆς ἀληθείας ἁπτόμενος. θήσω δ' αὐτοὺς
ἀμφοτέρους, ὡς παρέλαβον.

XIX. Τινὲς μὲν οὖν φασιν ὅτι θυσίας ἐπιστάσης
πατρίου, ἣν ἔδει τὸ Φαβίων ἐπιτελέσαι γένος, οἱ
μὲν ἄνδρες ἐξῆλθον ὀλίγους ἐπαγόμενοι πελάτας
ἐπὶ τὰ ἱερά, καὶ προῄεσαν οὔτε διερευνώμενοι τὰς
ὁδοὺς οὔτε ὑπὸ σημείαις τεταγμένοι κατὰ λόχους,
ῥαθύμως δὲ[1] καὶ ἀφυλάκτως ὡς ἐν εἰρήνῃ τε καὶ διὰ
2 φιλίας γῆς πορευόμενοι. οἱ δὲ Τυρρηνοὶ προεγνω-
κότες αὐτῶν τὴν ἔξοδον ἐλόχησαν τῆς ὁδοῦ χωρίον
μέρει τῆς στρατιᾶς, τὴν δὲ λοιπὴν δύναμιν συντεταγμένην ἔχοντες οὐ πολλῷ ὕστερον ἠκολούθουν.
ὡς δ' ἐπλησίασαν οἱ Φάβιοι ταῖς ἐνέδραις, ἐξαναστάντες τοῦ λόχου οἱ Τυρρηνοὶ προσπίπτουσιν
αὐτοῖς, οἱ μὲν κατὰ μέτωπον, οἱ δ' ἐκ τῶν πλαγίων,
καὶ μετ' οὐ πολὺ ἡ τῶν ἄλλων Τυρρηνῶν δύναμις
προσέβαλεν ἐκ τῶν κατόπιν· καὶ περιστάντες αὐτοῖς πανταχόθεν, οἱ μὲν σφενδόναις, οἱ δὲ τόξοις,
οἱ δὲ σαυνίοις τε καὶ λόγχαις στοχαζόμενοι, τῷ
3 πλήθει τῶν βελῶν ἅπαντας κατειργάσαντο. οὗτος
μὲν οὖν ἧττον ἔμοιγε πιθανὸς φαίνεται εἶναι λόγος.
οὔτε γὰρ εἰκὸς ἀπὸ στρατοπέδου θυσίας ἕνεκα τοὺς
ὑπὸ ταῖς σημείαις τοσούτους ἄνδρας εἰς τὴν πόλιν
ἀναστρέφειν ἄνευ ψηφίσματος βουλῆς, δυναμένων

δὲ B : τε AC.

preparing to set out against the Tyrrhenians with another force of equal size; but while he was making his preparations and losing time, the fortress on the Cremera was destroyed by the enemy and the entire Fabian clan perished. Concerning the disaster that befell these men two accounts are current, one less probable and the other coming nearer to the truth. I shall give them both as I have received them.

XIX. Some say that when the time was at hand for a traditional sacrifice which devolved upon the Fabian clan, the men set out from the fortress, attended by a few clients, to perform the rites, and proceeded without reconnoitring the roads or marching ranged in centuries under their standards, but negligently and unguardedly as in time of peace and as if they were passing through friendly territory. The Tyrrhenians, having learned of their departure in advance, placed one part of their army in ambush at a spot along the road, and followed soon after with the rest of their forces in regular formation. When the Fabii drew near the ambuscade, the Tyrrhenians who were lying in wait there rose up and fell upon them, some in front and others in flank, and a little later the rest of the Tyrrhenian force attacked them from the rear; and surrounding them on all sides and shooting at them, some with slings, some with bows, and others hurling javelins and spears, they overwhelmed them all with the multitude of their missiles. Now this account seems to me to be the less credible. For not only is it improbable that so many men serving under the standards would have returned from the camp to the city because of a sacrifice without a decree from the senate, when the rites might have

τῶν ἱερουργιῶν καὶ δι’ ἑτέρων ἐπιτελεσθῆναι τῶν
μετεχόντων μὲν τοῦ αὐτοῦ γένους, προβεβηκότων
δὲ ταῖς ἡλικίαις· οὔτ’ εἰ πάντες ἀπεληλύθεσαν ἐκ
τῆς πόλεως, καὶ μηδεμία μοῖρα τοῦ Φαβίων γένους
ἐν τοῖς ἐφεστίοις ὑπελείπετο, πάντας εἰκὸς ἦν τοὺς
κατέχοντας τὸ φρούριον ἐκλιπεῖν αὐτοῦ τὴν φυλα-
κήν· ἤρκουν γὰρ ἂν καὶ τρεῖς ἢ τέτταρες ἀφικόμενοι
συντελέσαι περὶ τοῦ γένους ὅλου τὰ ἱερά. διὰ μὲν
δὴ ταύτας τὰς αἰτίας οὐκ ἔδοξέ μοι πιστὸς εἶναι
ὁ[1] λόγος.

XX. Ὁ δ’ ἕτερος, ὃν ἀληθέστερον εἶναι νομίζω
περί τε τῆς ἀπωλείας τῶν ἀνδρῶν καὶ τῆς ἁλώσεως
τοῦ φρουρίου, τοιόσδε τίς ἐστιν. ἐξιόντων ἐπὶ τὰς
προνομὰς τῶν ἀνδρῶν πολλάκις καὶ διὰ τὸ κατ-
ορθοῦν ἐν ταῖς πείραις συνεχῶς προσωτέρω προ-
χωρούντων οἱ Τυρρηνοὶ παρεσκευασμένοι στρατιὰν
συχνὴν ἐν τοῖς ἔγγιστα χωρίοις λαθόντες τοὺς
πολεμίους κατεστρατοπέδευσαν. ἔπειτ’ ἀποστέλλοντες ἐκ τῶν χωρίων ποίμνας τε καὶ βουκόλια
καὶ φορβάδων ἀγέλας ἵππων ἐπὶ νομὴν τῷ λόγῳ,
προυκαλοῦντο τοὺς ἄνδρας ἐπὶ ταῦτα· οἱ δ’ ἐξιόντες
τούς τε ἀνθρώπους συνήρπαζον καὶ τὰ βοσκήματα
2 περιήλαυνον. τοῦτο συνεχῶς οἱ Τυρρηνοὶ ποιοῦντες
καὶ προαγόμενοι τοὺς πολεμίους ἀεὶ προσωτέρω
τοῦ χάρακος, ἐπειδὴ διέφθειραν αὐτῶν τὸ προ-
νοητικὸν τοῦ ἀσφαλοῦς ταῖς συνεχέσιν ὠφελείαις
δελεάσαντες, ἐγκαθίζουσι λόχους ἐν τοῖς ἐπικαίροις
τῶν χωρίων νύκτωρ, καὶ ἕτεροι τὰς ὑπερδεξίους
τῶν πεδίων καταλαμβάνονται σκοπάς[2]· τῇ δ’ ἑξῆς
ἡμέρᾳ προπέμψαντες ὀλίγους τινὰς ἐνόπλους ὡς
δὴ φυλακῆς ἕνεκα τῶν νομέων, ἀφῆκαν ἐκ τῶν

[1] ὁ B : ὅδε ὁ R.   [2] Suidas : σκοπάς O.

been performed by others of the same clan who were advanced in years; but even if they had all gone from the city and no part of the Fabian clan was left in their homes, it is improbable that all who held the fortress would have abandoned the guarding of it, since even three or four of them would have sufficed to return to Rome and perform the rites for the whole clan. For these reasons, then, this account has not seemed to me to be credible.

XX. The other account[1] concerning the destruction of the Fabii and the capture of the fortress, which I regard as being nearer to the truth, is somewhat as follows. As the men went out frequently to forage and, encouraged by the continued success of their forays, advanced ever farther, the Tyrrhenians got ready a numerous army and encamped in the near neighbourhood unperceived by the enemy. Then, sending out of their strongholds flocks of sheep, herds of cattle, and droves of mares as if to pasture, they lured the garrison out to these; and the men, coming out, seized the herdsmen and rounded up the cattle. The Tyrrhenians kept doing this and drawing the enemy ever farther away from their camp; then, when they had destroyed in them all thought for their safety by enticing them with constant booty, they placed ambuscades at night in the most suitable positions, while others occupied the heights that commanded the plains. The next day, sending ahead a few armed men, as if to serve as a guard for the herdsmen, they drove out a large number of herds

---

[1] For chaps. 20-22 cf. Livy ii. 50.

3 χωρίων[1] πολλὰς ἀγέλας. ὡς δ' ἀπηγγέλη τοῖς
Φαβίοις ὅτι τοὺς πλησίον ὑπερβαλόντες λόφους ἐν
ὀλίγῳ δή τινι χρόνῳ μεστὸν εὑρήσουσι τὸ πεδίον
παντοίων βοτῶν καὶ τὴν φυλάττουσαν αὐτὰ[2] χεῖρα
οὐχ ἱκανήν, ἐξῆλθον ἐκ τοῦ φρουρίου φυλακὴν τὴν
ἀρκοῦσαν ἐν αὐτῷ καταλιπόντες· καὶ διανύσαντες
σπουδῇ καὶ μετὰ προθυμίας τὴν ὁδὸν ἐπιφαίνον-
ται τοῖς φύλαξι τῶν βοσκημάτων συντεταγμένοι·
κἀκεῖνοι οὐ δεξάμενοι αὐτοὺς ἔφευγον. οἱ δὲ Φάβιοι, ὡς ἐν ἀσφαλεῖ δὴ ὄντες, τούς τε νομεῖς συν-
4 ελάμβανον καὶ τὰ βοσκήματα περιήλαυνον. ἐν
δὲ τούτῳ οἱ Τυρρηνοὶ ἐκ τῆς ἐνέδρας ἀναστάντες
κατὰ πολλὰ χωρία προσπίπτουσιν αὐτοῖς πανταχόθεν. καὶ οἱ μὲν πλείους τῶν Ῥωμαίων ἐσκεδασ-
μένοι καὶ ἀλλήλοις ἀμύνειν οὐχ οἷοί τε ὄντες,
ἐνταῦθα ἀπόλλυνται. ὅσοι δ' αὐτῶν συνεστηκό-
τες ἦσαν. προθυμούμενοί τι καταλαβέσθαι χωρίον
ἀσφαλὲς καὶ πρὸς τὰ ὄρη σπεύδοντες εἰς ἕτερον
ἐμπίπτουσι λόχον ἐν ὕλαις καὶ νάπαις ὑποκαθ-
ήμενον. καὶ γίνεται αὐτῶν μάχη καρτερὰ καὶ
φόνος ἐξ ἑκατέρων πολύς. ἀπεώσαντο δ' οὖν καὶ
τούτους ὅμως,[3] καὶ πληρώσαντες τὴν φάραγγα[4]
νεκρῶν ἀνέδραμον ἐπὶ λόφον οὐ ῥᾴδιον ἁλῶναι·
ἐν ᾧ τὴν ἐπιοῦσαν νύκτα ἄποροι τῶν ἀναγκαίων
ηὐλίσαντο.

XXI. Τῇ δ' ἑξῆς ἡμέρᾳ μαθόντες τὴν κατασχοῦ-
σαν τοὺς σφετέρους τύχην οἱ κατέχοντες τὸ φρούριον, καὶ ὅτι τὸ μὲν πλεῖον ἀπόλωλε τῆς στρατιᾶς
μέρος ἐν ταῖς ἁρπαγαῖς, τὸ δὲ κράτιστον ἐν ὄρει
πολιορκεῖται κατακεκλεισμένον ἐρήμῳ, καὶ εἰ μὴ

---

[1] χωρίων Cmg, Sintenis : φρουρίων O.
[2] Steph. : αὐτῶν Ba, αὐτὸ ABb.

from their strongholds. When word was brought to the Fabii that if they went over the neighbouring hills they would in a very short time find the plain covered with cattle of all sorts with a guard insufficient to defend them, they went out of the fortress, leaving an adequate garrison there. And covering the distance speedily in their eagerness, they appeared before the guards of the cattle in battle array. These did not await their attack, but fled, and the Fabii, thinking themselves now quite secure, set about seizing the herdsmen and rounding up the cattle. Thereupon the Tyrrhenians, rising up from ambush in many places, fell upon them from all sides. The greater part of the Romans, being scattered and unable to assist one another, were killed upon the spot; but those who were in a body, being eager to reach a secure position and hastening toward the hills, fell into another ambuscade that lay concealed in the woods and glens. Here a sharp battle took place between them and there was great slaughter on both sides. But nevertheless they repulsed even these foes, and after filling the ravine with dead bodies, they ran up to the top of a hill that was not easy to take, and there passed the following night in want of the necessary provisions.

XXI. The next day those who were holding the fortress, upon being informed of the disaster that had befallen their companions—namely, that the greater part of the army had been destroyed in their pursuit of plunder and the bravest of them were shut up and besieged on a lonely mountain, and that if some aid

---

³ ὅμως Ba (?), Portus : ὁμόσε ABb.
⁴ Sylburg : φάλαγγα O.

ταχεῖά τις αὐτοῖς ἥξει[1] βοήθεια, σπάνει τῶν ἀναγκαίων φθάσουσιν ἐξαιρεθέντες, ἐξῄεσαν κατὰ σπουδὴν ὀλίγους πάνυ καταλιπόντες ἐν τῷ φρουρίῳ[2]
φύλακας. καὶ αὐτοὺς οἱ Τυρρηνοί, πρὶν ἢ συμμῖξαι
τοῖς ἑτέροις, ἐπικαταδραμόντες ἐκ τῶν χωρίων
κυκλοῦνταί τε καὶ πολλὰ γενναῖα ἔργα ἀποδειξα-
2 μένους διαφθείρουσιν ἅπαντας σὺν χρόνῳ. μετ' οὐ
πολὺ δὲ καὶ οἱ τὸν λόφον καταλαβόμενοι λιμῷ τε
καὶ δίψῃ πιεζόμενοι ὁμόσε χωρεῖν τοῖς πολεμίοις
ἔγνωσαν· καὶ συμπεσόντες ὀλίγοι πρὸς πολλοὺς
ἕωθεν ἀρξάμενοι μέχρι νυκτὸς ἐμάχοντο· καὶ τοσοῦτον ἐποίησαν τῶν πολεμίων φόνον ὥστε τοὺς
σωροὺς τῶν νεκρῶν ἐμποδὼν αὐτοῖς εἶναι τῆς μάχης
πολλαχῇ κεχυμένους. οἱ δὲ Τυρρηνοὶ πλεῖον ἢ τὸ
τρίτον τῆς στρατιᾶς μέρος ἀπολωλεκότες καὶ περὶ
τοῦ λοιποῦ δείσαντες, μικρὸν ἀνασχόντες τὰ ὅπλα
διὰ τῶν ἀνακλητικῶν ἐπεκηρυκεύοντο πρὸς τοὺς
ἄνδρας, ἄδειαν αὐτοῖς ὑπισχνούμενοι καὶ δίοδον ἐὰν
3 τὰ ὅπλα ἀποθῶνται καὶ τὸ φρούριον ἐκλίπωσιν. οὐ
προσδεξαμένων δὲ τῶν ἀνδρῶν τὰς προκλήσεις,
ἀλλὰ τὸν εὐγενῆ θάνατον αἱρουμένων, ἐπῄεσαν αὐτοῖς αὖθις ἐκ διαδοχῆς, συστάδην μὲν καὶ ἐκ χειρὸς
οὐκέτι μαχόμενοι, πρόσωθεν δὲ βάλλοντες ἀθρόοι
λόγχαις καὶ χερμάσι, καὶ ἦν νιφετῷ παραπλήσιος
ἡ πληθὺς τῶν βελῶν. οἱ δὲ Ῥωμαῖοι συστρεφό-
μενοι κατὰ λόχους προσέτρεχον αὐτοῖς οὐχ ὑφιστα-
μένοις καὶ πολλὰς πληγὰς λαμβάνοντες ὑπὸ τῶν
4 πέριξ ὑπέμενον. ὡς δὲ τά τε ξίφη πολλοῖς ἄχρηστα
ἦν, τὰ μὲν ἀπεστομωμένα τὰς ἀκμάς, τὰ δὲ κατ-
εαγότα, καὶ τῶν ἀσπίδων τὰ πέριξ ἴτυος ἐχόμενα

---

[1] ἥξει ACmg : ἔσται B, om. C.
[2] φρουρίῳ Cmg : χωρίῳ O.

did not reach them promptly they would soon be destroyed for want of provisions—set out in haste, leaving very few in the fortress to guard it. These troops, before they could join their companions, were surrounded by the Tyrrhenians, who rushed down upon them from their strongholds ; and though they displayed many feats of valour, they were in time all destroyed. Not long afterwards those also who had seized the hill, being oppressed by both hunger and thirst, resolved to charge the enemy ; and engaging, a few against many, they continued fighting from morning till night, and made so great a slaughter of the enemy that the heaps of dead bodies piled up in many places were a hindrance to them in fighting. Indeed, the Tyrrhenians had lost above a third part of their army, and fearing for the rest, they now gave the signal for a retreat and stopped fighting for a short time ; and sending heralds to the men, they offered them their lives and a safe-conduct if they would lay down their arms and evacuate the fortress. When the others refused their offer and chose the death befitting men of noble birth, the Tyrrhenians renewed the struggle, attacking them in relays, though no longer fighting at close quarters in hand-to-hand combat, but standing in a body and hurling javelins and stones at them from a distance ; and the multitude of missiles was like a snow-storm. The Romans, massing by companies, rushed upon their foes, who did not stand their ground, and though they received many wounds from those surrounding them, they stood firm. But when the swords of many had become useless, some having their edges blunted and others being broken, and the borders of their shields

διετέθρυπτο, ἔξαιμοί τε οἱ πλείους καὶ καταβελεῖς
καὶ παράλυτοι τὰ μέλη διὰ πλῆθος τραυμάτων
ἦσαν, καταφρονήσαντες αὐτῶν οἱ Τυρρηνοὶ χωροῦσιν ὁμόσε· καὶ οἱ Ῥωμαῖοι προσπίπτοντες ὥσπερ
θηρία δόρατά τε αὐτῶν ἐπιλαμβανόμενοι κατέκλων,
καὶ ξίφη δραττόμενοι κατὰ τὰς ἀκμὰς ἀπέσπων,
καὶ περικυλίοντες εἰς τὴν γῆν τὰ σώματα συνεφύ-
ροντο θυμῷ τὸ πλεῖον ἢ δυνάμει διαγωνιζόμενοι.
5 ὥστε οὐκέτι συνῇεσαν αὐτοῖς εἰς χεῖρας οἱ πολέμιοι,
τό τε καρτερικὸν ἐκπληττόμενοι τῶν ἀνδρῶν καὶ
τὴν ἀπόνοιαν ἣν προσειλήφεσαν κατὰ τὴν ἀπό-
γνωσιν τοῦ ζῆν δεδιότες· ἀλλ' ἀποστάντες αὖθις
ἔβαλλον ἀθρόοι καὶ ξύλοις καὶ λίθοις καὶ ὅτῳ ἄλλῳ
ἐντύχοιεν, καὶ τελευτῶντες ἐγκατέχωσαν αὐτοὺς
τῷ πλήθει τῶν βελῶν. διαφθείραντες δὲ τοὺς
ἄνδρας ἔθεον ἐπὶ τὸ φρούριον, ἔχοντες τὰς τῶν
ἐπιφανεστάτων κεφαλάς, ὡς ἐξ ἐφόδου τοὺς ἐκεῖ
6 παραληψόμενοι. οὐ μὴν ἐχώρησέ γε αὐτοῖς κατὰ
τὴν[1] ἐλπίδα τὸ ἔργον· οἱ γὰρ καταλειφθέντες ἐν
αὐτῷ ζηλώσαντες τὸ εὐγενὲς τοῦ θανάτου τῶν τε
ἑταίρων καὶ τῶν[2] συγγενῶν ἐξῆλθον ὀλίγοι παντά-
πασιν ὄντες, καὶ πολὺν ἀγωνισάμενοι χρόνον τὸν
αὐτὸν τρόπον τοῖς ἑτέροις ἅπαντες διεφθάρησαν·
τὸ δὲ χωρίον ἔρημον οἱ Τυρρηνοὶ παρέλαβον. ἐμοὶ
μὲν δὴ ὁ λόγος οὗτος πιστότερος ἐφαίνετο πολὺ
τοῦ προτέρου· φέρονται δ' ἐν γραφαῖς Ῥωμαίων
ἀξιοχρέοις ἀμφότεροι.

XXII. Τὸ δὲ συναπτόμενον τούτοις ὑπό τινων
οὔτ' ἀληθὲς ὂν οὔτε πιθανόν, ἐκ παρακούσματος

---

[1] κατὰ τὴν O : κατ' Jacoby.　　[2] τῶν added by Sylburg.

next the rims were hacked in pieces, and the men themselves were for the most part bled white and overwhelmed by missiles and their limbs paralysed by reason of the multitude of their wounds, the Tyrrhenians scorned them and came to close quarters. Then the Romans, rushing at them like wild beasts, seized their spears and broke them, grasped their swords by the edges and wrenched them out of their hands, and twisting the bodies of their antagonists, fell with them to the ground, locked in close embrace, fighting with greater rage than strength. Hence the enemy, astonished at their endurance and terrified at the madness that had seized them in their despair of life, no longer ventured to come to grips with them, but retiring again, stood in a body and hurled at them sticks, stones, and anything else they could lay their hands on, and at last buried them under the multitude of missiles. After destroying these men they ran to the fortress, carrying with them the heads of the most prominent, expecting to take the men there prisoners at their first onset. However, the attempt did not turn out according to their hopes ; for the men who had been left there, emulating the noble death of their comrades and kinsmen, came out of the fortress, though very few in number, and after fighting for a considerable time were all destroyed in the same manner as the others ; and the place was empty of men when the Tyrrhenians took it. To me now this account appears much more credible than the former ; but both of them are to be found in Roman writings of good authority.

XXII. The addition to this account which has been made by certain writers, though neither true nor

δέ τινος πεπλασμένον ὑπὸ[1] τοῦ πλήθους,[2] ἄξιον μὴ παραλιπεῖν ἀνεξέταστον. λέγουσι γὰρ δή τινες, τῶν ἓξ καὶ τριακοσίων Φαβίων ἀπολομένων, ὅτι ἓν μόνον ἐλείφθη τοῦ γένους παιδίον, πρᾶγμα οὐ μόνον
2 ἀπίθανον, ἀλλὰ καὶ ἀδύνατον εἰσάγοντες. οὔτε γὰρ ἀτέκνους τε καὶ ἀγάμους ἅπαντας εἶναι δυνατὸν ἦν τοὺς ἐξελθόντας εἰς τὸ φρούριον Φαβίους. ὁ γὰρ ἀρχαῖος αὐτῶν νόμος γαμεῖν τε ἠνάγκαζε τοὺς ἐν ἡλικίᾳ καὶ τὰ γεννώμενα πάντα ἐπάναγκες τρέφειν· ὃν οὐκ ἂν δήπου κατέλυσαν οἱ Φάβιοι μόνοι πεφυλαγμένον ἄχρι τῆς ἑαυτῶν ἡλικίας ὑπὸ
3 τῶν πατέρων. εἰ δὲ δὴ καὶ τοῦτο θείη τις, ἀλλ' ἐκεῖνό γε οὐκ ἂν ἔτι συγχωρήσειε, τὸ μηδ' ἀδελφοὺς αὐτῶν εἶναί τισιν ἡλικίαν ἔτι παίδων ἔχοντας. μύθοις γὰρ δὴ ταῦτά γε καὶ πλάσμασιν ἔοικε θεατρικοῖς. οἱ δὲ πατέρες αὐτῶν, ὅσοι παῖδας ἔτι ποιεῖν εἶχον ἡλικίαν, τοσαύτης κατασχούσης τὸ γένος ἐρημίας οὐκ ἂν ἑκόντες τε καὶ ἄκοντες ἑτέρους παῖδας ἐποιήσαντο, ἵνα μήτε ἱερὰ ἐκλειφθῇ πατρῷα μήτε δόξα τηλικαύτη διαφθαρῇ γένους;
4 εἰ μὴ ἄρα οὐδὲ πατέρες αὐτῶν τισιν ἐλείποντο, ἀλλὰ πάντα εἰς ταὐτὸ συνῆλθεν ἐπὶ τῶν ἓξ καὶ τριακοσίων ἀνδρῶν ἐκείνων τὰ ἀδύνατα—μὴ παῖδας αὐτοῖς καταλειφθῆναι νηπίους, μὴ γυναῖκας ἐγκύους, μὴ ἀδελφοὺς ἀνήβους, μὴ πατέρας ἐν ἀκμῇ·
5 ταύτῃ μὲν δὴ τὸν λόγον ἐξετάζων οὐκ ἀληθῆ νενόμικα, ἐκεῖνον δ' ἀληθῆ· τῶν τριῶν ἀδελφῶν, Καίσωνός τε καὶ Κοΐντου καὶ Μάρκου τῶν ὑπατευ-

---

[1] Reiske : ἀπὸ O. [2] πλήθους B : ἀληθοῦς R.

plausible, but invented by the multitude from some
false report, does not deserve to be passed over without examination. For some report that after the three
hundred and six Fabii had been slain, there was only
one boy left out of the whole clan, thereby introducing a detail that is not only improbable, but even
impossible; for it is not possible that all the Fabii who
went out to the fortress were unmarried and childless.
For not only did the ancient law of the Romans
oblige all of the proper age to marry, but they were
forced also to rear all their children; and surely the
Fabii would not have been the only persons to violate
a law which had been observed by their ancestors
down to their time. But even if one were to admit
this assumption, yet he would never make the further
admission that none of them had any brothers still
in their childhood. Why, such situations resemble
myths and fictions of the stage! Besides, would not
as many of their fathers as were still of an age to beget
children, now that so great a desolation had come
upon their clan, have begotten other children both
willingly and unwillingly, in order that neither the
sacrifices of their ancestors might be abandoned nor
the great reputation of the clan be extinguished?
Unless, indeed, none even of their fathers were left
and all the conditions which would render it impossible
to perpetuate the clan combined together in the case
of those three hundred and six men—namely, that
they left behind them no infant children, no wives
with child, no brothers still under age, no fathers in
the prime of life. Testing the story by such reasoning, I have come to the conclusion that it is not true,
but that the following is the true account. Of the
three brothers, Caeso, Quintus, and Marcus, who had

σάντων τὰς συνεχεῖς ἑπτὰ ὑπατείας, ἐγκαταλειφ-
θῆναι πείθομαι Μάρκῳ παιδίον, καὶ τοῦτ᾽ εἶναι τὸ
B λεγόμενον[1] ἐκ τοῦ Φαβίων οἴκου λοιπόν. οὐδὲν
δὲ[2] κωλύει τῷ μηκέτι τῶν ἄλλων ἐπιφανῆ τινα καὶ
λαμπρὸν ἔξω τοῦ ἑνὸς τοῦδε ἀνδρωθέντος γενέσθαι
ταύτην παραστῆναι τοῖς πολλοῖς τὴν δόξαν ὅτι
μόνος ἐκεῖνος ἐκ τοῦ Φαβίων γένους ἐστὶ λοιπός
—οὐχ ὡς μηδενὸς ἄλλου ὄντος, ἀλλ᾽ ὡς μηδενὸς ἐκείνοις ὁμοίου—ἀρετῇ τεκμαιρομένοις τὸ
συγγενές, οὐ φύσει. καὶ περὶ μὲν τούτων ταῦθ᾽
ἱκανά.

XXIII. Οἱ δ᾽ οὖν[3] Τυρρηνοὶ τούς τε ἄνδρας διαφθείραντες καὶ τὸ ἐν τῇ Κρεμέρᾳ φρούριον παραλαβόντες ἐπὶ τὴν ἄλλην στρατιὰν τῶν Ῥωμαίων
ἦγον τὰς δυνάμεις. ἔτυχε δ᾽ οὐ μακρὰν κατ-
εστρατοπεδευκὼς ὁ ἕτερος τῶν ὑπάτων Μενήνιος
οὐκ ἐν ἀσφαλεῖ χωρίῳ· καὶ ὅτε ἡ Φαβίων συγγένεια
καὶ τὸ πελατικὸν αὐτῶν ἀπώλλυντο, τριάκοντά που
σταδίους ἀπεῖχεν ἀφ᾽ οὗ τὸ πάθος ἐγένετο τόπου,
δόξαν τε οὐκ ὀλίγοις παρέσχε, γνοὺς ἐν οἵοις κακοῖς ἦσαν οἱ Φάβιοι, μηδεμίαν αὐτῶν ποιήσασθαι
φροντίδα τῆς τε ἀρετῆς καὶ δόξης τοῖς ἀνδράσι
2 φθονῶν. τοιγαροῦν μετὰ ταῦτα ὑπαχθεὶς ὑπὸ τῶν
δημάρχων εἰς δίκην ἐπὶ ταύτῃ μάλιστα τῇ αἰτίᾳ
ἑάλω. σφόδρα γὰρ ἐπένθησεν ἡ Ῥωμαίων πόλις
ἀνδρῶν τοσούτων καὶ τοιούτων ἀρετὰς ἀποκειρα-
μένη, καὶ πρὸς ἅπαν τὸ δόξαν αὐτοῖς αἴτιον
γεγονέναι τῆς τοιαύτης συμφορᾶς πικρῶς καὶ
ἀπαραιτήτως εἶχεν· τὴν δ᾽ ἡμέραν ἐκείνην ἐν ᾗ τὸ

---

[1] λεγόμενον O : λεγόμενον μόνον Kiessling.
[2] δὲ added by Sintenis.
[3] δ᾽ οὖν Hertlein : γοῦν R, om. Ba.

been consuls for seven years in succession, I believe that Marcus left one young son, and that this boy was the one who is reported to have been the survivor[1] of the Fabian house. There is no reason why it should not have been because no one else of the clan became famous and illustrious except this one son, when he had grown to manhood,[2] that most people came to hold the belief that he was the only survivor of the Fabian clan—not, indeed, that there was no other, but that there was none like those famous three—judging kinship on the basis of merit, not of birth. But enough on this subject.

XXIII. After the Tyrrhenians,[3] then, had destroyed the Fabii and taken the fortress on the Cremera, they led their forces against the other army of the Romans. It chanced that Menenius, one of the consuls, lay encamped not far away in an insecure position; and when the Fabian clan and their clients perished, he was only some thirty stades from the place where the disaster occurred—a circumstance which gave many people reason to believe that, though aware of the dire straits of the Fabii, he had shown no concern for them because of the envy he felt of their valour and reputation. Accordingly, when he was later brought to trial by the tribunes, this was the chief ground for his condemnation. For the people of Rome deeply mourned their having shorn themselves of the valour of so many and so brave men and were severe and inexorable toward all whom they suspected of having been responsible for so great a calamity; and they regard the day on

---

[1] Or, following Kiessling, " the sole survivor."
[2] He was consul ten years later ; see chap. 59.
[3] For chaps. 23 f. *cf.* Livy ii. 51, 1-3.

πάθος ἐγένετο μέλαινάν τε καὶ ἀποφράδα τίθεται
καὶ οὐδενὸς ἂν ἔργου ἐν ταύτῃ χρηστοῦ ἄρξαιτο,
3 τὴν τότε συμβᾶσαν αὐτῇ τύχην ὀττευόμενη. ὡς
δὲ πλησίον ἐγένοντο τῶν Ῥωμαίων οἱ Τυρρηνοί,
συνιδόντες αὐτῶν τὸ στρατόπεδον (ἦν δ᾽ ὑπὸ λαγόνι
κείμενον ὄρους) τῆς τε ἀπειρίας τοῦ στρατηγοῦ
κατεφρόνησαν καὶ τὸ δοθὲν ὑπὸ τῆς τύχης πλεονέκτημα[1] ἀγαπητῶς ἔλαβον. καὶ αὐτίκα τοὺς
ἱππεῖς ἀναλαβόντες κατὰ τὴν ἑτέραν πλευρὰν τοῦ
λόφου οὐδενὸς κωλύοντος ἀνέβησαν ἐπὶ τὴν κορυ-
φήν. καταλαβόμενοι δὲ τὸν ὑπὲρ κεφαλῆς[2] τῶν
Ῥωμαίων κόρυμβον ἔθεντο ἐν τούτῳ τὰ ὅπλα, καὶ
τὴν ἄλλην δύναμιν ἀσφαλῶς ἀναβιβάσαντες ὑψηλῷ
χάρακι καὶ βαθείᾳ τάφρῳ τὴν παρεμβολὴν ὠχυρώ-
4 σαντο. εἰ μὲν οὖν συνιδὼν ὁ Μενήνιος οἷον ἔδωκε
πλεονέκτημα τοῖς πολεμίοις μετέγνω τε τὴν
ἁμαρτάδα καὶ εἰς ἀσφαλέστερον ἀπήγαγε[3] χωρίον
τὴν στρατιάν, σοφὸς ἂν ἦν, νῦν δὲ δι᾽ αἰσχύνης
λαμβάνων τὸ δοκεῖν ἡμαρτηκέναι καὶ τὸ αὔθαδες
πρὸς τοὺς μεταδιδάσκοντας φυλάττων, μετ᾽[4] αἰσχύ-
5 νης ἄξιον πτῶμα ἔπεσεν. οἷα γὰρ ἐξ ὑπερδεξίων
αὐτοῦ τόπων οἱ πολέμιοι τὰς ἐξόδους ἑκάστοτε
ποιούμενοι πολλὰ ἐπλεονέκτουν, ἀγοράς τ᾽ αὐτῶν
ἀγομένας ὑπὸ τῶν ἐμπόρων ἁρπάζοντες καὶ τοῖς
ἐπὶ χιλὸν ἢ ὕδωρ ἐκπορευομένοις ἐπιτιθέμενοι· καὶ
περιειστήκει τῷ μὲν ὑπάτῳ μήτε καιροῦ εἶναι
κυρίῳ ἐν ᾧ τὸν ἀγῶνα ἔμελλε ποιεῖσθαι μήτε τόπου
—ἃ δοκεῖ μεγάλα εἶναι κατηγορήματα ἡγεμόνων
στρατηγίας ἀπείρων—τοῖς δὲ Τυρρηνοῖς ἀμφότερα
6 ὡς ἐβούλοντο εἶχε ταῦτα. καὶ οὐδὲ τότε ἀπανα-

---

[1] πλεονέκτημα R : om. B.
[2] ὑπὲρ κεφαλῆς B : ὑπὲρ τῆς κεφαλῆς R.

which the disaster occurred as black and inauspicious and will begin no useful labour on it, looking upon the disaster which then occurred on that day as a bad omen. When the Tyrrhenians came near the Romans and observed the situation of their camp, which lay under a flank of a hill, they felt contempt for the inexperience of the general and gladly grasped the advantage presented to them by Fortune. They at once marched up the opposite side of the hill with their horse and gained the summit without opposition. Then, having thus possessed themselves of the height above the Romans, they made camp there, brought up the rest of their army in safety, and fortified the camp with a high palisade and a deep ditch. Now if Menenius, when he perceived what an advantage he had given the enemy, had repented of his error and removed his army to a safer position, he would have been wise; but as it was, being ashamed to be thought to have made a mistake, and maintaining an obstinate front toward those who advised him to change his plans, he came a merited fall which brought disgrace as well. For as the enemy were constantly sending out detachments from places that commanded his camp, they had many advantages, not only seizing the provisions which the merchants were bringing to the Romans, but also attacking his men as they went out for forage or for water; and it had come to the point where the consul did not have it in his power to choose either the time or the place of combat—which seems to be strong evidence of the inexperience of a general—whereas the Tyrrhenians could do both as they wished. And not even then

---

³ Sintenis : ἀπῆγε O.
⁴ μετὰ ABC : εἰς D, om. Jacoby.

στῆσαι[1] τὴν στρατιὰν ὁ Μενήνιος ὑπέμεινεν, ἀλλ'
ἐξαγαγὼν παρέταξεν ὡς εἰς μάχην, καταφρονήσας
τῶν τὰ συμφέροντα ὑποτιθεμένων. καὶ οἱ Τυρρηνοὶ τὴν ἄνοιαν τοῦ στρατηγοῦ μέγα εὐτύχημα
ἡγησάμενοι κατέβαινον ἐκ τοῦ χάρακος οὐκ ἐλάτ-
7 τους ἢ διπλάσιοι τῶν πολεμίων ὄντες. ὡς δὲ
συνέπεσον ἀλλήλοις, φόνος ἐγίγνετο[2] τῶν Ῥωμαίων
πολὺς οὐ δυναμένων ἐν τῇ τάξει μένειν. ἐξεώθουν[3]
γὰρ αὐτοὺς οἱ Τυρρηνοὶ τοῦ τε χωρίου τὴν φύσιν
ἔχοντες σύμμαχον καὶ τῶν ἐφεστηκότων κατόπιν
(ἐτάξαντο γὰρ ἐπὶ βάθος) ἐμπτώσει πολλῇ συν-
εργούμενοι. πεσόντων δὲ τῶν[4] ἐπιφανεστάτων λοχαγῶν ἡ λοιπὴ τῶν Ῥωμαίων δύναμις ἐγκλίνασα
ἔφευγεν ἐπὶ τὸν χάρακα· οἱ δ' ἠκολούθουν, καὶ τάς
τε σημείας αὐτῶν ἀφαιροῦνται καὶ τοὺς τραυματίας συλλαμβάνουσι καὶ τῶν νεκρῶν γίνονται
8 κύριοι. καὶ κατακλείσαντες αὐτοὺς εἰς πολιορκίαν
καὶ δι' ὅλης τῆς λοιπῆς ἡμέρας προσβολὰς ποιησάμενοι πολλὰς καὶ οὐδὲ τὴν νύκτα ἀφέντες αἱροῦσι
τὸν χάρακα ἐκλιπόντων αὐτὸν τῶν ἔνδον, καὶ
γίνονται πολλῶν σωμάτων τε καὶ χρημάτων ἐγ-
κρατεῖς· οὐδὲ γὰρ ἀποσκευάσασθαι δύναμιν ἔσχον
οἱ φεύγοντες, ἀλλ' ἀγαπητῶς αὐτὰ τὰ σώματα
διέσωσαν, οὐδὲ τὰ ὅπλα πολλοὶ φυλάττοντες.

XXIV. Οἱ δ' ἐν τῇ Ῥώμῃ τήν τε ἀπώλειαν τῶν
σφετέρων καὶ τὴν ἅλωσιν τοῦ χάρακος μαθόντες
(ἧκον γὰρ οἱ πρῶτοι διασωθέντες ἐκ τῆς τροπῆς
πολλῆς[5] ἔτι νυκτὸς οὔσης) εἰς μέγαν θόρυβον ὥσπερ
εἰκὸς κατέστησαν· καὶ ὡς αὐτίκα δὴ μάλα τῶν
πολεμίων ἐπὶ σφᾶς ἐλευσομένων ἁρπάσαντες τὰ

---

[1] Gelenius : ἀπαναστῆναι O.   [2] ἐγίγνετο B : ἐγένετο A.
[3] Prou : ἐξάθουν O.

could Menenius bring himself to move his army away
from there; but leading out the troops, he drew them
up ready for battle, scorning all who offered salutary
advice. The Tyrrhenians, looking upon the folly of
the general as a piece of great good fortune, came
down from their camp with numbers fully twice those
of their foe. When they engaged, there was a great
slaughter of the Romans, who were unable to keep
their ranks. For they were forced back by the
Tyrrhenians, who not only had the terrain as an ally,
but were also helped by the vigorous pressure of those
who stood behind them, their army being drawn up
with deep files. When the most prominent centurions had fallen, the rest of the Roman army gave
way and fled to the camp; and the enemy pursued them, took away their standards, seized their
wounded, and got possession of their dead. Then
they shut them up in their camp and besieged them;
and delivering numerous attacks during all the rest
of the day, without desisting even at night, they
captured the camp, which the Romans had abandoned, and took many prisoners and a great quantity
of booty; for those who fled had not been able to
pack up their belongings, but were glad to escape
with their bare lives, many not keeping even their
arms.

XXIV. When those at Rome heard that their army
was destroyed and their camp taken—the first who
had saved themselves from the rout arrived while it
was still deep night—they fell into great confusion,
as may well be imagined; and expecting the enemy
to come against them at any moment, they seized

---

⁴ δὲ τῶν R : δὲ πολλῶν τῶν ACmg.
⁵ τροπῆς πολλῆς Kiessling : πολλῆς τροπῆς O.

ὅπλα, οἱ μὲν τὰ τείχη περιεστεφάνουν, οἱ δὲ πρὸ
τῶν πυλῶν ἐτάξαντο, οἱ δὲ τὰ μετέωρα τῆς πόλεως
2 κατελαμβάνοντο. ἦν δὲ δρόμος ἄτακτος ἀνὰ τὴν
πόλιν ὅλην[1] καὶ βοὴ συμμιγής, καὶ ἐπὶ τοῖς τέγεσι[2]
τῶν οἴκων εἰς ἀλκὴν καὶ ἀγῶνα εὐτρεπὴς ὁ κατ-
οικίδιος ὄχλος, πυρσοί τε συνεχεῖς, οἷα δὴ ἐν νυκτὶ
καὶ σκότῳ, διά τε ὑπολαμπάδων[3] καὶ ἀπὸ τεγῶν
τοσοῦτοι τὸ πλῆθος ᾔθοντο[4] ὥστε συναφὲς εἶναι
δοκεῖν τοῖς πρόσωθεν ὁρῶσι τὸ σέλας καὶ δόξαν
3 ἐμπιμπραμένης πόλεως παρασχεῖν. καὶ εἰ τότε οἱ
Τυρρηνοὶ τῶν ἐκ τοῦ χάρακος ὠφελειῶν ὑπεριδόν-
τες ἐκ ποδὸς τοῖς φεύγουσιν ἠκολούθησαν, ἅπασα
ἂν διέφθαρτο ἡ στρατεύσασα ἐπ' αὐτοὺς δύναμις·
νῦν δὲ πρὸς ἁρπαγάς τε τῶν ἐγκαταλειφθέντων
ἐν τῷ χάρακι τραπόμενοι καὶ ἀναπαύσει τὰ σώματα δόντες μεγάλου αὐχήματος ἑαυτοὺς ἐστέρη-
σαν. τῇ δ' ἑξῆς ἡμέρᾳ τὰς δυνάμεις ἄγοντες ἐπὶ
τὴν Ῥώμην καὶ σταδίους ἀμφὶ τοὺς ἑκκαίδεκα
ἀποσχόντες ὄρος ἐξ οὗ σύνοπτός ἐστιν ἡ Ῥώμη,
τὸ καλούμενον Ἰάνικλον, καταλαμβάνονται, ὅθεν
ὁρμώμενοι τὴν Ῥωμαίων χώραν ἦγόν τε καὶ

---

[1] ὅλην B : om. R. [2] Jacoby : στέγεσι O.

[3] νυκτὶ καὶ σκότῳ, διά τε ὑπολαμπάδων Post : νυκτὶ καὶ σκότῳ·
δίαιτά τε ὑπὸ λαμπάδων A, νυκτὶ σκότῳ (σκότος Bb) δίαιτάτε
(διαιτᾶται Bb) ὑπὸ λαμπάδων B, νυκτὶ καὶ σκοταίᾳ ταύτῃ ὑπὸ
λαμπάδων Jacoby.

[4] ᾔθοντο Capps : ἤροντο B, ἐπειρῶντο δρᾶν AC, ἐπυροῦντο
Steph.

---

[1] "Lantern" is here used in the architectural sense of
a light open structure set upon a roof to admit light and
air to the interior. The only other occurrence of the

their arms and some formed a circle about the walls,
others stationed themselves before the gates, and
still others occupied the heights in the city. There
was a disorderly running to and fro throughout the
entire city and a confused clamour; on the roofs
of the houses were the members of each household,
prepared to defend themselves and give battle; and
an uninterrupted succession of torches, as it was in
the night and dark, blazed through lanterns [1] and
from roofs, so many in number that to those seeing
them at a distance it seemed to be one continuous
blaze and gave the impression of a city on fire. And
if the Tyrrhenians at that time had scorned the booty
to be got from the camp and had followed on the heels
of the fleeing Romans, the whole army which had
taken the field against them would have been destroyed; but as it was, by turning to plundering
everything which had been left behind in the camp
and to resting their bodies, they deprived themselves
of a great opportunity for boasting. The next day
they led their forces against Rome, and when they
were about sixteen stades from the city, they occupied
the mount called Janiculum, from which the city is
in full view. And using that as a base of operations,
they pillaged the territory of the Romans without

word ὑπολαμπάς in extant literature is in a quotation from
Phylarchus found in Athenaeus (536 e). But in an inscription (*Inscript. Graec.* xi. 366 A, lines 14–48 *passim*) contain-
ing an account of the expenditures made on the hypostyle
hall at Delos the word occurs several times, as a detailed
list is given of the parts of the lantern that were repaired.
Remains of the lantern have been found and agree with the
references given in the inscription. See *Exploration archéo-
logique de Délos: Nouvelles recherches sur la salle hypostyle*,
Suppl. 2 (R. Vallois and G. Poulsen, Paris, 1914), pp. 10, 34,
38 f., 51 f.

ἔφερον ἀκώλυτοι κατὰ πολλὴν τῶν ἔνδον ὑπεροψίαν, μέχρι τοῦ παραγενέσθαι τὸν ἕτερον τῶν ὑπάτων 4 Ὁράτιον ἄγοντα τὴν ἐν Οὐολούσκοις δύναμιν. τότε δὴ ἐν τῷ ἀσφαλεῖ Ῥωμαῖοι νομίσαντες εἶναι καὶ τὴν ἐν τῇ πόλει νεότητα καθοπλίσαντες ἐξῆλθον εἰς τὴν ὕπαιθρον. ὡς δὲ τήν τε πρώτην μάχην ἀπὸ σταδίων ὀκτὼ τῆς πόλεως ποιησάμενοι παρὰ τὸ τῆς Ἐλπίδος ἱερὸν ἐνίκησάν τε καὶ ἀπεώσαντο τοὺς ἀντιταξαμένους, καὶ μετὰ ταύτην αὖθις ἑτέρᾳ[1] πλείονι δυνάμει τῶν Τυρρηνῶν ἐπελθόντων παρὰ ταῖς Κολλίναις καλουμέναις πύλαις[2] λαμπρῶς ἠγωνίσαντο, ἀνέπνευσαν[3] ἐκ τοῦ δέους· καὶ τὸ ἔτος τοῦτο ἐτελεύτα.

---

[1] ἑτέρᾳ ABC : ἑτέραν D.
[2] ποιησάμενοι after πύλαις deleted by Sintenis.

hindrance, holding those in the city in great contempt, till the other consul, Horatius, appeared with the army which had been among the Volscians. Then at last the Romans thought themselves safe, and arming the youth that were in the city, they took the field ; and having not only in the first battle, which was fought at the distance of eight stades from the city near the temple of Hope, overcome their opponents and driven them back, but also, after that engagement, having fought brilliantly with them again near the gate called the Colline, when the Tyrrhenians had come against them with another and larger army, they recovered from their fear. Thus ended that year.

---

³ καὶ before ἀνέπνευσαν deleted by Sylburg.

INDEX

INDEX

INDEX